The Resurrection of Theism

Prolegomena to Christian Apology

Second Edition

Stuart C. Hackett

Division Chairman, Philosophy of Religion
Trinity Evangelical Divinity School
Deerfield, Illinois

BAKER BOOK HOUSE

Grand Rapids, Michigan 49506

PHOTOLITHOPRINTED BY CUSHING - MALLOY, INC.
ANN ARBOR, MICHIGAN, UNITED STATES OF AMERICA

Affectionately Dedicated
to Three of My Dearest:
My Wife: Joan
My Parents: Mr. and Mrs. Ray T. Hackett,
without whose constant help and encouragement
this book would have been impossible

FOREWORD

EVER SINCE Immanuel Kant wrote his monumental *The Critique of Pure Reason,* theistic discussion has proceeded on the postulate—an assumption generally viewed as an unquestionable datum given ἐφάπαξ by the Koenigsberg titan—that the existence of God can be neither demonstrated nor disproved by reason. Roman Catholic theologians, to be sure, have refused to accept the Kantian criticism as have some outstanding Protestants, notably F. R. Tennant. By and large, however, the alleged demolition of the venerable "proofs" has been taken as a *fait accompli* by schools of all persuasion whether agnostic or liberal or neo-orthodox or even evangelical. Hence Dr. Hackett's thesis, developed with a competence born of intellectual acumen and thoroughgoing scholarship, is really an audacious challenge to what he deplores as a suicidal throwing wide open of the gates of Christian supernaturalism to the Trojan horse of illogicality. He therefore finds it necessary to engage in a polemical analysis of positions defended by some of the most distinguished thinkers of our modern era, ranging from D. C. Macintosh to Carl Henry. While his analysis may not be unanswerably devastating in every case, it is certainly incisive, deep-cutting enough to compel a re-examination of basic premises and sufficiently penetrating to show the cogency of the rational empiricism which Dr. Hackett himself espouses.

Thus no matter what conclusion one may draw concerning the success of this extraordinary attempt to rehabilitate the great tradition in theistic argument, he will be compelled to admire its daring, sweep, power, and lucidity. He will also admire its spiritual thrust and motivation; for here is a devout believer skillfully utilizing the resources of philosophy in order to bring sinful man inescapably face

5

to face with God's self-disclosure in Jesus Christ. In other words, reason for Dr. Hackett is propaedeutic to revelation; it is a means of evangelism.

As an adherent of Protestant orthodoxy, I urge that this work be studied in our circles with the care and attention which it eminently deserves. And I venture to predict for it a wide reading among circles which lie theologically far beyond the boundaries of evangelicalism.

VERNON C. GROUNDS, *President*
Conservative Baptist Theological
Seminary

PREFACE TO THE FIRST EDITION

Origin of the Present Work: the Need for a Rational Apologetic

The immediate historical stimulus of the present work consisted in the invitation to the author to deliver the Fall Lectures on Christian Thought for 1952 at the Conservative Baptist Theological Seminary. But the more basic motivation has come from a growing conviction on my part that the Christian world view both needs and embodies a thoroughgoing, rational apologetic as a manifestation of its relevance to the contemporary mind, together with the companion conviction that no existing system of Christian apology adequately meets this need. The underlying assertion of my whole argument, therefore, is that Christian faith should be defended in terms of criteria which center in rational objectivity as the norm of truth and evaluation. If, as Peter urges, believers in Christ are to give a reason for their hope to *every* man, then they can do it only in terms of criteria which ought to be acknowledged by all such men so far as they think and act rationally in their concourse with life and experience. This consideration means, in turn, that if Christian faith is obligatory for men, then it is so because it embodies objective truth for all rational minds.

Against such a view of the role of apologetics the objection is frequently brought that rational objectivity is impossible for real men and that therefore the whole enterprise we attempt is merely a glorious dream. Of course, all of us are conditioned to a certain extent by our accumulated beliefs and environmental pressures. But the very recognition of this conditioning is a significant step in the direction of eliminating its influence. Indeed, if rational objectivity were really not attainable, even this judgment itself, that we are conditioned by our beliefs, would fall short of rational objectivity and would therefore be eliminated by its own assertion. From such a line of argument as this, it must be concluded that either rational objectivity is possible or else knowledge itself is impossible and we are reduced to absolute skepticism. There is, therefore, no absurdity in the attempt to construct a rational system of Christian apologetics.

As over against the stimulus and conviction of apologetics thus conceived in terms of rational objectivity as a norm, there stands the morass of irrationalism and voluntarism that characterizes the great body of Christian apology at the present time, whether evangelical, liberal, or neo-orthodox. In another place, I have tried to analyze this frightening predicament of an apologetic which largely surrenders common ground as the basis for argument and which at the same time urges the contemporary mind to accept a view, the rational objectivity of which has either been obscured or, in some cases, wholly denied.[1] This sort of refusal to defend faith on the battlefield of a reasoned interpretation of experience is to my mind nothing short of suicide for the relevance of the Christian message. The present work is a firm protest against every such irrationalism, from whatever source. Nor is the protest without significant historical precedent; aside from the fact that no apologetic has succeeded in being totally irrationalist—not even that of Sören Kierkegaard—there have been many in the history of Christianity who have been fundamentally preoccupied with a rational approach to apologetics: men like Thomas Aquinas, Ramon Lull, Joseph Butler, James Orr, and F. R. Tennant. Doubtless history will record that such men have done more to hold back the forces of unbelief than has the whole school of irrationalism and the crucifixion of the intelligence.

Acknowledged Limitations

By way of anticipation I should like to eliminate certain possible criticisms of my work in advance. In the first place, the present argument embodies only the first part of my apologetic system: namely, the problem of epistemological approach and the apologetic of natural revelation. Two remarks are appropriate in this regard: first, the rest of the system is in process of completion and its ultimate

[1] *The Word of God in the Life of Man:* "Reason and Biblical Authority" (St. Paul, Minn.: Bethel College and Seminary, 1956).

publication will await the response to the present work. In the final analysis a complete system of Christian apologetics is contemplated in which there will be developed the apologetic of special revelation and the apologetic of synthesis. This last section will attempt to show the truth of Christian faith comparatively by a detailed analysis of the major religious and philosophical world views. In view of this same partial character of the argument that follows, a specific treatment of Christian faith itself does not appear. It will be well therefore to clarify my position as a committed Christian, lest any should infer my lack of faith by an absence of its acknowledgment in the text. I am, in fact, an adherent of evangelical orthodoxy: and the absence of any such confession in the text that follows is due solely to the fact that the confession is not basic to the argument as herein developed.

In the second place, it is acknowledged that in treating the various modes of approach to Christian apologetics, I have not been exhaustive in my analysis. Had I been writing a history, I should, for example, have treated the whole development of liberal apologetics from Schleiermacher onward, the European representatives of presuppositionalism, and the historical background of neo-orthodoxy. Aside from the fact that this material would have increased the technicality of an already involved discussion, this acknowledged omission may perhaps be overlooked on two grounds: first, on the ground that representatives of the main approaches have been discussed; second, on the ground that the positive argument for my own position aptly contrasts it with other possible viewpoints.

One further possible misunderstanding should be avoided. It will be seen that my position stresses rational argument as the adequate foundation for intelligent Christian conviction. On this point the system will speak for itself: but I should like to stress in advance that no one can be compelled to faith by rational evidences, since man is a volitional as well as a rational being. Still, the presentation of such evidences will serve at least two purposes in this context: the argument may, it is hoped, be the occasion of a reasonable faith and, at the same time, may by its very presentation emphasize more clearly the moral culpability of rejecting spiritual truth. On the other hand, no one maintains that only those may have efficacious Christian faith who understand in detail the rational basis for Christian truth. Yet without this objective basis as its foundation, faith would certainly not be efficacious; just as a man might stand on a skyscraper without understanding the principles of engineering involved in its structure, while at the same time it is indisputable that he could not stand there safely if such principles were not exemplified in the structure of the building.

Intellectual Indebtedness

The text itself will manifest the many thinkers to whom I have been indebted in my thinking. But I should like to express special appreciation to four men who have stimulated my interest in philosophy and apologetics: Dr. Edwin A. Burtt, of Cornell University, who first aroused my appetite for philosophy itself; Dr. Kenneth Kantzer, of Wheaton College, who directed my interest toward natural theology; Dr. Carl F. H. Henry, who inspired me with his personal devotion to Christian scholarship and who continues to inspire other young men through his teaching at Fuller Theological Seminary; and Dr. Vernon C. Grounds, president of Conservative Baptist Theological Seminary, who has exemplified for me an enlightened Christian conviction tempered with a deep Christian compassion. The last two men have been so kind as to read my manuscript with great care and to suggest numerous criticisms. But of course the convictions of the book are entirely my own and I assume full responsibility for any deficiencies in their formulation and expression.

An Envisioned Ministry

It is hoped that this work will lend itself to a number of significant ends. As a textbook, it should be useful in several fields: as a companion volume in apologetics or as a basic text; as the basis of a study of theism as over against alternative positions; and even as an introduction to philosophy, since, at some point or other, it deals with the major philosophical problems in epistemology and metaphysics and even, though to a lesser extent, in ethics.

But these considerations, important as I intend them to be, are after all secondary. The book is primarily a serious effort to reorient and communicate argumentative theism and rational apologetics to the contemporary mind. Whatever else may be the use for this work, it is my prayer that it might be above all an evangel and a summons to theism as the most adequate explanation of existence and destiny.

In the light of this purpose, I both urge and invite comments and criticisms alike from all whose interest is stirred, whether positively or negatively.

PREFACE TO THE SECOND EDITION

If, after the lapse of nearly half a millennium, Michelangelo were to reevaluate the aesthetic worth of the frescoes he created in the Sistine Chapel at Rome, it would be profoundly interesting to question what his retrospective judgment of it might be. I surmise that although he might be dissatisfied with certain elements of structure and detail, he would nevertheless be at peace with himself about the main impact of that cultural treasure, precisely because he would see it as having effectively communicated to the eyes of all beholders a message to which he himself remained deeply committed. And as I look back over the comparatively shorter span of a mere quarter of a century since *The Resurrection of Theism* was first made available to minds other than my own, my present judgment of its worth is not unlike that which I have supposed would be Michelangelo's response to the Sistine frescoes: I too communicated to the minds of all beholders a message to which I myself remain deeply committed. Although I have continued to meditate on all these themes while being deeply affected by my thorough investigation of opposing views, I can sincerely say that I nevertheless have nothing whatever to take back with regard to the main content and thrust of what I earnestly contended so long ago.

But, again like Michelangelo, I too am moderately dissatisfied with certain elements of structure and detail. Buoyed up by an unbridled youthful enthusiasm, I wrote with a vibrant optimism which tended to assume that virtually the only barrier between truth and commitment was the mist of unclear insight which hampered adequate understanding; and I therefore proceeded as if the only serious hindrances to a person's accurate philosophical judgment were those which diligent investigation could ultimately recognize and disarm. Over the years I have become increasingly and even painfully aware of the complexity of those varied factors which unwittingly condition a man's understanding: I still believe in the ideal of rational objectivity, but I now see it as a far more difficult goal to approximate, so that if I were writing the book today I would come to all the same conclusions, though I would claim many of them with a more guarded confidence.

In particular I would see my task more as that of persuading a fellow human being than as that of devastating a competing antagonist with *reductio ad absurdum* arguments and rhetorical flourishes. For that reason I have gone through the text and eliminated a kind of continuous thread of sarcasm and invective which, as I see it now, is counterproductive. The style is still aggressive and at times even strident, but I hope it will come across as noticeably less arrogant—that in any case is what I intend.

I think I also owe the reader an explanation of several references in the text of the book in which I refer to further volumes that would complete the system here begun. The details of my personal life brought many unanticipated changes which delayed those youthful plans. But my book of 1979, entitled *Oriental Philosophy: A Westerner's Guide to Eastern Thought,* should be interpreted as a partial fulfillment of those promises in relation to Oriental religious philosophies of classical China and India. And I am now actively at work producing what I hope will be my *magnum opus* in philosophical apologetics, a volume which explicitly fulfills at length my early plans for a full-orbed systematic treatment. It is my earnest hope that no personal circumstances will further delay the completion of that goal.

I am thankful to all those who through the years have noticed, discussed, or even rejected my views, though I cannot here respond to their many criticisms and helpful suggestions. But I am especially glad for those who have been personally stimulated and helped in their spiritual pilgrimage by *The Resurrection of Theism.* In particular I want to cite Professor William Lane Craig, now my colleague in philosophy of religion here at Trinity, who thought highly enough of the work to write a master's thesis largely devoted to its exposition, and to recommend the book to Baker Book House for republication. I also want to recognize, with equally profound gratitude, Roger H. Wasson of Precision Research Incorporated (Austin, Texas), for many years an earnest student and avowed advocate of my book and its positions, and probably as familiar with my thought on these themes as any other living person. During many bleak seasons of my life the encouragement I have derived from such sources has served to sustain me in what I view as my intellectual task.

Finally, I want to express my sincere gratitude to Baker Book House for the interest of its editors in making this book available to the reading public again. I hope and pray that the book will serve many useful pedagogical and personal needs.

STUART CORNELIUS HACKETT
Deerfield, Illinois
March, 1982

PERMISSION FOR QUOTATIONS

CLARK, T. & T.
   Barth, Karl. *The Doctrine of the Word of God.*
   Galloway, George. *The Philosophy of Religion.*
COLUMBIA UNIVERSITY PRESS
   Krikorian, Y. H. (Editor). *Naturalism and the Human Spirit.*
CONGER, G. P.
   Conger, G. P. *The Ideologies of Religion.*
WILLIAM B. EERDMANS PUBLISHING COMPANY
   Carnell, E. J. *An Introduction to Christian Apologetics.*
   ——. *A Philosophy of the Christian Religion.*
   Clark, G. H. *A Christian Philosophy of Education.*
   ——. *A Christian View of Men and Things.*
   Henry, C. F. H. *Remaking the Modern Mind.*
   ——. *The Drift of Western Thought.*
   ——. *The Protestant Dilemma.*
GREYSTONE PRESS
   Ghose, Sri Aurobindo. *The Life Divine.*
HARCOURT, BRACE & COMPANY INC.
   Broad, C. D. *Religion, Philosophy, and Psychical Research.*
HARPER & BROTHERS
   Balfour, A. J. *Theism and Thought.*
   Burtt, E. A. *Types of Religious Philosophy.*
   Macintosh, D. C. *The Problem of Religious Knowledge.*
   Trueblood, D. E. *The Logic of Belief.*
   Wild, John. *Introduction to Realistic Philosophy.*
HODDER & STOUGHTON, LTD.
   Balfour, A. J. *Theism and Thought.*
HENRY HOLT & COMPANY
   Bergson, Henri. *Creative Evolution.*
   Dewey, John. *Logic: The Theory of Inquiry.*
   ——. *Reconstruction in Philosophy.*
HOUGHTON MIFFLIN COMPANY
   Larrabee, H. A. *Reliable Knowledge.*
JOHNSEN PUBLISHING COMPANY
   Werkmeister, W. H. *An Introduction to Critical Thinking.*
J. B. LIPPINCOTT COMPANY
   Stace, W. T. *Religion and the Modern Mind.*
LONGMANS, GREEN, & COMPANY
   Balfour, A. J. *The Foundations of Belief.*
   Lecomte du Noüy, P. *Human Destiny.*

MACMILLAN COMPANY
Blanshard, Brand. *The Nature of Thought*, 2 volumes.
Emmet, D. M. *The Nature of Metaphysical Thinking.*
Schiller, F. C. S. *Formal Logic: A Scientific and Social Problem.*
Smith, N. K. *A Commentary to Kant's Critique of Pure Reason.*
Streeter, B. H. (Editor). *Foundations: A Statement of Christian Belief in Terms of Modern Thought.*
Taylor, A. E. *Does God Exist?*
Whitehead, A. N. *Process and Reality.*

NEWMAN PRESS
Phillips, R. P. *Modern Thomistic Philosophy*, volume 2.

OXFORD UNIVERSITY PRESS (New York and London)
Russell, Bertrand. *Religion and Science.*
———. *The Problems of Philosophy.*

PHILOSOPHICAL LIBRARY
Barth, Karl. *Dogmatics in Outline.*
Russell, Bertrand. *Dictionary of Mind, Matter, and Morals.*

PHILOSOPHICAL REVIEW
Kaufman, A. S. "The Analytic and the Synthetic: a Tenable 'Dualism.' "
Quine, W. V. "Two Dogmas of Empiricism."
Reichenbach, H. "Are Phenomenal Reports Absolutely Certain?"

PRESBYTERIAN AND REFORMED PUBLISHING COMPANY
VanTil, Cornelius. *Common Grace.*
———. *The Defence of the Faith.* (Here quoted from the informal mimeographed syllabi in which the chapters first appeared.)
Warfield, B. B. *The Inspiration and Authority of the Bible:* Introduction by Cornelius VanTil.

PRESBYTERIAN GUARDIAN PUBLISHING CORPORATION
The Infallible Word: Article by Cornelius VanTil—"Nature and Scripture."

FLEMING H. REVELL COMPANY
Morrison, A. C. *Man Does Not Stand Alone.*

PAUL R. REYNOLDS AND SON, 599 Fifth Avenue, New York 17, New York
James, William. *Pragmatism.*
———. *The Meaning of Truth.*

ROLAND PRESS COMPANY
Patterson, C. H. *Moral Standards.*

CHARLES SCRIBNER'S SONS
Baillie, John. *Our Knowledge of God.*
Barth, Karl. *The Knowledge of God and the Service of God.*
Galloway, George. *The Philosophy of Religion.*
Hocking, W. E. *Types of Philosophy.*
Maritain, Jacques. *The Degrees of Knowledge.*

SIMON & SCHUSTER
Russell, Bertrand. *Human Knowledge: Its Scope and Limits.*

WESTMINSTER PRESS
Brunner, Emil. *Revelation and Reason.*

W. A. WILDE COMPANY
Henry, C. F. H. *Notes on the Doctrine of God.*

YALE UNIVERSITY PRESS
Dewey, John. *A Common Faith.*
Hocking, W. E. *The Meaning of God in Human Experience.*

NOTE: Full bibliographical data on the above works appears in the appended Bibliography at the end of the text. Every effort has been made to secure permission for all quotations; in case of error, due permission will be sought upon notification.

INTRODUCTION

The Importance of Apologetics

IT IS PROBABLY IMPOSSIBLE to imagine the amount of intellectual energy that has been diverted from normal processes of arriving at intellectual conclusions because it has gone into rationalization of the doctrines entertained by historic religions."[1] Such, in brief, is the estimate of one of America's greatest twentieth-century philosophers concerning the enterprise upon which we are about to embark. It is precisely to such an abnormal task that we address ourselves in the entire discussion that follows: whether Mr. Dewey's opinion is justified will be for the world to decide.

But abnormal or not, the attempt to understand the world, the effort toward adjustment to the Ultimate Reality, the determination of action according to primary beliefs, the burning desire for cosmic security—all these things are characteristic, if not always completely self-conscious, human indulgences. And it is to the utmost rational direction of these very indulgences that a theistic philosophy is supremely oriented.

In the simplest terms, life and existence are possible only by an adjustment to environmental reality: and if a man fails to make any such adjustment, his doom is antecedently sealed. Every successful advance—judged by whatever standard—necessitates the correlation of a man's thoughts and actions to circumstances and conditions external to himself: every experience of life, from the nursing of the infant to the sober reflections and reactions of the mature individual who stands on the brink of eternity at death's door, involves the interaction of life with environmental forces. Indeed, to the extent that one fails to adjust to the vast complex of reality beyond him, he brings himself and all his goals to the abyss of extinction; there may

[1] J. Dewey, *A Common Faith*, p. 33.

19

even be those who, in given situations, make no environmental adjustment; but such men make shipwreck of their lives in the rockbound treachery that is the shore of natural law. And if anyone entertains an opinion to the contrary, doubtless it is because his opinion has not been tested by practice.

Now adjustment to reality, for rational selves, is ultimately impossible apart from a knowledge of the nature of reality: and philosophy—even in the guise of religion—attempts to answer three basic problems related to this cosmic adjustment that is so necessary.

(1) How is knowledge possible at all? Here philosophy is *epistemology:* the study of the origin, nature, and limits of knowledge.

(2) What is the ultimate nature of reality in terms of which a finally satisfactory adjustment can be made, and how is this ultimate reality related to the immediate realities of our experience? Here philosophy is *metaphysics:* the study of the nature of ultimate and subordinate reality, together with their mutual interrelations.

(3) Through what appropriate means can adjustment to the total complex of reality, both ultimate and subordinate, be made? Here philosophy is *ethics:* the study of value and conduct.

Now it would appear highly questionable that the attempt to answer these questions rationally is an abnormal procedure. For apart from some such answers—at least on an elemental scale—a fruitful adjustment to reality would be rationally impossible; and apart from some such adjustment, the prerogative of this-worldly existence itself must be surrendered.

Apologetics—from Greek, *apologia,* a verbal defense—sets for itself the task of defending some systematic answer to such basic questions as we have outlined. And since the defense of a system logically presupposes the system itself, it is presumed that apologetics would necessarily entail an account of the basis on which the system itself is formulated. In this broad sense, apologetics is practically coextensive with the whole philosophical enterprise: it is not a *mere* defense—it is rather a defense of conclusions which the rational analysis of human experience fully justifies. And for my part, I have no interest in the defense of beliefs that are otherwise grounded than through a rationally self-consistent interpretation of experiential data, at whatever level these data might appear. In any case, it is this broad meaning of apologetics that we intend in our whole subsequent discussion: and apologetics may therefore be defined as the systematic, rational formulation and defense of beliefs about knowledge, reality, and conduct. And in particular, Christian apologetics would consist in the attempt to show that only the Christian World View satisfactorily meets the ultimate demands of reason in its approach to experience. In the present volume, we set ourselves to the establishment and defense of theism; in subsequent volumes, we shall make a similar attempt with respect to theistic Christianity.

Summary of Procedure

The immediate task at hand will be to reach a general answer to the problems that surround and determine our necessary adjustment to reality. Accordingly, in Part I, our attention will be directed to the problem of knowledge, since an understanding of the basic principles or presuppositions of all thought is logically prior to the formulation of any systematic metaphysic. If a man is to apprehend rationally his place in the scheme of things so as to make that adjustment to the Ultimate Reality toward which he grasps in his innermost being, he must come to a comprehension of the conditions which make knowledge itself possible. It will be found that this possibility of knowing depends upon an innate structure of rationality with which the mind approaches and understands the data of experience. Such an epistemology, called *rational empiricism,* may be plausibly argued in the face of all the main objections commonly brought against it by showing that negative criticisms of this perspective presuppose the very foundations of knowledge which those criticisms purport to reject as inadequate.

In Part II, there is set forth the inadequacy of every major historical alternative to rational empiricism as the epistemological basis for a theistic world view. Objective and subjective empiricisms, pragmatism, and voluntaristic rationalism (called presuppositionalism) are each examined and each in turn eliminated as inadequate and self-contradictory.

In Part III, rational empiricism, having eliminated its proposed alternatives, attempts a twofold task: positively, to demonstrate the existence of the God of theism; negatively, to refute the whole range of principal objections that are customarily urged against such a demonstration. At the summit of rational analysis, theism will emerge victorious over her opponents so as to justify the age-old conclusion that God is the Ultimate Reality and that it is to Him that man's final and only adequate adjustment must be made.

Our path is long; but at the journey's end there lies that prize toward which—consciously or not—men are ever bending their efforts: the prize of a finally satisfactory relation to Reality itself! Nor will our philosophical voyage be without its own delights: to the mind in search of ultimate truth, every step of knowledge is a joy. The road to the promised land may lead through a long wilderness; but as with Israel, so with us: the bitter waters of Marah turn to sweetness, Elim yields its quiet rest from the weary desert, and Sinai peals forth with majestic thunder. To the task, then! And may the hazardous intricacy of the way not deter us while we strive for such an eternal prize as the knowledge of God Himself!

GENERAL TABLE OF CONTENTS

PART I

RATIONAL EMPIRICISM AS A BASIS FOR CHRISTIAN APOLOGETICS

PART II

AN EVALUATION OF ALTERNATIVE POSITIONS

PART III

NATURAL THEOLOGY AND THE EXISTENCE OF GOD

Section A

THE THEISTIC ARGUMENT FROM NATURAL REVELATION

Section B

AN ANSWER TO OBJECTIONS AGAINST THE THEISTIC ARGUMENTS

ANALYTICAL TABLE OF CONTENTS

PART I

RATIONAL EMPIRICISM AS A BASIS FOR CHRISTIAN APOLOGETICS

PART III

NATURAL THEOLOGY AND THE EXISTENCE OF GOD

Section A

THE THEISTIC ARGUMENT FROM NATURAL REVELATION

CHAPTER I. THE CLASSIFICATION OF THE ARGUMENTS

Section B
AN ANSWER TO OBJECTIONS AGAINST THE THEISTIC ARGUMENTS

CHAPTER I. THE TRANSCENDENTAL ARGUMENT OF MYSTICISM
Introduction

Part I

RATIONAL EMPIRICISM AS A BASIS
FOR CHRISTIAN APOLOGETICS

THE MEANING OF RATIONAL EMPIRICISM

BRIEF STATEMENT OF THE POSITION

Primary Meaning

R ATIONAL EMPIRICISM, as I profess it, is the doctrine that knowledge is possible only because it involves the combination of two elements: a mind that comes to experience with a structure of thought in terms of which it is necessarily disposed to understand that experience—this is the a priori or "before-experience" element; data upon which this structure of thought terminates to gain specific knowledge of particulars—this is the a posteriori or "after-experience" element.[1]

According to this position, knowledge would be impossible on either a purely rational or a purely empirical basis. For on the one hand, while the mind by its very nature has a categorical structure, it has at the outset no stock of innate content ideas, but must terminate upon experiential data to gain such content knowledge: the evolving of knowledge from the categorical structure alone is therefore impossible and pure rationalism is rejected. On the other hand, however, the data of experience would not be intelligible if the mind were a total blank at birth, devoid of all structure or aptitude. Indeed, on this basis, minds would be nothing but stones, and knowledge would be impossible. Thus the very first intelligible experience of a self presupposes an a priori structure, and pure empiricism is likewise rejected. Every act of knowledge, therefore, presupposes both the categorical structure of rationality and the relation of that structure to experienced data. Such a position does not imply that the experienced data, in every act of knowledge, must come from a source be-

[1]T. Christlieb, *Modern Doubt and Christian Belief*, p. 76: for a good brief statement of this general thesis.

yond the mind and thus have an external or sensuous origin: the fact of thought is itself a datum of experience, and from its possibility important conclusions may be drawn, not only about thought itself, but also about the formal conditions for the possible existence of all things. From the possibility of consistent thought, for example, we can conclude that if a statement about the real world is self-contradictory, it is false—and this not merely in the sense that the statement is internally absurd, but also in the sense that it is a false account of the real world itself. For if we assert that a self-contradiction is true, then we are rejecting a principle upon which the possibility of any assertion at all rests: the principle, namely, that a thing cannot both be and not be at the same time and in the same manner; and if this principle is false, no knowledge is possible—not even the knowledge that a self-contradiction is true. As well in that case to be a nonrational mound of dirt as a thinking man.

Subsidiary Implications

But in addition, the theory of rational empiricism involves, to my mind, certain further tenets which are not always espoused by those who class their epistemology under this rubric. Since the position involves epistemological dualism, it necessitates an espousal of the coherence theory of truth. Epistemological dualism is the doctrine that the immediate object present to the mind is not the independently existing reality—say a box or what have you—but a representative idea of this object. All that the mind knows directly are its ideas and nothing else. That rational empiricism involves this position seems obvious: if intelligible experience does not *exist* until the structure of the mind terminates upon data of experience, then it is clear that what the mind possesses is always a resultant concept or idea, never the independently existing object as such. But if such is the state of the whole gamut of intelligible experience, then either we must be skeptics about the knowledge of things as they exist independently, or we must maintain that true knowledge of such entities is possible by the systematic correlation of our various experiences into a self-consistent whole. Since, as will subsequently appear, skepticism is self-contradictory, the second alternative will necessarily be maintained. But the theory that the test of truth consists in such a systematic consistency of ideas in a logically coherent whole is precisely the coherence theory of truth.

With such a key to the possibility of knowledge, we assert that the categorical forms of thought are applicable for the attainment of knowledge in every sphere where intelligible propositions are formulable. The self-consistent application of the categorical structure determines and makes possible the cogitation of any real object whatsoever, from the lowest material constituent to the being of God Himself. There exists no real entity that does not yield itself to rational thought and analysis when the data pertinent to its being are presented in experience: there are no incomprehensible realities, no realms of being that thought cannot conquer if she but encounters them. There are undoubtedly vast ranges of data that thought, in man, does not comprehend; but should the data thus unknown present themselves before the bar of reason, thought need not fail to comprehend them. Reason therefore sweeps from her path all contenders for the status of unknowability. Indeed, she maintains that these contenders could not even state their claim intelligibly if it were not utterly false and absurd.

CRITICAL EXPOSITION OF THE KANTIAN THEORY

Positive Formulation

A priori categories.—Slightly more than a century and a half ago, the wise sage of Koenigsberg brought to birth a theory of human knowledge with which the whole development of philosophical research had been in conception and travail from the time of the earliest critical speculations. It was in the year 1781 that Immanuel Kant published the *Critique of Pure Reason*. In that book, Kant became the first systematic champion of rational empiricism. There had always been, since the height of the development of philosophy in Greece, the two schools of rationalism and empiricism—the former holding that all knowledge is innate and is merely brought to the surface of the mind upon the occasion of observation and reflection; the latter holding that all knowledge is derived from experience in observation and reflection and that the mind, at the start of its journey, is an empty receptacle waiting to be filled with the stuff of experience. For the rationalist, the mind was like a seed which needed only to be planted in the soil of experience in order to flower forth with all the data of knowledge. For the empiricist, the mind was no more than a blank sheet of paper or a wax tablet waiting to receive impressions from some source outside itself.

The lasting contribution of Kant—whatever else may dispose our minds against him—was the fact that he discerned the element of truth in both these positions. He saw that, although the empiricists were right in maintaining that the mind has no content of knowledge at birth, no innate ideas as such, they were all wrong in failing to cede to the rationalists that the mind does come to experience, not as a wax tablet, but with a rational structure in terms of which the world must be understood. The knowing self approaches experiential data with certain categories or forms of thought in terms of which it necessarily understands these data; these categories are not, indeed, filled with the stuff of experience, but they are the preconditions in terms of which any experience of the world becomes possible. Such a category, since it is a precondition of all possible experience that is intelligible, is said by Kant to be a priori in nature, while the content of our ideas, being gained from experience, is said to be a posteriori.

To sum up the whole matter in Kant's own words:

> While all judgments of experience are empirical (i.e., have their ground in immediate sense-perception), *vice versa,* all empirical judgments are not judgments of experience, but, besides the empirical, and in general besides what is given to the sensuous intuition, particular concepts must yet be superadded—concepts which have their origin quite a priori in the pure understanding, and under which every perception must be first of all subsumed and then by their means changed into experience.[2]

There is, then, Kant clearly maintains, both a rational and an empirical facet to the production of knowledge: while all knowledge, as consisting of ideas in consciousness, must come from experience, experience itself is possible only because the mind comes to the world with certain pure conceptions of the understanding in terms of which the world is intelligible. The categories, therefore, are forms of thought through which the mind, by its very structure, is necessarily disposed to understand the data of experience; or in Kant's own words, they "are conceptions of an object in general, by means of which its intuition is contemplated as determined . . ."[3]

[2]I. Kant, *Prolegomena to Any Future Metaphysics,* pp. 54, 55.
[3]*Critique of Pure Reason,* p. 75.

This a priori categorical element that is basic to all experience, Kant declared to be *synthetic* in character as distinguished from *analytic*.[4] While the current definition of these terms is a matter of some dispute, Kant's own meaning here is unmistakable:

> Analytical judgments (affirmative) are . . . those in which the connection of the predicate with the subject is cogitated through identity; those in which this connection is cogitated without identity are called synthetical judgments. The former may be called *explicative*, the latter augmentative judgments . . . that is, judgments which really add to, and do not merely analyze or explain the conceptions which make up the sum of our knowledge.[5]

An analytical judgment, in other words, is one in which the predicate is or may be logically implied in the subject, so that no new content of knowledge is involved beyond what is already contained in the subject: e.g., all men are men. A synthetical judgment, on the other hand, adds a new element to those contained in the subject, so that our knowledge—if the judgment is true—is actually increased beyond the extent which would be possible by mere analysis of the subject term: e.g., all men are fools. A further distinguishing characteristic consists in the fact that if an analytic judgment is negated, self-contradiction results directly, whereas this is not the case with a synthetic judgment.

Now Kant's contention is that all experiential judgments are synthetic in nature. For example, when I say that every event is an effect of some cause, I am saying something that exceeds what could be derived by analysis from the mere concept of an event as such: the relation here is not cogitated by way of identity, but rests on a factor that is imported. Such importation may take place either from the data of experience, in which case the judgment is a posteriori; or it may take place in terms of the basic presuppositions of all thought, i.e., in terms of the categories, in which case the judgment, as in the example cited, is a priori. From this it becomes evident that Kant's defense of a priori categories is an affirmation that all experiential knowledge rests on a *synthetic* a priori factor: synthetic because judgments based on the categories could not be ultimately established by derivation from the meaning of subject terms, a priori because

[4]*Ibid.*, p. 7f.; *Prolegomena*, p. 59.
[5]*Critique of Pure Reason*, p. 7 and note.

the mind brings the categories to the data of experience in the first place. Even a synthetic a posteriori judgment depends for its intelligibility on the ultimate character of the basic presuppositions which the mind thus brings to bear. Thus, for example, the statement—this desk is wooden—could not be asserted, according to Kant, unless the mind contained at the outset the basic principles which make any intelligible predication possible.

Derivation of the categories from the types of logical judgment.—But beyond this point Kant was likewise able to show in exactly what manner the nature and number of the a priori categories may be determined. Aristotle had propounded a list of categories, but he had, according to Kant, merely derived them in haphazard meditation on experience.[6] It is to the credit of Immanuel Kant that he made a simple observation which enables us to determine the nature and number of the categories precisely; at least, he indicated the general method by which such a deduction of the categories may be carried out.

The content of knowledge is made up, Kant observed, of judgments that we assert about the data of experience; a judgment being the affirmation or denial of some predicate to some subject—as when I say: clouds are beautiful, *clouds* being the subject and *beautiful* the predicate. If, therefore, the application of the categories to experience results in various types of logical judgment, then there must be an a priori category corresponding to each of the most basic types of logical judgment. In this way, Kant was able to derive a table of twelve categories which he deduced from the commonly accepted classification of logical judgments under headings of quantity, quality, relation, modality.

The table of these judgments, with their definitions, is as follows:

(1) Quantity
   (a) Universal: in which a predicate is affirmed or denied of a subject in every instance of the subject. (Example: All men are mortal.)
   (b) Particular: in which a predicate is affirmed or denied of a subject in some instances. (Example: Some men are mortal.)
   (c) Singular: in which a predicate is affirmed or denied of

⁶*Categoriae*, 1b25–2a10.

a subject in a concrete instance. (Example: Socrates is mortal.)

(2) Quality

  (a) Affirmative: in which a predicate is assigned to some subject. (Example: Man is a biped.)

  (b) Negative: in which a predicate is abstracted from some subject. (Example: No men are fish.)

  (c) Infinite: in which a single proposition assigns and abstracts predicates to some subject. (Example: Man is not-a-fly.)

(3) Relation

  (a) Categorical: in which a predicate is either assigned to, or abstracted from, some subject. (Examples: All husbands are men; no husbands are women; etc.)

  (b) Hypothetical: in which a consequent is connected with a condition. (Example: If I win the game, I shall be glad.)

  (c) Disjunctive: in which mutually exclusive alternatives are affirmed. (Example: Either I am home in bed, or I am at the college teaching.)

(4) Modality

  (a) Problematical: in which a predicate is assigned to, or abstracted from, some subject with possibility. (Example: John may, or may not, be sleeping.)

  (b) Assertorical: in which a predicate is assigned to, or abstracted from, some subject, simply. (Example: John is, or is not, sleeping.)

  (c) Apodictical: in which a predicate is assigned to, or abstracted from, some subject, necessarily. (Example: John must, or must not, be sleeping.)

Since the faculty of pronouncing such judgments upon experience exactly corresponds to and exhausts the whole power of thought, "there arise exactly so many pure conceptions of the understanding, applying a priori to objects of intuition in general, as there are logical functions in all possible judgments. . . . This division is made systematically from a common principle, namely, the faculty of judgment (which is just the same as the power of thought), and has not arisen rhapsodically from a search at haphazard after pure conceptions."[7] As Weldon puts the point: "Kant maintains that each form of judgment, when carefully considered, is found to assert between the concepts which it synthesizes just the kind of connection which is expressed by one of the concepts corresponding to his table of . . . categories."[8]

In this manner, Kant arrived at a list of twelve categories of the understanding which correspond systematically with the types of judgment as indicated above:

(1) Quantity	(3) Relation
(a) Unity	(a) Substance
(b) Plurality	(b) Causation
(c) Totality	(c) Reciprocity
(2) Quality	(4) Modality
(a) Reality	(a) Possibility
(b) Negation	(b) Existence
(c) Limitation	(c) Necessity[9]

Except for some critical alterations to be suggested in the sequel, the correspondence between the types of judgment and the derived categories is so sufficiently obvious that only a few illustrations of the correlation need to be cited. An especially clear example may be drawn from the relation of an hypothetical judgment to the underlying or basic category of causation. Such a judgment "asserts the kind of connection which is expressed in the conception of the relation of ground and consequent. . . . The bare formulation of an hypothetical proposition implies that I understand the relation of something conditioned to that which is its condition."[10] And so with every type of logical judgment: each basic type implies a previous possession, by the mind, of a synthetic a priori form of thought in terms of which the judgment itself—and hence an intelligible experience—is possible.

The one derivation that seems unusually difficult, as Kant himself affirms, is that of the category of reciprocity or community from the disjunctive judgment.[11] But a few observations will, I think,

[7]*Critique of Pure Reason*, pp. 61, 62.
[8]T. D. Weldon, *Introduction to Kant's Critique of Pure Reason*, p. 89.
[9]*Prolegomena*, p. 61.
[10]Weldon, *op. cit.*, p. 89.
[11]*Critique of Pure Reason*, p. 65.

remove the difficulty. In a disjunctive judgment, as distinguished from a mere alternative judgment, a number of situations are posited in such a way that they determine each other reciprocally—in an alternative judgment, both or all of the proposed situations may hold simultaneously, as in the proposition: Either I am studying or I am wearing a green shirt; in a true disjunctive, the situations are mutually exclusive, as in the example cited in the table above. That is, in a true disjunctive, if one alternative is affirmed, the others are excluded by implication.

Now the very making of such a judgment implies that I understand the relation of reciprocal causation: in a body, for example—and this is Kant's illustration—the various parts mutually attract, repel, and condition each other.[12] Nor is this category the same as that in which I understand the relation of ground and consequent simply: for this last relation is a unilateral one in which x causes y, whereas by the category of reciprocity I cogitate a mutual causal interaction *between* x and y. It is according to this category of reciprocity that the understanding represents to itself the parts of a whole "as having—each of them—an existence (as substances), independently of the others, and yet as united in one whole."[13]

One further remark may be made about the fact that the categories form triads. Each third category, Kant notes, "arises from the combination of the second with the first . . . Thus . . . Community [Reciprocity] is the causality of a substance, reciprocally determining and determined by other substances . . ."[14] But this does not mean that the third member is a deduced and not a primitive conception. For in connecting the first two to achieve the third, there is required a special exercise of the understanding, *not* contained simply in the exercise of the first two.[15]

Limitation of the categories.—Having made considerable concessions to apriorism, Kant then proceeds to place serious strictures on the categories in their applicability. The forms of thought are subject to two principal limitations: (1) First, they are legitimately applicable and significant only within the realm of possible sense experience, so that we cannot by their use pass beyond the limits of such experience to make affirmations about supposed realities which

[12]*Ibid.*, pp. 65, 66.
[13]*Ibid.*, p. 66.
[14]*Ibid.*, pp. 64, 65.
[15]*Ibid.*, p. 65.

transcend the realm of possible empirical intuition or sensation.[16] In fact, when any such attempt is made, the mind falls into a series of hopeless contradictions which Kant called the antinomies of pure reason.[17]

(2) Second, the categories give us no knowledge whatever of things-in-themselves beyond the bare fact of their existence as the cause of our sensations: only that is known by the categories which consists in things as they appear to us. In Kant's own terminology,[18] the categories give us no noumenal but only phenomenal knowledge: "Beyond objects of experience, i.e., concerning things as noumena, all positive knowledge was correctly denied to the speculative reason."[19]

Critical Alteration

Introductory remarks.—Lest there should be any misapprehension, allow me to say that I accept without reservation Kant's contentions both for a synthetic a priori factor in knowledge, and for the derivation of the categories involved in this factor from the basic types of logical judgment. I further accept Kant's doctrine that the synthetic a priori element in knowledge is strictly categorical and relational: i.e., the categories give us, of themselves, no content of knowledge concerning real existences which are independent of the mind; they are simply forms of thought to which such content must be extraneously furnished. As Kemp Smith says: "Their sole function is to serve in the interpretation of contents otherwise supplied."[20]

But while Kant's epistemology of rational empiricism is thus generally acceptable, its detail requires alteration along three lines: (1) the precise number of the categories may be reduced by the corresponding reduction of certain of the types of logical judgment to more basic types; (2) the legitimate application of the categories extends beyond their relation to actual or possible sense experience; (3) the categories are forms of things-in-themselves (noumena) as well as forms of thought, or of things as they appear to us (phenomena).

The numerical reduction of the categories.—If the number of basic

---

[16]*Ibid.*, pp. 84, 348.
[17]Cf. Part III, Section B, Chapter III.
[18]*Critique of Pure Reason*, pp. 161-167.
[19]Kant, *Critique of Practical Reason*, p. 153.
[20]Norman Kemp Smith, *A Commentary to Kant's Critique of Pure Reason*, p. xxxvi.

types of logical judgment can be reduced, this will, according to Kant's own principle, imply a correlated reduction in the number of presuppositions which are basic to all thought. The possibility of such a reduction must therefore be considered in connection with each of the four classes of judgment.

(1) Concerning judgments of quantity.—The problem in this class concerns whether a singular judgment may be regarded as either a universal or a particular, so that the category of totality would be a strict derivative from unity and plurality in combination.

The singular judgment certainly has affinities to both the universal and the particular: to the former, because the predicate refers to all that the subject term as such connotes; to the latter, because, if the subject be regarded as one of a class (Socrates, e.g., being a man), a singular judgment may be said to affirm a predicate of a subject in one particular instance.

Watson, as usually in his analysis, defends Kant here: while he admits that formal logic treats the individual judgment as universal and that this is justifiable "when we abstract from all the content of knowledge and deal only with the relation of whole and part, [it] is not admissible when we use the functions of judgment as a clue to all the modes of unity belonging to the constitution of thought."[21]

But this analysis appears fallacious: for, as Kant himself would admit, when we derive the categories, it is just the *form* of the judgment alone, and not the *content* of it that must be considered. And since a singular judgment is distinct from a universal *only* by considering the content of a given judgment, the derivation of a separate category from a singular judgment is unjustified.[22] I therefore conclude that the concept of totality is not a basic category, but is implied in the conjunction of the categories of unity and plurality.

(2) Concerning judgments of quality.—The problem in this class concerns whether the so-called infinite judgment is actually a separate type, or reduces to a negative judgment, so that the category of limitation is included in the conjunction of the categories of reality and negation and is not a distinct and basic form of thought.

Since the infinite judgment is somewhat difficult to comprehend, an illustration may be illuminating. Take the proposition: Man is not a fly. Now in this judgment it appears that we both assign and

[21] J. Watson, *Kant and His English Critics*, p. 69.
[22] Smith, *op. cit.*, p. 192.

abstract a predicate: we abstract the predicate *fly*, but we assign the predicate *not-a-fly*.[23] Since the infinite judgment thus combines in itself, by a single proposition, the elements of both affirmation and negation, it has been held by some Kantians that the derivation of a separate category here is justifiable.[24]

But as a matter of fact, it can be shown that the infinite judgment is not a separate type. For the term *not-a-fly*—to revert to our example—does not signify the nature of anything and is therefore not a true term. "As we should not take the trouble to affirm of man nothing in particular, the only point of the judgment must lie in denying of him something in particular; so that the meaning of the 'infinite' judgment . . . lies in the negative judgment."[25]

Since therefore the infinite judgment does not actually make a particular affirmation, it is merely a type of negative judgment.[26] I therefore conclude that since the infinite judgment reduces to the negative in this manner, the concept of limitation, as a basic form of thought, is not legitimately derived therefrom, but is already included in the conjunction of the categories of reality and negation.

(3) Concerning judgments of relation.—In this class, it is suggested, all the types reduce to simple categorical form.

For first, a hypothetical judgment can be stated as a categorical: If A is B, it is C, may be stated in the form, A that is B is C. In this case, it would then appear that a hypothetical judgment is already included as a derivative from the categorical. But this reduction seems to me to be invalid for the following reasons: (i) The notion or idea of a qualification of the subject A in the manner which appears in the second proposition would not have arisen if the mind possessed the category of existence or substance alone; for the attribution of such a limitation implies an understanding of the relation between ground and consequent such as appears most clearly in the hypothetical judgment. (ii) The form of the suggested categorical implies that the condition is fulfilled, that it is embodied in an instance: but it is of the nature of an ultimate category that the judgment from which it is derived have reference merely to the form, and not to the content of the judgment in specific instances: and only the true hypothetical thus connects a consequent with a

[23] Illustration from H. W. B. Joseph, *An Introduction to Logic*, p. 42.
[24] Watson, *op cit.*, p. 70.
[25] Joseph, *op. cit.*, pp. 42, 43.
[26] Cf. A. C. Ewing, *A Short Commentary on Kant's Critique of Pure Reason*, p. 142; Smith, *op. cit.*, p. 192.

condition which is not determined as fulfilled or embodied in actual instances.

(iii) Finally, the reduction is possible only in cases of strictly logical implication in which only three terms are involved. If more than three terms appear, the reduction is difficult, if not impossible. For example: If A is B, C is D. How can this form be reduced to a categorical proposition in the manner suggested? The following might be suggested: A is B means C is D. But this is not strictly a categorical proposition at all, but reverts to the hypothetical under a different format; for it clearly involves the connection of a condition with a consequence. Such a connection is not implied in a purely categorical proposition.

I conclude therefore, on these three grounds, that the reduction of the hypothetical to the categorical is illegitimate and that therefore the category of causation is not analytically implied in that of substance. In fact, the very notion of analytical implication appears to rest on that basic category of thought to which the hypothetical judgment corresponds.

But again, a disjunctive proposition may be stated as a series of hypotheticals. Take the disjunctive-alternative proposition: A is either B or C. If this proposition be considered as a simple alternative (i.e., in which neither of the alternatives would by its affirmation necessarily exclude the other), it may be stated as follows: If A is not B, it is C; If A is not C, it is B. If the proposition be considered as a true disjunctive (i.e., in which the affirmation of one alternative excludes the other), it may be stated as follows: If A is B, it is not C; If A is C, it is not B. Now if these reductions are legitimate, it would appear that the disjunctive reduces to the hypothetical, and that the category of reciprocity is already included in that of simple causation.

Yet here again the reduction seems to me to be invalid. (i) The combination of hypotheticals thus suggested would not arise unless the mind possessed already an understanding of such a reciprocal relation as is involved in the combinations as here stated. To express the disjunctive, in other words, a power of thought, distinct from that needed for expressing a strict hypothetical, is required: namely, that power by means of which the hypotheticals are thus mutually related in pairs. But this can only mean that the combination itself presupposes the disjunctive judgment as basic. After all, it takes all four hypotheticals to express the complete disjunctive idea: and no reason can be given for the combination if thought does not have a distinct capacity for thus relating proposed situations. Certainly a simple hypothetical implies no thought of mutual reciprocity: but this is implied in the disjunctive.

(ii) Even aside from the preceding point, the combined hypotheticals do not express all that is involved in the alternative-disjunctive type. In the case of the alternative pair, the original statement implies that at least one, perhaps both, of the situations is the case; whereas the two hypotheticals, if truly hypothetical, leave the situation completely indeterminate. In the case of the disjunctive pair, the statement implies that at least one of the situations is the case, and at least one is not the case; whereas again the hypotheticals do not rise to the expression of this implication.

I therefore conclude that the disjunctive is a distinct basic type of judgment and that therefore it represents a different aspect of the power of thought from that included in the hypothetical. It follows that the category of reciprocity does not reduce to that of causation as such.

(4) Concerning judgments of modality.—The real significance of these judgments is that they mark differences in the certainty with which we hold an opinion, so far as ordinary predication is concerned. But are they really distinct basic types of judgment?

Now there seems to be no point in distinguishing between an assertorical and a categorical proposition: the only problem, in my opinion, concerns whether the category derived from this type of judgment should be called *existence* or *substance*. The crux of the problem arises when we consider the fact that substances are not the only objective realities: beside substances, there are objective reals that we call *relations*. For example, when I say: This house is wooden, I make an affirmation about its substantial character; but when I say: This house is west of Mount Tabor, I make an affirmation about its relational character. Now both statements relate to an objective or existential situation: both refer to the reality in question.

Now if we should maintain that the proper category to derive from the assertorical or categorical judgment is substance, we would be denying the power of thought to make the type of relational judgments exemplified—which contradicts experience. On the other hand, the category existence would include both substances and relations: and I therefore conclude that the form of thought underlying a categorical or assertorical proposition is properly denominated by that very term, namely, *existence*.

With regard to problematical and apodictical judgments, however, no reduction seems possible. While it may be the case that on a deterministic view of the world, the *is* equals the *possible* equals the *necessary;* still we must retain these basic types of judgment for two reasons: (i) First, the deterministic view of the world has not been proved: and if it should be proved, it could only be by employing the very forms of thought that are disputed as basic types. To show that a deterministic metaphysic was the case, we should have to show, first, that it was logically possible, and second, that it was rationally necessary. But to do this we would necessarily employ these very categories to establish our case: we could hardly turn back on our own argument to deny that possibility and necessity (and their opposites by negation) were basic forms of thought. (ii) Second, to restate the same point in a different context: thought does cogitate things as possible or impossible, necessary or contingent. And even the Absolute Mind, if such there be, could be deprived of these forms of thought only on the supposition of a determinism which, as we have seen, cannot be established without the use of these very forms.

I therefore conclude that the apodictical and problematical judgments are basic types and that from them thought may posit the categories of necessity and contingency, possibility and impossibility.

When the suggested and established alterations are made, the following list of judgments and corresponding categories results:

Judgments	*Categories*
Quantity	Quantity
Universal	Unity
Particular	Plurality
Quality	Quality
Affirmative	Reality
Negative	Negation
Relation	Relation
Categorical (Assertorical)	Existence[27]

[27]Since the categorical and assertorical judgments involve the same power of thought, this type of judgment, with its corresponding category, may be classed either under relation or modality.

Hypothetical	Causation
Disjunctive	Reciprocity
Modality	Modality
Problematical	Possibility
Apodictical	Necessity

The application of the categories beyond the realm of sense.— Kant's position is that the categories are legitimately applicable only within the limits of sensuous content, only with respect to the possible experience of the sensuous world. Nothing qualifies as knowledge, on the speculative or theoretical level, unless it has sensuous content.

But can this position be consistently maintained? I think that it cannot for two definite reasons:

(1) The statement itself is either meaningless or self-contradictory. Either this statement is an item of speculative knowledge or not. If it is not, then it cannot form a legitimate basis for a theory of speculative knowledge, and it therefore is ultimately meaningless from an epistemological point of view. But if it is an item of speculative knowledge, then it is false: for this statement does not relate to sensuous content and is therefore, by its own assertion, not a true proposition of speculative knowledge. Thus we end up with the curious conclusion that the statement can only be true by being false—which is self-contradictory. In either case—whether the original proposition is or is not an item of speculative knowledge—Kant's position cannot be maintained without absurdity.

(2) The position reduces to that empiricism which Kant himself attempts to avoid. Kant maintains—with great cogency I think— that the knowledge situation involves a nonempirical element, namely, the categorical structure of the mind which is the precondition of all possible experience. Now either this theory of innate categories is an item of speculative knowledge or not. If it is not, then the whole theory is undermined *ipso facto:* for that which is not an item of speculative knowledge cannot be the basis of the possibility of speculative knowledge itself. If, on the other hand, I do have, or can have, a speculative knowledge of the categories, so that they may become the basis of an epistemological position, then my knowledge of these very categories is a knowledge devoid of sensuous content. In coming to a knowledge of the categories themselves I have

passed from an analysis of possible or actual experience to objects of knowledge which are distinguishable by the very absence of sensuous content. It follows that either there is no nonempirical factor in knowledge, or else it is false to say that all valid speculative knowledge is of an object with sensuous content: since the former is the very empiricism which Kant wished to avoid—and which we are ourselves about to refute in the sequel—the latter position ought logically to have been affirmed by him.

What is the ultimate issue of these considerations? It is, as we shall see, that no objection can be brought against the possibility of a speculative metaphysic on the ground that such speculative knowledge is possible only within the limits of sensation. But more of this point in Part III.

The application of the categories to the knowledge of things-in-themselves.—[28] Kant maintains that the categories give us no knowledge of things-in-themselves (noumena), but only a knowledge of things as they appear to us (phenomena) : the categories, in other words, are forms of thought only and not conditions for the objective or independent existence of things apart from their being known. He asserts in fact that there is no *Third Way:* "either experience makes these conceptions possible, or the conceptions make experience possible."[29] But since the first alternative is merely the empiricism that Kant has already rejected, he therefore affirms the second and maintains that the intelligible structure of the world is *imposed upon* the stuff of experience by the mind.

In a single paragraph Kant dismisses the *preformation system* as he calls it.[30] According to such a view in its best form—Kant's own statement of it is defective—the categories are both forms of thought and forms of things. They are "subjective aptitudes for thought implanted in us contemporaneously with our existence, which were so ordered and disposed by our Creator, that their exercise perfectly harmonizes with the laws of nature which regulate experience."[31]

Kant poses two objections against such a theory: (1) That there would be, in that case, no principle for determining the number of such aptitudes with precision. (2) That the categories "would in

---

[28]G. H. Clark, *A Christian View of Men and Things*, p. 314, has a good discussion on this problem.
[29]*Critique of Pure Reason*, p. 95.
[30]*Ibid.*, pp. 95, 96.
[31]*Ibid.*, p. 95.

this case entirely lose that character of *necessity* which is essentially involved in the very conception of them."[32] That is, if the categories are merely subjective aptitudes, how do I know that they are not merely valid for *me*, rather than being preconditions of all possible experience?

But can Kant's limitation of the categories to the knowledge of phenomena be consistently maintained? I think not for the following reasons:

(1) The position is self-contradictory and reduces to skepticism. When it is said that the categories give us no knowledge of noumena, these noumena are asserted to exist as the origin or cause for the raw materials of sensation. But in thus admitting the existence of noumenal reality, I have already admitted that the application of the categories effects some knowledge of things-in-themselves—which is contrary to the hypothesis. In fact, that the categories yield no knowledge of things-in-themselves would be an unintelligible proposition if it were not false: since it assumes that very knowledge of noumenal reality which it denies.

If, to escape this predicament, I retreat to the position that the categories cannot even conclude the existence of a noumenal reality, the difficulty is not actually alleviated. For either there is, or there is not, a noumenal reality distinct from the phenomenal. Now the position that there is no such noumenal reality is identical with a form of solipsism which asserts that only the succession of ideas is real. Apart from the fact that this position is itself logically untenable,[33] such a doctrine cannot deny that the categories give us knowledge of things-in-themselves: for on this view my knowledge of things is precisely a knowledge of them as they are in themselves, since they are nothing but my experience of them in the succession of ideas. It is therefore logically absurd for the solipsist to deny noumenal knowledge. Hence, such a denial is logically possible only if one rejects solipsism and by that very fact asserts that noumenal reality does exist. But this is Kant's original argument which has already been shown to be self-contradictory. It turns out that the very statement that the categories cannot give us a knowledge of the existence of noumenal reality suggests its own falsity. If there were no noumenal reality, and if I therefore had no knowledge of it whatever, it would never occur to me to deny the possibility of knowing

[32]*Idem.*
[33]Cf. pp. 198-200.

such a reality. It follows that the contention is false that the categories yield no knowledge of the existence of noumena.

I conclude that Kant's limitation of the categories to the knowledge of phenomena reduces to self-contradictory skepticism and is therefore untenable. The categories do give us a knowledge of things-in-themselves. The precise mode of this knowledge will form the substance of Chapter IV of this part.

(2) The preformation system must therefore be maintained, nor are Kant's objections to it of any serious consequence. As for his insistence that there would, on this view, be no way of determining the number of categories; the derivation of such categories from the various types of logical judgment is just as applicable on the preformation view as it is for Kant's own position. As for the suggestion that the categories might be valid only for me instead of being preconditions for all possible experience; not only does this point press with equal force upon Kant, but we have already shown that such a skepticism is self-contradictory and invalid: the very statement —the categories are valid only for me—could not be true unless it were false. Even God does not snatch the categories out of the blue: if the categories are actually preconditions of intelligibility, they are just as essential for divine thought as for human. That the categories are implanted aptitudes does not impugn their absolute necessity, if only we remember that the same categories are presupposed in any intelligent experience whatever; so that their implantation proceeds according to that very necessity itself.

Conclusion.—With the modifications that have now been suggested, we stand ready to defend rational empiricism as the only adequate epistemology. To such a defense we forthwith proceed.

CHAPTER II

POSITIVE DEFENSE OF THE SYNTHETIC A PRIORI NATURE OF THE CATE-GORICAL STRUCTURE

The Basic Argument

How, IT MAY BE ASKED, can we argue that the knowledge experience does involve a synthetic a priori factor? As a matter of fact, there is only one basic argument in terms of which this assertion can be vindicated. It consists in showing, positively, that intelligible experience is possible only in terms of such a factor; and negatively, that the denial of the synthetic a priori is either self-contradictory or meaningless.

It is admitted at the outset that this argument is, in a very real sense, circular: that is, it depends upon the operation of the very categories that it is designed to prove. But this fact merely confirms the theory itself as a part of speculative knowledge: for the theory itself holds that no knowledge—hence, not even that of itself—is possible apart from the application of the categorical structure to data of experience. And if anyone should attempt to refute our position without using these very same categories, his refutation would be meaningless.

Hence, there is, strictly speaking, no proof of the categories in terms of more basic principles, since the categories themselves are the basic principles of intelligibility. Our task therefore is simply to show that every knowledge experience does presuppose a synthetic a priori factor: that even the opponent of rational empiricism can state his case only on the supposition that it is false.

Intelligible Experience Presupposes the
Synthetic A Priori

Kant himself propounded this argument: "The objective validity of the categories, as a priori conceptions, will rest upon this, that experience (as far as regards the form of thought) is possible only by their means. For in that case they apply necessarily and a priori to objects of experience, because only through them can an object of experience be thought."[1]

The gist of the argument is this: either the categories are thus a priori or they are derived from experience. But an experiential derivation of the categories is impossible because only by their means can an object be thought in the first place. Since the categories are preconditions of all possible knowledge, they cannot have been derived from an experience of particular objects: the very first experience would be unintelligible without a structure of mind to analyze it.

At the same time, it is to be granted that the categories arise as ideas in consciousness only upon the occasion of observation and reflection. But this is a far different thing from saying that such categories are derived from observation and reflection—any more than the water in a spraygun is derived from the push on its pump, although admittedly it rises into the atmosphere upon the occasion of such a push. And just as the spray would not exist without both the water and the push, so knowledge could not exist without both the innate categories and the data of experience. Such "a proof by reference to the possibility of experience is a proof of the principle by showing that it is presupposed in all empirical judgments so that if we did not accept it we should have to adopt the position of the absolute skeptic."[2]

After all, either thought starts with some general principles with which the mind is initially equipped, or it cannot start at all. Thought consists of ideas and judgments, as we have seen: and the very first act of judging presupposes that the thinker has a structure of thought in terms of which subject and predicate may be united according to certain relations.

As Bergson—whose defense of the synthetic a priori is most brilliant, though defective as we shall see—puts the point:

[1] *Critique of Pure Reason*, p. 73.
[2] Ewing, *op. cit.*, p. 68.

Intelligence, therefore, naturally makes use of relations of like with like, of content to container, of cause to effect, etc., which are implied in every phrase in which there is a subject, an attribute and a verb, expressed or understood. . . . May one say that it has innate knowledge of each of these relations in particular? In whatever way we make the analysis of thought, we always end with one or several general categories, of which the mind possesses innate knowledge since it makes a natural use of them. . . . What is innate in intellect . . . is the tendency to establish relations, and this tendency implies the natural knowledge of certain very general relations, a kind of stuff that the activity of each particular intellect will cut up into more special relations.[3]

In other words, our first intelligible experiences, our first acts of judgment, would not occur without such innate equipment, although perhaps Bergson is mistaken in calling this equipment innate knowledge as such. But judgments do in fact begin in our experience: we do assert and deny predicates of subjects. It follows that the general principles or categories, which are presupposed in every act of thought, must be innate: not as ideas in consciousness, but as forms by which thought operates.

An illustration may clarify the point: Every intelligent action presupposes tools or means to its fulfillment. Suppose, for example, that I am going to build a garage. Now I will need means to accomplish this end: and the means will be of two types. First, I will need materials with which to build: wood, nails, cement, glass, paint, etc. Second, I will need carpenter tools to manipulate these materials: hammer, saw, plane, etc.

Now it is to the tools that I would direct your attention at the moment. You might say that I could acquire the tools from an extraneous source: certainly I was not born with a hammer in my hand. But I was born with a hand or two: and the acquisition of extraneous tools presupposes that I have this constitutional equipment to acquire them. More than that, it presupposes a knowledge of my environment and the capacity to make judgments about that environment: for example, the judgment that certain materials and tools are adaptable as means to the building of a garage, or even that a garage is adaptable as means to some other end, and so forth. Ultimately, it

[3]H. Bergson, *Creative Evolution*, pp. 148, 151.

is just the faculty of judgment itself that is presupposed prior to experience, even for the simple task of building a garage.

Now you might say that I could get a garage built without using my hands or even lifting a finger, namely, by getting others to do the work. And you would be right—very much so in my case. But if I do get others thus to work for me, I must still employ the power of judgment in a number of ways: to conceive the building of a garage and its possibility, to make my intention known to the persons I wish to employ, etc. And in general, every intelligent action presupposes the mind's power of judging with respect to presented data of experience.

But, as we have already seen previously, the power of judging presupposes the mind's initial possession, as tools or forms of thought, of the basic relations which make intelligent judgment possible. Thus from such an intelligent action as the building of a garage, I reach, by process of inference, the necessity of a synthetic a priori element in knowing. Indeed, it may be said that if intelligence did not possess the determinate conditions which make judgments possible—i.e., the categories—there would be no way of distinguishing it from non-intelligence: in fact, there would be no way of distinguishing anything from something else, since such a distinction ultimately presupposes the mind's innate power of thought. It can only be concluded therefore, that the mind does come to experiential data with a categorical structure which it necessarily employs in understanding these data; or that intelligible experience is impossible: and since this last is self-contradictory by rendering itself unintelligible, the former alternative must stand.

The whole point of our argument reaches its climax when we realize that we could not understand a definition of knowledge itself if we did not know what it was to know something: so that hopeless skepticism results unless we admit the synthetic a priori: "Knowledge . . . is, strictly speaking, indefinable in the sense that its meaning could not be conveyed to anyone who did not already know what the experience of knowing was. To know what knowledge is, you must first know what it is to know something."[4] This predicament serves to illustrate clearly the fact that knowledge could not begin unless the basic presuppositions of intelligibility itself were a priori characteristic of rationality.

[4]H. A. Larrabee, *Reliable Knowledge*, p. 5.

Even the professing empiricists somehow find themselves rather perplexed by just such problems as this one. Thus C. I. Lewis—whose attempts to refute the synthetic a priori are almost notoriously well known—raises a whole host of questions which cannot be solved without repudiating the empirical viewpoint:

> Is it requisite to knowledge that the warrant of it be complete and sufficient to justify what is believed? In part, our empirical cognitions are based upon sense data, at least in typical cases. But that these by themselves do not constitute justification of the belief is suggested by the fact of illusion. Typically there must be some reliance upon other and like empirical beliefs, taken as antecedently assured. Must this kind of ground of our belief also lie within our apprehension if the belief is to be justified as knowledge? And must this ground itself be likewise grounded? And must this ground of the ground be warranted, and the warrant of it lie within our apprehension—and so on; unless or until we come to something in such regress, which is given and self-warranting and is sufficient for all which it must support? And if so, can any empirical cognition possible to us stand up under this requirement?[5]

Lewis, I think, never succeeds in answering these problems, although he spends hundreds of pages in the attempt. But this observation about empiricism brings us to the negative part of our basic argument.

The Denial of the Synthetic A Priori Is Either Self-contradictory or Meaningless

If the mind does not approach experience with an innate categorical structure, then, since it is indisputable that we do think in terms of certain categories, this synthetic element must have been derived from the data of experience: i.e., all synthetic knowledge must be traced to a purely empirical origin. But this, it is evident, is simply the affirmation that the only alternative to synthetic apriorism is empiricism.

Now empiricism, therefore, is the doctrine that all synthetic knowledge is derived from sense experience. But either this statement itself is an item of synthetic knowledge or it is not. If it is not an item of synthetic knowledge, then it must be an analytic statement, in which case it is either a mere tautology, or a definition arbitrarily

[5] C. I. Lewis, *An Analysis of Knowledge and Valuation*, p. 28.

proposed without experiential justification. Now if it is a mere tautology, then it is actually meaningless as the basis for a theory of knowledge. As Joad suggests,[6] a tautology is a saying again of what has been said. And "if we were to ask the question, what is the same thing that, having been said once already, is said again by the verification principle [i.e., by the basic tenet of empiricism], I do not know what the answer may be."[7] Nor will the situation be helped by maintaining that in the statement of the empirical theory the predicate is tautologous with respect to the subject, as: knowledge *is* the content derived from sense experience; for this statement could be a tautology only on grounds that establish the identity between subject and predicate, since the identity does not appear from the proposition itself, else there would be no argument about epistemology. And if the statement must be thus supported by grounds, it is not an analytic identity or tautology.

The principle is not therefore an obvious tautology: and hence it must be either a purely arbitrary definition, or an analytic derivative from such a definition, and thus be tautological merely by hypothesis or supposition. But in this case, it is a very strange statement indeed: for while a mere definition does not profess to tell us anything about the world of sense, the principle of empiricism professes to tell us *everything* about it. Furthermore, as an arbitrary definition, it is no more than an expression of the determination of certain persons to use words in a certain manner: it therefore tells us nothing about the criteria of genuine knowledge, which must transcend individual preference or collapse; and the theory is consequently meaningless as a basis for epistemology.[8]

But suppose then that the empirical theory is an item of synthetic knowledge. By its very assertion it must therefore be arrived at by induction from sensory facts, or else it is false. Now in point of fact, there are no relevant sense experiences of which it is a generalization. To quote Joad again: "I cannot . . . conceive what kind of *sense*-experience would verify the principle that the meaning of a statement is wholly verifiable in terms of the sense-experiences which verify it."[9] And furthermore, if the empirical formula *were* a generalization, it could not be asserted to be universally the case, since

[6]C. E. M. Joad, *A Critique of Logical Positivism*, p. 68.
[7]*Idem.*
[8]Cf. *ibid.*, p. 69.
[9]*Ibid.*, p. 66.

it would then rest on an induction from a limited number of particulars: yet it claims to be true of *all* synthetic knowledge and is thus not intended as an empirical generalization.

It follows that the empirical principle is false: for there are no relevant sensory experiences which could conceivably verify it; and if there were, it could not be universally asserted because it would then rest on a partial induction. Thus we reach the curious result that if the empirical principle is an item of synthetic knowledge, its truth involves its falsity—which is self-contradictory.

Putting the two parts of our argument together: the denial of the synthetic a priori is thus shown to be either self-contradictory or meaningless for epistemology in general. And this was the point we set out to demonstrate.

But a still deeper contradiction now bursts upon the empirical horizon. If the empirical principle is neither analytic, nor synthetic a posteriori, as we have shown, then it must be a synthetic a priori statement, for this is the only remaining alternative. But in this case the empirical theory again turns back upon itself: for the whole affirmation of the theory, from a negative point of view, is the denial that any synthetic a priori knowledge is possible. In general then, it may be asserted that every denial of the synthetic a priori works itself around to self-contradiction by necessarily affirming that very factor which it denied, or else rendering its own meaning unintelligible.

In conclusion, the basic argument for the synthetic a priori factor in knowledge has been established: it has been shown both that intelligible experience is impossible without this factor and that every denial of it involves its affirmation and thus suffers self-contradiction. Were it not for the factor that the empiricist denies, neither he nor anyone else could even understand the very denial itself.

Illustrations

There are, in fact, an indefinite number of ways in which to illustrate or exemplify this basic argument for our position. But perhaps the three following examples or modes of inference will suffice:

Every attempt to derive the categories from the data of experience presupposes their use in the attempted derivation.—If I attempt, for example, to derive the category of causation from experience, I find that I have already used this very structure of thought to infer the presence of an object and thus make the possibility of existential experience intelligible. And the passage in thought, furthermore, from objects of experience to the conclusion of the causal category, would itself presuppose the whole power of judging—and hence the categorical structure—in terms of which such a movement of thought is possible. If in fact a basic category like causation were derived from the data of experience, would it ever occur to me to raise any question about the mode in which the derivation might be possible?

Clark gives an interesting illustration of our point by posing a situation in which a child is supposed to learn to count by using marbles. The truth seems to be that unless the child comes to experience with at least the categories of unity and plurality, he can never learn to count. For suppose he had six marbles; yet he does not know this, for he is going to *learn* to count. Now he cannot learn by dividing these marbles into various groups, for he would have to know how to count to divide them significantly. And in fact, he would have ultimately to possess the whole categorical structure of rationality in order to have an intelligible experience of the marbles at all.

But perhaps someone will help the child by taking away five of the six marbles and leaving him only one: for he certainly must learn what one marble is if he is going to count six of them. But how does he know that it *is* one marble unless he already has the concept or category of unity as a structure of rationality when he comes to the marbles in the first place?[10]

And so generally with the forms of thought which, like unity, make mathematical reasoning possible. In fact, if mathematical truths were gained by induction from experience alone, they would occupy the status of empirical generalizations. But as Russell says: "The general propositions of mathematics, such as 'two and two always make four,' can obviously be known with certainty by consideration of a single instance. . . ."[11]

The logical laws of identity, contradiction, excluded middle, and so on, cannot have been derived from the data of experience.—Such logical laws prescribe, on our view, the self-consistent mode according to which the categories, in their interaction, ideally operate. Take the law of contradiction, for example, according to which a thing can-

[10]Clark, *op. cit.*, pp. 306, 307.
[11]B. Russell, *Problems of Philosophy*, p. 131.

not both be and not be at the same time and in the same manner. Now if pure empiricism were correct, we ought to be able to deduce this law from our experience with objects. But the fact of the matter is that I could not be aware of sensing any particular object at all without first being able to distinguish it as this and not that, as one thing rather than another. But I must already be employing the law of contradiction in order to do this, since it is that law whereby I know that a thing cannot be two different objects simultaneously and in the same sense; thus I employ the law at the very beginning of experience with objects.[12]

Furthermore, the mere cogitation of the law of contradiction is sufficient to establish its universality and necessity: but if it were derived from experience, it would not possess this a priori character, but would be an inductive generalization. As Clark has put it: "Empiricism therefore is conclusively shown to be skeptical because the law of contradiction cannot be abstracted or obtained from temporally conditioned particulars. And without the law of contradiction it is impossible to say anything meaningful."[13]

But if necessary logical laws do not, as we have shown, have a purely empirical origin, they must rest on the structure of thought itself, or—what is the same thing—the synthetic a priori. And if it be said that such laws are analytic, then the answer is that an analytic statement is either a tautology or a definition. What meaning the former alternative would have here, I certainly do not know, nor do I think that any empiricist knows either: for I could not recognize a tautology unless I already possessed the laws of logic to discern the relation between the subject and predicate of one single proposition, or between one proposition and another. Nor, on the other hand, could I formulate an intelligible propositional definition without the same laws of logic. That these laws are analytic a priori therefore seems to me to be absurd. Such laws must therefore be based on a synthetic a priori.

Universal and necessary judgments about reality would be impossible on a purely empirical basis.—Bertrand Russell—not entirely without inconsistency—develops this point at some length in his epoch-making volume on *Human Knowledge: Its Scope and Limits.* What we learn by perception, he points out, is always particular and

---

[12]Cf. E. J. Carnell, *Introduction to Christian Apologetics*, p. 162, for a good statement of this point.

[13]Clark, *op. cit.*, p. 308.

if we have any universal knowledge, it will have to come from another source.[14] Induction will never give us a universal that is normative for tomorrow: yet this is just what science needs to predict the future:

> We most certainly do need *some* universal proposition or propositions. . . . Whatever these principles of inference may be, they certainly cannot be logically deduced from facts of experience. Either, therefore, we know something independently of experience, or science is moonshine.[15]

Now the only other source than experience must be sought in a propensity of the mind itself: we must therefore come to experience with a certain propensity of structure in terms of which universal and necessary judgments are possible; nor can our knowledge of the principles involved in this structure be based upon experience as such.[16]

If it occurs to someone to deny that universal and necessary propositions are possible, then the following analysis will serve to show him his mistake. In the first place, this proposition itself—no universal and necessary propositions are possible—is either true or false. If the proposition is false, it is refuted at once. Suppose then that it is true: but in this case, since it asserts, or better denies, the predicate universally and necessarily, it is, by its own criterion, false—which is self-contradictory. And if, to escape this conclusion, we allege that the statement is an empirical generalization, no easing of the situation will result: for I dare say that no one has an idea what the revelant sense facts are of which it is the generalization; in fact, what sense facts could possibly prove the impossibility of any negative proposition of this type, even if the proof were inductive?

In the second place, take the very proposition that no universal proposition is attainable by induction from particulars. Now this statement is, I think, hardly susceptible of reasonable doubt: for no induction rests on all possible instances, so that a universal proposition cannot be justified by appeal to such instances as are experienced. But this very proposition itself is a universal proposition: and therefore it cannot have been arrived at by empirical induction from particulars.

But now a statement of this kind has only two other possible bases:

[14]*Op. cit.*, p. 504.
[15]*Ibid.*, pp. 504, 505.
[16]*Ibid.*, p. 507.

either it is an arbitrary definition, or it rests ultimately on principles which the mind itself brings to experience. Yet it is certainly not an arbitrary definition, for it commends itself as true to all rational minds. It follows that the universality and necessity of the original proposition are based upon the structure which rationality possesses antecedently to contact with the data of experience: the statement therefore rests on a synthetic a priori basis.

I therefore conclude that universal and necessary propositions lie at the base of all knowledge and acquire these characteristics from the innate categorical structure which reason brings to the data of experience.

Conclusion

In the light of our basic argument and its illustrations, it may be concluded that knowledge is either impossible, or else it is possible in terms of a synthetic a priori structure that the mind initially brings to the data of experience: since the former position embodies a self-contradictory skepticism, the latter must be affirmed. Rational empiricism has thus far shown itself to be plausible.

CHAPTER III

AN ANSWER TO OBJECTIONS AGAINST RATIONAL EMPIRICISM

Introduction

WHILE THE POSITIVE ARGUMENT for rational empiricism is intended to be a sufficient vindication of its all-inclusive epistemological validity, the case for our position would not be critically complete without a consideration of the major objections that are usually urged against the theory in philosophical circles. Such objections emanate from four particular sources which embody alternative theories with respect to the possibility of knowledge.

(1) *Rationalism* urges that synthetic apriorism has embraced too little: not only the forms of thought are innate, but so also is the universal content of knowledge.

(2) *Empiricism* urges that synthetic apriorism has embraced too much: there are indeed a priori principles of knowledge, but they are analytic or definitional rather than synthetic.

(3) *Pragmatism* contends that rational empiricism neglects the presumed fact that forms of thought arise as instruments for manipulating particular problem situations, rather than being synthetic categories which descend upon experience by a priori necessity.

(4) *Intuitionism,* finally, asserts that while the basic forms of thought are synthetic a priori factors, these forms are not coextensive with the whole range of knowledge: the inner truth of things is unknowable by intellect which must therefore be supplemented by suprarational intuition.

It is to the consideration of such contentions as these that our attention must now be directed.

FROM THE VANTAGE POINT OF RATIONALISM
The Objection Stated

The first opponent to rational empiricism, then, is the rationalist. While he would quite readily and gladly accept our defense of the synthetic a priori factor in knowing, this premature joy of his is transcended by the disappointing affirmation of ours that the categorical structure must terminate on the data of experience to gain existential and objective content knowledge. To him, the argument has not pressed forward to its ultimate conclusion that all genuine knowledge—with respect to both form and content—is innate in the mind of the knower and needs only to be called to the surface of experience upon the occasion of observation and reflection. For the rationalist, the individual mind, spider-like, spins forth knowledge in its entirety from within its own bowels.

The first great proponent of this theory, to give it anything approaching adequate expression, was Plato himself (427-347 B.C.). True knowledge, according to Plato, is knowledge of the form or universal.[1] But these forms antedate our experience of knowing in a twofold way: (1) First, the whole realm of forms (universals) exists eternally apart both from the particular world of our experience and from our knowledge of such forms—and with this general contention of Plato, we have, in the present work, no particular dispute.[2] (2) But in the second place, the knowledge of this whole realm of universals has somehow already been implanted in the soul at birth: so that a given knowledge experience—if it is true knowledge—consists in recalling, upon the proper occasion of observation and reflection, what was already known.[3]

In support of the doctrine that all knowledge is innate—knowledge consisting, as it does, of universals—Plato urges a number of arguments, the most important of which are the following:

(1) First, no true universal can be abstracted from sensible particulars: so that either we have to deny the possibility of knowledge, or maintain that the mind brings the whole stock of universals a priori to the data of experience or sensation. There are, for example, no absolute equals in nature: yet, when presented with approximate equals, the mind forms the idea of absolute equality.[4] And this

[1]*Republic*, 476f.
[2]*Ibid.*, 500, 517.
[3]*Phaedo*, 73; *Meno*, 81f.
[4]*Phaedo*, 74.

can only mean that prior to experience "we must have had a knowledge of absolute equality, or we could not have referred to that standard the equals which are derived from the senses."[5] And so with our whole knowledge of universals:

> Must we not allow, that when I or anyone, looking at any object, observes that the thing which he sees aims at being some other thing, but falls short of, and cannot be, that other thing, but is inferior, he who makes this observation must have had a previous knowledge of that to which the other, although similar, was inferior?[6]

(2) Second, knowledge must be innate because "if you put a question to a person in a right way, he will give a true answer of himself, but how could he do this unless there were knowledge and right reason already in him?"[7] That is, the fact that a person can give correct answers about a subject of which he has had no previous learning in this life implies that he already has a knowledge of the subject and merely calls it to mind upon the occasion of the proper questions.[8] And thus Plato says of the servant boy whom he used as an example in the *Meno:*

> If there have been always true thoughts in him . . . which only need to be awakened by putting questions to him, his soul must have always possessed this knowledge. . . . The truth of all things always existed in the soul . . .[9]

The essentials of this type of solution to the problem of knowledge are propounded by E. J. Carnell, though of course he would hold as against Plato that knowledge was implanted in the soul by creation:[10] Plato himself, despite the clear statement just quoted, seems to be ambiguous on this point. According to Carnell, the a priori element in knowing must extend not only to the categorical structure, but to the content of knowledge by way of universals.[11] The standards, for example, of truth, goodness, and beauty are "in the intelligible soul, to be perceived by an analysis of the content of rationality itself."[12] Nor does this mean merely that the norms of knowledge are

[5] *Ibid.,* 75.
[6] *Ibid.,* 74.
[7] *Ibid.,* 73.
[8] *Meno,* 85, 86.
[9] *Ibid.,* 86.
[10] Cf. also Clark, *op. cit.,* p. 321, although the theory is not there developed in detail.
[11] Carnell, *op. cit.,* p. 152f.
[12] *Ibid.,* p. 153.

innate as structures or aptitudes; but rather also that the whole content of truth, in universals, is thus imbedded in the soul and needs
merely to be called to the surface. Man possesses, by his very nature
as a rational being, a body of ideas.[13] And this content knowledge
is apparently to be conceived, along Platonic lines, as the whole body
of intelligible forms.[14]

As applied to the knowledge of God, for example, this rationalistic
theory would imply, as Carnell maintains, that "because we *know*
God's existence and nature in our heart, we *recognize* Him in His
handiwork. Thus the heavens declare the glory of God, for they
constantly remind us that God exists. . . . If man did not know what
to look for when he observed nature, it would be pointless for Paul
to look upon nature as a means to bring all men under condemna-
tion."[15]

The Objection Answered

Positive objections to the rationalistic position.—(1) The most
basic objection to the rationalistic theory is this: that only that can
be declared innate, or a priori in the mind, which is necessarily presupposed in the mind's power of knowing; and that, since the whole
range of universals is not thus presupposed, it cannot be said to be
innate.

For what is presupposed in the mind's power of knowing? While
this question has been answered at some length in the preceding
discussion, a summary will be helpful in the present context. The
power of judgment exhausts, as we have seen, the mind's whole power
of thought in general: for knowing consists precisely in a series of
self-consistent judgments. It follows that only that factor which is
presupposed in the capacity of judgment may be legitimately called
innate. Now this capacity of judgment, as has been previously shown,
presupposes precisely that categorical structure of thought in which
a basic thought form corresponds to each basic type of logical judgment. And this means that only the categorical structure of thought
may therefore be called innate, since this structure, and nothing
more, is required, conjointly with the data of experience, to account
for the possibility of knowledge.

Now it is granted that the categories themselves, when they arise

[13]*Ibid.*, p. 161.
[14]*Ibid.*, p. 162.
[15]*Ibid.*, pp. 169, 170. (The reference to Paul is in Rom. 1:20.)

as ideas in consciousness subsequently to observation and reflection may properly be called universal or general ideas. But it is denied: (a) that the mind's innate equipment extends beyond the categorical structure to the whole range of universals, for not all the universals are presupposed in the possibility of knowledge: the universal idea of *cheese,* for example, is not thus presupposed; (b) that the categorical structure may be correctly designated as a series of ideas prior to contact with experiential data: the categories are rather to be described as modes of thought, or as ways in which rationality and intelligence necessarily function. Of course, the categories might be called ideas or concepts if it were clear that this describes their character only after their intercourse with experience.

(2) In the second place, the rationalistic theory is untenable because no intelligible meaning can be ascribed to the phrase *innate idea,* except that which limits the phrase to the categorical structure we have defended.

The following meanings seem to exhaust the possibilities:

(i) An idea of which the mind is conscious at birth: but—not to mention the fact that this theory has never been seriously propounded —this is manifestly false. The mind has no conscious ideas prior to its contact with experience.

(ii) An idea of which all men may become conscious upon occasion of the appropriate experience. But on this ground, only that is *required* to be innate which makes intelligible experience itself possible: namely, the categorical structure, as we have already shown. This structure, plus more or less common data of experience, are all that may be required to explain the universality of certain content ideas or universals.

(iii) An idea which the soul acquired prior to birth and which, being lodged in the memory, is called into consciousness upon the occurrence of the appropriate experience. This suggestion fails to solve the problem at all, but merely succeeds rather in raising it to a different level. If the mind has a memory stock at birth, then this memory stock must exist either by virtue of the soul's previous conscious experience, or by virtue of a creative act which implanted the ideas conjointly with an intelligence fitted to receive them: and in either case we must assume that the mind's capacity to receive these ideas was at least logically prior to the ideas themselves.

But what is presupposed in the mind's capacity to receive ideas?

Precisely the categorical structure and nothing more, beyond the fact of existence itself. So whether the soul's alleged innate ideas are to be explained by previous conscious experience or by a creative act, it is presupposed that originally these ideas were imparted to a mind fitted by its structure to receive them. And if this is the case, since all universals represent realities of our present experience, then there is no real ground for assuming anything more than the categorical structure as the innate basis of the mind's present conscious experience.

It follows that the phrase *innate idea* has no ultimately intelligible meaning, if it purports to connote anything more than the structure of rationality which the mind brings to the data of experience.

(3) In the third place, the mind obviously has no knowledge of particulars except through contact with the data of experience: and if knowledge does not embrace particulars, self-contradictory skepticism is the result. Even if it were true that all universals are innate, still the mind has no *particular* knowledge apart from experience: even if I knew *man-ness,* I would not know this or that *real man* before contacting him in experience.

As a matter of fact, however, knowledge either embraces particulars or not: If it does, then it is false to say that all knowledge is innate, for the knowledge of absolutely every real object in particular would then be derived from the data of experience, and not from the mind itself, occasion or no occasion.

But suppose knowledge does not embrace particulars—and this, incidentally, seems to me to be the implication of Plato's whole theory of knowledge, since true knowledge is of the form or universal only, according to him: In this case, the position is tantamount to the assertion that no real or particular object is knowable. And since all objects which exist independently of the mind are presumably particular objects or relations, the rationalist is actually asserting that knowledge of independently existing reality is impossible. But this last position is nothing but a solipsistic and self-contradictory skepticism: since if reality is unknowable, then this assertion, embodying just such knowledge, is false.

In either case, the theory of innate knowledge is shown to be ultimately inadequate.

(4) Finally, the rationalist theory is untenable because it is self-contradictory in that its denial of empirically derived knowledge

implies just that origin of content ideas from experience which the theory denies. It appears that some knowledge from particulars must be the ground for our denying that ideas, as universals, may be derived from sense-experience: for if there *were* no empirical knowledge of particulars, such a denial would be unintelligible. Why bother to deny that our ideas originate from a source which, by hypothesis, is unknowable? This very denial implies that—universal or not—our ideas of particulars are not merely occasioned but *originated* from the mind's contact with experiential data. At the very least, the rationalist must admit that I know particulars as the *occasion* of my ideas: otherwise his whole theory reduces to a solipsistic gymnastic. But if *this* empirical knowledge is granted, then there is not only no objection to the position that the whole content of our ideas originates from the data of experience, but more than that: the admission contradicts the original denial that knowledge could be derived from sense-experience.

Answer to Plato's arguments.—But what about Plato's arguments for the rationalistic view? The preceding analysis already refutes them by implication. (1) The assertion that no true universal can be derived from sensible particulars is self-contradictory by implying that very knowledge of such particulars that it ostensibly denies. (2) The theory of knowledge as recollection merely postpones the problem and presupposes an original state of the soul in which, by its categorical structure, it was fitted to receive content ideas: and in this case, there is no reason why *all* its content ideas may not be thus derived from contact with the mind's present experiential data.

Conclusion.—I therefore conclude that the innate factor, presupposed by the possibility of knowledge, extends merely to the categorical structure of rationality, and that therefore the rationalist objection is invalid.

From the Vantage Point of Empiricism
The Empirical Assertion

Its general character.—Contemporary empiricists generally conspire together in a repudiation of the synthetic a priori as we have attempted to defend it. Thus Reichenbach, in a paper read to the Eastern Division of the American Philosophical Association in 1951, declares: "Modern empiricism has shown Kant's thesis [of the synthetic a priori] to be fallacious. There is no synthetic a priori; what

reason contributes to knowledge are analytical principles only."[16]
And C. I. Lewis, in his long and erudite *Analysis of Knowledge
and Valuation,* declares, when he turns to consider the synthetic
a priori, that the problem is "a dead, or nearly dead, issue; conviction that all a priori truth is analytic being now quite general."[17]
In fairness to Lewis, I think I ought to mention that apparently
some transition on this subject has characterized his thought since
his book was published. In a personal letter to me, dated June 26,
1953, he writes: "I have no clear and settled opinion whether there
are synthetic judgments a priori, but suspect either view is defensible
on the issue, for a *plausible* definition of 'analytic'—different in the
two cases. Such definitions are not 'arbitrary' . . ."

Its detailed exposition.—But how can the empiricist assertion here
be stated in detail? Taking Lewis as an exemplary proponent, the
objection would run as follows:

While Kant contended for the synthetic a priori, the fact is that
all a priori knowledge is purely analytic; i.e., it "can be asserted exclusively by reference to defined or definable meanings."[18] In other
words, every statement that can be determined as true "without reference to any particular experience of sense"[19] is an explication of the
meanings of terms or propositions: "There are no other sources of
knowledge than the one hand data of sense and on the other hand
our own intended meanings."[20] Thus every analytic statement is
true with reference to the meanings of the terms involved; every synthetic statement is true with reference to the data of sense as expli-
cated through meanings.

On the other hand, Lewis does not take logical positivist ground:
meanings are not creatures of mere linguistic convention, so that
they may be a matter of purely arbitrary definition.[21] Linguistic
symbols themselves may be subject to arbitrary rules or convention,
but the freedom to manipulate "does not extend to the meanings
which are symbolized. . . . An analytic statement says something; and
something whose factuality is independent even though it is not
existential in significance."[22]

[16]*Philosophical Review,* April, 1952, p. 147.
[17]*Op. cit.,* p. 158.
[18]*Ibid.,* p. 35, cf. p. ix.
[19]*Ibid.,* p. 35.
[20]*Idem.*
[21]*Ibid.,* p. ix.
[22]*Idem.*

What, then, may be said about the alleged synthetic a priori? I think Lewis, if he were still in the frame of mind expressed by his *Analysis of Knowledge and Valuation,* would answer as follows: When we make a statement—like, every event is the effect of some cause—what we say is either analytic (i.e., determinable with reference to the meaning of the term *event*) or synthetic (i.e., determinable from factors not included in such meaning).

Now the proponent of synthetic apriorism argues that we cannot conceive an uncaused event, etc., but that such a state of mind could not arise from the consideration of sense data alone: But if this contention is true, then the assertion—every event is the effect of some cause—is analytic; precisely because a characteristic without which a given predicate could not be thought, actually enters into the definition of the predicate: in this case, causation entering into the definition of *event.* As Lewis puts the point:

> Any character in the absence of which we should refuse to apply a term, is of the essence. It is included in the signification of the term; and any definition which does not entail such an essential character represents a faulty analysis of the meaning in question . . .[23]

It follows that if an uncaused event is inconceivable, then *being caused* is a part of the definition of *event,* so that the assertion, though a priori, is analytic. If, on the other hand, we maintain that an uncaused event *is* conceivable, our original assertion—every event is the effect of some cause—while it may be synthetic, is certainly not a priori; for necessity enters into the very meaning of the synthetic a priori. In either case, then, there is no synthetic a priori.

The Empirical Compromise

If, as we shall endeavor to show, the empiricist is required to retreat after all to the synthetic a priori to save his position from utter insignificance, he has yet one last stand short of the rational empiricism which we ourselves espouse: he may hold that while the forms of thought are synthetic a priori for the possibility of intelligible experience, they are merely psychologically inevitable and impose no conditions on objective reality itself; these forms are therefore not inescapably possessed of absolute universality or necessity.

[23]*Ibid.,* p. 163.

This view is propounded by Tennant in his *Philosophical Theology*. Thus he writes:

> If there be any necessity characterizing our empirical knowledge, it is but that of the psychological inevitableness, for us men, of the synthetic forms . . . which our minds supply when constituting objects and judging about them. . . . Synthetic judgments a priori are valid, because our minds cannot but give certain forms to what they apprehend.[24]

For ought we know, the synthetic forms "may be regarded as but expressing 'rules of the game' we call thinking. . . . If so, these laws of thought are not *necessarily* laws of reality also."[25]

Refutation of the Objections

At the outset, we may debar any serious consideration of the compromise suggested by Tennant. It is in fact merely the old Kantian assertion that the categories do not necessarily give us a knowledge of things-in-themselves: the conditions of rational intelligibility are not necessarily conditions of objective existence. Since this objection has already been refuted in our analysis of Kant—and since, in fact, it will come up for constant discussion and refutation in the sequel; no consideration will be given to the suggestion in the present context other than to mention that it is self-contradictory by applying its own assertion universally: in the end, it reduces to complete skepticism.

Our only task, then, will be to deal with the empirical assertion itself as we have defined it: the choice must be either for *no* synthetic a priori, or for such a synthetic a priori as imposes conditions, not merely of intelligibility, but of existence itself.

The empirical debate.—With regard therefore to the assertion that all a priori truths are analytic, it should be initially indicated that the empiricists themselves are in somewhat of a muddle on this question. One of their most important spokesmen—whose name is withheld at his own request—wrote me that he shares a certain negative attitude with the synthetic apriorists:

> Both of us wonder on what basis certain statements are said to be true by virtue of the meanings of terms, only the "synthetic apriorists" go on to conclude that some of them are therefore

[24] *Op. cit.*, I, p. 408.
[25] *Ibid.*, pp. 205, 206.

synthetic a priori while I tend to avoid the use of both "analytic" and "synthetic" as obscure terms. . . . This . . . is an area in which my views are undergoing development at the present moment, so that I hesitate to deliver myself of any view that I might expect to remain mine for a very long time.

Since 1950, at least two of the world's outstanding empiricists (broadly defined) have thrown the whole problem of the relation between synthetic and analytic into an unstable equilibrium. In that year, Morton White published in *John Dewey: Philosopher of Science and Freedom* his now famous essay called "The Analytic and the Synthetic: an Untenable Dualism." In this essay, White shows—conclusively, I think—that the whole distinction between analytic and synthetic is unintelligible and obscure on a purely empirical basis.

In order to understand the meaning of the analytic, White maintains that we should have to understand the meaning of synonymy, else a definition would be unintelligible. But then we would have to understand synonymy itself by an analytic definition, and we are right back where we started with the analytic. In fact, every attempted definition presupposes that either analyticity or synonymy is understood to begin with.[26]

Similar considerations are urged by W. V. Quine, White's colleague at Harvard, in his essay, "Two Dogmas of Empiricism."[27] After a masterful criticism of the distinction between analytic and synthetic, Quine concludes:

> For all its a priori reasonableness, a boundary between analytic and synthetic statements simply has not been drawn. That there is such a distinction to be drawn at all is an unempirical dogma of empiricists, a metaphysical article of faith.[28]

Both Quine and White leave the obvious conclusion to their argument unexpressed. For it seems clear that their concessions actually yield the palm of victory to synthetic apriorism. If every definition presupposes ultimately that certain meanings—at least that of *meaning* or *synonymy*—are understood initially, then the fact that meanings *are* understood presupposes an innate factor of knowing, or a synthetic a priori. And we presume White and Quine know what they are talking about when they speak of meaning, or analyticity.

[26]*Op. cit.*, pp. 319-323.
[27]*Philosophical Review*, January, 1951.
[28]*Ibid.*, p. 34.

But they have already shown that no one knows what he is talking about unless he initially understands the meaning of *meaning* itself. The whole discussion, since it shows that this understanding is impossible on a purely empirical basis, argues for a synthetic a priori.

In a letter from Quine, dated August 21, 1953, he demurs this conclusion:

> My misgivings over the distinction between analytic and synthetic do not support the claim for a synthetic a priori. They tend rather, by questioning the distinction, to cast doubt on the meaningfulness of the claim that there is (and equally of the claim that there is not) a synthetic a priori.

But this answer is hardly possible except in terms of a complete and self-contradictory skepticism: for, by the law of contradiction, either there is, or there is not, a synthetic a priori—regardless of what that a priori may be. And the law of contradiction itself can hardly be suspended without this act bringing one either to self-contradiction or meaninglessness: if the law were not universally valid, Quine's whole discussion would be quite unintelligible, both to himself and to all the rest of us. And thus it is that empiricism has rendered itself implausible in the persons of two of its outstanding representatives. Either the whole debate is unintelligible or the basic tenet of empiricism is false.

In the *Philosophical Review,* July, 1953, A. S. Kaufman has attempted to answer White and Quine in his article: "The Analytic and the Synthetic: a Tenable 'Dualism.' " He urges that despite the difficulties suggested, "men are able to fix the distinction [between analytic and synthetic] whenever it becomes important to do so."[29] He then goes on to point out that when once the definition of a concept is arbitrarily selected, the distinction between analytic and synthetic is determinable within the context of the definition.[30] "We *make* sentences analytic or synthetic by *fixing the meanings* of component expressions."[31]

But it seems to me that Kaufman has either missed the point of White and Quine, or else he has surrendered the philosophical distinction of the view he defends: for the whole point is that we could not fix a meaning at all if at least the meaning of *meaning* were not

[29]*Op. cit.,* p. 423.
[30]*Ibid.,* p. 425.
[31]*Ibid.,* p. 426.

fixed and understood to begin with. If, as Kaufman suggests, it is possible to distinguish between analytic and synthetic—and if it were not possible, no statement would be intelligible or meaningful, then it can only be in terms of a synthetic a priori that repudiates its empiricist background.

And even if we overlook this point, then we still have the problem of how an arbitrarily fixed meaning can have any real significance in a discussion of the possibility of human knowledge: indeed, unless there are some meanings which are fixed apart from experience on the empirical level, intelligible predication seems hopeless. How futile it is for an empiricist to expound his view! For neither he nor we shall be able to understand him, since, by his own presuppositions, we cannot understand the meaning of understanding or meaning itself! If no meanings are necessarily fixed, ...!

The argument of Lewis.—That there are such fixed meanings is freely admitted by C. I. Lewis, whose argument against the synthetic a priori must now be considered.

The empiricist holds that all a priori truth is analytic; i.e., it is determinable in terms of defined or definable meanings. And it is further asserted that every predicate, which must when considered be assigned to a given subject, is analytic with respect to the meaning of the subject term.

Now suppose we grant this premise for the sake of argument. If all a priori truth is analytic in the sense defined, then how are we to explain the origin of such analytic a priori truth? If an analytic proposition is true by reference to the meaning of the terms, the following alternatives seem possible (I exclude here any statement of formal logic, such as, x is x—questions of this kind not being in dispute here) :

(a) The proposition is true by reference to other more basic analytic a priori statements from which it is logically derived.

(b) The proposition is true because the meaning of the terms involved has been arbitrarily fixed for the convenience of discussion.

(c) The proposition is true by reference to a body of fixed meanings that are not subject to arbitration.

Now consider these alternatives:

(a) The first alternative obviously does not constitute an ultimate explanation, since it merely raises the question as to where the more basic a priori truths originated. It follows that only the two remaining alternatives are finally possible: either all meanings are ultimately a matter of purely arbitrary definition, or they rest on some absolutely fixed set of meanings.

(b) But the idea that the meaning of terms is arbitrarily fixed is open to objection on two grounds.

(i) It assumes, as we have shown, that we have genuine a priori knowledge of *meaning* or *synonymy* or what have you: but this is precisely what the theory denies. If I do not know what meaning is to begin with, no definition—arbitrary or not—is possible. But if I do have an initial and fixed knowledge of what meaning is—what, in other words, is basic to the mind's power of making predications— then it is false that all meanings are arbitrarily determined.

(ii) If all meanings are purely arbitrary, then no basis for a non-skeptical theory of knowledge seems possible. The very statement— all meanings are purely arbitrary—is either analytic or synthetic. If it is analytic, then it is itself a purely arbitrary statement, since an analytic statement is precisely one whose truth rests on meaning. But a purely arbitrary and groundless assumption will hardly make good its claim to philosophical significance except by employing propositions which contravene its own premises.

Suppose then that the statement is synthetic—and I cannot imagine how it could be, for it professes to tell us, not merely something about the way we use language, but something about meaning itself —if, I say, the statement is synthetic, then it is false on two counts. First, because it is cast in universal form—a form that is unjustified on a synthetic a posteriori basis: empirical induction cannot rise to a universal. Second, because it then is not a definition, or a part of the definition, of *meaning* itself; for, by its own assertion, all definitional statements are purely arbitrary and are *not* derived from experience. And if the statement fails to tell me anything essential about meaning, then it is false to say that all meanings are purely arbitrary.

(c) We therefore revert to the final alternative: that analytic a priori statements are true, in the final analysis, by reference to a body of fixed meanings that are not subject to arbitration; this, in fact, is the position of Lewis.

But this view—which is the only plausible one, as I think—implies the very synthetic a priori which Lewis would apparently like to escape. And in fact, my differences with Lewis at this point are probably of a purely semantic nature.

How can I show that this position, espoused by Lewis, does involve belief in the synthetic a priori? Well, if the mind comes to the data of experience with a set of fixed meanings—meanings not subject to arbitration—then these meanings, which are thus admittedly a priori, must ultimately rest on a synthetic basis: and this precisely because *our most ultimate meanings cannot be determined as true in an analytic fashion.*

An illustration will help: let *x* equal a specific event in the space-time universe. Now suppose I say: *x* is the effect of some cause. Is this statement analytic or synthetic? This, of course, depends on more basic meanings to which we subscribe. But suppose I say that the statement is analytic by reference to a more basic meaning-proposition: every event is the effect of some cause. Now is *this* statement analytic or synthetic? And so on.

The series of analytic statements may theoretically regress in this fashion indefinitely: but the essential point is that every analytic proposition *is* analytic by reference to more basic meanings. Now since the series in such a regression of analytic meanings is not infinite—if it were, none of us would ever reach a first intelligible predication—we must come ultimately to some basic presuppositions or fixed meanings that cannot be analytic for the simple reason that *there are no more basic meanings to which they may be referred:* such a priori ultimates may and must therefore be synthetic and *at the same time* both universal and necessary because they are the basic presuppositions of all thought.

Now the validity of such basic propositions—which the presuppositions become when formulated as judgments in consciousness—could not be determined by analysis from their subject-terms without assuming that there were still more basic propositions than the ones under consideration. Suppose I take, as a basic proposition, the following: every reality is completely determined by the presence of determinate conditions. But now either this statement is determined as true by an analysis of the meaning of *reality* or not; yet on the other hand *if* the statement is true, it is presupposed in my understanding of a reality, and *vice versa.* This consideration serves to show that the ultimate synthetic a priori factor in knowing is complex in nature, and not reducible to a single element: there must be a series of basic propositions which are interdependent. How can we determine this series with any precision? The question has already been answered if we recall that the basic meanings determine the possibility of predication, and that therefore some basic category of thought corresponds to each most basic type of judgment or predication.

I therefore conclude that if predication rests on fixed meanings—as is conclusively the case—there is no recourse but to espouse faith in the synthetic a priori; indeed, if there *were* no synthetic a priori, nobody could espouse faith in anything!

One final word about the position of Lewis: after asserting the factual independence of the basic meanings, then he declares that these meanings are *not existential;* this point seems ambiguous. If it means merely that the basic presuppositions of thought are not derived from the data of experience, this is certainly true, as we have attempted to demonstrate. But if it means that these meanings, thus basic to thought, are not necessarily basic to objective existence, then this is merely the old Kantian contention in disguise; and thought has no recourse but to dismiss it as already discredited.

Conclusion.—In the light of the above considerations, I conclude that intelligible predication does presuppose a complex synthetic a priori factor and that therefore the empiricist objection is totally invalid; indeed, the objection itself would be unintelligible if it were not false.

FROM THE VANTAGE POINT OF PRAGMATISM

Formulation of the Objections

Pragmatism—the theory that the workability of an idea both tests and ultimately constitutes its truth—has likewise spoken its piece against synthetic apriorism as follows:

(1) If the mind comes to experience with a priori categories which are the basic presuppositions of all thought, how can the difference between true and false beliefs be discerned, since the categories operate equally in both? As Dewey puts it:

> [The categories] descend equally upon that which is finally ascertained to be valid knowledge and that which is specious and turns out to be false—as the rain from Heaven descends equally upon the just and the unjust. . . . [This] precludes the theory from ability to account (given its premises) for the differ-

ence between true and false beliefs, since the categories of "thought" are equally operative in both.[32]

The result is that the theory has to go outside its premises to distinguish between true and false beliefs: it has to "fall back upon the actual operations of inquiry by which beliefs are grounded and tested."[33] But in this case, the theory should have begun with these very operations.[34]

(2) And this brings us to a further objection: the theory "ignores the fundamental considerations which define reflective operations. . . . The occurrence of existential problematic situations, and the occurrence of existential operations which are directed by ideas and whose consequences test the validity of ideas."[35] That is, synthetic apriorism bypasses the fact that inquiry assumed its definitive function by facing problem-situations. On the other hand, Dewey—our pragmatic spokesman—does admit that reflection is involved in the attainment of all knowledge.[36]

(3) The theory assumes, in the next place, that reflective operations are moving toward a final, all-comprehensive unity, a goal of complete knowledge.[37] But as a matter of fact, no such unification is in reality approached; "it is always a unification of the subject-matter which constitutes an individual problematic situation. It is not unification at large."[38] Consequently, synthetic apriorism goes "beyond empirically verifiable limits" in positing such an ultimate unification.[39]

(4) This allegedly false ideal of unification suggests a further objection: the theory propounds the claim "that the world is rational through and through since science is the disclosure of an order of uniform, because necessary, laws."[40] But the laws to which appeal is made are in actuality "instrumentalities for control of individualized situations. . . . The alleged rationality of the universe as a whole is another case of generalization beyond the limiting conditions of grounded inquiry . . ."[41] In other words, since the laws in

[32]J. Dewey, Logic: the Theory of Inquiry, p. 530.
[33]Ibid., pp. 530, 531.
[34]Idem.
[35]Ibid., p. 531.
[36]Idem.
[37]Idem.
[38]Idem.
[39]Idem.
[40]Idem.
[41]Ibid., pp. 531, 532.

question are instruments for facing specific situations, there is no ground for asserting that the universe, so far as it does not bear on such situations, is characterized by this same rationality.

And what is more serious: if the universe is really rational in the sense suggested, why should there be any problematic situations at all—as obviously there are? Why should the rational order not, in every case, bare itself to the eye of a correlated mind?[42]

(5) One final objection is suggested by Schiller: even if we could assume the existence of basic categories of thought, the precise determination of their number and significance a priori would be impossible, because these factors depend on the content of a given judgment, so that the range of categories would be as broad as that of distinct problems in the separate sciences.[43]

While the sciences, to a greater or lesser extent, use the common forms of predication, they all *"mean them in the senses appropriate to their own subject-matter."*[44] Thus, to understand the senses in which *is* or *being* may be predicated, we must understand the matter or content of the predication. The logician would therefore have to be omniscient to make a complete list of the categories. But this is absurd; it is inconsistent with his own claim to have abstracted the form of truth from its content; and it fails to take into account the possibility that new problems needing new categories might arise.[45]

Refutation of the Objections

(1) As for the charge that synthetic apriorism has no basis for distinguishing between truth and falsity—it is admitted at once that our theory does go outside its basic a priori premises, in part, to make the distinction of truth and falsity possible, for knowledge at every level involves a combination of both a priori and a posteriori factors, both a categorical and an experiential basis. And it is only in the context of such a combination that truth or falsity can be distinguished. Dewey's point *would* apply to a pure apriorism like that propounded by a Platonic rationalist, but not to the rational empiricism that we have ourselves defended.

But more positively, how can our position both account for the possibility of error and also make the distinction therefore between

[42]*Ibid.*, p. 532.
[43]F. C. S. Schiller, *Formal Logic*, p. 41.
[44]*Idem.*
[45]*Ibid.*, pp. 41, 42.

truth and falsity? This point will be expounded at length in the following chapter; hence, only a brief answer is presented here. (a) Error is possible because the categorical structure may be mistakenly applied to the experiential data. Such misapplication is possible from a great variety of personal motivations. But its general ground is twofold: first, the categories themselves may not be consistently correlated in their applications: as when we accept as true a series of propositions among which there are logical self-contradictions. In the same way, we may add a column of figures and obtain a wrong answer. But second, the application of the categories, while in itself perfectly consistent, may be based upon insufficient experiential data: as when I conclude from a burning fire that it must have been started with a match.

(b) Considering these same points from an opposite point of view, we may indicate how it is possible to distinguish truth from falsity; here again, the test is the twofold one of systematic coherence. A proposition is true or false depending on whether or not: (i) it results from a self-consistent application of the categorical structure; and if it be asked how this itself may be determined, the answer is: by further analysis, just as a mistake in arithmetic may be corrected or avoided by executing the problem again to obtain an ultimately coherent result; i.e., a result free from self-contradiction. (ii) It rests on sufficient data of experience as systematically correlated by the categorical structure of the mind itself. Thus, for example, I determine the length of a desk by taking a number of measurements and correlating the results in self-consistent fashion. Of course, in any such problem I do assume that the desk at any given moment has a determinate length. But this proposition can be denied only by the self-contradictory skeptic.

It is concluded that synthetic apriorism *can* distinguish truth and falsity and that therefore the first pragmatic objection is invalid. Whether or not the pragmatist himself can make this same distinction consistently with his premises will form food for our thought in the following chapter.

(2) As for the charge that our theory ignores the fact that inquiry assumed its definitive function by facing problem-situations—synthetic apriorism, as I profess it, is guilty of no such negligence. The fact is that it starts with just the operations of reflective inquiry and asks what the possibility of such intelligent predications ultimately

presupposes: that this possibility of knowledge rests ultimately on certain basic presuppositions that the mind brings to experience has already been shown in sufficient detail in preceding sections. Furthermore, as was also previously pointed out, the fact that the principles of thought come to the forefront of consciousness only by contact with experience in no way implies that these ultimate categories themselves were *derived* from such experience.

Dewey himself admits that reflection is involved in all knowledge; but it has already been shown that if we grant this premise, the very first act of knowledge implies a synthetic a priori factor in knowing. Nor do I see how the premise itself can be intelligibly denied. The objection is consequently unjustified.

(3) As for the charge that synthetic apriorism assumes that knowledge is moving toward a final, all-comprehensive unification—whereas in fact it moves only toward a unity that is prescribed by a specific problem-situation:

This unification is admittedly an ideal; yet it is a fact that we *do* strive for such unification in our explanations. The very presence of a complex reality poses a problematic situation for thought in its attempt to explain the world. The whole history of philosophy is the successive embodiment of more or less systematic attempts to reach a unified world-view in which reality is explicable in terms of certain posited principles. In fact, our basis for impugning a given philosophy must always be that it fails to achieve that unification in which all the particular data of experience are explicable.

But even more pertinent is the remark that Dewey's own criticism of synthetic apriorism assumes just such an ideal unification as he ostensibly denies; his criticism assumes that there is a body of truth about the nature of thought and that some approximation to this truth is possible. Otherwise, I do not know why Dewey should have made the criticisms I am now discussing; much less do I understand why he should have been one of the most prolific philosophical writers of the twentieth century. Dewey's point is therefore self-contradictory, since it assumes the very unification which it denies.

To state this last point differently, the very assertion that the alleged unification goes beyond empirically verifiable limits is itself guilty of its own accusation and is therefore self-contradictory. Either this statement itself is supported by empirical data or not. But the former alternative is, by the very nature of the statement, inadmissible: what empirical data could possibly support it? The statement is therefore not supported by empirical data; but then it is subject to its own accusation and is self-contradictory. And surely a self-contradictory allegation is no refutation of any theory whatever except its own.

(4) As for the assertion that the rationality of the world is beyond empirical verification and is therefore an unjustified assumption—exactly the same contradiction is here embodied as in that just pointed out with respect to the preceding objection.

Furthermore, it is impossible to deny the rationality of the world, in whole or in part, without self-contradiction, for either the world (or any given part of it) is rational or not. If it is declared to be not rational, then it follows at once that it *is* rational: which is self-contradictory. For if truth were on the side of its nonrationality, then it could not be asserted that this was the case, since such an assertion is itself a rational one or not. If it is not rational, then it is false; and if it is a rational assertion, then it is also false—in the first case because it would be meaningless and could lay no claim to truth; in the second case because it would then contradict its own assertion. In brief: the denial of the world's rationality is either unintelligible, or as itself an intelligible statement about the world, undercuts its own structure. The world must therefore be rational, so that the identification of the real with the rational is thoroughly justified.

As for the query concerning why there should be problems at all in a rational universe—it is not the existence of problems, but only the existence of insoluble problems, that would make an insuperable difficulty at this point. But it is precisely the contention of rational empiricism, as I profess it, that there are no ultimately insoluble problems. That problems exist, for a finite intelligence, is traceable to the fact that rationality, in such a finite being, involves a process in which data are *progressively* apprehended in categorical fashion; and to the fact that, as previously explained, an erroneous application to experience is possible. For an ultimate mind—and to such our argument will eventually lead—no such problems would exist: for such a mind would apprehend the whole content of experiential data in a timelessly necessary intuition.

(5) As for the assertion that the number of categories is indeterminable since it would depend on the *content* of given judgments—

We have already pointed out precisely how the number of categories may be determined: all those presuppositions are categories without which the whole range of intelligible predication would be impossible, so that these presuppositions are determinable from the basic types of logical judgment. If there were no such basic presuppositions, predications would be initially impossible.

It is to be admitted that the precise and exact significance of a given predication depends on the content of the judgment itself: but this does not mean that there are not basic categories which make the act of predication itself possible. Thus if I make the assertion—if life is present, moisture is its cause—the exact causal relation between moisture and life is discernible only from experiential data; but that I make the judgment at all implies ultimately that my mind is so oriented as to understand things in terms of ground and consequent.

Could there be any new categories? Obviously not, unless the basic types of logical judgment are themselves determinable in an entirely different fashion from what we have outlined, for a category is precisely a basic presupposition of *all* thought or intelligible predication; so that thought does not exist unless the whole categorical structure is present. Only such an ultimate presupposition can legitimately be granted a synthetic a priori status and thus be correctly called a category.

Since therefore the whole range of objections suggested is thus shown to be invalid, I conclude that the pragmatic opposition to synthetic apriorism is unjustified. Pragmatism—like rationalism and empiricism before it—stands silent before the bar of reason.

FROM THE VANTAGE POINT OF INTUITIONISM
The Meaning of Intuitionism in Epistemology

Intuitionism, as expounded by Bergson for example, is the epistemological doctrine that intellect requires supplementation, extension, and transcension in a higher faculty of knowledge, called intuition, which alone is adequate for an insight into the reality of things as they are.

This view by no means repudiates the synthetic a priori factor of intellectual knowledge; what it does maintain is that reality, in its mobility and process, transcends the power of intellectual knowledge even as constituted in part by such an a priori element.

The principal exponent of this type of objection to rational empiricism has been Henri Bergson, and it is consequently to his arguments that we now turn.

Formulation of the Objections

So far as I am able to determine, Bergson poses two main criticisms of synthetic apriorism as we have espoused it.

(1) First Objection: the forms of intellect are not coextensive with the matter of knowledge.

Kant failed to realize, maintains Bergson, that as science moves upward from the realm of matter to those of life and mind, "it becomes less and less objective, more and more symbolical. . . ."[46] If this is the case, "then as it is indeed necessary to perceive a thing somehow in order to symbolize it, there would be an intuition of the psychical, and more generally of the vital, which the intellect would transpose and translate, no doubt, but which would nonetheless transcend the intellect. . . . There would be, in other words, a supra-intellectual intuition."[47]

If we are to have a knowledge that grasps things from within in their true meaning, the intellect must be supplemented, especially in our knowledge of life and mind: the *matter* of the knowledge we may have is much greater than that knowledge, if any, which is amenable to intellect alone. Intellect cannot give us "a knowledge from within, that could grasp them [facts] in their springing forth instead of taking them already sprung. . . ."[48]

But why is intellect so defective in its attempt to grasp the reality of things? The general answer to this question is that intellect, because it functions by means of fixed concepts, can never pierce to an apprehension of the process of things.[49] "Whatever is fluid in the real will escape it in part, and whatever is life in the living will escape it altogether."[50] But in particular, intellect does not gain adequate knowledge of the changing reality because it divides its objects into fixed units, conceives their mobility as a series of immobilities put together.[51]

Or to put it differently: the intellect perceives things under the

[46]H. Bergson, *Creative Evolution*, p. 359.
[47]*Ibid.*, p. 360.
[48]*Ibid.*, p. 361.
[49]*Ibid.*, p. 153.
[50]*Idem.*
[51]*Ibid.*, pp. 154, 155.

form of discontinuity by means of concepts which are stable and outside each other.[52] "The intellect is characterized by the unlimited power of decomposing according to any law and recomposing into any system."[53] And even as a man thus literally torn apart would no longer be a living, real man when his parts were subsequently placed in juxtaposition; just so intellect, for the very reason that it can think an object only by tearing it into parts through conception, can never, by placing these concepts in juxtaposition, gain a knowledge of the object as a changing whole. Once put a steak through a meat grinder and it will never be the same steak again!

Intellect, therefore, cannot grasp the meaning of becoming or change: it is "at ease only in the discontinuous, in the immobile, in the dead. *The intellect is characterized by a natural inability to comprehend life.*"[54]

Intuition, on the other hand, leads us to this very knowledge in respect to which intellect is so impotent. What does Bergson mean by intuition? He defines it as a development from instinct, or the power of grasping at definite objects immediately *as if* they were known when in fact they are not—as when the newborn child acts as if the mother's breast were a thing known to it.[55] With this background, Bergson tells us: "By intuition I mean instinct that has become distinterested, self-conscious, capable of reflecting upon its object and enlarging it indefinitely."[56] Intuition, in brief, is merely the power of grasping the reality of things directly, but this power as abstracted from the instinctive fixation to some particular object.

How is intuition related to intelligence? The relation is basically twofold: (i) It is from intelligence "that has come the push that made it rise to the point it has reached. Without intelligence, it would have remained in the form of instinct, riveted to the special object of its practical interest."[57] (ii) But when intuition is once achieved, it then turns back on intelligence and uses the latter's own mechanism "to show how intellectual molds cease to be strictly applicable. . . ."[58]

But suppose someone objects that the only way to go beyond in-

[52]*Ibid.*, p. 160.
[53]*Ibid.*, p. 157.
[54]*Ibid.*, p. 165.
[55]*Ibid.*, pp. 147-149.
[56]*Ibid.*, p. 176.
[57]*Ibid.*, p. 178.
[58]*Ibid.*, p. 177.

telligence is by the use of intelligence itself, since "all that is clear in your consciousness is intelligence."[59] The answer is that this reasoning "would prove the impossibility of acquiring any new habit. It is of the essence of reasoning to shut us up in the circle of the given. But action breaks the circle."[60]

Furthermore, intuition is an extension of the powers of intelligence which, though mere reasoning on the powers of intelligence would never accomplish it, would yet not appear unreasonable when once achieved.[61] Just so, the discussion of walking will never yield the rules of swimming; but if you jump in the water, you must either go beyond the rules of walking, or—if you persist in treating water like solid earth—drown.[62] Similarly, when knowledge ventures to swim in the sea of change and mobility, it must either transcend its conceptual rules of "walking" or perish.

(2) *Second Objection: the categorical structure of intellect might have been entirely different.*

If the forms of the understanding are absolute, irreducible, and inexplicable, then "the whole of our knowledge becomes relative to certain requirements of the mind that probably might have been entirely different from what they are: for an intellect differently shaped, knowledge would have been different."[63] The only escape is to view the intellect as relative to the needs of action, from which therefore the forms of the intellect may be deduced: "This form is therefore neither irreducible nor inexplicable. . . . Knowledge ceases to be a product of the intellect and becomes, in a certain sense, part and parcel of reality."[64]

Bergson forbears to answer the charge that he begs the question in explaining intellect by action, when this latter presupposes intellect: and it is doubtful that he ever succeeds in answering this accusation.

Refutation of the Objections

First objection: general refutation.—The assertion that the forms or categories of intellect are not coextensive with the matter of knowledge is either self-contradictory or meaningless. Either this

[59]*Ibid.*, p. 192.
[60]*Idem.*
[61]*Ibid.*, pp. 192, 193.
[62]*Ibid.*, p. 193.
[63]*Ibid.*, p. 152.
[64]*Ibid.*, pp. 152, 153.

assertion is rationally comprehensible or not: and this by the intellect. If it is not thus comprehensible, it is meaningless. If it is thus comprehensible, it is self-contradictory: for it assumes that I have an intelligible concept of the matter of knowledge, else I could make no such assertion. But this must then mean that intelligible conception *is* coextensive with the whole range of being. It follows that the original assertion, by its own implication, is false; so that the assertion is self-contradictory by necessarily presupposing the very knowledge it denies. I therefore conclude that the proposition which denies intellect the capacity to know any datum whatever, is either self-contradictory or meaningless.

In like manner, and by a precisely similar analysis, the assertion that there is a suprarational intuition for the knowing of reality is also either self-contradictory or meaningless. For either this assertion is unintelligible or else the realities it asserts are the proper objects of intellectual conception: and in this last case, the alleged suprarational faculty of knowing has disappeared. Bergson himself speaks of intuition as reflecting upon its object: but this is precisely the function of intellect, so that the supposedly suprarational faculty is merely intellect itself in exercise.

And in general, we may conclude that every attempt to mark off a territory from which reason is excluded by the nature of the subject matter as such, *ipso facto* admits this very reason itself.

First objection: specific applications of the refutation.— (i) The assertion, for example, that the essence of things as changing and developing is unknowable by intellect is unintelligible apart from its falsity: for if I do not have a clear concept of change or development, the sentence strikes me as water strikes a stone: it is meaningless. But if I do have such concepts, then the proposition is false since it denies me just these concepts.

(ii) Again, the assertion that the intellect—because it proceeds through fixed concepts—is insufficient for understanding things as living and organic overlooks three obvious facts: (a) That unless knowledge consists of fixed concepts it does not exist: for the knowledge of something not fixed and definite is the knowledge of nothing in particular and hence of nothing at all. (b) That it is possible to have a fixed concept of change and process themselves: indeed, Bergson's own theory, as we have seen, would be unintelligible on any other supposition. (c) That only the most basic concepts, only the presuppositions of all thought, are absolutely fixed: less adequate concepts of existing things may be replaced by the more adequate through interaction with the data of experience.

(iii) Bergson, as we noted, attempted to answer the objection that the only transcension of intellect must employ intellect and is therefore impossible. But his answer is inadequate.

The objection, he insists, would prove the impossibility of forming any new habit of action. But this assertion is obviously false since the formation of a new habit—if it is a rational or telic act—presupposes intelligence in the very nature of the case: unless I conceive what I am attempting to achieve, and adapt present means to that end, the formation of a new habit, on a rational or deliberate basis, *will* be impossible. And thus Bergson's point turns back on him, just as his imagined intuition was supposed to turn back on intellect itself.

As for the illustration about walking and swimming: the same *basic* principles of motion apply and are essential in both pursuits—otherwise neither one would be possible: it is only the *specific* application to the environment that varies. Just so with the principles of thought. The same basic principles operate in all knowledge—otherwise knowledge would be impossible. It is only the specific application of the principles that varies from the apprehension of one thing to that of another at a different level of reality.

Second objection.—The assertion that the basic forms of thought might have been different is doubly self-contradictory. (i) For it is of the nature of a category that it is a *basic* presupposition of *all* thought: if therefore, such a category might have been different, then it would not be such a basic presupposition, and hence not a category. But this is self-contradictory. In fact, the only alternative to the absolute necessity of the basic forms of thought is the doctrine that knowledge is impossible—which again impugns its own assertion.

(ii) Furthermore, there is no way to make the original assertion —that the categories might have been different—without assuming that just the present categories are absolute and changeless: for if there were no such starting points of thought, this predication or any other would be impossible. In making the assertion we make, we presuppose precisely the truth that we deny. But this point has already been fully supported in previous contexts.

In concession to Bergson, there is a sense in which we deduce the forms of intellect from action. We begin with the fact of possible knowledge and then proceed to infer what this possibility implies. But this process of inference does not mean that the forms of thought are prescribed by action, as Bergson seems to suggest: for the very possibility of inference from action, and indeed of action itself so far as it is rational, depends upon the mind's a priori possession of the basic forms of thought which make inference, or any other intelligent action, possible.

Conclusion.—Since the objections of intuitionism reduce, on every line of argument, to either self-contradiction or meaninglessness, I conclude that synthetic apriorism has emerged as preferable to this proposed alternative.

Conclusion

Since the whole range of objections to rational empiricism has been thus weighed in the balances and found wanting, I conclude that rational empiricism, as I have defined it, stands yet unscathed by its erstwhile opponents. It remains to determine and similarly support the corollaries of such of view: and to this task we forthwith proceed.

Chapter IV

COROLLARIES OF RATIONAL EMPIRICISM

Concerning Epistemology Proper

First Corollary: Epistemological Dualism

Formulation of the theory.—Epistemological dualism, as mentioned in our previous summary of rational empiricism, is the doctrine that the immediate object present to the mind in any knowledge experience, is not the independently existing reality, but is rather a representative idea of that reality.

The immediate object of knowledge is always an idea that is ontologically distinct from the object to which it refers: and this is true of any object of knowledge whatsoever. When, for example, I have knowledge of a house, the house is not directly given in or to consciousness: what *is* given is an idea about the house which I take as its more or less adequate representative in consciousness.

Nor is there any exception to this dualism in the mind's knowledge of itself or of its own ideas. When I make a given idea the object of thought—when, for example, I make the concept of triangularity an object of conscious meditation—still, my idea about the concept is not the concept itself as such, but a judgment that refers to that concept. Nor does this lead to an infinite regress of ideas: for, while the series of such dualisms may be indefinitely expanded—as when I think about triangularity, then about angles, then about lines, then about points, etc.—still the number of such steps is ever being cut off by practical expedience, on the one hand; and on the other, the number of such implications from any given context of thought is not infiinte, but comes to rest in those basic categories with which the mind functions *before* they become objects of knowledge.

Similarly, when I make my self the object of thought: I am ontologically distinct from the particular concept of my self that I form. Otherwise, the self could not exist apart from my possessing a concept of it. And this is obviously false, for on this supposition, infants all the time, and the rest of us most of the time, would be selfless, which is absurd. The concept of my self that I possess in consciousness from time to time is not my very self, but a representative idea of that self.

Why is this theory a necessary corollary of the rational empiricism which we have established? According to our original theory, all knowledge is a combination of categorical and experiential elements. In other words, knowledge is a resultant: it does not *exist* until the mind *applies* the categories to the data of experience, whether external or internal. It follows at once that the immediate object of knowledge, being such a resultant, is not the independently existing object itself, but an idea which represents this object in consciousness. But this is precisely epistemological dualism, which is therefore a necessary implication of rational empiricism on any but purely subjectivist or solipsistic grounds. (Solipsism, the doctrine that for each self the world is within his mind, will be refuted in the sequel.)

On what rational basis may the theory of epistemological dualism be established and accepted? Its principal grounds are three: (1) First, it is in accord with the accepted scientific analysis of the way in which our perceptions of the external world reach us. According to such an analysis, external objects in some way impinge upon the sensory organ—eye, ear, etc. Through a series of neural and other physicochemical changes, the effects of this impingement are transmitted to the central nervous system and, in the case of what becomes a conscious impression, to the brain itself. And it is only in conjunction with this point in the physical series that an object appears in consciousness as perceived. Such an object is therefore obviously *not* the original object that presumably impinged upon the sensory mechanism.

At the level of brain activity, physical science surrenders the reins of analysis: the exact relation between brain activity and consciousness being left for the philosopher or psychologist to determine.[1] But the scientific analysis of perception has shown us that—whatever the relation between brain-events and mind-events—a perception is not ontologically identical with the externally existing object.

[1]Cf. Part III, Section A, Chapter IV, notes on the metaphysical argument.

(2) Second, epistemological dualism, being a corollary of rational empiricism, is supported by the whole weight of argumentation that has established the truth of the latter theory: if a premise is true (rational empiricism), so also is its necessary implication.

(3) Finally, epistemological dualism may be established by reducing proposed alternatives to a self-contradiction. It is to this task that we now turn.

Proposed alternatives.—Very casual meditation will serve to convince one that the logically possible alternative theories—so far as the terms of the knowledge situation are concerned—are the following:

(1) The idea and the object are ontologically distinct. (Dualism.)

(2) The idea and the object are numerically identical (or if we accept a critical position: there is a partial numerical identity), but the object is real apart from the knowledge of it. (Monism.)

(3) The idea alone is real, there being no independent object apart from the knowledge present in consciousness. (Solipsism, or Subjective Idealism.)

(4) The object alone is real, the presence of conscious ideas being a pure illusion. (Illusionism.)

(5) Neither idea nor object exists. (Nihilism.)

If therefore the last four positions can be exposed as inadequate, the first—namely, epistemological dualism—will be established. Nor does this reasoning commit the fallacy of consequent, according to which a conclusion is accepted merely because those results are present which ought to be present *if* the theory were true. For this fallacy occurs only when some other possible circumstances might produce the same result. A match, for example, may cause a fire; but it cannot therefore be concluded that wherever fire is present, it was caused by a match: for there are other causes which might produce fire—lightning, for instance.

But in the case of the above epistemological alternatives, there *are* no other logically possible explanations than those mentioned. Consequently, the destruction of the remaining logically possible alternatives will involve the truth of epistemological dualism—unless we are ready to accept that self-refuting skepticism according to which no solution to the problem is possible.

Consider the theories in reverse order:

(1) (2) *Nihilism* and *Illusionism,* as we have called them, have

not usually been presented as serious theories: indeed, they are so untenable that the very statement of them is practically sufficient for their refutation.

Nihilism is directly self-contradictory and therefore invalid: for if neither ideas nor objects exist—and these are all the realities that would exist if they did—then by hypothesis this theory does not exist and therefore requires no refutation. Surely no one will maintain that we should refute nothing. And if he does, then he at least exists to refute the objection.

Illusionism suffers a similar fate. For if consciousness is a pure illusion, then even the illusion itself does not exist, since no illusions exist except in consciousness. Again, this theory itself, being a series of ideas in consciousness, does not exist. In both these ways, illusionism reduces to self-contradiction.

(3) *Solipsism* or *Subjective Idealism*. (a) Even if solipsism were true, epistemological dualism would still follow. Solipsism teaches that for each self the world of experience and reality is in his mind and has only subjective existence. But either this self and its world of ideas are ontologically identical or not. Suppose they are identical: self and ideas are the same. But they cannot be identical if monism is true: for either the world's separate existence would then be illusory, or that of the self would be thus illusory, since I do in fact appear to know these realities (?) as distinct.

In the first case, there is a difference between the real object and the idea, because the *illusion* of the world's existence is obviously not the same thing as the self, else there would be no ground conceivable for calling the former an illusion. In the second case, there is the same difference: for the illusion of the self's existence could not be the same thing as the world, and for the same reason just mentioned, namely, that on such terms there would be no ground for speaking of an illusion at all. There is further the added point that the position then reduces to nihilism: for by hypothesis the world of experience has no objective existence; and if there is no self or subject, it has no subjective existence either. Since these two exhaust the possibilities, it follows that the world of experience has *no* existence. And this is precisely the theory of nihilism which has already been refuted. Thus, in either case, solipsism involves epistemological dualism.

Suppose then that the self and its world of ideas are distinct. In this case epistemological dualism follows at once. For the essence of the theory will then be that ideas are projected by the self. And since only the self has ultimate actual existence, it follows that the real object and the ideas of it are distinct. And this is the dualistic assertion.

Thus, whether solipsism identifies self and world or distinguishes them, epistemological dualism holds its validity.

But in fact, solipsism itself is untenable: (a) Because the world appears to have a separate existence from my consciousness: and there is no way of accounting for this illusion if the world is actually the projection of my consciousness. For such an illusion would have to reduce ultimately to an act of will—in which case it would not be an illusion, and then solipsism itself would collapse; or it would spring from an extraneous cause, in which case the self is not the only reality.

(b) Solipsism cannot account for the fact that in perception we seem at least to be affected involuntarily. As Wild puts it: "We cannot make or provide ourselves with external sensations of our own making when we are in an unbefuddled state."[2]

(4) *Monism* is open to the following objections:

(a) The very way in which the monistic theory is formulated establishes its falsity. Beginning with the facts of consciousness, the monist in epistemology attempts to find correlates for these facts in the real, external world. But this very procedure assumes that the fact in consciousness is distinct from the fact as independently existing in the external world. Otherwise, the monist would have no motivation to formulate his theory, since it attempts to correlate the two. Thus when perception is said to be the identical presence of the object to the mind, what is said would be unintelligible if it were not false: for since my only knowledge of the external world in particular springs ultimately from perceptions, if the percept and the object were numerically one, I would never have any reason for saying so.

Nor is the situation saved by appeal to so-called critical monism, which asserts the percept and object to be partially the same numerically, partially different. For prior to critical determination, for ought I know, the whole percept may be numerically distinct from the object; furthermore, the fact that I critically consider the percept

[2] J. Wild, *Introduction to Realistic Philosophy*, p. 436.

to determine its relation to the object, implies at once that percept and object are distinct.

(b) As previously indicated, the theory contradicts the scientific analysis of our perception of external objects.

(c) The theory fails to account for *pure sensory illusion:* as when I see double by pressing the eyeball; although, in fact, other percepts tell me the object is not double. But if monism were true, then the same object would be both double and not double in the same manner—which is self-contradictory.

(d) The theory overlooks the fact that ideas and physical objects have mutually exclusive attributes. A physical object has, for instance, extension and weight, while an idea has neither. An idea, on the other hand, is clear or confused, adequate or inadequate, while none of these predicates may be similarly predicated of physical objects. Yet if monism were true, if perception were the identical presence of the object to the mind, the object and the percept would have the same attributes—which is absurd.

(e) Wild presents a further list of objections as follows: (i) If monism were true, why should we not sense everything with any given sense?, though in fact each sense senses only one kind of thing.[3] (ii) There are many things in the world—like ultraviolet light— that we do not sense at all: our very knowledge of these assumes our idea of them to be distinct from the realities themselves.[4] (iii) Sensation depends, in many cases, on physical influences which emanate *from* the object: thus, for instance, I cannot see colors at night. But this implies that the object itself and my percept of it are distinct.[5]

(f) Finally, monism cannot explain the existence of qualities like color, smell, etc. Scientific analysis reduces all the aspects of external objects to quantitative proportions: a color, for example, is not in the object as such, but depends for its existence upon a relation to the percipient's sensory mechanism. But if perception were the *identical* presence of the object, no experience of qualities would be possible at all—which is obviously ridiculous. Consequently, either the scientific analysis of qualities must be surrendered, or monism must be impugned. Since scientific analysis *may* be questionable here, I do not press this last argument as completely decisive.

[3]*Ibid.,* p. 414.
[4]*Idem.*
[5]*Idem.*

Conclusion.—Thus every alternative to epistemological dualism reduces ultimately to self-contradiction. And since the alternatives considered exhaust the possibilities, we must conclude that the dualistic theory is completely substantiated.

Second Corollary: the Coherence Theory of Truth

A. Formulation of the Theory

Definition and meaning.—The coherence theory of truth, as I profess it, is the theory that the truth or falsity of any proposition whatever is to be tested and determined by the consideration of: (i) whether or not the proposition results from a self-consistent application of the categorical structure to experiential data; and (ii) whether or not such proposition is systematically correlated both with the data in question and with the whole body of previously established propositions.

Thus the test is twofold and may be presented in question form: (i) Have the basic presuppositions of all thought (the synthetic a priori categories) been applied with self-consistency, i.e., without internal self-contradiction? (ii) Is the proposition consistently correlated, both with the whole range of available data directly pertinent to the entity or situation in question, and with the whole body of propositions previously established in similar fashion?

Consider the following proposition: I am twenty-eight years of age. How is the truth of this proposition to be tested, according to the coherence theory? In the following manner: First, is the proposition internally free from self-contradiction so far as the meanings of its terms are concerned? Have I predicated of myself something that is consistently possible in accordance with the meaning of the subject-term, *I*? Is there anything about being a human *I* that would analytically preclude my being a certain age? Apparently, the proposition meets this first test successfully.

Second, does the proposition fit in with the whole range of directly pertinent data about myself and with the whole body of previously established propositions? For example: do the testimonies of my grandparents and parents, or other possible witnesses, substantiate or cohere with this proposition? Is the fact on record, through the recording of my birth date at the bureau of vital statistics in the district where I was born? And so the questions may be raised. If I find that the whole range of available data confirms the original proposition in every case, or that apparently contrary cases have some alternative and coherent explanation, I am provisionally justified in accepting the proposition as true. Of course, a whole cluster of previously accepted propositions is likewise pertinent, but in a less immediate sense: e.g., that age is determinable, or that coherence is a reliable test, or, ultimately, that knowledge is possible.

From the foregoing definition and illustration a number of general implications about the coherence theory of truth may be drawn:

(1) The theory depends upon synthetic apriorism. For if the knowing mind had no a priori structure of rationality, the coherence test could not be applied: there would, for example, be no basic presuppositions of all thought in terms of which initial propositions could be either tested or correlated to the body of propositions taken to be valid.

(2) The theory of coherence itself is no exception to its own truth. It too, as a formulated theory, is to be tested in the same manner. But how, you say, is this possible? How could I apply the theory if I did not first formulate it, and how, if it is true, could I formulate it if I did not know its truth to begin with?

The answer is that the coherence theory is merely the formulation, in consciousness, of the way in which the a priori categorical structure ideally functions from the outset in the manipulation of experiential data. It is not then that I need to know the theory to begin with, but that the theory is a conscious description of the way in which I do in fact *think* to begin with. The whole argument for synthetic apriorism is therefore an argument for the coherence theory of truth: and just as the a priori categories as such were established by showing that without them knowledge would be impossible, so the coherence theory is established in the same way by showing that rational nature does in fact test its propositions in this manner and that if valid knowledge were not thus attainable, skepticism would result.

(3) The theory does not appeal to certain axioms as self-evident. In fact, no proposition is self-evident as such. If it is a *basic* proposition, its validity is demonstrated by showing that if the proposition were not true, knowledge would be impossible. It is sometimes said, for example, that the law of contradiction is self-evident because its reaffirmation is involved in its denial. But as Blanshard points out, this argument is itself an appeal to coherence:

The demonstration lies in showing that acceptance of the law is necessary on pain of incoherence. The argument is: *if* the law of contradiction holds, then within the system governed by it even the assertion that it does not hold assumes that it does. The incoherence is between the principle of the system and the content of a proposition supposed to be made within it.[6]

(4) Our knowledge of the truth of any proposition of fact concerning which error is possible is provisional and subject to revision by the continued application of the coherence test to broader ranges of data.

There are, indeed, some propositions about which error is impossible from a logical point of view. In general, these are of two classes: (i) All synthetic a priori propositions when they are formulated consistently (i.e., propositions consistently expressing, or derived from, the basic categories which make all thought possible). Such propositions are, when correctly formulated, not provisional but certain, for the possibility of knowledge itself rests upon their validity, else they would not be the basic propositions we presumed they were.

(ii) Propositions which describe an initial perceptual experience: e.g., I feel cold; or this chair feels hard to me; or I experience this paper as white. Such propositions, since they merely describe my actual state of consciousness, do not admit of being false, provided they are genuinely descriptive.

But when I make transition to statements such as: The room *is* cold; the chair *is* hard; the paper *is* white; then the situation changes. And in general, all synthetic a posteriori judgments, so far as they make an assertion about a presumed objective and independent reality, are provisional in nature because they depend for their *absolute* justification upon the whole range of experiential data—which, in fact, is not simultaneously available to a finite self. The important exception to this rule occurs when it is possible to reduce all logically conceivable alternatives of a given proposition to self-contradiction. In such a case, the synthetic statement, even though a posteriori, may be taken as absolutely demonstrated. The significance of this exception will become increasingly evident as our argument progresses.

Relation of the theory to epistemological dualism.—If, as we have shown, the mind is directly aware of representative ideas alone and not of the independently existing object as such, it follows that either

[6] B. Blanshard, *The Nature of Thought*, vol. II, pp. 252, 253.

knowledge is impossible, or that valid knowledge of the independent object can be had by the systematic correlation of ideas in the manner suggested by the coherence theory of truth. Since skepticism is self-contradictory—since, in fact, it can only state its case intelligibly by appealing to that very possibility of knowledge which it denies, truth must be attainable by the test of coherence. And if someone here objects to our argument assuming the validity of the coherence test, I will ask him to state an intelligible argument that does not; in fact, I call every opponent to the bar of this very challenge!

Answer to objections.—While the major objections to the coherence theory have already been anticipated and answered in our formulation of the theory itself, some attention should be given to specific further criticisms. Blanshard[7] gives a typical catalogue, but his answer to the catalogue of such objections seems to me to be tragic, since it leaves the coherence theory itself in a state of hypothetical validity.[8] No such theory of truth will, in our opinion, be sufficient: if the tests of truth are not absolutely normative, all predication is ultimately hopeless and unintelligible.

The most important of these objections—so far as they have not appeared already in our discussion—are the following:

(1) That the theory actually reduces to *correspondence* since the truth of knowledge as a whole is measured by its approximation to an absolute system.[9] We answer: (a) That if the coherence test did not concrete in a knowledge that involved a partial representative correspondence both to objects as independently existing and to objects as possibly known by an absolute mind, skepticism would result. (b) That it is precisely the point of the coherence theory to prescribe the mode by which the correspondence of our representative ideas with independent objects may be ascertained. No one doubts, I presume, that a true proposition must embody such a correspondence: it is when correspondence is allegedly established as itself the test of truth, that difficulty, as we shall presently note, ensues.

(2) That a system of thought can be fully coherent without being true.[10] We answer: (a) That the objection is self-contradictory. For either the proposed system is known to be false or not: if it is not, there is no ground for the objection; if it is known to be false, then

[7]*Ibid.*, p. 269f.
[8]*Ibid.*, p. 291.
[9]*Ibid.*, p. 272.
[10]*Ibid.*, p. 275.

it is *ipso facto* not a perfectly coherent system in the sense in which we have defined coherence. For our theory holds "that one system only is true, namely the system in which everything real and possible is coherently included."[11] Any ground that impugned the truth of a system would by that very fact impugn the system's claim to coherence.

(b) Nor could there be two or more systems that meet the test of coherence. Each such system would omit at least one fact: namely, the fact that explanation is possible in terms of the alternate theories, nor could it include this fact without contradicting itself.[12] If, on the other hand, there is some rational basis for believing one system as over against the others, only the system that was thus characterized would be an approximation of ideal and perfect coherence. It follows that there could be no more than one ultimately coherent system, although it is granted at once that, with the exceptions noted previously, the correlation of our propositions with this system may be only approximative.

B. Proposed Alternatives

There are three ways in which the coherence theory of truth may be supported: (i) by showing, positively, that knowledge is possible only on the assumption of the theory's validity; (ii) by showing, negatively, that specific objections to the theory are invalid; and (iii) again negatively, that proposed alternative theories of truth are inadequate. Our discussion has already embodied the first two types of evidence, so that there remains only the consideration of the third.

Aside from the so-called self-evidence theory which has already been discarded, there are two proposed alternative theories: (1) The Correspondence theory, according to which a proposition is true if it corresponds to a fact. (2) The Pragmatic theory, according to which a proposition's truth is its practical workability as a plan of action.

The correspondence theory of truth.— (1) The theory formulated.

The theory is best expressed in the words of one of its own proponents, Bertrand Russell. He speaks of "the correspondence theory of truth, according to which the truth of basic propositions depends on their relation to some occurrence, and the truth of other proposi-

[11]*Ibid.*, pp. 275, 276.
[12]*Ibid.*, p. 277.

tions depends upon their syntactical relations to basic propositions. For my part, I adhere firmly to . . . this theory."[13]

But if basic truth is thus a correspondence with fact, how do I get to this correspondence? In all candor, Russell admits "that while we don't get as many facts as we should like, we do arrive at some: we get at our own feelings and sensations, which seem to be verifications of our previous beliefs."[14] In any case, the truth of a proposition is to be tested by its correspondence with an objective factual situation.

(2) The theory refuted

(a) If epistemological dualism is true—as we have attempted to show, then there is no way in which the mind can actually transcend its ideas to determine whether they correspond with some "solid chunk of fact," as Blanshard calls it.[15] The mind has only its ideas to compare, so that while the goal of a true proposition is the adequate representational concept of some independent fact or situation, the only way of defining the proposition *as* true, or declaring it to be thus an adequate representation of the object, must consist in the systematic correlation of our ideas in a self-consistent whole: and this is precisely the coherence theory as I profess it. In other words, the only way of testing correspondence is by coherence, so that the former is not an adequate theory of truth.

Russell's own critical realism should convince him of this fact. Indeed, his very formulation of the correspondence theory implies its inadequacy. The facts we do get at, he maintains, are our own feelings and sensations. But if this is the case, it is implicitly admitted that we do not "get at" independently existing objects, so that the truth about them must either be impossible—which is skepticism —or else determinable by the coherence propositions which interpret experiential data.

And with respect to sensations and feelings themselves; as soon as we formulate even a descriptive proposition about them, we surrender the possibility of *observing* any correspondence between proposition and fact: we never can get outside our circle of propositions to see if they correspond with the presumed separate feeling or sensation. After all, even such a feeling or sensation does not exist for us until it becomes the object of intelligible experience: and such an experience always consists in a judgment or a series of judg-

[13]B. Russell, *Dictionary of Mind, Matter and Morals*, p. 260.
[14]*Ibid.*, p. 259.
[15]*Op. cit.*, II, p. 228.

ments. At least I cannot recall ever having had a sensation that I did not experience as the object of intelligence. And if anyone can thus recall a sensation, his very recalling it proves that it existed first as an intelligible experience so far as he was and is concerned: certainly we cannot recall from memory what was not first in consciousness as an idea.

As Blanshard puts the point: "What the [correspondence] theory takes as fact and actually uses as such is another judgment or set of judgments, and what provides the verification is the coherence between the initial judgment and these."[16] Epistemological dualism therefore renders the correspondence theory untenable: the theory itself would be unintelligible if it were not inadequate, since the only test of the theory itself is its self-consistent coherence with experiential data. There surely are no solid facts to which the correspondence theory itself corresponds.

(b) But suppose, for the sake of argument, that epistemological monism is true—a position that Russell himself repudiates; in this case, there certainly is no ground for maintaining the correspondence theory. If perception is the identical presence of the object to the mind, there would be no conceivable mode, nor indeed any intelligible meaning, for asserting any correspondence between percept and object. But if we accept the reality of both ideas and objects, the relation between them must be either dualistic or monistic; since the correspondence theory of truth is unsustained in either framework, it is legitimate to conclude its invalidity.

The pragmatic theory of truth.— (1) The theory formulated.

The principal exponents of the pragmatic theory in America have been William James and John Dewey.

According to these thinkers, a proposition is true if it brings us into a satisfactory relation with our experience. Thus Dewey writes:

> If ideas . . . or propositions are instrumental to an active reorganization of the given environment, to a removal of some specific trouble and perplexity, then the test of their validity and value lies in accomplishing this work. If they succeed in their office . . . they are true. . . . The hypothesis that works is the *true* one; and *truth* is an abstract noun applied to the collection of cases, actual, foreseen and desired, that receive confirmation in their works and consequences.[17]

[16] *Idem.*
[17] J. Dewey, *Reconstruction in Philosophy*, pp. 156, 157.

While the views of James are specifically different from Dewey's in their precise application, it seems to me that the former holds the same general theory about truth as the latter.

Thus he writes:

> Ideas . . . become true just in so far as they help us to get into satisfactory relation with other parts of our experience. . . . . Any idea that will carry us prosperously from any one part of our experience to any other part . . . is true for just so much, true in so far forth, true *instrumentally*.[18]

James admits that this theory of truth involves the following implications: (i) An idea is not true *as such*, but *becomes* true: its truth is in fact identical with the process of its verification.[19] (ii) Workability in experience is therefore the very meaning of an idea's truth.[20] (iii) Pragmatism involves epistemological dualism: in fact, this position "lies at the base of the pragmatist definition of truth."[21] And it is by workability as a criterion that the correspondence of idea and object is established.[22]

Pragmatism maintains then that the truth of a proposition is its instrumental workability as a plan of action, either for thought or for activity in the physical environment: workability is not merely a test of truth's presence: it is truth itself.

(2) The theory refuted. May I say, by way of prolegomena, that the pragmatic theory of truth has been subjected to such thorough refutation that no more than a brief catalogue of objections needs to be cited. The most thorough refutation known to me is that of Blanshard in his *Nature of Thought*, Volume I, page 349f. The pragmatic theory is unacceptable for the following reasons:

(a) Pragmatism is self-contradictory in at least the following ways:

(i) The truth of an idea could be identified with its workability only on the basis of a presumed knowledge of workability, the truth of which knowledge must therefore be determined by some other criterion than workability itself. But in this case the hypothesis that the truth of an idea is its workability would be false at its most crucial point—which is self-contradictory.

If the true is the workable, what is the workable? Either I have

---

[18]W. James, *Pragmatism*, p. 58.
[19]W. James, *The Meaning of Truth*, p. vi.
[20]*Ibid.*, pp. vi, vii.
[21]*Ibid.*, pp. 217, 218.
[22]*Ibid.*, pp. 218-220.

a true knowledge of workability or not. If not, then the pragmatic theory is unintelligible. But if I do have such a true knowledge, then workability cannot be the ultimate concept for the definition of truth. It follows that, in either case, the hypothesis that the true is the workable is contravened: workability as a *test* for truth necessarily transcends itself in a higher definition of the meaning of truth itself.

If it be said that *workability* should be defined as satisfactory adjustment to environment, then the same questions may be asked about this satisfactory adjustment, and so on to an infinite regress; *unless* I come at last to a synthetic a priori, the validity of which brings us ultimately to the coherence, rather than the pragmatic theory of truth. It therefore appears that the very intelligibility of the pragmatic theory impugns its sufficiency.

(ii) If a given proposition is true only through the process of verification and not as such, then an infinite regress of ideas is involved so that knowledge becomes impossible—which is self-contradictory. For what constitutes the truth of the principles of verification? They also become true only by being verified and so on to infinity! Unless we finally reach principles which are true *as such* and not by *becoming* true, we can never have knowledge of anything: but the reality of such principles would and does refute the pragmatic theory.[23]

Pragmatism itself—being a proposition or set of propositions—is in precisely the same predicament. For if it *becomes* true only by verification, and if verification, on the pragmatic theory, involves an infinite regress of propositions, it follows that pragmatism itself is not true and never can become true; but in this case it is false—which again is self-contradictory. Furthermore, if it be asked what principles might be used to verify the pragmatic theory itself, I have no idea what the answer might be except in terms which would repudiate the theory propounded.

(iii) Even if these difficulties could be overcome, pragmatism would share the self-contradiction that we have already found in empiricism. For no series of partial verifications could ever justify a universal and necessary proposition. But then two curious results would ensue: first, the proposition just mentioned could not be universally true—which is absurd; second, pragmatism itself would not

"Cf. Blanshard, *op. cit.*, I, p. 367.

be universally true and would therefore be inadequate as a theory of truth.

(b) A proposition asserts a present attribute or past situation and not a future expectancy. A historical statement, for example, is obviously either true or false as such: it is meaningless to say that it becomes true or false. Either Napoleon spat in a puddle at 10:04 A.M. on the morning of August 12, 1811, or he did not. A proposition about such a situation cannot be said to *become* true or false: otherwise, why should I take the trouble to determine *whether* any historical statement *is* true?

But the same holds, as Blanshard points out,[24] of any proposition about the present situation as well. If I say: Vinegar is sour; I do not mean the same thing as if I had said: If I taste vinegar, I will experience sourness. For if the two propositions were analytically identical—as the pragmatist must hold that they are—I would never test the former by the action suggested in the latter. Either the vinegar is sour or it is not. And if not, it is the last vinegar I buy from *that* store!

(c) Again, intelligent action implies, as we have shown repeatedly, the antecedent possession, as modes of thought that may become conscious ideas, of some truth not derived from action itself: namely, the basic presuppositions of all thought; so that these cannot *become* true through verification in action, since action, if it is intelligent, presupposes their functioning. Consequently, the pragmatic theory cannot account for the possibility of the very action it regards as basic.

(d) If the pragmatist, with James, accepts epistemological dualism: we have already shown repeatedly that this position makes the coherence theory of truth the only alternative of skepticism.

(e) Finally, the very mode, by which pragmatists attempt to establish their theory, indicates its falsity: they attempt to show that it is a systematically consistent theory of truth, that it is not self-contradictory, that it explains the whole range of data involved in the knowledge situation. But this entire process implies that the systematic consistency at which the theory aims is itself the test in terms of which a theory or set of judgments should be accepted: and such is precisely the coherence theory of truth. To put the point briefly: the only grounds for believing pragmatism are necessarily considera-

---

[24]*Ibid.*, p. 356.

tions which involve the repudiation of that very pragmatism as decisively inadequate.

I therefore conclude that, since pragmatism reduces, on every line of analysis, to self-contradiction; and since the very grounds on which it rests constitute its refutation; it is totally unsustained as a theory of truth.

Conclusion.—Since neither of the proposed alternatives to coherence meets the tests of rational analysis, and since both of them are intelligible only in terms of the coherence they ostensibly repudiate, therefore, the coherence theory of truth has met the test of ultimate adequacy.

Concerning the Relation of Epistemology to Metaphysics
The Logical Primacy of Epistemology

The corollary of our whole discussion up to this point is clearly this: that valid assertions concerning the nature of reality, whether about the immediate realities of experience or about the relation of these to the basic and ultimate reality, can be established only in the context of an epistemology which delineates the basic presuppositions for the possibility of knowledge itself. In other words, epistemology, from our vantage point as knowers, is logically prior and basic to metaphysics, which is therefore the second object of philosophical attention and not the first. Before an elaboration of *what* we can ultimately know is possible, there must exist a comprehensive understanding of *how* we know any object whatsoever, if our metaphysical dogmas are to transcend belief in knowledge.

Of course, there is a certain sense in which *being,* as a *fact,* is in our experience prior to knowing: not only does our knowing presuppose the fact of our existence as knowers, but, when once the basis of knowledge is made clear, conclusions are reached which indicate that the material universe (and its ultimate metaphysical ground) existed long before human knowers appeared on the cosmic scene. But this is a far different thing from contending that our basic metaphysical beliefs must be determined prior to any discussion of the presuppositions of possible knowledge. For this last contention would be to rest our most crucial beliefs on a nonrational basis. It may be the case that, Ultimate Reality being what it is, the possibility of knowledge is what it is: but this does not mean that our *knowledge* of the Ultimate Reality is basic to the understanding, initially, of the principles of knowledge. Indeed, that metaphysical knowledge would be impossible without the prior possession of the basic categories themselves. And if such be the case, then it is self-contradictory to say that the knowledge of the metaphysical ultimate is logically basic to the knowledge of knowledge itself. It is, I suggest, the *fact* of the Ultimate Reality, not the *knowledge* of this fact, that is basic to all existence and to knowing itself. And would not the suggestion be premature: the far-reaching implication might be asserted even here that this means that in the final analysis being and knowledge coincide in the ultimate reality. But more of this in a subsequent context.

But, it may be insisted, you seem to be arguing that I could not know anything without understanding its rational basis, and on these grounds I will involve myself in an infinite regress that makes knowledge impossible, since the principles of knowledge themselves require a rational basis and so on. The answer to this objection is twofold:

(i) First, there is a sense in which we do possess knowledge apart from an understanding of its rational basis. That is, we become aware of ourselves as knowing subjects, capable of understanding and positing meaningful predications. Beginning with this fact that in our experience knowledge is possible, we raise the question—if we are speculatively inclined: how is the possibility of knowledge ultimately to be explained? In answer to this question, we are led finally to the whole structure of epistemology that has formed the substance of our previous discussion. Since such an epistemology concludes a synthetic a priori factor in knowledge, no such infinite regress of rational bases, as the objection charges, is involved in our knowing: the mind *comes* to the data of experience with the basic structure of thought.

(ii) Second, it is possible to maintain a whole nexus of true beliefs without understanding their rational basis in detail: just as a man may fly to Chicago in a United Mainliner without a detailed understanding of the principles of science involved in the possibility of flight. But just as it is in terms of the validity of these very principles that he *can* fly, so it is in terms of the principles of knowledge that a man can entertain a true belief; although in both cases the detailed understanding of these principles may be absent. It is, in fact, a cardinal point in our epistemology that we *use* the basic presuppositions of thought long before the principles themselves become clearly formulated in consciousness. If this were not so, knowledge could never begin.

Epistemology, therefore, I take to be logically prior to the establishment of any basic metaphysical theory: to know what *being* is, we must first know what *knowing* is, if our metaphysical view is to commend itself as rational and transcend mere belief in demonstrative knowledge.

The Establishment of a Common Ground

Since epistemology is logically prior to metaphysics, and since knowing presupposes, as we have seen, both a categorical structure and experiential data, it follows that there is a common basis or ground in terms of which rational and universally acceptable propositions about reality — whether ultimate or subordinate — may be reached.

An adequate metaphysic should be such that it commends itself to all knowing minds, insofar as they determine their beliefs rationally. Such a metaphysic should embody principles that all men ought rationally to accept. If, for example, naturalism—the doctrine that nature alone, as the space-time nexus, is real—should be true, it ought to be rationally obligatory on all intelligent knowers, *qua* rational, to accept it. If, on the other hand, theism—the doctrine that nature's reality is subordinated to that of a transcendent Being—should be true, it ought to be able to commend itself as similarly obligating acceptance. In this last case, the validity of what has been called natural or rational theology will have been fully justified.[25]

[25]For a detailed development of this theme, consult Part II, Chapter III; Part III entire.

Part II

AN EVALUATION OF ALTERNATIVE POSITIONS

CHAPTER I

THE EMPIRICAL APPROACH

OBJECTIVE EMPIRICISM: THE ROMAN CATHOLIC POSITION:
THOMISM

Formulation of the Position

A. The General Nature of Knowledge

SUMMARY STATEMENT.—The first of several major alternatives to rational empiricism, as a mode to the knowledge of the Ultimate Reality, confronts us in the objective empiricism that was first given detailed theological exposition by Thomas Aquinas (A.D. 1225-1274), and in modern times has become the official philosophical position of the Roman Catholic Church. According to this position, the origin, nature, and limits of natural knowledge (i.e., of knowledge apart from special or supernatural revelation) may be described as follows:

Knowing originates in a process of abstraction whereby the sense data are freed from their particular or individual elements through the active intellect and then concreted in the potential intellect as intelligible species or universal ideas. The whole of knowledge is therefore derived, on the natural level, from the data and objects of sense: so that there are neither innate ideas nor innate categories in the mind at the start of experience.

On the other hand, the intellect is active and does have a certain initial structure in the sense that it has the capacity, or intellectual light, whereby, through participation in the Divine Intellect, the abstraction of the universal from the particular takes place.

As to its nature, then, knowledge consists in an apprehension and possession by the mind of the universal ideas or intelligible species that are exemplified in particular sense objects. Such a position is rightly called *objective empiricism: objective,* because it holds to an externally real referent from a consideration of which all knowledge originates: namely, the concrete entity apparent to sense; *empiricism,* because all knowledge is thus mediated through the senses or the sensory mechanism. Still, however, the level of knowledge is reached only when the intellect apprehends the particular object through a knowledge of its universal form: ideas are, by their very nature, universal, so that knowledge would be impossible if there were not an abstracting power whereby the universal is known *from* the particular object.

The initial objects of knowledge are the so-called first principles, such as the ideas of being and unity: these principles are not innate but are merely the first objects to be abstracted from contact with sensible things, although the aptitude for forming these principles is wrought into the very nature of the intellect.

The origin and nature of knowledge being thus described, the implied limitation of knowledge may be stated as a corollary: strictly speaking, knowledge is confined within the limits prescribed by the objects of sense. Only abstractions from sensible things can form a basis for valid knowledge in the first instance.[1]

Working "from the outside in," as a true empiricist ought to do here, knowledge may be described as a concourse between two *factors:* the sense data, on the one hand; and the intellect, both active and passive, on the other. The *process* of this concourse consists in the abstraction, initially of the first principles, subsequently of the universal ideas or intelligible species. It is to the detailed consideration of these factors and this process that our attention is now directed.

The factors of knowledge.— (1) The Intellect

(a) Passive Intellect: At the outset, it must be noted that the intellect is passive, i.e., it contains no innate species or inborn knowledge. The intellect, to employ an oft-repeated metaphor, is like a wax tablet at birth. "The human intellect . . . is in potentiality [i.e., a state of passivity] with regard to things intelligible, and is at first *like a clean tablet on which nothing* is written."[2]

Nor does this mean merely that the soul is passive in receiving the intelligibles, but it means rather that she is "naturally deprived of them."[3] Such a passive state is far from ideal, and in consequence it

---

[1] E. Gilson, *The Philosophy of St. Thomas Aquinas,* p. 230.
[2] *Basic Writings of Saint Thomas Aquinas,* vol. I, pp. 747-748; *Summa Theologica,* I, qu. 7a, art. 2.
[3] Gilson, *op. cit.,* p. 235.

is asserted that "the necessity of assuming a certain passivity at the beginning of our intellectual knowledge rests . . . upon the extreme imperfection of our intellect."[4]

(b) Active Intellect: While the soul is thus completely passive with respect to the origin of knowledge, yet its passage to a knowledge of ideas—or from potency to act, as the Thomists say—involves also an *activity* of the intellect. Since ideas are universal and *sensa* are particular, there must be a special faculty which abstracts the form or universal idea of the object.[5] Such capacity, of abstracting from particular objects their universal form, is called the faculty of active or agent intellect.[6]

This intellectual light, as Thomas calls it, is:

> A participated likeness of the uncreated light [of the Divine Intellect]. . . . But since besides the intellectual light which is in us, intelligible species, which are derived from things, are required in order that we may have knowledge of material things, therefore this knowledge is not due merely to a participation . . . as the Platonists held.[7]

(2) The Sense Data: The sensible objects in some way impinge upon the senses, which are in immediate contact with things. "All our knowledge begins with the senses. Therefore intellectual knowledge (knowledge by means of ideas) must undoubtedly be derived from sense-knowledge."[8] All knowledge therefore stems from an empirical basis.

The process of knowledge.— (1) The First Principles

The initial objects of knowledge are certain first principles, like *being* and *unity*, which form the basis of all further knowledge: "Human reasoning, in the order of inquiry and discovery, proceeds from certain things absolutely understood—namely, the first principles. . ."[9]

It should not be thought, however, that these principles are innate: they are merely "the first concepts formed by our intellect when we come into contact with the sensible . . . the first intelligibles which our intellect can reach in starting from sensible experience. The intellection of these principles is no more innate than the conclusions

[4]*Idem.*
[5]J. Maritain, *Introduction to Philosophy*, p. 171.
[6]Gilson, *op. cit.*, pp. 235, 236.
[7]Aquinas, *op. cit.*, p. 804; *Summa*, I, qu. 84, art. 5.
[8]Maritain, *op. cit.*, p. 171.
[9]Aquinas, *op. cit.*, p. 759; *Summa*, I, qu. 79, art. 8.

of deductive arguments. . ."[10] Like all other knowledge, the apprehension of these principles is possible only by abstraction of their definitions from sensible matter.[11] While the aptitude for forming these principles is in the soul initially,[12] the actual apprehension of them presupposes the "intervention of the sensible."[13] Thus the knowledge of being, unity, etc., is built upon and derived from sense objects: *"principium nostrae cognitionis est a sensu* [our knowledge of principles is from sense]."[14]

(2) The Intelligible Species

When once the first principles have been thus abstracted, they serve as tools for the abstracting of the whole range of universals in terms of which knowledge becomes actual: "We abstract universal forms from their particular conditions; which is to make them actually intelligible."[15] Knowledge is, in fact, an apprehension of particulars through their universal forms, and of universals by abstraction from their concrete particular instances.

B. The Resultant Knowledge of God

Knowledge of God through His effects.—Since all knowledge, on the natural level, is derived from sense experience, knowledge of God is no exception: "The only road which can lead us to a knowledge of the Creator must be cut through the things of sense. The immediate access to the Cause being barred to us, it remains for us to divine it with the help of its effects."[16]

The knowledge of God's existence is therefore neither self-evident to us nor innate in our intellect: it is rather achieved through an analysis of the objects of sense in accordance with the process of knowledge already described in the preceding section.[17] The demonstration of God's existence, according to Thomas, is fivefold and rests on analysis successively of motion, efficient causation, necessity and contingency, the gradations of the good, and the governance of the world.[18] The consideration of these various effects leads to a knowledge that their Cause exists and is of such and such a character.

Yet no knowledge of the *essence* of God (i.e., of God as He is in

---

[10]Gilson, *op. cit.*, p. 246.
[11]*Ibid.*, pp. 246, 247.
[12]*Ibid.*, p. 247.
[13]*Idem.*
[14]*Idem.*
[15]Aquinas, *op. cit.*, p. 752; *Summa*, I, qu. 79, art. 4.
[16]Gilson, *op. cit.*, p. 64.
[17]Aquinas, *op. cit.*, *Summa*, I, qu. 2, art. 1f.
[18]*Ibid.*, *Summa*, I, qu. 2, art. 3, cf. Part III of present work.

Himself, considered independently of the mere fact of His existence, etc.) is possible in this way.[19] From the knowledge of an effect, no perfect knowledge of the cause is possible, especially in a case like the knowledge of God where the effects are not proportioned to the cause: "yet from every effect the existence of the cause can be clearly demonstrated."[20]

The entities which we regard as God's effects, can never give us a knowledge of His essence therefore, because they do not equal the power of God the cause; and God's essence can be known only through the knowledge of His whole power:

> From the knowledge of sensible things the whole power of God cannot be known; nor therefore can His essence be seen. But because they are His effects and depend on their cause, we can be led from them so far as to know of God *whether He exists,* and to know of Him what must necessarily belong to Him, as the first cause of all things, exceeding all things caused by Him.[21]

There is likewise a further difficulty which makes the knowledge of God through sensible things imperfect: not only are the effects a mere partial embodiment of God's power, they are of an entirely different kind. For the idea of God is the notion of an immaterial or nonsensible substance: how then can any passage be possible from sensible things to immaterial substance?[22]

It is true that the intellect abstracts the forms or ideas from sensible objects, but immaterial substances are *not forms:* "However much our intellect may abstract the quiddity [form, whatness] of a material thing from matter, it could never arrive at anything like an immaterial substance."[23] Thus we can never acquire any perfect knowledge of God by such a process of abstraction, although *some* sort of knowledge of immaterial substance, and consequently of God, *is* possible in this manner. This knowledge proceeds by analogy.[24]

The analogy of being.—While God as cause and creatures as effects are essentially distinct, so that no knowledge of God's essence is possible from a knowledge of His effects, still there is *some* analogy between uncreated Being and created being.

[19]*Ibid.*, pp. 12, 13; *Summa,* I, qu. 1, art. 7.
[20]*Ibid.*, p. 21; *Summa,* I, qu. 2, art. 2.
[21]*Ibid.*, p. 109; *Summa,* I, qu. 12, art. 12.
[22]*Ibid.*, p. 848, f.; *Summa,* I, qu. 88, art. 2.
[23]*Idem.*
[24]*Idem.*

When God's existence as the first cause has once been established, there is *ipso facto* established a certain analogy or proportion between God and creatures:

> Because God confers upon all things all their perfections, we are able to discover in all things their resemblance and unlikeness to God. . . . It is the creature which . . . resembles the Creator. But this resemblance is none the less real, and would suffice to prevent our assertions concerning God from being completely equivocal. In speaking of God and created things in the same terms, we use these terms in a sense of at least partially common meaning. . . .[25]

Thus the whole range of predicates ascribed to God has analogical significance: i.e., the meaning of the predicates is different when applied to God, from the meaning of the same predicates when applied to creatures; yet there is a principle which warrants the common applicability of the terms to both God and creatures. This principle, in general, is the fact that God, as the first cause, contains formally (or in some cases only virtually) the archetypes or ideas that are being realized by the whole range of creatures.

Consequently, no affirmation applies to God in the same sense as to creatures: in fact, nothing at all can be predicated of God and of creatures in a univocal, or same-meaning, sense.[26] The result is that predications about God fail "to contain or even grasp the reality signified."[27]

Does this analogical character of the predications make God unknowable? Such a conclusion would seem natural. And Maritain speaks of the situation in a manner that suggests this very implication: "God is known by the natural reason analogically, so that we perceive the divine perfections in the mirror of creatures, without asserting any unity of nature, common measure, or proportion, or mixture or confusion of any kind between God and created things."[28] And again: "The infinite abyss of difference of nature which divides Him [God] from all is crossed by ananoetic [analogical] intellection; but the analogous concepts of which it makes use avow in that very use their impotence to enclose or delimit the reality they thus describe."[29] To speak thus of the impotence of analogous concepts, and

[25]Gilson, *op. cit.*, pp. 109, 110.
[26]*Ibid.*, pp. 108, 109.
[27]*Ibid.*, p. 109.
[28]*Op. cit.*, p. 259.
[29]J. Maritain, *The Degrees of Knowledge*, pp. 276, 277.

of there being no proportion between God and creatures, would seem to imply that God is incomprehensible.

But still an analogy is insisted upon which renders predicates about God partially meaningful: our descriptive statements are not sheer equivocation.

The crux of the problem arises when we realize that God must be an absolute unity, whereas the assertions we make about His nature are multiple and distinct. There is no particular problem when negations are made—as in the assertions that God is eternal, or infinite—for such definitions aim at the exclusion of limitations. But what about the ascription of positive analogical perfections? Do *they* not impugn the divine simplicity? No: just as the intellect forms the resemblance of any unity in terms of multiple conceptions, so here; but "if the intellect affirms the unity of an object by complex propositions, whatever is diverse and complex in the propositions must be referred to the intellect making them, but the unity described by them, must be referred to the object."[30]

What are the types of analogy, and what, in particular, is the analogy that God bears to creatures?

There are two basic types of analogy, according to Thomistic thinkers: (1) Analogy of *attribution,* in which a term is predicated of a number of particulars, only one of which possesses the property intrinsically and formally, the others possessing the property only extrinsically by virtue of their relation to the first. Thus *health* is predicated of man intrinsically and formally; of air, color, food, exercise, etc., by virtue of their relations to man.[31]   (2) Analogy of *proportionality,* in which a term is predicated of a number of particulars intrinsically, in a way that is simply different but proportionally the same in all. Such intrinsic meaning may be metaphorical and virtual on the one hand, or formal and proper on the other. An instance of the former would be: The lion is to the beasts as a king to his subjects; of the latter, The life-principle in man is to his vital operations as that in plants is to theirs.[32]

The analogy of God or Being to creatures is then: (1) Proper analogy of proportionality: since the analogous notion of being is intrinsic formally in all the analogates, all creatures possessing being.[33] This does not mean that the properties of created beings bear

[30]Gilson, *op. cit.,* pp. 110, 111.
[31]Phillips, R. P. *Modern Thomistic Philosophy,* II, pp. 168, 169.
[32]*Idem.*
[33]*Ibid.,* p. 173.

the *same* relation to their being as those of uncreated Being to its being, but merely that the relation subsists in each case in a manner appropriate to the two types of being.[34] If we ask how we know that any such analogy exists, since we do not know the modality of the properties of uncreated Being, the answer is that we know this because created being is itself derived from uncreated Being, which therefore contains the perfections proper to all created being formally; so that terms drawn from the relative perfections of created things "can be used as analogies to say something about the absolute being on which they are dependent for their actualization."[35] Thus we can predicate of God such things as unity, being, goodness, truth, intelligence, will.

(2) Analogy of attribution (though not in the strictest sense) : "inasmuch as this notion of being is found in a higher degree in substance than in accidents, and in God than in creatures, so that accidents are dependent on substance for their existence, and creatures on God both for essence and existence."[36] In addition, a whole host of predications about God embody a metaphorical analogy of attribution, as when God is called Father to indicate the idea of dependence.

Conclusion.—It follows from our entire analysis that God, according to objective empiricism, is known through His effects or creatures by means of analogical predication which, though it gives us some knowledge about God in this indirect way, yet fails to lead us to a knowledge of His essence.

Criticism of Objective Empiricism

Of the general theory of knowledge.—(1) The entire Thomistic theory of knowledge rests on a strict empiricism that has already been refuted in connection with our defense of rational empiricism in the preceding section. The whole range of objections against any theory that denies the synthetic a priori or the innate categories, falls with all its devastating weight on the very basis of Thomist reasoning to the knowledge of God. And as we have shown in our previous discussion that on the grounds of empiricism knowledge becomes impossible and self-contradictory skepticism ensues, it is hardly to be expected that a theory which embraces this type of epistemology can

[34]D. M. Emmet, *The Nature of Metaphysical Thinking*, pp. 176, 177.
[35]*Ibid.*, p. 177.
[36]Phillips, *op. cit.*, p. 173.

ever lead us to a knowledge of the Ultimate Reality or God—and that for the simple reason that apart from the synthetic a priori *no* knowledge of anything at all is possible. Thus Thomism stands with its foundation cut from beneath it, so that the whole superstructure of its reasoning collapses.

(2) But with respect to the Thomistic formulation in particular: how, for example, can it be affirmed both that the active intellect abstracts the universals from sensa and that there are no innate categories, or forms of thought, or first principles? If the intellect does abstract the form in this manner, it must proceed either on the basis of proclivities or structures inherent within it, or on the basis of similar tendencies derived from sense experience itself; that it proceeds without any such proclivities is not a possible alternative, since then it would never act at all to abstract the universal.

But of the two alternatives, one is contradictory of the original affirmation and the other makes knowledge impossible. If the proclivities or structures are inherent in the nature of intellect as basic categories which make intellection possible, then it follows that the mind *does* come to sense experience with certain forms of thought in terms of which it is disposed to understand that experience: but this contradicts the assertion that there *are* no such innate forms of thought.

If, on the other hand, the forms of thought are said to be derived from sense experience itself—and this is apparently the Thomist contention—then the very first act of knowledge would be impossible: significant thought cannot begin unless the intellect has the basic forms of thought that make initial predication possible. Unless the proclivities or tendencies of intelligence are innate, the very first universals could never be abstracted, and knowledge would be impossible—which is self-contradictory skepticism.

(3) Again, if there are no innate categories of thought, why, as the Thomist maintains, should the active intellect concrete initially the so-called first principles? The answer is that these principles are the basis of all further knowledge: but why should they not also be the basis of a conscious knowledge of the principles themselves? The distinction between the basis of knowledge in the one case from that in the other is purely arbitrary. And the only satisfactory explanation is that the intellect must operate with such first principles in the initial act of knowledge: not, of course, in the sense that these prin-

ciples are present from the beginning as ideas in consciousness, but rather in the sense that they are modes of thought wrought into the very structure of intellect itself. But this is a repudiation of empiricist moorings.

After all, if the first principles are the initial achievements of intellect, there must be some structure within the intellect which causes the abstraction of intelligibles in this order. The Thomists themselves admit this when they assert that the aptitude for the formation of first principles is in the soul initially. But what is this, if not the admission that the principles themselves are innate structures of intellect which rise gradually to consciousness through external or internal experience? The potentiality of intellect to achieve these principles is inexplicable on any other basis, especially when we realize that just these principles are in fact basic to *all* knowledge.

But can it really be said that the categories or first principles are the first concepts formed upon contact with sensibles? By the formation of a concept, I understand the clear apprehension of this concept in consciousness. But experience hardly supports the position that the basic categories are the first concretions of conscious knowledge: it seems rather to be the case that particulars are known first and that only after long concourse with experience do the categories themselves appear before consciousness as apprehensible concepts. Indeed, the vast majority of persons probably never achieve a clear understanding of the first principles of thought.

Yet thought, from its first act, employs these principles as structures or modes: the intellect is initially disposed to interpret the data of experience in a certain way. Just so, for example, people think syllogistically from premises to conclusion without having necessarily any knowledge of syllogistic rules. Now the fact that the first principles or basic categories *are* the modes whereby intellect functions without their being necessarily present in consciousness means that these categories are innate as part of the constitution of intellect itself.

In conclusion it should be asserted that the epistemology of objective empiricism is self-contradictory and invalid, and that knowledge is possible only in terms of a theory which grants intellect an innate structure of rationality with which it manipulates the data of experience.

Of the knowledge of God.—The knowledge of God is just as impossible on a purely empirical basis as is the knowledge of anything else. The proofs of God's existence, for example, either beg the question or rest on the universal validity of certain basic categories—especially causality, necessity-contingence, and existence—which cannot have been derived from sense experience, as we have shown.

Again, Thomism asserts that while God's existence can be known from His effects, no knowledge of the essence of God is possible in this way, because of the extreme disproportion, in this case, between effects and Cause. But if all natural knowledge is derived by abstraction from sensa, how can this assertion itself be justified? How can the assertion—that a knowledge of God's essence is impossible through effects—be valid knowledge? If sensa are the only source of natural knowledge, how can we assert either that God's essence cannot be known through His effects, or that any disproportion exists between God and creatures? Such assertions are untenable in a twofold way:

(i) First, the assertions are self-contradictory. If I do not know the essence of God, how can I assert that it is unknowable through a knowledge of effects? Either such an assertion is a valid predication about God or not. But if it is a valid predication, it must be an assertion about God as He is in Himself, or what is the same thing, as He is essentially: but then some knowledge of God's essence is given, and hence the original assertion contradicts itself. For its truth involves its falsity: if it is really and essentially true that no essential knowledge of God is possible through His effects, then even this assertion must be false. The appeal to analogy in this context will be considered below.

(ii) Second, such assertions imply a nonempirical source of knowledge: if I know God to be disproportionate to creatures, and if this disproportion cannot be discerned from the mere consideration of God's effects, then I must have this knowledge from some other source. The only such sources which occur to me are the mind itself or some supernatural revelation: either this knowledge is innate or it is communicated directly by God.

But either of these principles would, if admitted in this context, undermine the whole theory of objective empiricism, according to which there are no innate ideas or intelligibles, and according to which also the knowledge of God's existence and certain of His characteristics is possible apart from special revelation of the kind suggested. In any case, suppose that this necessary knowledge were derived from some other source than sensible effects: the knowledge itself, from whatever source, would be an effect of God and not God Himself. As an effect, it could not, by hypothesis, give us any knowledge of God's essence. Every allegation against the possibility of essential knowledge of God from His effects is therefore a declaration that the knowledge of God is impossible: for every conceivable source of that knowledge is itself an effect. Suppose, for example, that God should now supravene upon the course of experience and tell me by special revelation that His essence is unknowable from effects: it would be easy for me to decide that it was the Devil, and not God, who thus spoke. For not only is it the case that the statement would be unintelligible if it were not false—since I would not then know the meaning of the word *essence* here—but what is more: the statement itself, as a particular propositional affirmation, is itself an effect, so that it would cancel itself out by implication. And if the statement is nothing particular and hence not an effect, it is nothing at all.

But again: if the essence of God is unknowable through His effects, how can we assert His existence? As Carnell urges,[37] how can we know that a thing exists if we do not and cannot know what it is? Either God exists essentially or not: if He does, then His essence is knowable through effects. If He does not, then my assertion is not applicable and therefore has no real meaning.

The same point can be made in still another way: how may we question the possibility of essential knowledge of God from effects on the ground that God, as immaterial substance, could never be adequately known through sensibles? Such an assertion assumes that very essential knowledge of God which it ostensibly denies: for how do we know that God is an immaterial substance? There is no conceivable source for this knowledge that would not itself be an effect.

From such considerations it would appear to follow that either essential knowledge of God is possible through an analysis of His effects, or no knowledge of God is possible at all.

Thomists attempt to escape the difficulties suggested above by an appeal to analogical predication: all knowledge of God is analogical rather than univocal.

But what is the status of this assertion itself? If all knowledge of God is analogical, then the knowledge, that it is analogical, is also

[37] *Introduction to Christian Apologetics*, p. 150.

analogical, and so on to an infinite regress. If the asserted analogy between God and creatures, or Being and beings, does not describe a relation that holds *essentially* of God, then there is no basis for proposing the analogy at all, nor does it yield any real knowledge of God. But if the analogy does describe a relation that holds essentially of God, then the assertion of the analogy is false: for it would then not be true that all knowledge of God is analogical, the analogy itself posing an insuperable and decisive exception.

Nor is there any escape from this predicament by asserting that God, as the cause, must bear some analogy to His effects: for if all knowledge of God is analogical, *cause* is also predicated analogically; so that no essential knowledge of God is communicated by the statement that God is the first cause. Yet it is only in terms of just such an essential knowledge that any analogy between God and creatures may be asserted. Hence, as Clark maintains,[38] when the existence of God is concluded from sensible things, it is not actually *God's* existence that is concluded.

The denial of a univocal element in predications about God therefore reduces analogical predication to sheer equivocation and makes God unknowable: the only thing that makes any analogy meaningful is a univocal element or point of likeness which can be clearly specified. But the Thomists deny just such a univocal element. It follows that no predication about God actually describes God as He is essentially or even as He is analogically with respect to creatures: for the knowledge of God's essence is required to assert the analogy.[39]

Even if we admit that an analogy between God and creatures exists on the basis of the relation of causation, how, as Emmet asks,[40] could we derive analogies of the nature of the cause from the effects in terms of the assumption that God contains formally all the perfections of creatures? Why must God be wise and good to cause wisdom and goodness, and not material and vegetable to cause matter and plants?

The answer, on Thomist lines, is that God contains *formally* those perfections consonant with His perfect and simple being, and only *virtually* (i.e., in such a way as not to pertain to His essential nature) those properties necessary to bring bodies to perfection. But on what basis can such a distinction be made? Any answer that is given

[38]*Christian View of Men and Things,* p. 312.
[39]So Clark, *op. cit.,* p. 311; Carnell, *op. cit.,* p. 147.
[40]*Op. cit.,* p. 182.

would appear to discredit the whole Thomistic position. The only bases for the distinction which occur to me are the following:

(i) That the knowledge of God's formal perfections is innate—but Thomism denies innate knowledge.

(ii) That this knowledge results from special revelation—but Thomism asserts that some knowledge of God is possible without special revelation—and the knowledge of which formal perfections are actually in God is basic to such a natural knowledge of God through effects.

(iii) That this knowledge of God's formal perfections is possible through analysis of God's effects—but Thomism denies that any such essential knowledge of God is possible through an analysis of God's effects.

The conclusion appears to be that there is no principle in terms of which Thomism can consistently make the distinction between formal and virtual perfections.

Conclusion.—I therefore conclude that objective empiricism is untenable as an approach to Christian apology, both because its basic empiricism is self-contradictory and because its doctrine of analogy makes the knowledge of God impossible. The whole position therefore concretes in both a general and a religious skepticism which is *ipso facto* invalid.

SUBJECTIVE EMPIRICISM

Formulation of the Position

A. Summary Statement

The second alternative that confronts us as a possible basis for Christian apology is that of an empiricism which turns its eye inward to the mind's experience of immediate awareness. Whereas objective empiricism attempted to find a basis for the knowledge of God by an analysis of external objects presented to sense, subjective empiricism attempts to find such a basis in an alleged immediate or direct awareness of God through inner, intuitive experience.

God is known, not by a process of inference primarily—if at all—but by a direct and intimate personal encounter in which the soul confronts God in immediate subjective experience; apart from such experiences, there is no knowledge, strictly speaking, of the Divine Reality. This position is appropriately denominated *subjective empiricism: subjective,* because it bases the knowledge of God on inner personal encounter; *empiricism*, because the encounter presents God as an object of direct experience analogous to the impinging of external objects on the sensory mechanism.

Such a subjective empiricism is propounded by a school of thought that cuts across the lines of nearly all the great ethnic religions and is called, from such a general point of view, mysticism. Christianity, like others among the world's living religions, has had its own succession of mystical thinkers who affirmed that God was to be known only through an internal and immediate experience of His presence. But the principal exponents of this position in the twentieth century, so far as Christianity is concerned, have appeared in the ranks of the liberal and neo-orthodox wings of professing Christendom; although even some of the evangelicals have had leanings in this direction.[41] Certainly the influence of subjective empiricism has had its greatest impact through the two first-mentioned movements.

In our analysis we shall present the position through a select few of its spokesmen: D. C. Macintosh will serve as a representative from the ranks of liberalism; John Baillie, Karl Barth, and Emil Brunner will typify the neo-orthodox stand on this point.

B. The Liberal Spokesman: D. C. Macintosh

Macintosh, both in general and religious epistemology, accepts a position that he calls *critical monistic realism.*

General epistemology.—In general theory of knowledge this position means that an external object is truly known to the extent that there is a numerical identity between the object as perceived and the object as independently existing. While some of the qualities in any given percept are subjectively contributed and conditioned:

> In normal sense-perception physical things are presented within the field of immediate experience and observation. . . . There can be affirmed (at least partially, i.e., to some extent) a numerical oneness, an existential identity between the object as perceived and the object as independently existing.[42]

Religious epistemology.—In the field of religious knowledge, a precisely analogous situation holds. In normal religious experience the self is aware of a Divine Factor or Reality which is truly known precisely to the extent that there is a numerical oneness between the

[41] So Dr. Timothy Fetler, Professor of Philosophy at the Bible Institute of Los Angeles: "Christian Apologetics and Modern Thought," 1953, *passim.*
[42] *The Problem of Religious Knowledge*, p. 5.

object *as experienced* and the object as *independently existing.* Thus
Macintosh writes:

> In religious experience at its best, divine reality (divine proc-
> esses and a divine factor) is presented with sufficient immediacy
> to make possible for man a genuine acquaintance with (experi-
> ential knowledge of) that divine reality. . . . There is . . . a
> partial identity or overlapping of the divine as immediately ex-
> perienced and the divine as independently real.[43]

With respect to this Divine Reality, three things may be affirmed:
(1) *Realism:* that it exists independently of human selves;[44] (2)
Critical Realism: that our experience of it may have some "quality
or qualities of an exclusively subjective nature";[45] (3) Critical *Monistic* Realism: that there is a partial numerical or existential oneness
between the Religious Object as experienced and that same Object
as independently existing.

How may we distinguish in our experience of the Divine Reality
between subjective and objective elements? According to Macintosh,
God is, at least, that cosmic factor which makes for the realization of
eternal and absolute ideals or values which coincide "with the qualities of character which spiritual religion tends to ascribe to its ideal
object."[46] Such a factor is neither to be identified with the human
self or selves, nor with reality as a whole: not the former because
persons are the products of the value-producing factor and are being
educated *toward* ideal ends which are therefore not exclusively human; not the latter "since not all reality is making for the realization
of absolutely valid ideas."[47] The divine factor is therefore distinct
from both human selves and from reality as a whole.

Now it is just the spiritually ideal which constitutes the appropriate criterion for distinguishing between subjective and objective in
our experience of the religious Object: "The truly divine is the
spiritually ideal, and this it is which is the true criterion of the genu-
ineness of all that claims to be revelation of the specifically divine."[48]

God therefore, as the cosmic factor making for the realization of
absolute values, is known through a direct and immediate experience

[43]*Ibid.,* pp. 175, 178.
[44]*Ibid.,* p. 11.
[45]*Idem.*
[46]*Ibid.,* pp. 163-165.
[47]*Ibid.,* pp. 164, 165.
[48]*Ibid.,* pp. 176, 177.

which is partially identical with, partially distinct from, the independently existing Divine Reality.

C. The Neo-orthodox Spokesmen: Baillie, Barth, Brunner

Denial of the inferential knowledge of God.—It is a matter of basic agreement among neo-orthodox thinkers that God cannot be known through the inferential processes of human thought; so that the procedure of all natural theology, in attempting to establish the existence of God and to know certain of His attributes from the natural revelation alone, is wholly fallacious.

Just because God is known in direct personal encounter, it is not possible to consider objectively the question of His existence. So Barth writes:

> It is not a matter here of observing, analyzing, considering and judging an object, where the knower is permitted to consider himself disinterested, free and superior in his relation to his object. . . . Knowledge of God . . . does not therefore permit the man who knows . . . to maintain an independent and secure position over against God so that from this he may form thoughts about God which are in varying degrees true.[49]

And Baillie, in similar spirit, declares that:

> It is not as the result of an inference of any kind, whether explicit or implicit, whether laboriously excogitated or swiftly intuited, that the knowledge of God's reality comes to us: It comes rather through our direct personal encounter with Him.[50]

Why this rejection of the inferential knowledge of God? (a) Baillie's answer is that all argumentative or inferential theism starts from the assumption that atheism is a possible position: arguments for God assume a situation "in which God is not yet."[51] But as a matter of fact, the Divine Other confronts man with the challenge of His holy presence from the beginning, and there is thus no way of standing aside to consider whether the Challenger exists, any more than we can genuinely debate the question whether any other reality we thus confront in direct experience exists. And thus Baillie rhetorically asks:

[49] K. Barth, *The Knowledge of God and the Service of God*, pp. 103, 104.
[50] J. Baillie, *Our Knowledge of God*, p. 143.
[51] *Ibid.*, p. 176.

How can I, who in this very moment that I write am conscious of a demand being made *now* upon my life by God and His Christ, stand aside from the situation of responsibility thus created in order coldly to debate the question whether the God who thus claims me so much as exists?[52]

(b) The answer of Barth and Brunner differs from that of Baillie with respect to this question. Their assertion is actually twofold: (i) First—and this point is especially proffered by Brunner—while God is clearly manifested in the natural revelation, no knowledge of God is thereby possible, because the human mind shares the natural corruption and depravity of man's whole being in revolt against God. So Brunner: "The only reason why man can be a sinner is because God reveals Himself to him [in natural revelation]; it is because he is a sinner that the revelation cannot issue in the knowledge of God."[53]

Baillie aptly presents Barth's position here by representing the latter as affirming of man that "his humanity has been so totally corrupted by sin that no more than a cat is he able to hear God's voice until, through faith in Christ, the image and similitude of God are created in him afresh. And with the rest of his human nature his reason also has been totally corrupted. . . ."[54]

(ii) Second, the God reached by thought and inference does not bring a knowledge of the true God. The God known by man's natural powers, says Barth, will be something like a supreme Being or absolute nature: but "this absolute and supreme being, the ultimate and most profound, has nothing to do with God. . . . Man is able to think this being; but he has not thereby thought God."[55]

Brunner, though not so extreme here, takes similar ground. When I think my way to God, I never get beyond the circle of my thought:

> Even God is here part of *my* rational world, in which *I* am the center. . . . *I* introduce God into the world of my thought. Nothing happens that breaks through the circle of my self-isolation. I am alone with my truth, even with my idea of God. . . . The God whom I conceive myself cannot give me truth because He gives me nothing at all.[56]

[52]*Ibid.*, p. 175.
[53]E. Brunner, *Revelation and Reason*, p. 65.
[54]Baillie, *op. cit.*, p. 20.
[55]K. Barth, *Dogmatics in Outline*, p. 23.
[56]*Op. cit.*, pp. 366, 367.

It is only in a personal encounter with God that the circle of such isolation can be broken.[57]

On the other hand, Brunner accords, as over against Barth, at least some negative value to argumentative theism: while the certainty of our knowledge of God does not depend on the processes of proof,[58] and while the God of the proofs is a mere intellectual abstraction and not the God of faith,[59] the "proofs" at least show that "by thinking we do not necessarily fall away from faith in God, but rather that we are led toward Him. . . ."[60] Yet this salute to argumentative theism seems little more than a passing gesture, since in another passage Brunner affirms: "We must decide either for proof or for trust, either for rational evidence or for personal encounter. . . ."[61]

Positive doctrine of divine encounter.— (1) The Knowledge of God.

More positively, the knowledge of God is an intensely personal experience in which man finds himself directly confronted with God in Christ through the divine revelation. Nor is the revelation distinct from the experience: revelation *is* personal encounter between the divine and human subjects; and the revelation is not revelation apart from this relation to the subject, God. "The revelation actually consists in the meeting of two subjects, the divine and the human, the self-communication of God to man."[62]

Faith which knows God, then, is not related to a doctrine as its object: "It is wholly a personal relationship: my trustful obedience to Him who meets me as the gracious Lord."[63] Knowing God is thus an experience of God's presence, and "this truth is neither subjective nor objective, but it is both at once: it is the truth which may be described, in other words, as the encounter of the human 'I' with God's 'Thou' in Jesus Christ."[64] That is, the experience itself is a subjective one, but it is related to the objective reality of God.

Under what conditions does the Divine Other confront man? (i) According to Baillie, God confronts *all* men from the *beginning* of their self-conscious experience: "The only humanity known to us is a humanity which has already, in some degree at least, been con-

[57]*Ibid.,* p. 371.
[58]*Ibid.,* p. 340.
[59]*Ibid.,* pp. 340, 341.
[60]*Idem.*
[61]*Ibid.,* p. 179.
[62]*Ibid.,* pp. 33, 48.
[63]*Ibid.,* p. 36.
[64]*Ibid.,* p. 171.

fronted with the reality of God and disturbed by the challenge of His holy presence. . . . Not one of us has been left quite alone by God . . . we have been sought out from the beginning."[65] Baillie appeals to the fact that no matter how far back he goes in memory, he never arrives at an atheistic mentality;[66] nor is this his own experience alone, since all men are confronted with God in their recognition of a moral imperative that constitutes a claim so sovereign "that the least attempt to deny it awakens in us a sense of sin and shame. . . ."[67] In the framework of such a universal moral demand—which is the very heart of the universal confrontation of man with God—Baillie constructs a moral argument for God, which he considers as a "demonstration that the recognition of such an unconditional obligation does in fact contain in itself the recognition of a holy God who is its source."[68]

(ii) For Barth and Brunner, on the other hand, it is not the case that all men are directly confronted with God from the beginning: the Divine Encounter is rather the experience only of those who have been specially influenced and regenerated by the Holy Spirit through a recognition of the Lordship of Christ.[69] Apart from such special and exceptional revelation, Barth, at least, holds that the hearts of men are stony and totally unreceptive.[70] Brunner's position on this point seems to me to be ambiguous.

(2) The Divine Initiative

The knowledge of God therefore depends entirely on the initiative of God, and not at all on human efforts to know the Divine Other. Thus Brunner declares "that man has no power at his own disposal to enable him to acquire this knowledge. . . . God cannot be found by thought. . . . The fact that this inner movement arises in the heart of man, a movement which is the very opposite of the sinful striving for autonomy or independence: this is the work of the Holy Spirit."[71]

And Barth is unusually clear on this point: the man who believes, thinks rigorously and consistently, makes a conscious decision: "but *the fact that* he did come to this decision, *that* he really believed, and

---

[65]*Op. cit.*, p. 17.
[66]Reference, pp. 4-6.
[67]*Ibid.*, p. 159.
[68]*Ibid.*, p. 244.
[69]*Op. cit.*, p. 171 (Brunner).
[70]Barth, *Knowledge of God*, p. 109.
[71]*Op. cit.*, pp. 24, 179.

that he actually had freedom to enter this new life of obedience and hope—all this was not the work of *his* spirit, but the work of the *Holy* Spirit."[72] And in another work: "Knowledge of God is a knowledge completely effected and determined from the side of its object, from the side of God."[73]

On the other hand, Brunner and Baillie, at least, grant some instrumental significance to ordinary knowledge as a propaedeutic to the immediate knowledge of God. While the object of faith, according to Brunner, is not a proposition or even a doctrine about God, when once God has revealed Himself in direct encounter, "every 'something' points to 'Himself,' and in so doing is subordinated to Him. . . . All acts of objective, positive knowledge are therefore merely a preparation for this, and take a secondary position; they are not the perception of faith itself."[74] Ordinary knowledge becomes a set of pointer-readings which refer us to God when once He is known at the higher level of encounter.

Baillie's doctrine is similar, except that, since the Divine confrontation is universal, the instrumental character of natural revelation is likewise universal: the immediate knowledge of God is a *mediated immediacy*. While we do not know God *through* the world, "we know Him with the world; and in knowing Him with the world, we know Him as its ground. Nature is not an argument for God, but it is a sacrament of Him."[75] This doctrine seems self-contradictory, but this appearance can be transcended by "the conception of history as something that happens in the present. . . . "[76] The historical Christ, for example, mediates the knowledge of God: but we do not argue from Christ to God; rather it is in Christ that we see God. "In Christ we know God not by argument but by personal acquaintance. In Christ God comes to us directly."[77] In a similar way God is known immediately through the mediation of our knowledge of the world and things.

(3) God as Incomprehensible

The God of revelation is an absolute mystery to human thought:

> The absolute of thought is not truly mysterious because it can be thought. But God cannot be found by thought . . . and

[72]*Knowledge of God*, p. 109.
[73]*Dogmatics in Outline*, p. 24.
[74]*Op. cit.*, p. 36.
[75]*Op. cit.*, p. 178.
[76]*Ibid.*, p. 189.
[77]*Ibid.*, pp. 196, 197.

in this He shows Himself to be the absolute Mystery who can be understood only through His own self-revelation.[78]

Barth is particularly articulate here. Just because God is known to us through intimate personal encounter, "He meets us as the One who is hidden, the One about whom we must admit that we do not know what we are saying when we try to say who He is."[79] God is eternal, infinite, incomprehensible, omnipotent. But all these predicates mean that God is above all concepts and opinions.[80] And every predicate we assert of God is true in an incomprehensible way.[81]

Yet the encounter of the soul with God somehow transcends our uncertainty in intimate knowledge of Himself, and this "in the midst of the uncertainty which is and remains our portion."[82] This leaves man entirely dependent on the *moment* of revelation for the knowledge of God, and even there clouds of mystery abound: "Our assurance of the knowability of God's Word cannot be great enough, but yet at the same time this assurance is limited to the moment when God speaks."[83] Apart from a recognition that God is incomprehensible, knowledge of Him is impossible:

> If we do not wish to end by really defining ourselves, when we think we are defining God, we can only . . . hold fast to the incomprehensible majesty in which God meets us in His revelation. . . .[84]

Criticism of the Position

A. Of the General Position

It is no part of my intention to deny the possibility of an inner, subjective experience of God without the mediation of sense objects: my remarks against subjective empiricism must not therefore be taken as involving such a denial.

But while God may be known subjectively, this does not mean that He is known without inference or the mediation of representative ideas. If epistemological dualism is true, as we have attempted to show, then every reality is known through the mediation of such

---

[78]Brunner, *op. cit.*, p. 24.
[79]*Knowledge of God*, p. 27.
[80]*Ibid.*, p. 28.
[81]*Ibid.*, p. 31.
[82]*Ibid.*, p. 29.
[83]Barth, *The Doctrine of the Word of God*, p. 260.
[84]Barth, *Knowledge of God*, p. 33.

representative ideas, else it is not known at all. This point is developed at length in Part III, Section B, Chapter I; and the reader is referred to that chapter for a detailed exposition.

By way of brief summary, however, even a subjective or inner knowledge must be mediated by the categories of thought as we have outlined them previously. In fact, there *is* no personal encounter with God that does not involve inference by an application of the categories. How could I recognize my experience as an experience of God unless it was represented in thought by a coherent concept with categorical structure? To have a determinate experience of God implies that I have isolated Him in thought from other objects of my experience. But such a process is both rational and inferential.

The basic defect of subjective empiricism is its over-all self-contradictory character. God, it is asserted, is known, not by inference or rational process, but by direct encounter. But is this assertion itself an inference or not? If it is an inference, then it tells us nothing about God, for it asserts that no inferential knowledge of God is possible. Hence its truth involves its falsity: which is self-contradictory. If the assertion is not an inference, what is the ground of its truth? As a proposition, it is not a direct experience of God (or anything else) ; so the only conclusion is that the assertion is baseless. But an assertion for which by definition there is no conceivable basis is a false assertion, perhaps even an unintelligible one.

The same point may be differently expressed. Suppose we grant that the mystic has an intuitive knowledge of God; yet he cannot conclude from this experience that God is knowable only in this way. And that for two reasons: (1) Such a conclusion would be an inference and would by definition be devoid of any knowledge of God. (2) The conclusion would, even if consistent with the mystic's denial of inferential knowledge, involve the fallacy of consequent: just because the mystic knows God in direct encounter, this does not mean that the knowledge of God is possible only in this way. Because x leads to the knowledge of y, it cannot be asserted that *only* x does so, unless all alternatives reduce to self-contradiction. But such a process is impossible for the mystic who denies the validity of inferential knowledge with respect to God. The mystic, then, has no ground except his experience in terms of which to deny the inferential knowledge of God, since every other ground would itself be an inference, as would the mystic's own denial. If therefore the ex-

perience of God cannot refute the possibility of knowing God infer-
entially, the mystic cannot refute such knowledge at all.

But even more seriously: in strict logic, the mystic who denies the
inferential knowledge of God can say nothing about his experience
either to himself or to anyone else: for every such statement would be
an inference and would refute the denial of the inferential knowledge of God. And still more basically: could the mystic be spoken
of as having an experience at all? To have an intelligible experience
is all the same as the understanding of particular data through a series of systematically consistent propositions in thought. Unless the
mystic is ready to say that his own religious experience is unintelligible, he cannot deny the validity of an inferential knowledge of God.
But in fact, he cannot even say that his experience is either religious
or an experience.

Thus the very assertion—that God is unknowable by inference
but knowable by direct encounter—is therefore shown to be self-
contradictory.

Finally, if all these difficulties could be transcended, how could
one discern between a false and true experience of God in his own
life, or among the conflicting claims of various mystics whose allega-
tions rest on a purely intuitional basis? Either reason and coherence
must be introduced here, or chaos rules the waves on the sea of religious experience:

> The tests of intuitions, however, are not purely intuitional,
> but rational and analytical. We cannot validate one intuition
> by the simple expedient of calling in another intuition. In order
> to draw the line between mysticism and delusion, between the
> false prophet and the true, it is always necessary eventually to
> invoke the aid of discursive reason.[85]

B. Of the Position as expounded by Macintosh

In the first place, the position rests on a critical monistic realism in
general epistemology which has already been refuted in Part I. No
detailed repetition of the arguments there presented will appear in
the present context. Suffice it to say: (1) That the knowledge of
any reality whatsoever is mediated in terms of representative ideas
whose objective validity is determined in each case by the test of
systematic coherence. (2) That the very admission that monistic

---

[85]Larrabee, *Reliable Knowledge*, p. 68.

realism must be critical assumes that percept and object are *not* identical as monism insists that they must, at least in part, be. (3) That there is no possible basis for criticizing a percept which would not involve some other criterion of knowledge than a direct or monistic experience: if the percept is not completely self-validating, then some further criterion of knowledge must intervene to distinguish objective and subjective. This criterion can only be the test of coherence among the whole body of percepts in a given sense context. But in this case, monistic experience is no longer the criterion of knowledge.

The same general criticisms apply against critical monistic realism in religious epistemology. Macintosh himself admits only a parital monism, as we have seen: but the only basis for distinguishing among subjective and objective aspects of our God-idea is some criterion of truth other than direct experience itself. This is implicitly admitted in Macintosh's assertion that the *spiritual ideal* is the criterion for making such distinctions. But such an admission undermines the whole monistic structure and makes the knowledge of the true God an inference from our experience of God as critically discerned with reference to absolute values. Thus the whole structure of monism turns out to be invalid as a mode of approach to the knowledge of God.

How, again, can we possibly maintain that God and my idea of Him are to any extent numerically identical? The criticisms in general epistemology apply equally here. My idea is not God; it is rather a concept that represents Him and the validity of which is to be tested by systematic coherence. Macintosh himself seems to admit this representative character of a given God-idea: "Our God-idea is a human construct and a projection, but it is this in order that it may represent an objective Reality which is obviously neither mere construct nor mere projection."[86]

I conclude that subjective empiricism, as expounded by Macintosh, brings us the knowledge of God, if at all, only at the expense of self-denial! And this of course means that it brings us no knowledge of God at all.

C. Of the Position as Expounded by Neo-orthodoxy

(1) At the outset the denial that God can be known through in-

[86]*Op. cit.,* p. 143.

ferential processes of thought is self-contradictory, as shown above: for the statement itself is either an inference about God or it is meaningless. And it cannot be the former without turning back upon itself.

(2) But such denial makes the knowledge of God self-contradictory and impossible in still another way. For I could not know an object as God without discerning the determinate character of my experience. But to recognize an object as this rather than that, as something rather than nothing, as God rather than nausea, already involves inference based on the application of the rational categories. But since inference is denied to be a means to the knowledge of God, such knowledge must be impossible, so that God is indistinguishable from the idea of anything else.

(3) Nor is it true, as Baillie asserts, that argumentative theism assumes a possible atheism. What it does assume is the gamut of common human experience as interpretable by rationality: and its very goal is to show that, in terms of available rational and experiential data, atheism is logically impossible. In Part III, this very feat is attempted in detail.

Furthermore, atheism is a volitional possibility: a man can will to disbelieve in God. Otherwise, how account for naturalism? To say that the naturalist really believes in God all the time is at least psychologically false. To say that he holds views which are ultimately invalid on any but theistic grounds is certainly true, I think; but then the knowledge of God's reality would be an inference from these views—in which case argumentative theism is established as the mode for the knowledge of God. Baillie himself is inconsistent in his denial that the knowledge of God is inferential: for even *he* uses the moral argument to "demonstrate" that the moral imperative implies the reality of God.

(4) The suggestion of Barth and Brunner—that man cannot have inferential knowledge of God because he is a sinner—will be discussed in Chapter III, since it is an assertion which contributes "body and soul" to the position we there criticize. Sufficient to ask at present: why is the natural revelation a revelation at all if God is not known thereby? Such an assertion is open to two obvious criticisms: (i) It contradicts the denial of inference as a means to the knowledge of God. If there *is* a natural revelation, and if God is not known *immediately* through it, it must be a revelation because it contains fac-

tors which *could*, under other circumstances, be means to the knowledge of God. But this is the same as saying that inference could, in such circumstances, move from nature to God: hence the very existence of a natural revelation that fails to present God immediately repudiates the denial that the knowledge of God is inferential.

(ii) If nothing is revealed in the natural revelation, how, on neo-orthodox terms, can it be called a revelation at all? For revelation is held to be nonexistent until the message of God "strikes home." But if nature fails thus to strike home, in what conceivable neo-orthodox sense is it a revelation? Any answer to this question will *ipso facto* destroy the denial of the inferential knowledge of God. For to call nature a revelation at all must mean that there is *something* about nature from which inference could be made to God.

(5) Barth claims that the absolute of thought has nothing to do with God. Now not only is such a statement self-contradictory, as anyone might discern from our previous discussion, but it practically destroys all knowledge of God. For thought does reach attributes for God that coincide with those of the God of the Christian revelation: attributes of omnipotence or eternity, for example. But every inferred attribute of God has, by definition, nothing to do with the true God: and by thus paring away one attribute after another, the knowledge of God will be largely destroyed.

It might be replied that at least the attributes of which we have knowledge only from special revelation would remain: but (i) The intelligent understanding of this revelation will by that very process of understanding remove the whole content of the revelation to the sphere of thought. (ii) That very special revelation itself declares God to be eternal, omnipotent, etc.—and these attributes, being likewise posited by thought of the absolute, have no relation to the true God; and it follows that the alleged revelation is itself unreliable. (iii) It is questionable whether a special revelation would be intelligible were I not previously convinced that a being existed who might thus be revealed.

(6) Brunner's point, on the other hand, is that a rational knowledge of God leaves me alone with my truth, since it is a conclusion which I make myself. But how does personal encounter help here— I am still alone, but worse than that, I am desolate—for I cannot communicate my knowledge, or make any inference about it, without self-contradiction? As soon as I *think* God, He is gone! And if I *fail*

to think Him, how do I know that He was ever there? On such grounds I am more than alone with truth: I am alone without it; for truth is a characteristic of propositions or judgments. And by hypothesis no judgment or inference about God can give me a knowledge of God in the final analysis.

Furthermore, how can Brunner consistently hold that the theistic proofs lead us *toward God?* If the knowledge of God simply cannot be had by thought, how can thought lead me toward it? If this were possible, I might eventually arrive thus at the knowledge of God and be in the embarrassing predicament of having refuted my own original theory.

(7) If the initiative for the knowledge of God is totally divine, if man has *no* power to enable him to achieve such knowledge, how can the revelation be received when it comes? It can fall on a man like mud on a stone, but neither stone nor such a man will be any the worse or better for wear. To have something revealed implies at least a receptive rational nature—so that man does have some part, else his position as a recipient of divine revelation will be unintelligible.

Nor will an appeal to the ministry of the Holy Spirit solve this problem. For if men are really stones, as Barth seems to suggest, if they are actually devoid of a capacity for the knowledge of God, why does not the Holy Spirit make His revelation to stones in the first place? The very fact that I am not a stone and that God speaks to me implies that as a rational man I have a capacity for knowing the God who thus speaks to me in rational modes. Indeed, a God who speaks to stones is no more intelligent than a lunatic who speaks to the walls of his cell!

(8) A word may be said about Baillie's doctrine of *mediated immediacy*. Baillie asserts that nature, while it is not the means to a knowledge of God, is none the less a sacrament of Him. But can anything be a sacrament of God which does not contain a characteristic from which God might be inferred? To be sure, arbitrary symbols may be assigned to meanings in the construction of an artificial language by a semantic logician: but in such a case, the meaning is *purely* arbitrary. Nature, on the other hand, is held to *contain within itself* elements that are symbolic of God: can this mean anything less than that nature, the world-whole, may be a means to infer God's existence?

Baillie appeals to the knowledge of God in Christ as an analogy to save his doctrine of mediated immediacy from the type of contradiction I have just outlined. But the reason that Christians know God *in* Christ, rather than by inference *from* Christ, is that for them Christ is Himself God. What then of the world of things? The only conceivable way in which this world could thus mediate an immediate knowledge of God is by being, like Christ, itself God. Not only does pantheism ensue; but again the knowledge of God is inferential: for the world is not *obviously* God. And if I assert it to be such, it must be the result of some complex inference.

(9) The Barthian assertion, that God is incomprehensible, involves self-contradiction, for this very assertion is itself either a meaningful predication or an unintelligible assertion; and in either case the original statement is contravened. It can hardly be said that we know God if we do not know what we are saying when we try to say who He is: and if this statement itself were true, it would involve its own falsity.

(10) Finally, the whole exposition proffered by neo-orthodox thinkers implicitly undermines its own theoretical structure. These thinkers spend laborious hours and hundreds of pages attempting to explain their own theory about the knowledge of God, and to explain it in rationally intelligible terms. The whole aim of their efforts is the rational defense of their position. But if their theories are true, they are by that very fact false! For they maintain that any such rational knowledge of God on an inferential basis is absurd and impossible. What effort, then, do these scholars expend on such a futile and hopeless task? The very statement of the subjective empiricist theory would be unintelligible if it were not basically false.

D. Conclusion

I conclude that, since subjective empiricism is basically fraught with a complex of self-contradictions at nearly every level, such a position gives us no alternative to rational empiricism as a means to metaphysical knowledge in general or as a means to the knowledge of God in particular.

And with empiricist theology, both in its objective and subjective forms, thus shown to be critically defective, consideration may be directed to the next alternative approach.

CHAPTER II

THE PRAGMATIC APPROACH

FORMULATION OF THE POSITION

The General Nature of Religious Pragmatism

THE NEXT ALTERNATIVE of rational empiricism to engage our attention is religious pragmatism. Such a position holds that while the existence of the Divine Reality or God may not admit proof on purely theoretical or speculative grounds, this Reality may nevertheless be asserted to exist on valuational grounds, or in terms of the practical effect of theistic belief in human experience. In the context of this view, then, theism is preferable to naturalism or agnosticism because it makes a greater appeal to all the energies of our active nature; it is better, in the end, to risk chance of error than loss of truth, especially when that truth serves, as does belief in God, to enrich and ennoble human life.

By far the most brilliant exponent of this general position was William James, whose views have been subjected to constant restatement since the time they were most clearly formulated in *The Will to Believe*. But within the context of Christianity the great proponent of religious pragmatism was A. J. Balfour, whose influence, even on the thinking of James, was by no means inconsequential. And since our interest, in this Part, lies in evaluating alternative approaches to *Christian* apology, it is to Balfour that we turn to meet our next rival.

Exposition of Balfour's Position

The grounds of philosophic doubt.—Philosophy, according to Balfour's view, is a critical study of the grounds of belief.[1] But from a purely theoretical point of view, all our beliefs, whether scientific

[1] Macintosh, *Problem of Religious Knowledge*, p. 307.

or religious, are susceptibile of doubt for two principal and supplementary reasons:

(1) In the first place, every attempt to prove our beliefs rests on still more general and ultimate beliefs which, in the final analysis, rest on themselves: i.e., they can be established only on grounds which assume their truth. Thus Macintosh expounds Balfour's view on causation: "So far as the law of universal causation is concerned, unless we first believe in the law we can have no reason for believing in the observations upon which it is supposed to be based."[2] And thus with all our most fundamental beliefs.

(2) In the second place, all of our beliefs—especially the most general and basic ones—are determined by nonrational causes and have arisen proximately from nonrational sources.[3] And this is as true of scientific beliefs as of any others. In all honesty we must admit "the scientific truth that at the root of every rational process lies an irrational one; that reason, from a scientific point of view, is itself a natural product; and that the whole material on which it works is due to causes, physical, physiological, and social. . . ."[4] Thus we may say "that every belief is without exception causally determined, and, in the last resort, determined by antecedents which are not beliefs, nor indeed psychical events of any kind, but belong wholly to the nonrational world of matter and motion."[5]

Since all our beliefs are thus determined by nonrational causes beyond our control, they are all open to theoretical doubt. But despite these skeptical considerations, we have a practical need for beliefs in the guidance of life: we therefore accept beliefs on valuational grounds precisely because of our subjective needs.[6]

The resultant argument for God.—What are the implications of Balfour's analysis with respect to the knowledge of God?

Well, in the first place, the most that we can claim for theism, on an argumentative basis, is that it embodies reasonable religious belief. Religious and scientific faith stand on equal footing from a theoretical point of view: strictly speaking, knowledge is impossible in both cases. Yet just as this fact does not impede our acceptance of scientific dicta, neither should it prevent our espousal of religious

[2]*Idem.* Reference: Balfour, *A Defence of Philosophic Doubt*, pp. 71, 145, 146.
[3]Balfour, *Foundations of Belief*, pp. 193f., 330f.
[4]*Ibid.*, pp. 331, 332.
[5]Balfour, *Theism and Thought*, p. 21.
[6]*Foundations, passim;* cf. Macintosh, p. 308.

faith, if, like science, that faith is workable in maintaining the value of our highest beliefs.[7]

To put the matter more positively, we must choose between theism, on the one hand, and the consignment of the whole body of our reflective beliefs to meaninglessness, on the other: if we are to believe in anything, we must believe in God.[8]

All our beliefs are determined ultimately by factors which, in their natural context, are nonrational; this we have already seen. Now the naturalistic position "rejects the notion that these nonrational beginnings are, or ever have been, subjected to rational guidance."[9] Thus science, if committed to naturalism, admits "the unqualified nonrationality of its own origins."[10]

But now: either scientific beliefs are true or not. If they *are* true, then by what coincidence are they thus, if their nonrational origin does not presuppose intelligent guidance? Nor will it help to say that objective tests may be applied to determine the correctness of a given scientific belief: for "what tests can we apply to it which have not the same origins and do not suffer therefore from the same defects?"[11]

If, on the other hand, scientific beliefs do not embody rational truth, "the conclusion of the argument has shattered its premises; and scientific naturalism perishes through the very completeness with which it has destroyed any theory of origins which involves a belief in reason, purpose, or design."[12]

It is frequently objected, Balfour notes, that natural selection provides a suitable substitute for creative design and hence a sufficient reason for accepting the truth of scientific belief without appeal to theism.[13] But this factor is possessed of two basic defects which make it an insufficient explanation: (1) First, natural selection *begins too late* "to provide human reason with even the imitation of a reasonable origin."[14] It does not explain the environment of life, the production of life itself, or the organic complexes within which variations take place.[15] (2) Second, natural selection *ends too soon* to ex-

[7]*Theism and Thought*, pp. 249, 250, *et passim*.
[8]*Foundations*, pp. 331, 332.
[9]*Theism and Thought*, p. 22.
[10]*Idem*.
[11]*Idem*.
[12]*Idem*.
[13]*Ibid.*, p. 24f.
[14]*Ibid.*, p. 26f.
[15]*Idem*.

plain the validity of our highest reflective beliefs. The supreme values of love, beauty, and knowledge have, in their highest expression, no serious consequence in the struggle for existence.[16] How, for example, on the naturalistic hypothesis, could such a chance variation as beauty—which possesses no appreciable survival value—play such a large part in the higher life of the race?[17]

And what of intellectual knowledge itself? If knowledge never pushed beyond the bounds within which it effectively fosters the multiplication of the species, natural selection might pose a reasonable explanation.[18] But not so: the very questions about the limits of knowledge, or about the nature of Ultimate Reality, involve the use of intellect for a purpose not "contemplated" by selection and not productive of race survival.[19]

What may be concluded from our analysis? Unless we are prepared to surrender the validity of our highest ideals of knowledge, beauty, and morality, we must posit, beyond the nonrational origins which determine belief, a guiding intelligence, a "Supreme Reason" in whom we must thus believe, if we are to believe in anything. The choice then must be determined on valuational grounds: either we believe in God, or the whole structure of all our beliefs sinks to nonrational dimensions:

> If naturalism be true . . . all that gives dignity to life, all that gives value to effort, shrinks and fades under the pitiless glare of a creed like this; and even curiosity, the hardiest among the nobler passions of the soul, must languish under the conviction that neither for this generation nor for any that shall come after it, neither in this life nor in another, will the tie be wholly loosened by which reason, not less than appetite, is held in hereditary bondage to the service of our material needs.[20]

CRITICISM OF THE POSITION

Of Religious Pragmatism in General

Insofar as this general view rests—as it does in large measure—on the pragmatic theory of truth, it has already been subjected to analysis and thorough refutation in Part I, Chapter IV.

In the specifically religious context, it may be remarked that in

[16]*Ibid.*, pp. 26-28.
[17]*Ibid.*, p. 31.
[18]*Theism and Humanism*, p. 257.
[19]*Ibid.*, p. 258.
[20]*Foundations*, p. 78.

any field of investigation our belief must be more than mere choice. While we *do* often choose our beliefs, and while we frequently choose them carelessly, when the question is raised, why *ought* we to believe such and such, the answer cannot be given in terms of a valuationally grounded choice, except that as rational men we should choose a coherent, rather than an incoherent, belief. I *ought* to believe a given proposition, not because I should prefer it to be true, nor because it would justify prejudices which are already in my possession; but rather because it is grounded in rational and experiential factors of which it is a self-consistent interpretation. A belief ought to be the relation of the mind to some objective situation which is assumed to be real independently of the wishes of the percipient. *If* we suspect that a belief *is* determined purely by subjective need and on valuational grounds, we at once clothe it with suspicion. And while the belief may turn out to have been true, it will not, by any stretch of imagination, be thus true on such pragmatic grounds.

With specific reference to the religious object, then, we believe (or disbelieve) in God's real existence on the basis of objective factors in our experience, as these factors are interpreted by the mind's categorical structure.

When it is said that we should believe in God because of the practical effect which this belief will have in implementing our welfare, how do we know, on pragmatic grounds, what effects actually advance our welfare? In order to accept theism on this basis, we would have to possess a comparatively a priori knowledge of what constitutes our welfare. But this knowledge is possible only if I already possess the ultimate metaphysical truth which the theory attempts to achieve: for my welfare is definable only in terms of an adjustment to reality at its highest level, which, if theism be true, is God. It follows that in order to believe in God on the basis of the practical effect of this belief, I must already believe in God on other grounds: and if this is the case, the pragmatic theory of truth is superfluous. Pragmatism can be a basis for theism only on grounds which refute its character as an ultimate basis for that very theism.

Of Balfour's Position

(1) If it is really true that all our beliefs are determined by non-rational and material factors beyond our control, then, since every belief is thus determined, it is neither true nor false: it just *is,* like

any other effect of the causal nexus. Now since this first assertion itself is presumably a belief, it shares the fate of its comrades: it is neither true nor false, it just *is*. It follows that the belief is not true: and this in terms of its own assertion. Since therefore the belief is both self-contradictory and meaningless by thus being neither true nor false, it is its own refutation. Furthermore, we should have to conclude, on this line of argument, that there *is* no truth; and this in itself is likewise self-contradictory by impugning its own allegation. By just such a process of reasoning, the basic tenet of Balfour's entire argument is brought into serious question.

(2) Balfour *himself* is inconsistent in holding to the determination of beliefs by nonrational factors. If beliefs are thus determined, how *choose* between theism and meaninglessness? if by the theory itself, we have no choice in our beliefs. The very fact that Balfour propounds this premise to *defend* theism involves the falsity of the hypothesis that beliefs are thus determined in the way suggested: to defend a proposition is to assume that beliefs ought to be determined, both ultimately and proximately, on grounds which are rational. Otherwise Balfour's own reasoning from premises to conclusion is so much wasted effort. Since Balfour's whole argument rests on the premise which is thus refuted, the argument collapses.

(3) If all beliefs are open to doubt from a purely theoretical point of view, so then is *this* belief itself open to such doubt, in which case it is false, for it cannot be universally asserted. Thus the denial that theoretical knowledge is possible cannot rest on the grounds alleged: and in any case, the assertion of such an impossibility is self-contradictory, since, if it were true, the statement itself would not be true. Balfour's own analysis implies the validity of our criticism: for he attempts to establish skepticism itself on grounds which are rational—a procedure which assumes the very possibility of the theoretic knowledge it denies. There cannot, in other words, be grounds for doubting all our beliefs, unless some of our beliefs are ultimately not susceptible of doubt—but this is self-contradictory.

(4) That beliefs rest on ultimate grounds which can be established only on the assumption of their own truth is no cause for skepticism, as we have established at length in Part I. It is rather cause for accepting a rational empiricism which espouses belief in an a priori categorical structure for rationality. Either we come to experience with certain forms of thought in terms of which we are disposed to

understand that experience, or knowledge could not begin; yet it does begin and this last alternative is self-contradictory, so that the former must be affirmed. Furthermore, Balfour's admission of such primitive grounds of belief, is inconsistent both with the doctrine that all beliefs are causally determined by nonrational factors, and with the assertion that we accept beliefs on the basis of subjective practical need.

(5) Skepticism about the knowledge of God is as self-contradictory as skepticism in general. If the theoretical knowledge of God is impossible, so is this assertion: for the statement itself is just such an allegation about God. Nor do any of Balfour's other criteria justify the assertion: (i) I have no idea what nonrational causes would concrete in such a belief; for the assertion necessarily springs, not from determinate conditions, but from the lack of them. (ii) And the criterion of practical effect in maintaining our highest beliefs would require, not the denial of such theoretical knowledge of God, but the affirmation of it: if the existence of God is demonstrable, the practical effects, which would accompany such belief, would far outweigh those of any hypothetical or pragmatic theism.

(6) With regard to Balfour's specific argument for theism: I heartily agree both that we must choose between theism and meaninglessness, and that the appearance of knowing beings requires explanation in terms of an ultimate intelligent will. This last point comes up for detailed discussion in Part III.

But the choice of theism must be determined, not by purely valuational considerations, but by a self-consistent interpretation of experienced data through an application of the mind's categorical structure. This implies again the falsity of Balfour's basic tenet that beliefs are completely determined by nonrational factors: and since his whole orientation of the theistic argument rests precisely on this point, his analysis fails to do more than foreshadow an adequate theistic argumentation.

One final word concerning Balfour's criticisms of natural selection: while there is much truth, as we shall later show, in the assertion that selection begins too late to be an adequate explanation of the apparent presence of design in the universe; still the suggestion that natural selection ends too soon to explain our highest beliefs, while it may be true, seems a questionable basis for argument. For an entity, once produced by natural selection, may admit of accidental functions, not prescribed by selection itself, without this fact as such requiring the principle of selection to be supplemented. In this way intellect might perform functions of no survival value without this requiring the abandonment of the principle of selection.

Conclusion

Since religious pragmatism is thus freighted with self-contradiction, and since it can be the basis for theism only on the supposition that theism is already believed on other grounds, I conclude that such a position is not a valid alternative to rational empiricism as a means to the knowledge of God.

CHAPTER III

THE APPROACH OF VOLUNTARISTIC RATIONALISM: PRESUPPOSITIONALISM

THE MEANINGS OF PRESUPPOSITIONALISM

PRESUPPOSITIONALISM, as a method in philosophy, refers to three rather distinct claims with regard to the validity of basic assumptions. The first of these—which we may term *metaphysical* presuppositionalism—is the claim that the only proper method of constructing a philosophical world view consists in holding that the metaphysical ultimate in any such view does not admit of verification or proof, but must be accepted as a basic, axiomatic assumption or presupposition. Every metaphysical system, it is claimed, commences with some ultimate of explanation—say God or physical substance—and it is unreasonable to require proof of this first principle, since it is the point where argumentation begins. It is just because a first principle is the starting point of explanation that no proof of the principle can possibly be given: for every argument that is adduced proceeds upon the assumption that the ultimate reality described as such principle is an adequate starting-point. The individual must start by accepting the basic ultimate in any system, if he is ever to end up with the over-all structure of explanation that the system professes to provide.

Thus the Christian does not, and indeed cannot, commence his system by proving the existence of God: he must start by assuming the existence of the God who has revealed Himself in Scripture. With this assumption or hypothesis, he may be able to offer an explanation of reality, but he can never offer to establish the validity of this ultimate starting-point, since all argumentation within the system is intelligible only when one accepts the assumption itself. The same could be said with reference to the presupposition of the naturalist, who holds that nature, as the space-time nexus, is the only and ultimate reality. To ask the naturalist to prove the validity of his assumption that nature is ultimate is to ask a meaningless question; he may be able to offer a coherent explanation of reality in terms of this ultimate assumption; but he cannot prove the assumption itself, since any argument, if he is consistent, will assume the validity of that very assumption.

To call this general approach to the structure of philosophical world views by the name metaphysical presuppositionalism is therefore an appropriate designation, since the position rigorously insists that any first reality must be assumed, not proved. An equally appropriate designation is *voluntaristic rationalism: voluntaristic,* because the acceptance of the basic postulate is a volitional or willful act for which, in the final analysis, no rational evidence can be given, since every such argument, to be valid within the system, must rest ultimately on just this very postulate; *rationalism,* because, when the basic metaphysical postulate is taken as assumed, the attempt is made to show that in terms of this postulate, as applied by the basic logical laws (likewise dependent upon the ultimate postulate), a self-consistent explanation of reality becomes possible in a degree to which it is not possible in terms of other basic postulates.

Analytical or *logical* presuppositionalism, in the second place, is that method of testing the adequacy of a world view, however derived originally, by assuming its truth hypothetically and attempting to show, by application of proper logical analysis, whether or not its basic principles lead to a self-consistent position that is at the same time correlated with the whole gamut of experiential data. Basically, this procedure involves, not the assumption of a metaphysical starting-point, but the assumption of an epistemological ground, common to all rational beings, in terms of which the adequacy of any speculative doctrine may be tested with something approaching final authority. We assume, in such an approach, a universal structure of rationality, both in the mind and in the real world—such a structure, in fact, as we have defended in our espousal of rational empiricism in Part I.

In such terms, which in fact merely embody that coherence theory of truth already established, an adequate defense for a philosophical system would proceed as follows: First, it would attempt to show that all available experiential data can be explained coherently by the basic principle or principles of the system; or at least, that this can be done more adequately in terms of these principles than in terms of any others. Second, the defense would attempt to show that the over-all structure of the system itself is internally free from self-contradiction—it must, for example, have no explanation in terms of which the simultaneous disappearance of the gingham dog and the calico cat are to be accounted for by asserting that they ate each other up—all the aspects of the system must be free from such inconsistency. Finally, such adequate defense must undertake to show that all rival systems of explanation are deficient, either by way of self-contradiction, or by way of inadequacy in the explanation of the total gamut of experience. Surely, we can argue, in terms acceptable to all rational beings and on the grounds of the rational empiricism we have already espoused, that a system which is satisfactory with respect to these three criteria is the system that ought to be accepted by the rational man. Such, precisely, is the drive of our defense for Christian theism.

Nor will it be difficult to see that such an analytical presuppositionalism is basically inconsistent with any ultimate acceptance of the metaphysical presuppositionalism which argues that the acceptance of a first metaphysical principle is a matter of unjustifiable assumption: for here we are offering to show exactly the validity and necessity of the first metaphysical principle itself by indicating that obviously its acceptance is the only basis on which an intelligible explanation of experience can ultimately be given. Of course, there is a starting-point; but it is not the assumption of the first reality: it is rather the epistemological starting-point of rational empiricism. It may be both interesting and comforting to hold at the same time both that we must assume God's existense in order to arrive at it, and that we can show that only God's existence postulates an adequate explanation of reality—it may, I say, be interesting and comforting, but it is not rational!

Categorical or *experiential* presuppositionalism, finally, is the method of showing that a consistent application of the rational categories to the totality of available data must conclude the validity and truth of some ultimate metaphysical principle. This procedure is similar to that of the preceding type, except that with analytical presuppositionalism we were attempting to test the validity of a system of thought regarded as already constructed, whereas categorical presuppositionalism attempts a more positive approach to experience with the goal of showing that the data available imply definitively the existence of some ultimate real. The former approach, briefly, was a negative method for testing the structure of a world view; while the present approach is a method, cast in the same mold, for arriving at that world view by a positive interpretation of experience.

Thus, for example, theism asserts that the only adequate explanation for the intelligibility of experience is the truth of the proposition that God exists. Some Christian thinkers, realizing this point, have consequently declared the impossibility of proving the existence of God; since if God's existence is presupposed in any order of intelligibility, then such existence cannot be argued on the basis of such intelligibility. Thus E. J. Carnell argues: "By the very nature of the case, a fulcrum able to support the weight of a proof for God would have to be God Himself. God gets in the way of all demonstration of deity, for His existence is the *sine qua non* for all demonstration. ..."[1] But this is indeed a strange objection: it is quite true that, if theism be correct, then the existence of God is metaphysically basic to all rational structure. But the individual does not start with this knowledge when he approaches experience—it is the fact of God's existence, not the knowledge of it, which makes rational structure, whether in argument or in reality, possible. And it is the very showing that the rationality of existence presupposes God that constitutes the demonstration of His existence. Proof for God is possible just because all men start with a rational experience which, if rationally interpreted, leads to the conclusion that God exists.

Presumably, it is superfluous to indicate that here again our position is inconsistent with an espousal of metaphysical presuppositionalism. For we do not propose to assume the first principle of reality in order to arrive at it: we shall rather propose to show that reality itself, categorically interpreted, establishes the validity of that very first principle.

METAPHYSICAL PRESUPPOSITIONALISM AS A METHOD IN CHRISTIAN APOLOGETICS

The General Position

The last alternative of rational empiricism to claim our consideration is therefore confronted in the attempt to show that God is

[1] E. J. Carnell, *Introduction to Christian Apologetics*, p. 159.

known in terms of a structure of thought that becomes adequately intelligible only through an initial volitional presupposition or postulation of His existence.

It is difficult to define the common position of the contemporary presuppositionalists, since their own ranks are by no means entirely in agreement on the basic approach to Christian apology. But in general, the position embraces the following points:

(1) One must start by assuming the existence of the Christian God who has spoken in Scripture, if ever he is to get to the assurance that the Christian world view is valid and true—the validity of this first principle must be assumed.

(2) It is therefore impossible to infer or imply the existence of God by means of epistemological and experiential data that are, or can be, common to all men—there is no such thing as a common ground between Christianity and non-Christianity, so that this ground could become the starting-point of a Christian apologetic.

(3) Although God has clearly and unmistakably revealed Himself in nature and in the self, it is impossible for the natural man to see God as the conclusion to the syllogism of experience, since his view is distorted by sin; consequently, man needs special revelation before he can interpret even the natural revelation as implying the existence of God. Nor should this be taken to mean that the Christian world view is not rational; it is rational, but only to the person who initially assumes the truth of its first principle or God, the person who stands within the framework of special revelation, the person, in short, who is himself a Christian.

The chief contemporary exponents of this general position are Cornelius VanTil, Carl F. H. Henry, Edward John Carnell, and Gordon H. Clark.

Detailed Exposition of the Theory

Presupposing the metaphysical ultimate.—The first and most basic assertion of presuppositionalism is that one must start with the assumption that the God who has spoken in Scripture is the true God. Indeed, the acceptance of an ultimate metaphysical starting-point determines one's whole methodology and his conclusions. Thus Carnell writes:

> A man's attitude toward what he considers to be the highest logical ultimate in reality determines the validity of his synoptic

starting-point, his method, and his conclusion. The Christian
. . . [has] chosen as his logical starting-point the existence of the
God who has revealed Himself in Scripture.[2]

Thus also VanTil urges that in order to interpret reality correctly,
man must work within the propositional revelation of Scripture:[3]
"for the human mind to know any fact truly, it must presuppose the
existence of God."[4] It is also asserted that the Bible itself must be
received on authority alone without appeal to rational foundations,
for "if we must determine the foundations of authority we no longer
accept authority on authority."[5]

Clark takes this same general presuppositionalist ground when he
asserts:

> If everything is to be demonstrated, the demonstration turns
> out to be either circular or an infinite regress. Both are unsatis-
> factory. Therefore some things cannot be demonstrated. These
> are first principles which themselves are the basis or beginning
> of argument; and if they are the beginning they cannot have
> been previously argued. To require a proof of a first principle
> is to misunderstand the whole procedure. . . . The Calvinists
> begin with God and revelation.[6]

After all, Clark argues in another place, the first principle of a metaphysical system cannot be demonstrated—and that just because it *is*
first: "It is the first principle that provides the basis for demonstrat-
ing subordinate propositions. Now if such be the case, the thoughtful person is forced to make a voluntary choice."[7] Thus the person
who tries to begin with facts and reason to God is guilty of basic misunderstanding. In the Christian world view, "unless a thinker begins
with God, he can never end with God, or get the facts either."[8]

And so, finally, Henry argues that "you must begin with God, not
only to get to God, but to get to anything . . . the existence of God is
the necessary presupposition for the affirmation of intelligibility anywhere."[9] Nor, apparently, does Henry mean merely that the existence of God is the only ultimately adequate interpretation of an in-

[2]*Ibid.*, p. 212; synoptic starting-point equals epistemological starting-point in my
parlance.
[3]In B. B. Warfield, *The Inspiration and Authority of the Bible*, pp. 30, 31.
[4]C. VanTil, *Junior Systematics*, p. 19.
[5]VanTil, *Christian Apologetics*, p. 18.
[6]Clark, *Christian View*, p. 259.
[7]*A Christian Philosophy of Education*, p. 41.
[8]*Ibid.*, p. 38.
[9]C. F. H. Henry, *Remaking the Modern Mind*, pp. 226, 227.

telligibility which we take as given—as though from the intelligibility of the world we could argue to God. The contention is rather that we must assume God's existence in order ultimately to apprehend intelligibility at all.

The Christian God, therefore, must be taken as a basic, unproved assumption, if we wish to arrive at a true knowledge of God: this basic postulate is a matter of choice or volition. The grounds of that volition—if there can consistently be any—will be discussed in a later context.

Denial of common ground and the rejection of rational proof for God.—It follows at once that if the Christian and the non-Christian part company with the espousal of opposing *first* principles, there can be no common ground, at the level of philosophical system, in terms of which the two can meet to accept the same implications of the facts with which they are both confronted: there is no area of agreement, therefore, in terms of which the Christian can prove the truth of the Christian God to an unbeliever.

VanTil and Carnell both expound this point at considerable length. Thus VanTil asserts that "in Christian theism we have a system of interpretation that is so different from all other systems of interpretation that we cannot find a common ground between them on the basis of which an argument with respect to the truth may be undertaken."[10] The fact is that while the Christian and the non-Christian are confronted with the same God-interpreted facts objectively, yet epistemologically they have nothing in common.[11] The reason for this is that a fact and its ultimate interpretation are epistemologically inseparable: and while the non-Christian interprets facts according to immanentistic categories that imply man himself as the ultimate reference point, the Christian interprets them according to divine categories which imply the God of the Bible as the ultimate reference point.[12] VanTil calls the former type of reasoning *univocal,* the latter *analogical.*[13] All true predication must be of the latter type: i.e., it must be a restatement of the facts as God-interpreted.

Carnell's position is generically similar: "The very nature of Christianity demands that there be no common ground between the system of the godly and the system of the ungodly. . . ."[14] But Carnell differs

---

[10]*Apologetics*, p. 28.
[11]*Ibid.*, pp. 28, 29; cf. Warfield, p. 20; *Common Grace*, p. 5.
[12]*Apologetics*, pp. 28-30; Warfield, p. 22f.
[13]*Systematics*, p. 86.
[14]*Op. cit.*, p. 212; cf. also Clark, *Christian Philosophy of Education*, p. 164.

sharply with VanTil by holding that there is *some* interpretive content common to Christian and non-Christian at the scientific level: "There is no problem of common ground here, for scientific conclusions as such do not depend for their meaning upon one's logical starting-point. . . . It would be absurd to suggest that Christians have a science all their own. . . ."[15] This interpretive common content disappears, however, as soon as we move to the metaphysical level and relate facts to our logical starting-point.[16] VanTil's reply to Carnell here—quite justly, I think—would be that "if it be first granted that man can correctly interpret an aspect or dimension of reality while making man the final reference point then there is no justification for denying him the same competence in the field of religion. . . ."[17]

The inevitable correlate of the denial of common ground is the repudiation of any argument from common-to-all factors to the existence of God; and this involves, of course, the repudiation of all argumentative theism and natural theology, except for the Christian who *already* believes in God.

The sinful distortion of general revelation.—The third basic assertion of presuppositionalism attempts to explain why it is that no argument for God is possible on the basis of the revelation of God in nature and man: the answer is that man's intellect is distorted by sin, so that, while nature clearly reveals God, man's intellectual distortion obscures the revelation and makes so-called natural theology impossible.

This view stems back, in modern theology at least, to Calvin himself: such is our carnal stupidity, he claims, that while God is clearly revealed in His works, we derive no advantage from these natural revelations.[18] This seems evident from the fact that very few men posit God as the explanation of the world on a natural basis, and those who do cannot agree.[19] All this shows "the horrible blindness of the human mind."[20] It follows, according to Calvin, that while the natural revelation renders inexcusable the whole of the human race, we must turn to Scripture "as another and better assistance, properly to direct us to the Creator of the world."[21] Yet no more can man know the existence of God from Scripture than from nature

[15]*Ibid.*, p. 214.
[16]*Ibid.*, pp. 211, 214.
[17]Warfield, p. 37.
[18]*Institutes*, I, pp. 58, 65, 66.
[19]*Ibid.*, pp. 67, 68.
[20]*Idem.*
[21]*Ibid.*, p. 71.

unless the Holy Spirit imparts to him that saving faith in terms of which the authority of Scripture may be accepted.[22] Thus Calvin's position reduces to a faith-reason formulation such that only those know the existence of the Creator, or *can* know it, to whom the Spirit has imparted faith.

Writings of the metaphysical presuppositionalists abound in variations on this basic theme. So Carnell: "All men have the *rationes* by which means they know that God exists. But, being in defection by their sins, what they see is vitiated."[23]

And VanTil: "The sinner is like the man with colored glasses on his nose. Assuming the truth of Scripture, we must hold that the facts speak plainly of God. . . . But all is yellow to the jaundiced eye. . . . Since sin has come into the world, God's interpretation of the facts must come in finished, written form. . . ."[24] The fact is, man ought to infer from nature to God by analogical reasoning, but he *cannot*.[25] Thus, because man is a sinner, he needs special revelation in order to interpret natural revelation correctly.[26]

And Henry, whose exposition on this point is abundant: Man has even an innate knowledge of God, not to mention the revelation of God in external nature.[27] But "man's nature as finite creature in sin is not such that, from the side of human initiative, it is possible for him reliably to attain the great metaphysical verities. . . ."[28] Because man is thus in sinful rebellion against God, special revelation is needed.[29] If there were no general revelation, man could not be a sinner; yet this does not presuppose natural theology, "or the notion that the theistic evidences lead man to an accurate and for some purposes adequate view of God. For such an estimate does not take sin soberly enough."[30]

What is the precise extent of sinful distortion? VanTil holds that the distortion, strictly speaking, is complete: the natural man cannot reason correctly on any level of thought.[31] Even logic is not the same

---

[22]*Ibid.*, pp. 80, 81.
[23]*Op. cit.*, p. 171; cf. his *Philosophy of the Christian Religion*, p. 278; Clark, *Christian View*, pp. 251, 252.
[24]Warfield, pp. 20, 22; cf. *Apologetics*, p. 19; *Common Grace*, p. 7.
[25]*Systematics*, pp. 86-89.
[26]*Ibid.*, p. 94; *Apologetics*, p. 19.
[27]*The Drift of Western Thought*, pp. 96, 103. cf. *Remaking*, p. 201.
[28]*Drift*, p. 96.
[29]*Notes on the Doctrine of God*, p. 66.
[30]*Ibid.*, p. 68.
[31]Warfield, p. 37f.

for Christian and non-Christian, and "the syllogistic process must be followed in frank subordination to the notion of a self-sufficient God."[32] The Christian view may thus contain even what, from a human logical point of view, are self-contradictory propositions.

But the other presuppositionalists have not been so ready thus to sacrifice reason. So Henry writes that "the Biblical view . . . does not dethrone reason as an instrument, for that premise would make it impossible for anyone to think anything—even this sentence."[33] And again: "the validity of implications is the same for all minds."[34] And as for Carnell and Clark, their whole system is built on the universality of logical laws and the rational categories.[35] Yet man's sinful predicament may be defined negatively by saying that he cannot properly interpret the natural revelation so as to infer the existence of God: apparently the distortion is therefore a volitional matter which has become so constitutional as to impose an inability.

On the other hand, the presuppositionalists do not hesitate to cite data which *are* intended to show to all rational minds the insufficiency of theistic arguments to establish the existence of God: in this context, even the arguments of an unregenerate Hume are made the basis of appeal.[36]

In the light of man's sinful predicament, what, finally, is the ground for man's choice of the basic postulate of Christian theism? The answer seems to be that the ground of choice is an efficient act of God in which the sinner's sinful distortion is rectified, at least in part and principle, though such a regenerate person may think at times according to his old sinful nature.[37] Thus Henry writes, for example: "The supernatural regeneration of sinners secures the acceptance of the divine revelation as true."[38]

VanTil is exceedingly clear on this point:

> It is therefore the Holy Spirit bearing witness by and with the Word in our hearts that alone effects the required Copernican revolution and makes us both Christians and theists. . . . It is only when the Holy Spirit gives man a new heart that he will accept the evidence of Scripture about itself and about nature

[32]*Common Grace*, pp. 27, 28.
[33]*Notes*, p. 65.
[34]*Remaking*, p. 233.
[35]Clark, *Christian View*, pp. 231, 232, 256, 268; Carnell, *Introduction*, pp. 70, 83.
[36]Carnell, *Introduction*, p. 129f.; Clark, *Christian Philosophy of Education*, p. 37f.; Henry, *Remaking*, pp. 198-200.
[37]Carnell, *Philosophy of the Christian Religion*, p. 278.
[38]*Drift*, p. 117.

for what it really is. . . . If sinful man is to be saved he must be saved against his will. . . . So an entrance has to be forced.[39]

Positive approach to apologetics.—If, then, the first principle of any metaphysic must be presupposed; if, further, there is no common ground as a basis for argument; and if, finally, man, while he ought to do so, nevertheless cannot distill God from the general revelation; how is any apologetic at all possible?

In general, while strictly speaking there is no epistemological point of contact, there is a formal point of contact between the believer and the unbeliever in terms of which apologetic reasoning may be carried on. The most common term used to denote this formal point of contact is the *image of God.* Just because man, even though a sinner, is yet a creature made in God's image in an intellectual and moral sense, every human being is metaphysically accessible to the influence of God.[40] And it is this very image that keeps man from consistently moving to the nihilism of every non-Christian position: "Christianity can see in every such view, by its inability to work itself out into a comprehensive nihilism, that struggle with the innate image of God which drives every naturalistic philosopher to something less than a consistent outworking of his position."[41] Carnell, in rather more generous fashion, grants not only the formal contact posed by the image of God, but also that posed by the facts of nature, though both together are inadequate.[42]

In terms of such a formal point of contact, an apologetic becomes possible. Believer and unbeliever may reason together "by placing themselves in turn upon their opponent's position for argument's sake. The argument will then be one from consequences. . . ."[43] The argument will then proceed on the basis of coherence and will be twofold: first, it will point out the internal coherence of Christian theism; second, it will set forth the internal incoherence of every non-Christian position.[44]

Does this mean, then, that the Christian and the non-Christian do have a true epistemological, as distinguished from a formal, point of contact? VanTil's answer is emphatically: no—the agreement is

[39]"Nature and Scripture," pp. 272, 273; Warfield, p. 33.
[40]VanTil, *Apologetics*, p. 38.
[41]Henry, *Drift*, p. 99.
[42]*Introduction*, pp. 218, 219.
[43]VanTil, *Apologetics*, p. 38.
[44]*Ibid.*, p. 41; cf. also Clark, *Christian View*, pp. 29-33, 318f.; *Christian Philosophy of Education*, p. 41f.

still only formal; in fact, "a non-Christian could not recognize the fact of coherence if he were to do so by his own principle of interpretation. . . . The non-Christian does not realize this. . . ."[45]

Among the other presuppositionalists, coherence seems to be granted a status, as the test for truth, which appears to transcend a purely formal point of contact. This is especially true in the positions of Carnell and Clark.[46]

The detailed working out of the Christian apologetic by these various thinkers is too complex for treatment here, but one point of special interest should be indicated. Both Clark and Carnell reintroduce theistic argumentation on an a priori basis, even though they ostensibly repudiate the efforts of the natural mind to distill God from the general revelation.

Carnell, for example, passes in argumentation from the values grounded in the moral categories of the human mind to the assertion of God's existence as a time- and space-transcending being that supports the eternal validity of these values.[47] Nor does Carnell intend this argument to have force only for the regenerate mind, for he comments: "The fact of these data makes the postulation of God's existence both scientifically and rationally satisfying."[48] And in a long passage in his *Introduction to Christian Apologetics*, clear affirmation is presented that man does have a knowledge of God's existence on the basis of the general revelation.[49]

Clark's procedure is similar. Although he holds with the Calvinist tradition that "sin has so vitiated human powers that man can read neither the heavens nor his own heart aright,"[50] still he too argues with great zeal for the theistic position. He holds, for example, that the existence of God is the best explanation for the fact that all men possess the rational categories in common and that they find these categories to be the very principles whereby the real world is constituted.[51] And he further sees God as the implication of the time- and space-transcending character of true propositions.[52] Nor does Clark intend any more than Carnell that this argumentation will be valued and valid only for a regenerate mind: in fact, he ad-

[45]*Apologetics*, p. 42.
[46]Cf. above references to Clark; Carnell, *Philosophy of the Christian Religion*, pp. 5, 306, 449, 450.
[47]*Ibid.*, pp. 270, 271.
[48]*Ibid.*, pp. 272, 273.
[49]*Ibid.*, p. 157f.
[50]*Christian View*, pp. 251, 252.
[51]*Ibid.*, pp. 316-318.
[52]*Ibid.*, p. 321

mittedly borrows the bulk of the argument from certain idealist philosophers who presumably would not be classed as regenerate.

On the other hand, both men claim that the argument falls short of demonstration and is merely hypothetical in nature as a proof by coherence.[53] Thus Clark states:

> No demonstration of God is possible; our belief is a voluntary choice; but if one must choose without a strict proof, none the less it is possible to have sane reasons of some sort to justify the choice. Ultimately these reasons reduce to the principle of consistency. A postulate must be chosen such that it makes possible a harmony or a system in all our thoughts, words, and actions.[54]

CRITICISM OF METAPHYSICAL PRESUPPOSITIONALISM

Prefatory Remarks

It should be apparent that no exception is taken to the presuppositionalist methodology as long as it be construed in an analytical or categorical manner; that is, as a test for truth, or as a means for showing what the facts of experience imply with regard to the basic or ultimate reality. It is rather against the stronghold of the *metaphysical* presuppositionalists that our attack is intended to be directed. And it should be made *very clear* that any criticism of the position of the thinkers who propound this system is to be taken on a strictly philosophical level: no personal implications are intended, since it is always the argument and not the men that I would criticize: it is to the insufficiency of their approach as a basis for Christian apologetics that we address ourselves, and by no means to the grandeur of their persons.

As for the precise methodology of our criticism: the most feasible procedure will be the consideration of the basic assertions in the order in which they have been set forth in our positive formulation.

Detailed Criticism

Concerning the assertion that the basic metaphysical postulate is insusceptible of proof.— (1) In the first place, the assertion involves a basic misunderstanding concerning epistemology. It is granted that any argument starts with something as given: that such is the case we

[53]*Ibid.*, p. 318; Carnell, *Introduction*, p. 170.
[54]*Christian Philosophy of Education*, pp. 48, 49.

have already attempted to establish in Part I of the present work. Yet argument thus starts, not with a basic metaphysical ultimate—say God, or matter in motion—but with a common basis of rationality and experience in terms of which the validity of one's metaphysical assertion is to be justified. Men—if Christian theism be correct—come to experience with a rational structure of mind which, when consistently applied to that experience, yields the conclusion that God exists as theism construes that existence. On the Christian view experience would be unintelligible if God did not exist: but it is the fact of God's existence, not the original knowledge of it, which makes the intelligibility of experience possible. Unbelievers, after all, do, like Christians, apprehend their experience as rational: what they fail to do is to carry through this apprehension to its highest explanation in the affirmation of God's reality; or else they volitionally reject the conviction they may thus reach by a logical interpretation of the ultimate possibility of existence.

But how can we prove that argument starts, not with the assumption of a metaphysical ultimate, but with a basic epistemological structure common to all minds as rational and with a common world of facts?

(a) In the first place, the assertion—that no basic metaphysical assertion is susceptible of proof—is self-contradictory. According to this view, as we have seen, the basic metaphysical postulate or first principle determines the whole balance or remainder of the system—it even determines the validity of the epistemological starting-point or of the basic forms of thought. But what about the assertion itself? Is it intended to be true of *every* metaphysical system or not? Does it hold for naturalism as well as for theism? Is it true universally?

If it is thus universally true, then the following remarks are appropriate: (i) First, here is a truth that cuts across every basic metaphysical postulate and every complex metaphysical world view: it is therefore a truth which is valid, not in terms of a particular metaphysical postulate, but in terms of an epistemological starting-point which all the systems necessarily share. The only conceivable ground on which it could be maintained that the assertion derives its validity from the basic metaphysical postulate would be that all these postulates are ultimately identical, that naturalism and theism, for example, are really the same view in the end: an identity that would bring little comfort to either naturalist or theist, and that would, in fact, be logically impossible.

(ii) Second, the truth of the assertion is epistemologically basic to the acceptance of any metaphysical world view whatsoever: I will not be moved to choose a world view unless I know that a choice is involved; I will have no way of selecting a basic metaphysical ultimate. At any given point in my experience, I either espouse a world view or not. But if I do, it is because, according to the theory, I chose it at some previous time; and if I do not, I am confronted with the choice now. But I could not come to a world view at all in these terms, if I did not realize that a choice was possible. It follows that prior to the acceptance of a basic metaphysic, there must be *at least* a knowledge that a choice is possible. Consequently, it is false to say that the acceptance of a metaphysical ultimate is epistemologically ultimate.

Suppose, on the other hand, that the assertion is not intended to be true universally, but only within the context of a given metaphysical world view. It follows at once that the assertion is false: for it *claims* to make an allegation about every metaphysical postulate whatsoever, i.e., to be a statement which is true irrespective of the metaphysical position with which it is affiliated.

Nor will it help to say that the statement is intended to be universally true, but only within the context of metaphysical view *x*. For (i) then the statement would be unintelligible to everyone who did not hold view *x*—which is obviously false; (ii) view *x* itself could have been chosen only in terms of a knowledge of the truth of this statement itself, as we have already shown; (iii) all the problems that arise about the original assertion arise likewise about this explanation: is this explanation intended to be universally true, and so on to infinity?

Whether therefore the original assertion is taken to be universally true or not, it involves its own falsehood and is therefore self-contradictory.

(b) In the second place, the original proposition would be unintelligible if it were not false. If it is actually the case that the espousal of a first metaphysical principle is epistemologically basic—that such espousal determines the very forms of thought—then the statement would be unintelligible except to the person within the context of whose metaphysical position the proposition is propounded. But as a matter of fact, I think the statement will commend itself as rationally intelligible to any person whatever who is possessed of normal powers of ratiocination.

The only escape from this predicament would be to hold that the forms of thought or intelligibility are common to all systems: but this either destroys the original assertion by finding a common epistemological starting-point in terms of which a metaphysical ultimate is established, or it reduces to the absurdity that all metaphysical systems are basically identical, as we suggested previously.

I therefore conclude that the assertion—that the basic metaphysical postulate of any system is insusceptible of proof—is self-contradictory and invalid.

(2) As against this same assertion, I urge in the next place that if the espousal of a metaphysical ultimate is epistemologically basic—if, that is, the first principle of thought is a *metaphysical* principle—no rational basis for a choice of this principle can consistently be given. For the validity of this basis itself is determined by my metaphysical first principle: so that the only basis of the choice rests on a previous espousal of the position. It follows that either the choice is purely gratuitous and arbitrary, or that it is not actually a choice at all but the effect of completely determining extraneous factors. That Christian presuppositionalism eventually works itself around to this last alternative will be noted in a subsequent context.

But in point of fact, with the possible exception of VanTil, the presuppositionalists are inconsistent by attempting to construct just such a rational basis for accepting theism as ought logically to be rejected. If the internal self-consistency of the Christian view can be exhibited and the skeptical character of other positions displayed, this procedure either constitutes a rational justification for the metaphysical ultimate or not. If it does then there *is* a rational basis that underlies the acceptance of the theistic postulate. And if the procedure does *not* constitute a rational justification for theism, it is a meaningless exercise. The same may be affirmed with respect to the reintroduction of the theistic arguments by Clark and Carnell; and in fact, it may be asserted generally that every apologetic attempt either assumes that the metaphysical view of theism can be rationally established, or such attempt is not an apologetic at all.

Concerning the denial of common ground.—Since this position is a corollary to that just considered, the objections already cited apply here with equal force. Hence the denial actually makes a rational apologetic impossible and any apologetic at all devoid of fruitful issue.

(1) If—to consider VanTil's view first—the non-Christian uses one set of categories and the Christian another, there is no ground for argument or discussion. Nor will appeal to the formal point of contact or image of God help in this connection: for *if* this formal point actually makes fruitful argument possible, it is a *real* and *common* epistemological ground on the basis of which conclusions may be validly drawn—but this is precisely what VanTil denies. Either there is a true common basis for argument or not; if there is, fruitful argument is possible, but the denial of common ground is set aside; if there is no such true basis, argument is impossible.

Nor can the non-Christian place himself within the framework of the Christian world view to discern its internal self-consistency. For his categories are, by the theory itself, immanentistic and distorted: even his concept of coherence is wrong; and if not, it constitutes a *real* common ground. To say that the non-Chrisitan could not recognize coherence on his principle is to say either that he cannot recognize it at all—in which case there is no apologetic; or that he *has* a principle beside his own in terms of which such recognition is possible—in which case this principle constitutes common ground.

(2) As for Carnell's position: if believer and unbeliever have *any* interpretive content in common, as Carnell admits, there is no reason in principle for denying the non-Christian the possibility of achieving such content in metaphysics. How could believer and unbeliever have any interpretive content in common—say in science? Since all such content is determined by the validity of certain epistemological principles in terms of which facts are interpreted, such common content would imply that believer and unbeliever alike have the capacity for interpreting data according to universally valid first principles of knowledge. And what objection can possibly be given against the extension of this capacity to the highest level of ex-

planation in metaphysics? Whatever answer may be given to this last question, it will be inconsistent with Carnell's own attempt to establish an argument for theism.

With the denial of common ground apologetics becomes no more than the unfolding of a belief already possessed and devoid of all universally valid rational basis: in which case presuppositionalism is not a basis for the knowledge of God, but the denial that any such basis actually exists. And on such grounds, it is scarcely likely that a thinking man would decide for theism.

Concerning the sinful distortion of the general revelation.—Presuppositionalism holds that althougfi God is clearly revealed in nature, man's intellect is so distorted by sin that he *cannot* distill God from this revelation which nevertheless leaves man a sinner without excuse. Immediately the following problems confront such an outlook:

(1) How can the theistic arguments themselves be impugned by reason? When the presuppositionalists argue against the theistic proofs, they intend, I suppose, that their arguments are valid on a universal rational basis: the natural mind is so distorted that it cannot see the plain evidence of the natural revelation, but it is not so distorted that it cannot see the invalidity of the time-worn proofs for God. That the criticisms of argumentative theism *are* intended to be universally acceptable is confirmed by the fact that the presuppositionalists literally import as objections the arguments of such skeptics as Hume himself. Now all this is but to say that the natural mind is both competent and incompetent with respect to exactly the same data and in the same context.

Surely consistency would demand that if the unregenerate man cannot see God in nature, neither can he see the inadequacy of those arguments which attempt to infer God's existence to explain nature.

And the inconsistency is far worse. For, after showing me the critical inadequacy of theistic argumentation, the holder of this view asks me to move over to his revelational position where he will ask me to believe the very doctrine that he has just shown is lacking in respect to objective evidence; namely, that God *is* the Creator of all reality beyond himself and that the purposive aspects of nature *are* integrated in the eternal plan of God.

(2) How, as we have already queried in other contexts, can any fruitful arguments for theism be introduced at all? If man's intellect is thus distorted, any admission that he can see at all the consistency of the Christian position will ultimately repudiate the rejection of the general revelation as a basis for the knowledge of God. For to see this consistency *is* to move toward theism on the basis of natural revelation.

(3) Does this distortion involve reason as an instrument or not? (a) If it does—and this is the view of VanTil—self-contradiction is immediately involved. For only the instrumentality of reason can make this assertion itself intelligible, so that the statement can only be true by being false—which is absurd.   (b) If it does not—and this is the view of Carnell, Clark, and Henry—how can common ground and natural theology be consistently rejected? If all men have the same reason as an instrument and the same facts of natural revelation, on what grounds can the *possibility* of natural theology be denied? If it be answered that men volitionally refuse to use reason in understanding nature theistically, this is certainly true in unnumbered cases: but it involves the abandonment of presuppositionalism itself, since then it will be affirmed that while man *could* know God from nature, he *wills* not to.

(4) How does special revelation really help the natural man to know the existence of God? Every objection against man's ability to interpret the natural revelation will hold equally against the special revelation.

VanTil and Henry admit this point: and thus they press to the conclusion suggested by Calvin that only the regenerated person can truly know the existence of God. Nor does the initiative rest with man at all in the final analysis: after all, there is no basis on which he can of himself repent, even under *influences* of the Spirit. Since he is unregenerate, such influences will be on a precisely equal footing with both the general and the special revelations for him. The regeneration that is requisite to a knowledge of God's existence is therefore completely effected and determined from the divine side.

But more than this: such a doctrine of absolute electionism is part of a larger framework of sovereignty in terms of which every act of man and every event in the universe is completely determined and effected from the divine side with no measure of autonomy for rational selves. Since acts of men are determined by beliefs, and since, on the theory of presuppositionalism itself, a belief is *possible* only in the framework of a metaphysical world view that is ultimately given without rational foundation; then every *belief* and hence every *act* of man stems back finally to the ultimate metaphysical Real which is admitted by the theory to be God. Thus every act of man, as well as every event in the universe, is completely determined and effected from the divine side.

But such a rigid determinism is incompatible with a theism that makes God's nature the embodiment and norm of absolute goodness as over against the acknowledged evils of existence. If God is absolute goodness, He cannot be the cause of evil as such; but if every event in the universe is completely determined from the divine side, then God is precisely the cause of evil, which He cannot be, consistently with His goodness.

In this situation, the following alternatives are possible: (i) We may deny the absolute goodness of God: but then the God we thus posit is certainly not the Christian God. (ii) We may deny the reality of evil: but this is impossible, since at least the *illusion* of evil exists, and this in itself is an actual evil in the universe of a God who efficiently causes all things as such. (Cf. Part III, Section B, Chapter IV, for a discussion of the whole question of evil.)   (iii) We may accept a logical self-contradiction and maintain that God is both absolute goodness and yet the efficient cause of evil: but this is irrationalism and skepticism at its worst, for it asserts actually that the whole problem is insoluble. And such an assertion is self-contradictory on any line of argument whatever, for it involves its own denial.

(iv) The obvious and only remaining alternative is to deny our original determinism, and hold that evils spring from conditions which contained these evils only contingently: in particular, with regard to human moral evils, we would then hold that they spring from moral freedom, and that the acts and the beliefs which characterize men are *truly* chosen and *ought* to be chosen on rational grounds alone. But when we thus posit rational and moral freedom, we have left the presuppositionalist hypothesis far behind us: for it is *man* who chooses now; and if he chooses theism, it should be on the ground that a consistent rational interpretation of the data of experience has led him to this position as the only thoroughly logical alternative. A man may choose theism on a lesser ground, but every such ground ultimately comes to rest in such a supreme rational basis.

Thus the presuppositionalist approach lands one ultimately in an extreme Calvinistic atmosphere. If one feels comfortable here, let him remain with this God who has created rational men as mere puppets of His sovereignty. But if it seem to be the case that man is under *obligation* to believe the Gospel and that *he* must accept Christ as Saviour *before* the Spirit of God regenerates the heart—if, I say, man is a moral and rational agent confronted with a revelation for the acceptance of which he is morally and rationally responsible— then let the presuppositionalist framework be consigned to the ir-rationalism that is written so plainly through its structure!

But the final repudiation in this present context consists in the observation that the denial of the knowledge of God from the general revelation is inconsistent with that very revelation in Scripture to which the presuppositionalists make their greatest appeal. While a proponent of the present theory denies that man can imply God's existence from the general revelation, yet the psalmist declares: "The heavens declare the glory of God; and the firmament showeth his handiwork. Day unto day uttereth speech, and night unto night show-eth knowledge. There is no speech nor language, where their voice is not heard" (Ps. 19:1-3). And in the letter to the Romans Paul lays the foundation of Gentile responsibility squarely on the shoul-ders of natural theology, for he declares that "the invisible things of him are clearly seen from the creation of the world when they are considered by the things that are made, even his eternal power and deity, so that they are without excuse" (Rom. 1:20). Surely man is not responsible to God on the basis of natural revelation, if he can-not see that such revelation implies God's existence. Otherwise the passage is unintelligible. And again in Acts Paul declares that God has given a witness to all the nations in terms of the natural revela-tion (Acts 14), and that in God men have their very being, if only they would discern this fact (Acts 17).

Paul never suggests, nor is it the doctrine of Scripture, that man in his sin *cannot* imply God's existence from the facts of nature. What he does clearly teach is that, although man is intellectually able to take this step, he volitionally wills, at some point, to reject the evi-dence: "And according as they did not approve of having God in their knowledge, God gave them up to a reprobate mind" (Rom. 1:28). Man ought to see God in nature, but he *wills* not to.

Concerning the positive approach to apologetics.—The relevant criticisms in this connection have already been cited in previous contexts. But by way of summary: if there is any formal point of contact which makes apologetics possible, it is necessarily a true common ground and presuppositionalism is repudiated. And if the *rationes* and the facts of nature are common to all men as rational, there is no reason, in principle, why conclusions based on such premises may not reach true judgments about ultimate reality.

One additional point about the approach of Clark and Carnell: Both thinkers, when they reintroduce the arguments for theism, hold that theism is not a demonstrated truth, but only a verifiable hypothesis: now in scientific terminology, this means that theism would be a *possible* interpretation, but that it had not been shown to be the only possible one. This last is required if we are to transcend verification in demonstration.

Yet both men attempt to meet just the requisites of demonstration itself: for they try to show, not only that theism is a self-consistent interpretation of reality, but that every lesser view reduces to skepticism and self-contradiction. Now if it can be shown that every logically possible alternative to theism is thus self-contradictory, then theism will no longer be verified hypothesis, but demonstrated certainty.

Conclusion

I therefore conclude that since metaphysical presuppositionalism is thus entangled in such a mass of self-contradictions, it forms no valid approach to the knowledge of God. And with the principal alternatives to rational empiricism having been thus shown to be critically inadequate, we may now proceed to consider experience itself to determine whether God is real!

Part III

NATURAL THEOLOGY AND THE EXISTENCE
OF GOD

SECTION A
THE THEISTIC ARGUMENT FROM NATURAL REVELATION

CHAPTER I

THE CLASSIFICATION OF THE ARGUMENTS

INTRODUCTORY REMARKS

THE PROBLEM now is to attempt the establishment of theism on the basis of rational empiricism as an adequate account of epistemology: to show that in terms of experiential considerations which all men ought to acknowledge, insofar as they are rational, the theistic explanation of reality is the only one which can logically be accepted and believed by a reasoning mind that applies the categories of thought to the whole gamut of human experience as common to the community of rational selves.

Lest there should be any misunderstanding about the orientation of the discussion, a precise explanation of theism is requisite. By theism I understand that metaphysical philosophy which explains the total space-time universe by positing as its ground an absolutely necessary being, whose nature is that of personal intelligence and absolute goodness, and who, though he sustains the existence and functioning of that universe, nevertheless transcends it in the timeless necessity of His being. That theism has not always been defined in this way is undoubtedly true. Yet this, in my opinion, is the theism which a rational interpretation of experience will yield.

It will be alleged by some that the use of the term *natural revelation* is prejudicial in a twofold way: first, because it presupposes the establishment of theism by suggesting at the outset the conclusion that is to be established; namely, that the gamut of human experience does reveal the existence of God; second, because it suggests that, granting the validity of theistic argumentation, there is some other more specialized form of revelation.

In point of fact, however, no prejudgment of conclusion is intended to be imported at this point. The term *revelation* is used, not to imply the conclusion, but to indicate the end to which the discussion is teleologically directed. But more importantly, the whole phrase *natural revelation* is employed to clarify the fact that the entire argument proceeds solely on the basis of experiential considerations common to all rational selves, and not on the basis of any appeal to some specialized supernatural revelation in the experience of certain individuals.

On the other hand, it is certainly not my intention to discredit either the idea or the reality of such a special revelation: this consideration, however, is simply not a part of my present purpose. That a theism based on natural revelation may be supplemented by special revelatory acts is a position that I share: but that such a special revelation must be given initially, from a logical point of view, before the revelation in nature can be decisively significant, is a position that has already been repudiated. It seems rather to be the case that men must have some natural knowledge about God before special revelatory acts themselves can achieve ultimate significance:

> Without general [natural] revelation, special revelation would lack that basis in the fundamental knowledge of God as the mighty and wise, righteous and good, maker and ruler of all things, apart from which the further revelation of this great God's interventions in the world for the salvation of sinners could not be either intelligible, credible or operative.[1]

The plan of procedure will be as follows: first, to offer a detailed positive formulation of the progressive argument for theism; second, to consider the objections against such a structure of argument and to attempt to answer them. While such a method has the disadvantage of rendering either section incomplete without the other, it has also certain compensating merits. It enables the reader to gain, in the positive formulation, a synthetic view of the whole argument, unencumbered by an excess detail of critical remarks. And what is of equal importance, our method makes it possible for the reader, who is perplexed about specific objections to theism, to find, in the section on objections, a specialized treatment of the various particular criticisms.

Only two significant departures from this method will occur. In the discussion of the ontological argument, criticism of its structure

[1]B. B. Warfield, *The Inspiration and Authority of the Bible*, p. 75—although no implication is intended that the author's whole argument is shared by Warfield.

is so decisive that the validity of the argument can be maintained only through a basic alteration in that structure. A similar departure will be made in the consideration of the teleological argument as it relates specifically to the nature of rational and moral being: in these instances, criticism of the argument requires analytical consideration before its positive impact can be fully discerned.

THE CLASSIFICATION OF THE ARGUMENTS

Traditionally, the arguments for theism have been variously classified: but the most common arrangement is their separation into two groups by application of the terms a priori and a posteriori; the former group being considered *before,* or *apart from,* any appeal to the particular data of experience, and the latter group being based rather on just such an appeal.

A priori: the Ontological argument, or the argument from the idea of absolute existence.—This attempted proof undertakes to show that the mere conception in the mind, of an absolutely necessary being, involves both the conceived attribute of existence and the objective reality of the being itself. In brief, the idea of God is asserted to involve his actual or real existence. Consequently, the argument is called a priori because it rests solely on the mind's necessary conception of the relationship among the rational categories, and not at all on an appeal to particular experienced facts.

A posteriori: the cosmological, causal, or aetiological argument; or the argument from the fact of particular existence.—This argument moves from the admission of any particular existence whatever to the assertion that there exists an absolutely necessary being as its ground and ultimate cause. The argument is denominated *causal,* because it rests on the validity of the causal category according to which nothing could exist apart from the presence of completely determinate conditions of its being—the word *aetiological* is applied with similar motivation, since it is derived from the Greek *aitios* which means causal or causative. The movement of thought involved is further called *cosmological* because, while the argument generally rests on the mere admission that anything at all exists, still the broadest area of supposedly contingent reality to which the argument may be applied is the world or *cosmos* itself in the widest sense.

A posteriori: the teleological argument, or the argument from the nature of total existence.—This most complex type of theistic argumentation attempts to show that the detailed character of the experienced world embodies such adaptations of means to ends and such transcension of the possibilities of a material base, that the whole is explicable only in terms of a personal intelligent will whose nature is goodness and whose ultimate purpose the universe is progressively realizing. The argument has two basic orientations in proportion as it focuses attention on the universe as a whole or on man in particular. In the first orientation—the macrocosmic—thought moves from the sum total of what appear to be adaptations in nature and from the progressiveness of the cosmic process through levels of matter, life, and mind to the positing of an intelligent will as the sole sufficient explanation of this macrocosm.

In the second orientation—the microcosmic—thought moves from the distinctive character of mind or personality and from the nature of values as absolute to the positing of a Mind with absolute goodness as the sole sufficient explanation of man the microcosm. This phase of the teleological argument is often called the anthropological or moral argument. But its decisive significance depends upon its status as the climax of the whole process of teleological, and ultimately of theistic, argumentation.

The Necessary Synthesis of A priori and A posteriori Elements

Our whole discussion of epistemology should have made it clear that a bifurcation of arguments as a priori and a posteriori would involve the cessation of significant discussion before it began; for every valid piece of argumentation must involve both of these elements if it is to have ontological significance. Such argumentation must be a priori because resting on the categorical structure of the mind independently of particular experiences—every rational self, as we have shown, comes to the particular data of experience with a structure of rationality in terms of which it is necessarily disposed to understand experience and apart from which such experience could not exist; a posteriori because no content of knowledge about real and independent existences can be derived from the categories themselves and their interrelations—the knowledge of such real existences, the achievement of objective content knowledge, must result from the application of the categorical structure to the world of experience.

Consequently, no argument for God—or for anything else that is objectively actual apart from the mind—is valid on either of these bases alone, so that a purely empirical argument, or a purely rational argument, would both be invalid. This means that all the great arguments for theism, if they are to be logically cogent, must embody both rational and experiential considerations. And lest any misapprehension should occur here, it is conceded at once that the a priori ontological argument is therefore invalid.

Chapter II

THE ONTOLOGICAL ARGUMENT: OR THE ARGUMENT FROM THE IDEA OF ABSOLUTE EXISTENCE

Formulation of the Argument

The General Movement of Thought

THIS ARGUMENT attempts to show that the ontological or actual existence of God is implied in the idea of God that we must rationally conceive. The idea of an absolutely infinite being could not be the idea that it is unless such a being existed in reality; for if such a being had a merely conceptual or ideal existence, it would not be the object of our idea of an absolutely infinite being, and that just for the reason that the idea of such a being necessarily involves the concept of actual existence. On any other supposition the being conceived would be less than absolutely infinite. But men do have a concept of the absolutely infinite being: consequently, such a being must actually exist.

The Anselmic Formulation

The distinction of being the first thinker clearly to formulate the ontological argument has usually been attributed to Saint Anselm of Canterbury (A.D. 1033-1109). Indeed, his statement of the argument is so illuminating that it bears consideration in his own words as follows:

> We believe that thou [God] art a being than which nothing greater can be conceived. Or is there no such nature, since the fool hath said in his heart, there is no God? (Psalm 14:1). But, at any rate, this very fool, when he hears of this being of which I speak—a being than which nothing greater can be conceived—

understands what he hears, and what he understands is in his understanding. . . . And assuredly, that than which nothing greater can be conceived, cannot exist in the understanding alone: For suppose it exists in the understanding alone: then it can be conceived to exist in reality; which is greater. Therefore, if that, than which nothing greater can be conceived, exists in the understanding alone, the very being, than which nothing greater can be conceived, is one, than which a greater can be conceived. But obviously this is impossible. Hence, there is no doubt that there exists such a being, than which nothing greater can be conceived, and it exists both in the understanding and in reality.[1]

It is important to note carefully the movement of thought in this argumentation. Anselm rightly takes it as given that I can in some way form a clear conception of that than which nothing greater can be conceived. But such a being could not exist in the understanding alone, since then it would not exist as conceived: for obviously, a being that exists in the understanding alone is not a being than which nothing greater can be conceived. That is, the very concept of such a being implies the necessity of its existence, since otherwise I would be denying the consistent and logical character of the conception itself. Anselm would admit that in any other case it would be impossible to argue from conceptual to actual existence; but he would assert that in this one case alone, namely, in the conception of that than which nothing greater can be conceived, existence attaches to the very concept itself. Since this is the case, the conclusion that such a being necessarily exists is an inevitable movement of thought.

The Alternate Formulation of Descartes

Perhaps the most famous alternative expression of the ontological argument is to be found in the writings of Descartes (A.D. 1596-1650). Descartes states the argument with considerable clarity, and his statement is especially illuminating by reason of the fact that it embodies a mathematical analogy in some of its formulations.

From the fact that I cannot conceive God without existence, it follows that existence is inseparable from Him, and hence that He really exists; not that my thought can bring this to pass

[1]Anselm. *Proslogium; Monologium; An Appendix in Behalf of the Fool by Gaunilon, and Cur Deus Homo,* pp. 7, 8.

or impose any necessity on things, but, on the contrary, because the necessity which lies in the thing itself, i.e., the necessity of the existence of God determines me to think in this way. For it is not within my power to think of God without existence (that is of a supremely perfect Being devoid of a supreme perfection . . .) .

I saw very well that if we suppose a triangle to be given, the three angles must certainly be equal to two right angles; but for all that I saw no reason to be assured that there was any such triangle in existence, while on the contrary, on reverting to the examination of the idea which I had of a Perfect Being, I found that in this case existence was implied in it in the same manner in which the equality of its three angles to two right angles is implied in the idea of a triangle. . . . Consequently, it is at least as certain that God, who is a Being so perfect, is, or exists, as any demonstration of geometry can possibly be.[2]

The same general movement of thought characterizes this formulation as pervaded that of Anselm. But the terminology and the analogy are deserving of special attention. Descartes speaks of an idea of a Perfect Being: and here his statement is at a disadvantage compared with that of Anselm, since the positive idea of perfection is not nearly so clear a concept as the negative one of that than which nothing greater can be conceived. Be that as it may, Descartes avers that the very concept of perfection implies existence. When, in other words, I contemplate the idea of perfection, I consider that existence must be one of its attributes; since a being perfect in every way except that it did not exist would be less perfect than one which had the added attribute of such existence. This conclusion, maintains Descartes, is at least as certain as the conclusion that, given the idea of a triangle, the sum of its angles must be equal to two right angles: the development of implications is the same in either case.

Note further that an attempt is made, with dubious success, to anticipate and answer the objection that the mere self-consistency of an idea is made, in the ontological argument, to impose an existential necessity. It is not that my thought imposes any necessity on things, Descartes claims, but rather that the necessity of God's existence determines my thought. In other words, the mere conception of *any* given entity does not involve the actual existence of the entity as such: but in the case of the idea of God, or of an absolutely

[2]*Descartes Selections,* pp. 140-141, 33.

perfect being, the situation is altered; for the concept itself cannot be consistently thought without implying actual existence. Instead of my thought determining the objective necessity of God's existence, it is rather this very necessity of existence that determines my concept of God. Whether this is an adequate answer to the anticipated objection is a point that now calls for detailed consideration.

CRITICISM OF THE ARGUMENT
The Principle Objection

The objection stated.—The most important charge against the ontological argument is that it is a simple case of the fallacy of *petitio principii* or begging the question, for it possesses cogency only by assuming as a premise that very passage, from conceptual to actual existence, which it is the point of the argument to prove. If I take it as given that an adequate idea of God involves as such the absolute necessity of God's objective existence, then I certainly can conclude that the concept of God does imply the actual necessity of his existence; for I have merely stated a redundancy. But the fact is that it is just such a movement from thought to reality that the argument should establish: to assume the desired conclusion as an essential premise is wholly arbitrary and gratuitous.

Gaunilon's criticism.—The above criticism was stated, for substance, by the monk Gaunilon during Anselm's own lifetime. Thus Gaunilon urged that if the argument were a valid movement of thought, it would involve peculiar and wholly ridiculous results: if God exists necessarily and objectively, merely because He exists in my understanding as that than which nothing greater can be conceived, "could it not with equal justice be said that I have in my understanding all manner of unreal objects, having absolutely no existence in themselves, because I understand these things if one speaks of them, whatever they may be?"[3] If I can argue from my clear concept of God to His actual existence, could I not create a whole universe in the same way? Nor is it a sufficient answer to say that while such a passage of thought is not legitimate in the case of any other concept, it is legitimate in the case of the concept of God: for this is just what the argument ought to prove and it fails to do so.

Nor can the ontological argument be urged by observing that if such a being did not exist, it would not be that than which nothing

[3] Anselm, *op. cit.*, p. 146.

greater can be conceived: for here again I have smuggled in the objective existence that I ought to be proving. If God does not exist, He is not God: that is true enough. But whether He does actually exist is not established by the necessity that my concept of Him involves the idea of Him as necessarily existing. Thus unless we can begin our argument from some *conceded existential base,* we might argue with Gaunilon when he says: "I even deny or doubt that this being is greater than any real object."[4] In brief, all that the argument proves is a conceptual and not an objective or ontological necessity. Though Gaunilon failed to concede the point, it ought to be admitted that when I conceive God, I must conceive Him as necessarily existing. But only if I have already assumed that such a conceptual necessity imposes or implies actual existence, can I pass to the objective reality of the object of my concept.

Anselm attempted to answer Gaunilon's criticisms by simply restating the substance of the original argument. A being than which nothing greater can be conceived is by definition a being the nonexistence of which is inconceivable.[5] Now one either has this concept or not: if he does not have it, then "he does not conceive of the nonexistence of that of which he does not conceive."[6] On the other hand, "if he does conceive, he certainly conceives of a being which cannot be even conceived not to exist."[7]

Now while this analysis does answer the superficial remark of Gaunilon that all sorts of unreal things could be proved in this way— it being the case that the concept of God does involve the concept of Him as necessarily existing—it fails to answer the deeper objection that underlies Gaunilon's surface point. For while it is true that if I conceive God I must conceive Him as necessarily existing, this is not an argument but a mere analysis. All I have stated is a redundancy: I have said that the concept of a being, whose nonexistence is inconceivable, is the concept of a being whose nonexistence is inconceivable. Or in brief, I have stated an identity: but the statement of the identity proves absolutely nothing about the actual existence of the object itself, in this case, God. Only by assuming the passage from conceptual to actual existence can I prove this same passage.

[4]*Ibid.,* p. 150.
[5]*Ibid.,* p. 154.
[6]*Ibid.,* p. 159.
[7]*Idem.*

And thus the ontological argument hangs suspended in the mist of nothingness.

Kant's formulation of the objection.—Kant stated the argument so forcefully against the purely a priori form of the ontological argument that scarcely any modern thinker since his time has attempted to vindicate the argument on a priori grounds alone.

It is illegitimate, Kant urged in the first place, to argue from an a priori conception, the content of which embraces existence, to the actual existence of the thing.[8] The statement—an absolutely necessary being exists—is an identical judgment: i.e., it merely asserts that what necessarily exists necessarily does exist. Now "if I annihilate the predicate in thought, and retain the subject, a contradiction is the result."[9] As when I say: that which necessarily exists does not exist necessarily; or a gremlin is not a gremlin. "But if I suppress both subject and predicate in thought, no contradiction arises; for there is *nothing* at all, and therefore no means of forming a contradiction."[10] As when I say: an absolutely necessary being does not exist; or gremlins do not exist.

Now then, Kant asserts, it would be legitimate to argue from an a priori concept to the actual existence of its object, *only* if the annihilation of both subject and predicate in thought would leave a contradiction. And there is no such contradiction, logically speaking, in the proposition that an absolutely necessary being does not exist objectively. And if someone objects that there are some subjects which cannot be annihilated in thought, then Kant answers, rightly I think, that "this is nothing more than saying: There exist subjects which are absolutely necessary—the very hypothesis which you are called upon to establish."[11]

But in the next place, Kant attempts to show that objective or actual existence does not enter into the concept of a thing at all. The proposition, *x* exists, is either analytical (i.e., the predicate is implied in the subject), or synthetical (i.e., the predicate is an assertion not deducible from an analysis of the subject). If it is *analytical,* then nothing new is said or asserted beyond what the concept of *x* itself contains and either "the conception in your minds is identical with the thing itself [as actually existing], or you have supposed the

[8]*Critique of Pure Reason,* pp. 332, 333.
[9]*Ibid.,* p. 333.
[10]*Idem.*
[11]*Idem.*

existence of a thing to be possible and then inferred its existence from its internal possibility."[12] But the conception of a thing is obviously not its actual or objective existence as such; nor can the actual existence of a thing be identified with its mere possibility. In either case, it follows that actual existence is not part of the definition of a concept.

Suppose, then, that the proposition, *x* exists, is *synthetical* (and Kant would maintain this to be the case) : then it cannot be said that "the predicate of existence cannot be denied without contradiction— a property which is the characteristic of analytical propositions, alone."[13] That is, the denial of the predicate would be self-contradictory only if the predicate were already contained in the subject: but a synthetical proposition is precisely one in which this is not the case. It follows, here also, that actual existence does not enter into the definition of a concept.

It therefore appears that when I say, *x* actually exists, I am not expanding the concept of *x*, but am merely positing "the existence of the subject with all its predicates—I posit the *object* in relation to my *conception*."[14] The predicate *actual existence* does not enter into the concept of anything precisely because the concept merely includes the cogitation of the thing as possible. There is no difference, in fact, between the concept of a thing as real and the concept of it as possible. To use Kant's illustration, a hundred real dollars and a hundred possible dollars are conceptually identical. For on the supposition that this was not the case, my concept of the real dollars would not be an adequate concept of them, if conceptual and actual existence are different. "I could not affirm that the exact object of my conception had real existence."[15] For the object would differ from my conception of it by actually existing, unless the object happened to be just my conception and nothing else—a case not applicable to anything that really exists apart from the mind. It must therefore be that the real and the possible are conceptually identical and that consequently actual existence is not involved in the concept of anything whatsoever.

The sum of the whole matter turns out to be this: since actual existence is not included in the concept of anything, we cannot derive the actual existence of God from our concept of Him.

[12]*Ibid.*, p. 334.
[13]*Idem.*
[14]*Ibid.*, p. 335.
[15]*Ibid.*, p. 336.

Attempted Answers

W. G. T. Shedd attempts to answer this objection by saying: "If the idea of a thing implies that it may or may not exist, it does not follow from the idea that the thing does exist. But if the idea of a thing implies that it must exist, it does follow from the idea that the thing does exist."[16] But this statement does not appear to me to make any significant contribution to a defense of the ontological argument. The same alternative remains as always: either the statement begs the question, or it is a miserable tautology. If I assume as a premise that a thing must exist objectively, then it must exist thus—yet this is exactly the point that the argument should prove. If, on the other hand, I grant that the necessity is merely a conceptual one, I never can bridge the gap to objective existence without appeal to existential data. But it is just such an appeal that the ontological argument professes to transcend.

A further attempt to eliminate the objection has been formulated by endeavoring to show that either the ontological argument is valid, or self-contradictory skepticism results.[17] The ontological argument shows that if we conceive God, we must conceive Him as necessarily existing. Now "if what we are obliged to think is not necessarily real, there is an end to all proof and reasoning."[18] Hence, skepticism results.

But this attempt to escape the principal objection against the argument is entirely gratuitous. For the ontological argument does not prove but assumes that the conceptual existence of God involves as such His actual existence. The critic of ontological reasoning does not urge that the conception of God does not involve the concept of His necessary existence, but merely that this conceptual existence does not prove God's actual existence. If we conceive a being the nonexistence of which is inconceivable, then we do conceive such a being: and this is not denied. That the principal objection results in skepticism would be the case only if the objector denied that the concept of an absolutely necessary being was identical with itself. But this is not asserted: it is simply asserted that the concept of itself does not involve *actual* existence. And such a position is neither self-contradictory nor skeptical.

[16]*Dogmatic Theology,* I, pp. 226, 227.
[17]George Galloway, *The Philosophy of Religion,* p. 386. Stated for purposes of refutation.
[18]*Idem.*

Finally, we might point out that the allegation of skepticism *would* be valid if the conclusion of the ontological argument were founded on existential premises: if what we must think, when we begin with objective existential premises, is not objectively valid, then skepticism—the doctrine that knowledge is impossible—truly does result. But it is precisely the point of the ontological argument that it does not rest on any such existential premises.

I therefore conclude that the a priori ontological argument is invalid, since it is either a pointless tautology or an instance of the fallacy of *petitio principii* (begging the question).

RECONSTRUCTION

We will, however, make a serious mistake if we bypass the argument altogether, since it may be admissible on a posteriori and a priori grounds together. It will be recalled that we have already embraced an epistemological theory called rational empiricism: namely, that the mind comes to the data of experience with certain forms of thought in terms of which it is necessarily disposed to understand experience; and when it makes this approach, it finds a world constituted by the very categories with which it operates and a world which contains other selves, all of whom operate with the same rational categories. The question arises therefore: how are we to explain this adaptation of thought to the world of experience and this universality of the categorical structure? Since the categories are, in our experience, connected with a rational self, we may infer that their presence in the world and in other finite selves is to be similarly explained by reference to a Reason from which both finite selves and their world of experience are derived. In brief, the categorical structure of rationality and existence is grounded in the being of an eternal Reason or God.[19]

Such argumentation is indeed founded on an a priori basis in part, since it depends for its validity on the structure and operation of innate rational categories which characterize the mind before experience. But the argument, in this form, is not open to the objection of Kant that a passage is illicitly made from conceptual to actual existence. Rather the existence of God is concluded as an explanation for the possibility of any intelligible experience at all. Whether

[19]Cf. James Orr, *The Christian View of God and the World*, p. 104, for a similar argument. Also, Gordon H. Clark, *A Christian View of Men and Things*, p. 318.

any other explanation of the intelligibility of the world is possible is a subject that will be considered in the sequel: in fact, this formulation is substantially an aspect of the teleological argument, which will presently engage our utmost attention.

It may therefore be urged that we have so changed the structure of the original ontological argument that it is no longer the same movement of thought. This we readily admit: yet at the same time there is a common ground between both modes of thinking; namely, that some a priori basis is necessary in the establishment of God's existence. The mistake of Anselm and Descartes was that they sought this a priori element in the mind's idea of God, whereas they ought to have sought it in that categorical structure which makes intelligible experience possible.

CHAPTER III

THE COSMOLOGICAL ARGUMENT: THE ARGUMENT FROM THE FACT OF PARTICULAR EXISTENCE

FORMULATION OF THE ARGUMENT

UNLIKE THE ONTOLOGICAL ARGUMENT, in its purely a priori form, the present argument lays its foundations on an experiential basis. It urges that if we admit the fact of any particular existence whatsoever—myself, for example—we must logically admit an absolutely necessary being. Or as Kant puts it, though he himself opposed the argument: "If something exists, an absolutely necessary being exists. Now I, at least, exist. Consequently, there exists an absolutely necessary being."[1]

Now it will probably not occur to anyone to deny the existence of anything at all. But if it does, we can easily prove either that he is mistaken, or that his statement is not a refutation of the argument, or both. He is mistaken because he at least exists to effect the denial, which is therefore self-contradictory. His statement is not a refutation of the argument because, on the supposition of its truth, neither the denial nor the argument would exist to refute or be refuted.

This movement of thought from any particular existence to an absolutely necessary existence will become evident if we consider the following factors. Any given existing thing is either an effect or not, an effect being defined as an existence whose character and being are determined by antecedent and contemporaneous existences external to itself. Now if such an entity is not an effect, its character and being must be determined by factors within itself: and thus we conclude

---

[1]*Critique of Pure Reason*, p. 338; for a summary and refutation of Kant's criticism of the cosmological argument, cf. Section B below, Chapter III.

at once an absolutely necessary being, since such a being is precisely one whose determinate character is completely self-contained.

But suppose that a given entity *is* an effect. Its character and being must therefore, by definition, be determined by antecedent and contemporaneous existences external to itself: but these existences are again either effects or not, and so on. Now either the series of such effects and causes is infinite or not. But an infinite number of successive causes and effects—or any infinite number of actual existents—is rationally inconceivable. For no series of particular and determinate entities could ever add up to infinity. But if, on the other hand, the series of effects is not infinite, it must end in a cause which is self-contained, i.e., in an absolutely necessary being, or a being that contains within itself the conditions of its determinate character.

Thus, whether a given entity is an effect or not, we rationally conclude the existence of an absolutely necessary being.

It may be helpful to state the same reasoning in terms of a different vocabulary: any given entity is either contingent in its existence or not—contingency being defined, not as the absence of determinate conditions for existence (no actual entity being contingent in this way), but rather as the imposition of such determinate conditions from some extraneous source. If the entity is not contingent, the determinate conditions of its existence are self-contained and it is an absolutely necessary being.

If the entity *is* contingent, on the other hand, then its existence is determined by some extraneous source, which again is either contingent or not, and so on. But consider the alternatives: the series cannot be infinite, since an infinite series of determinate things is rationally inconceivable; but if it is not infinite, then it must be dependent or contingent upon a being whose determinate conditions of existence are self-contained and who therefore is an absolutely necessary being. Thus, whether a given entity is contingent or not, we rationally conclude the existence of an absolutely necessary being.

The Transition to Theism

But how, it might be queried, can this argument, to an absolutely necessary being, establish theism? For ought I know, *I* might be the absolutely necessary being, and so might the space-time universe, or some part of it. The establishment of theism from the cosmological argument—i.e., of theism so far as it asserts God's transcendence of the space-time universe in a timeless necessity of existence, it being involved in the general validity of the argument that the absolutely necessary being sustains the series of effects or contingents, so that this last is taken as established for theism—this establishment of theism, I assert, is possible in two ways which embody the same reasoning from different points of view: positively, from a consideration of what is meant by an absolutely necessary being; negatively, from a consideration of proposed claimants to absolute necessity of existence.

The positive argument.—An absolutely necessary being is one whose determinate character is completely self-contained, one that has within itself all the conditions of its existence and that faces no limitations which are not self-involved.

Now such a being must transcend the temporal series by reason of the fact that it must be absolutely changeless and devoid of succession, whereas the temporal series is characterized by just such marks of change and succession, for suppose the absolutely necessary being to be changeable and therefore subject to temporal succession. Such change would proceed either from within its own nature or from some extraneous cause. In the latter case, such a being would not be the absolutely necessary being, which, by definition, stands in no necessary relation that is not self-involved.

The alleged change must therefore proceed from the nature of the absolute being itself: but this is impossible, for such a change either springs from a determinate condition that is itself changeless and eternal, or from a determinate condition that has originated. But in the last case we have merely explained one change by another and hence shifted the problem without solving it. In the former case, a determinate condition that is itself changeless and eternal must have produced its necessary effect changelessly and eternally—in which case no change is involved at all.

Consequently, since change can, in the absolutely necessary being, be produced neither from an extraneous cause nor from a self-involved cause, the absolutely necessary being must be changeless and hence not subject to temporal succession.

But suppose, it may be objected, that the absolutely necessary being is changeless in his essential nature, but that he does experience a succession of moments in time: if this were possible, then we could not say that the absolutely necessary being transcends the temporal series and we would still fall short of theism. Now consider this proposed possibility.

If such a being is subject to succession of temporal moments, this succession of moments must either be a self-involved subjection or one that arises from some extraneous cause. But in the latter case, as we indicated above, such a being is not an absolutely necessary being. In the former case, this self-involved subjection to time must spring either from a changeless or a changeable determinate condition in the absolute being. In the last instance—that the determinate condition is changeable—we contradict the original hypothesis that the absolutely necessary being is changeless in its essential nature, since any determinate condition in such a being must be part of its essential nature.

In the first instance—that the determinate condition from which subjection to time springs is changeless—the subjection itself would be eternal. Now this would mean that the eternity of the absolutely necessary being would consist in an infinite series of successive moments: and we have already shown that such an infinite series is rationally inconceivable. Furthermore, if the determinate condition from which subjection to time springs is changeless, then self-contradiction results: for the condition, being itself a part of the nature of the absolutely necessary being, would itself be subject to time and would therefore change by passing through a succession of moments. This would yield then the curious result that the alleged changeless condition is a changeable and changing condition—which is self-contradictory.

It therefore follows that since an absolutely necessary being cannot be subject to temporal succession either from a self-involved or extraneous cause, such a being must completely transcend the temporal series.

What follows from this proof of such transcension? The world to be explained by positing the absolutely necessary being is itself either subject to the temporal series or not. If not, then it is not the world of our experience: for this last world is essentially characterized by temporal succession of effects, and it would thus result that this actual world of experience is left unexplained by the argument to an absolute being. If the world to be explained is subject to temporal succession, it follows that the world—which might then be that of our experience—is not the absolutely necessary being.

But might some part of the world be the absolute being for which we seek? Apparently and obviously not: for to be a part of the world-whole, such a being would be necessarily subject to that very temporality of succession which characterizes the world itself; else we would be making the self-contradictory assertion that some part of the world is not a part of the world.

Consequently, it follows from a positive consideration of what is meant by an absolutely necessary being that such a being transcends the temporal world and is thus identical in this respect with the God of the highest theism. Incidentally, a similar analysis can be made in terms of the concept of space, but because the analysis proceeds, almost point for point like that from the concept of time, it is here omitted.

The negative argument.—If anything less than a transcendent being were the absolutely necessary existence, it would have to be one of the following (proceeding from subjective to objective) : (1) myself, or some other self which exists in the world; (2) some other part of the space-time universe; (3) the space-time universe as a whole.

Could an *existing self* in the world be the absolutely necessary being? I hardly think that such a position can be seriously maintained in the final analysis. My very existence is contingent upon its relation to the whole causal nexus of reality: I have not always existed, and my present existence depends upon the conspiration of an indefinite number of external determinate conditions which sustain my being; consequently, I am not the absolutely necessary being, since my existence, being thus contingent, is *ipso facto* not absolutely necessary.

But suppose an objector urges solipsism—the doctrine that for each self the world is within his mind—and maintains that the whole world of his experience is the concretion of his own mind, so that he is the absolutely necessary being. While I think that this contention is not likely to be urged by a man in his right mind, it is nevertheless easy to show that the contention itself proves our original point, namely, that the absolutely necessary being transcends the world of experience.

For either the world that I thus create is distinct from my very self or not. If it is not distinct from my very self (e.g., as an idea is distinct from the mind that thinks it), then either its separate existence is illusory or mine is. Now if my separate existence is illusory, not only is the original solipsism contravened, but the world of experience is itself asserted to be the absolutely necessary being, since there is nothing else in existence—but this contention has already been refuted and will subsequently be subjected to further refutation. Suppose then that the world's separate existence is illusory and that I am the world of experience: the result is the same, since it is still asserted that the world of experience is the absolutely necessary being.

If, on the other hand, the world that I create *is* distinct from my very self, it follows at once that the absolutely necessary being is distinct from the world of experience, for the very reason that I am this being and I am distinct from it. Thus even the solipsist must conclude that the absolutely necessary being transcends the world of experience, and this on any line of argument he may select.

Furthermore, this self of mine which I as a solipsist posit to be the absolutely necessary being is subject to temporal succession, or at least to the illusion of it. But we have already shown in detail that the absolutely necessary being cannot be thus subject to succession, whether actually or by illusion. On this ground also, the self of a given individual cannot be the absolute being which thought necessarily concludes.

Of course, solipsism is itself untenable, in any case. For a world that I create is not really the actual world of experience, since this actual world appears, at least, to have objective and independent existence. If it be said that this appearance is an illusion, then the solipsist faces the hopeless problem of accounting for the origin of such an illusion in a world that he asserts to be his own creation by an act of will. For either the illusion springs directly from his will—in which case it ought to be no illusion at all, or it springs from another illusion and so on until it reaches a source in such an act of will. The only alternative is an infinite series of illusions with no ultimate explanation: and this series—here as elsewhere—is inconceivable. And is there not something strange in the notion that when a solipsist passes through the gates of death, he not only succumbs to the very effects which his own will imposed but leaves the rest of us, who do not actually exist, to bemoan his departure. And thus all reality vanishes in the oblivion of nonexistence!

I therefore conclude that on any line of argument whatever the self is not the absolutely necessary being.

Could the absolutely necessary being be some other *part of the space-time universe?* Obviously not. For a part of the space-time universe is, by definition, a thing or event to which the whole universe sustains an active and reciprocal causal relation; i.e., such a part is contingently related to the whole. But a being that is thus contingently related is by that very fact not the absolute being which we are seeking. To say that a thing is part of the universe is to say that it belongs to the temporal series and that it is therefore an event determined by its place in the series and not an existence determined from itself. To maintain therefore that some part of the universe is the absolute being which thought necessarily posits is self-contradictory, since it is the same as saying that some part of the universe is not a part of the universe.

Could the *space-time universe itself* be the absolutely necessary being? Again, obviously not. For the space-time universe is, by admission, a temporal series (from one point of view), or a series of contemporaneous interdependent entities (from an alternate point of view). Now either this series is finite in extent and thus depends for its existence upon a being that transcends the series itself, or the series is infinite. But an infinite series of actual existents, as we have mentioned so often, is logically absurd. And therefore the space-time universe does depend for its existence on a transcendent being that exists necessarily—and this is the point we set out to establish.

But suppose someone queries: how can you assert that because the parts of a series are contingent, therefore the whole series is contingent? Not only is this objection already answered by implication, but it is considered and answered in great detail in Section B, Chapter IV. Suffice it to say that even if this were a valid objection—which I demonstrate subsequently that it is not—a formulation of the cosmological argument is possible without this movement of thought.

John Wild formulates the argument in his *Introduction to Realistic Philosophy.* The following preliminary definitions are offered: (1) composite—anything consisting of intrinsic and distinct parts; (2) contingent—anything the existence of which is merely possible with respect to itself; (3) simple—that which lacks all composition; (4) necessary—that which is unable not to be.[2]

[2]John Wild, *Introduction to Realistic Philosophy*, p. 360.

The argument then runs as follows: whatever is composite is contingent; this follows from the fact that in any composite being, say one made up of parts x and y, x accounts for the x-ness of the thing, and y for the y-ness, but the togetherness of the two does not explain itself, since the union might be dissolved if it is really made up of parts. But in the next place, whatever is contingent must have an ultimate cause which is necessary: this follows from the fact that a contingent being is externally caused and from the fact that an infinite series of contingencies is absurd. Now the world of nature is composite, any supposition to the contrary being utterly devoid of experiential basis and therefore untenable. It follows that the world is contingent and therefore has an absolutely necessary cause that transcends it.[3]

That the world is not a self-sufficient existence receives striking scientific confirmation from the second law of thermo-dynamics, according to which the quantity of available energy in the world is constantly diminishing: "Because there is constant diffusion, and because there is no addition to the total energy, we must contemplate a final condition of absolute stagnation."[4] What does this concept imply about the world? It implies either that the original quantity of energy was infinite, or that the world in process had a beginning: since the first is logically ridiculous, the latter must be affirmed.

But more significantly, if the second law of thermo-dynamics is valid, then the space-time universe is not self-explanatory and therefore not the self-existent and absolutely necessary being: "the universe as we know it, by the aid of modern science, could not have originated without the action of a creative Source of energy outside itself. . . . But a creative Source of energy outside the natural order is God."[5] Of course, the law itself may be invalid: but no matter, for the case rests, as we have already indicated, on logical considerations which are valid independently of this or any other inductive scientific law.

Conclusion.—It therefore follows that the argument for an absolutely necessary being establishes a theism which asserts God to transcend the space-time universe in a timeless necessity of existence.

Historical Exponents of the Cosmological Argument

Since our development has proceeded rather largely without refer-

[3] *Ibid.*, pp. 360, 361.
[4] D. E. Trueblood, *The Logic of Belief*, p. 154.
[5] *Ibid.*, p. 159.

ence to proponents of the cosmological argument in the history of philosophy, a brief notice should be made of the historical prominence of this movement of thought. In ancient times, the essential structure of the argument was propounded by both Plato[6] and Aristotle,[7] although it is certainly doubtful that either of these thinkers was consistent, either in the formulation of the argument itself or in the maintenance of its validity within the structure of his over-all world view.

In medieval times, the argument was championed by a whole succession of Christian philosophers: most notably by Anselm,[8] whose formulation was Platonically oriented and depends upon the Platonic theory of ideas for its validity; and by Thomas Aquinas,[9] whose formulation was basically Aristotelian and whose philosophy is the official norm for contemporary Roman Catholic thinkers.

Even the *principal* proponents of the theoretical basis of the cosmological argument in modern times, are too numerous to mention: but Berkeley,[10] Descartes,[11] and Spinoza[12] have all propounded the argument, each in his own particular version and from the standpoint of differing metaphysical points of view. As previously mentioned, the argument is likewise defended by modern Catholic thinkers, references to whose works may be found in the Bibliography.

On the whole, the cosmological argument has probably, until the twentieth century at least, enjoyed a preponderance of popularity over all other types of theistic argumentation. Since the rise of modern evolutionary nautralism, however, it has been the argument next to be considered that has played the dominant role.

COGENCY OF THE ARGUMENT: CONCLUSION

Upon what structure does the cosmological argument rest for its cogency? In the first place, it rests upon that very a priori structure of rationality with which the mind approaches experience and without which intelligible experience itself does not exist. While the whole categorical structure is basic to the cosmological argument, the principal categories involved in the basis of the argument are the following: (1) causality, according to which every reality exists

[6]*Laws*, X, 896.
[7]*Metaphysics*, 994; 1071b-1072b; *Physics*, 259a.
[8]Anselm, *op. cit.*, pp. 37-45.
[9]*Summa Theologica*, I, qu. 2, art. 3.
[10]*Principles of Human Knowledge*, sections XXVI f., CXLVI f.
[11]*Descartes Selections*, pp. 118-124.
[12]*Ethics*, p. 9.

only through the presence of determinate conditions; (2) existence, according to which real entities are asserted; (3) unity, which is posited of the absolutely necessary being; (4) plurality, which is the characteristic of contingent being; (5) necessity-contingence, according to which a given reality is cogitated as infinite or finite.

In the second place, the argument has likewise an a posteriori or existential premise: for it reasons to the existence of an absolutely necessary being from the granted reality of some particular entity of experience.

In the third place, the basic movement of thought in the argument may be asserted without raising questions about the precise nature of the particular existence granted, although, as we have seen, some analysis of this kind is involved when the transition to theism is made.

The sum of the whole matter is this: that rationality and experience have together established the existence of an absolutely infinite being that transcends the world of experience and is its only sufficient explanation. And if such a being were not God, we should all be atheists!

CHAPTER IV

THE TELEOLOGICAL ARGUMENT: THE ARGUMENT FROM THE NATURE OF TOTAL EXISTENCE

GENERAL NATURE OF THE ARGUMENT

HAVING ESTABLISHED the existence of an absolutely necessary and transcendent being as the only sufficient ground of the total space-time universe, we then take up inquiry as to what the detailed character, of the universe as a whole and of our own existence in particular, might reveal to us concerning the nature of such an absolute being.

It is precisely to this question that the structure of the teleological argument[1] proffers an answer: for it urges, as mentioned previously, that the world embodies such adaptation of means to ends and such transcension of the possibilities inherent in matter, that it becomes necessary to explain the nature of the absolutely necessary being as a personal, intelligent will, characterized by absolute goodness and by an eternal purpose which the universe is progressively objectifying. The overwhelming force of these considerations will become more apparent when the phases of the argument are studied below in detail.

Now it is to be granted at once that the argument assumes that thought may rationally infer something about the cause of an entity from a consideration of its effect—something, too, which exceeds the bare assertion that the cause exists, though that in itself is by no means insignificant. Thus, for example, I look at my flute on the shelf yonder: it consists of a long metal tube possessing various apertures, two of which are open and the rest either open or closed de-

[1]Called *teleological* because it attempts to show that the universe evinces the progressive realization of ends or purposes. Greek: *telos*, meaning end, purpose, goal.

pending on the up or down position of the keys with which they are in juxtaposition. Now when I blow on the opening in the side of the tube and move my fingers over the keys—as I should be doing more often, were I not writing this book—music, or if you like, a succession of sounds, results.

What, now, may I infer about the cause of the flute? It seems to me that since the flute is of such intricate mechanical structure and since it is so obviously adapted or suited to the production of various sounds, I may infer that a *part* of the cause of the flute was an intelligent will that had some prevision of the effect it was to produce and of the end to which it should be adapted: for intelligence is characterized by just such adaptation of means to ends.

But, you urge, the only real reason that you believe the flute to have been made by an intelligent will is that you know that flutes are made by men, or that you have seen them in process of being made, or etc. On the contrary, while I have been playing the flute for a period that approaches twenty years, I have never seen a flute being made by an intelligent agent; nor did it ever occur to the man who sold me the flute, and has since kept it in operation, to tell me that the flute was thus made. In fact, I think I have never heard anyone on any occasion make such a statement as: flutes are made by intelligent agents.

How, indeed, could I know that flutes are thus made? Presumably the following alternatives exhaust the possibilities: (1) I either made the flute myself or I saw it being made by some other intelligent agent; (2) this knowledge is innate; (3) I received this knowledge from some other intelligent agent by way of testimony; (4) I infer this knowledge from the conspiration of the various parts of the flute to produce a given result.

Now consider these possibilities: (1) I did not make the flute, nor did I see it being made by another. And if I had seen some other flute being thus made, the analogy would not show that this flute was thus made except on grounds that would destroy the objection to my inference of intelligent will.[2]   (2) My knowledge that this flute was made by an intelligent will is not innate, the hypothesis of innate ideas having been already discredited.[3]   (3) I never received this knowledge from testimony: and if I had, this would not serve to convince me unless a careful scrutiny of the flute itself led me to

<hr>

[2] This point is elaborated at great length in Section B, Chapter IV, of this part.
[3] Part I, Chapter III.

the same conclusion. (4) It must therefore be that the reason I know this flute to have been produced by an intelligent will is this: that the conspiration of its intricate structure to produce a certain result is explicable only in terms of a force which adapted means to a previsioned end or ends. And intelligence is exactly this process of adaptation. I note in passing that this is exactly the kind of adaptation that, as we shall see, nature herself everywhere evinces.

But what else might I infer from the flute about its cause? The flute is impressed with apertures and decked with keys; further, it is made of a silver alloy. May I therefore infer that the intelligent will who made the flute is full of holes, covered with keys, and made of silver alloy? Obviously not, but the question is, *why* not? After all, *these* aspects of the flute require explanation in causal terms too.

The answer to this question is as follows: we take the matter of the flute for granted as means which the workman adapted to produce his anticipated end. It is not the *substance* of the flute that leads us to infer intelligent will as its explanation, but rather the arrangement of the substance to produce a certain result. We therefore impute to this aspect of the cause only that capacity which is required to explain the otherwise problematic effect: the capacity, that is, of intelligent will.

On the other hand, the flute could not exist apart from its matter: if there were no material elements that could be adapted to produce the complex structure of a flute, the intelligent will that we postulate could not have made such an instrument. Where then did the matter of the flute originate? The following alternatives seem possible: (1) The matter always existed, either in this form or some other (i.e., as silver, for example, or as some more basic elements from which silver itself is constituted), and in such a way as to have been adapted eternally to the production of such ends as the making of a flute. (2) The intelligent will that adapted the materials to its end created the materials with such potentialities. (3) The materials were thus brought into being by some other intelligent will and formed an environment for the particular intelligence that produced the flute.

Consider these possibilities. (1) That the matter always existed with such a potentiality is untenable on two counts: first, because the cosmological argument has already shown us that no part of the world, nor even the whole of it, is self-explanatory but depends for its existence on an absolutely necessary and transcendent being; second, because the existence of materials that *can be adapted* to intelligent ends, itself requires explanation in terms of intelligent will, just as the flute itself does. (2) The matter of the flute must therefore have been produced by an intelligent will: yet not any particular finite intelligence, as we have already demonstrated in the cosmological argument by showing that no particular finite self could be the absolutely necessary being.

(3) Consequently, the matter of the flute—or of anything else—admits of ultimate explanation only in terms of an absolutely necessary being essentially characterized by intelligent will: absolutely necessary to account for the sheer existence of contingent materials, intelligent will to account for the potential of matter for adaptation to previsioned ends.

But a still deeper note may be struck just at this point: for whence the existence of the particular intelligent will that made the flute from materials in its environment? Is not the fact that such an intelligence stands related to an environment which can be manipulated for the realization of ends, *itself* a case of previsioned adaptation of means to yield certain results? The environment and the intelligence act *as if* they had been themselves associated by intelligent will? Thus the flute, its intelligent maker, and its matter, all require final explanation in terms of an absolute intelligence that is distinct from the space-time universe.

It therefore appears that from the existence of the flute, thought has ultimately arrived at the existence of such an absolute intelligence. But note carefully that the argument maintains nothing so ridiculous as that every characteristic of the flute must be contained either eminently or virtually in this absolute and intelligent cause—as if God had a perfect hole in His head (or even a head, for that matter) simply because the flute has an opening near its top extremity. What is maintained is that God has such characteristics as are required to explain (1) the contingency of the flute's substance; (2) the adaptation of its matter to ends visualized by intelligence; and (3) the adaptation of particular finite intelligences themselves to the realization of previsioned ends in a material environment.

It appears at once from our prolonged illustration that the teleological argument is ultimately dependent upon the basic movement of thought contained in the cosmological: for the argument moves on the assumption that for any given entity or group of entities it is reasonable to suppose a sufficient explanation. This supposition lies at the very base of the cosmological argument and springs ultimately, as we have shown (Part I), from the structure of rationality itself.

FORMULATION OF THE ARGUMENT: MACROCOSMIC POINT OF VIEW

Introduction

If now the attribution of intelligent will to the absolutely necessary being is rationally demanded by the consideration of an object of human contrivance like a flute, what will be our reaction if we find that the whole world of nature itself is replete with particular instances of the adaptation of means to ends, and that, more importantly, the movement of the cosmic process itself likewise evinces this characteristic and unique mark of intelligence? Yet, when we subject nature to a detailed analysis, this universal presence of adaptedness is precisely what we discover.

Stated in progressive order, the general areas of nature, in which adaptation is conspicuously present, are the following:[4] (1) The fitness of the inorganic, material world to be an environment for both the production and maintenance of organic life. (2) The internal adaptedness of organic beings, both in the structure of their specialized functions and in their general orientation for self-maintenance or subservience to some other form of organic life. (3) The intelligibility of the world and its instrumentality in the realization of humanly previsioned ends. (4) The temporal progressiveness of the cosmic process through levels of matter, life, and mind, in an order of increasing valuational significance.

A word of explanation about this last point: while this statement appears to imply my belief in both cosmic and biological evolution, such an inference should not be made. The point of emphasis is on the fact that regardless of the proximate mode through which these levels appeared—whether evolution or direct creation—they *did* appear in the order suggested. The determination of this exact mode of production, while it may be significant, appears to me to be of

---

[4] I acknowledge a conscious dependence here on the work of F. R. Tennant, *Philosophical Theology*, II, p. 81f. But my detailed analysis differs markedly from that of Tennant and attempts to transcend the purely empirical and hypothetical status within which he tragically constricts the theistic explanation.

no *apologetic* significance whatever, so far as our present argument is concerned.

Analysis of the Areas of Adaptation

(1) *The Fitness of the Inorganic in the Production and Maintenance of Life*

The argument stated.—Regardless of the proximate mode whereby organisms were produced, it is universally conceded that the inorganic realm temporally preceded the organic and was the environment for the latter's appearance and sustenance.

But a vast complex of inorganic conditions, uncalculated in their precise extent, is essential to make the appearance and continued existence of life possible. In the case of the existence of life on the earth as now constituted, there would be included in such conditions "the size of the earth, the distance from the sun, the temperature and the life giving rays of the sun, the thickness of the earth's crust, the quantity of water, the amount of carbon dioxide, the volume of nitrogen. . . ."[5]

Nor is the situation appreciably altered by the assertion that had the inorganic conditions been different, other forms of life than the present ones, consonant with such conditions, would have appeared: for the existence of any forms of life would still depend on a complex multiplicity of conditions continuously maintained through long temporal periods.[6]

Now then, such a required complex of inorganic conditions is so intricately and essentially related to organic life that "there would seem to be a development of this fitness for life, involving convergence of innumerable events toward a result, *as if that result were an end to which the inorganic processes were means.*"[7] But such adaptation of a multiplicity of means in the production of an end is precisely the mark of intelligence or mind. Now surely it will not be argued that molecules and atoms possess the required intelligence and that *they* conspired of themselves to produce organic life: yet it is these material constituents that are most ultimate in the universe. If therefore the very structure of matter, and its complex ar-

[5]A. Cressy Morrison, *Man Does Not Stand Alone,* pp. 99-100. Numerous attempts have been made to detail these conditions; beside Morrison, see also P. Lecomte du Noüy, *Human Destiny.*

[6]Tennant, *op. cit.,* II, p. 87.

[7]*Ibid.,* p. 86, italics mine.

rangement in the space-time universe so as to be a fit environment of organic life, should require explanation in terms of intelligence, then that intelligence or mind must have an existence that transcends matter and its resultants: it must be, in other words, a transcendent mind that so oriented matter and its arrangements in the first place, that organic life might appear.[8]

The possibility of chance.—While intelligent will is a possible hypothesis for the explication of the complex interrelatedness of the organic and inorganic realms, is not the hypothesis of chance at least mathematically possible? In a game of dice, for example, the chance that I will throw double fours is only one to thirty-five. But now it is still possible to throw double fours even on the first try. And as a matter of fact, the chance against any particular throw at all is thirty-five to one. Even if the universe is unique, it might have resulted from a single throw.[9] And as a matter of fact, the universe is constantly "throwing its dice": by the law of averages, the complex of conditions required for organic life *could* therefore have occurred by chance concatenation. And in any case, as with the dice so here: any arrangement of the elements of the world would be altogether as improbable as any other.

This objection is fully considered and refuted in Section B, Chapter IV. But a brief summary of the answer is here in order because of its essential relation to our whole movement of thought. In the first place, before we even approach the objection itself, it is well to point out that the ultimacy of matter in motion has already been refuted in the cosmological argument, since such an ultimacy involves self-contradiction. In the present context it would involve such difficulties as the following:

If matter in motion is an ultimate explanation of reality, why have not organisms always existed? For at any given point of time the series would already have run through all possible configurations and thus all possible results would already have transpired. Yet it is conceded on all hands that organisms are not eternal. If the objector falls back on the thesis that the emergence of life has occurred repeatedly in past eternity—if, in brief, he falls back on the doctrine of the alternation of worlds or cycles of existence—he has not escaped the difficulty at all but merely moved it to a different level. For the series of cycles must then be infinite: and then the cycle we are now

[8] The possibility that there might be a plurality of such intelligent wills is considered and refuted in Section B, Chapter II.
[9] Cf. Tennant, *op. cit.*, II, p. 88.

in must already have transpired or else it must have existed from eternity. The former is manifestly ridiculous, and the latter contradicts the original hypothesis of cycles.

But to consider the hypothesis of chance on its own merits—and shall we first consider the dice, then the universe. While it is true that the chance of any given throw is one in thirty-six, it is also true that only thirty-six possible combinations exist: only that can be thrown with the dice that is already involved in their constituent make-up. It is further the case that in a series of throws every successive throw eliminates an increasingly large number of other possible orders in which the throws might have been executed. And it is finally the case that the only significant and "valuable" results of a series of throws are those which intelligence previsioned in setting the conditions of the game itself (e.g., winning the game, or spending an hour relaxing).

Now apply the analogy to the emergence of the organic in an inorganic environment. Assuming for the sake of argument that life is completely explicable in terms of material constituents alone—an assumption difficult enough in itself, since life is certainly more than a series of material elements in motion; assuming this, only such effects can result from the motion of material elements as are *already involved in the constituent make-up* of the elements themselves as possibilities. Consequently, if organsims do appear, as indeed they have, it is as if the original elements had themselves been adapted to the possibility of this production.

Will anyone argue that any conceivable constitution of material elements will inevitably produce life? I can myself imagine a universe in which this is not so: a universe, for example, of two perfectly homogeneous masses of spherical shape, endowed with gravitational attraction and devoid of initial velocity. The motion of such a universe will always be the same. It therefore appears to be false that any conceivable arrangement of material elements necessarily contains the possibility of organisms. If therefore such a possibility exists, it must be as a result of such an arrangement and constitution of the elements themselves as is only reasonably explicable in terms of an intelligent selection from among an indefinite number of other material constitutions and arrangements in which this possibility would *not* be contained.[10]

[10]Cf. W. E. Hocking, *Types of Philosophy*, pp. 107-114, for a similar argument.

But just as a game of dice does not consist in a single throw, so the production and maintenance of organic life in the universe is not the result of a single eruption of mindless matter: a game of dice consists in a succession of throws, and the universe consists in a succession of motions, on the naturalistic hypothesis. Now just as each throw of dice in succession eliminates an increasingly large number of other possible successions consonant with the make-up of the dice, so each motion of the elements does the same. Suppose then that by chance the possibility of organisms *was* contained in the original constitution of the elements *without* the activity of a previsioning intelligence, and suppose that organisms had been struck out at some fortuitous juncture: what is the possibility, in terms of pure chance, that the motion of the elements will sustain organic life through an indefinitely extended succession of subsequent motions? With each successive motion that sustains organic life, the hypothesis of its motion being explicable in terms of pure chance diminishes until we can say that it is almost infinitely improbable that the production and maintenance of organic beings is explicable in terms of pure chance.

Now someone will object that the destruction of life likewise becomes almost infinitely improbable: or flatly, that any arrangement of elements in a complex universe is almost infinitely improbable from the standpoint of chance. But this is precisely the point to emphasize: namely, that any explanation whatever of the elements of the world, in terms of pure chance, *is* almost infinitely improbable and is therefore not an explanation that ought to be accepted by a rational mind!

But horrors! We have forgotten the dice! After all, chance does explain a game of dice, doesn't it? Yet the answer is plainly that chance does not explain a game of dice, for the only significant results emerging from such a game are those previsioned by intelligence in setting the conditions of the game itself. All the possibilities of the dice—so far as the game is concerned—originated in a conscious adaptation of means to an end; namely, in this case, the amusement of the mind (or the advancement of one's bank account, or what have you) which results from an ignorance of the exact causal factors that produce a given combination on the dice. Furthermore, the throwing of dice is not even a game unless the ends to be realized are prescribed in advance and made possible by the conditions of the operations involved.

We therefore conclude that any chance explanation of the universe, and in particular of the complex interrelation between inorganic and organic existence, is almost infinitely improbable as an explanation. When we add to this the self-contradictory character of an assumed infinite series of motions, the improbability of a chance explanation becomes absolute. Consequently, we may affirm that a chance explanation of the fitness of the inorganic in the production and maintenance of life is absolutely improbable and that therefore such fitness is explicable only in terms of a transcendent intelligent will that endowed material elements with the necessary potentialities for their essential function in connection with the existence of the whole organic realm.

(2) The Internal Adaptedness of Organic Beings

The argument stated.—When attention is shifted from the general relation between inorganic and organic realms to a consideration of the latter sphere itself, a whole further range of adaptations appears. In general, adaptations within the organic realm are of two major types:

(a) Adaptation of the structure of various organs to subserve a given end: e.g., that of the eye to seeing, or of the ear to hearing. Just as the existence of life at all required the conspiration of a complex multiplicity of conditions, so with the structure of such specialized parts of a given organism: the structure of the part is so intricate and its functioning reciprocally with the rest of the organism so complicated that we can scarcely avoid the conclusion that the eye, for example, is constructed *as if* for the purpose of seeing. But of course, the construction of a thing to fulfill a purpose that is still future can only be the work of mind, or previsioning intelligence.

(b) Adaptation of the whole functioning of the organism to subserve either its own continued self-maintenance, or the benefit of some other organic being in its environment. A. E. Taylor expands this point at great length:

> The way in which a [biological] process shall take place appears to be determined not simply by reference to the earlier stages of natural process of which it is the continuation, but even more by reference to the later and still future results which are

to come out of the present. . . . The healthy organism in normal conditions continues the process by responding to the present situation with just that continuation which is valuable as preserving the individual organism or making for the continuance of the species.[11]

Such adaptations may be: (i) to the needs of the immediate future, as when a membrane on a given organism pushes oxygen inward, without regard to the purely mechanical laws of diffusion, wherever there is need for an extra supply of oxygen;[12] (ii) to the needs of the remote future, as when insects deposit eggs on "a particular kind of leaf which will supply suitable nourishment for the coming generation of grubs, though the insects themselves will die before the eggs are hatched."[13]

All nature is replete with just such prospective adaptation of the action of organisms to future needs: "Animal life seems to disclose intelligence everywhere adapting the present to the needs of the still unborn future, though, except in man, the directing intelligence does not appear to be embodied in the individual animal organism."[14]

Here again, the crucial point is that the adaptation of present action to future ends or needs is a function of intelligent will. Surely the membrane does not deliberately determine its own action with a view to organic needs, nor does the insect prevision its progeny in depositing its eggs where it does, as a man might set up a trust fund for his unborn child. Yet such actions do display just such deliberate determination. Thus the supposition of a transcendent intelligent will that guides these processes becomes unavoidable.

The possibility of chance.—It is often alleged that the theory of organic evolution discredits entirely any such mode of argumentation as we have attempted to propound: for evolution shows us how, through mutations and natural selection, both the special structure of particular organs and the apparent adaptedness of present functions to future ends may be explained in naturalistic terms without the supposition of a transcendent, or even an immanent, intelligence. Every case of such adaptation is explicable if only we grant credence to the supposition that in the long course of organic history only those variants or mutants were preserved that, by chance concatena-

[11]*Does God Exist?*, pp. 46, 47.
[12]*Ibid.*, pp. 47, 48.
[13]*Ibid.*, p. 48.
[14]*Ibid.*, pp. 54, 55.

tion of various factors, did adapt successfully to their total environment. It is no marvel, then, that the eye is adapted to seeing if it was itself generated from the environmental womb! Even a thinker like Tennant seems to make unusual concessions to this type of objection.

Now this objection is considered in detail at Section B, Chapter IV, of this part; and the reader is referred to that context for an expansion of the brief remarks that follow. Before the objection itself is even approached, it should be noted that it is antecedently exposed to the charge of immense improbability. It has already been shown that the existence of organic beings at all is absolutely inexplicable in terms of chance. Shall an attempt *now* be made to explain the adaptedness of the organic realm itself in terms of the same barren hypothesis? Is not such a procedure more desperate than it is rational?

But to consider the hypothesis on its own merits: suppose, for the sake of argument, that organic evolution affords a sufficient explanation, causally, of the proximate factors operative in the production of such specialized functions as are now in question: does the proximate mode by which a given end is achieved alter its character as an end? Suppose, for example, that the vertebrate eye was produced through a long series of mutations which were fit to survive: does this alter the fact that it is adapted to seeing? Or what is more significant, would not the whole evolutionary process itself, as related to the eye, appear to be adapted to the fulfillment of the anticipated functioning of sight? After all, in human life, we do not deny an end merely on the basis of its having been effected through a long series of proximate causes. We call an effect an end if its *resultant character* is such that it is only explicable as a previsioned goal, irrespective of the complexity of proximate causes involved.

As a matter of fact, however, such explanation in terms of organic evolution alone seems inadequate even at the level of proximate causes. The changes evolving any given adaptation would have to be explained as effected either through sudden mutations of marked degree or through minute variations.[15] In the former case the whole force of our teleological argument stares us in the face: if a structure is suddenly produced with an immense adaptive advantage and in an environment that has not evoked this effect in other cases, then does

[15]*Ibid.*, p. 60f.

it not immediately appear that the structure was produced with this adaptive advantage as an end? If the basic structure of the vertebrate eye is explicable as a sudden mutation, then teleology rises full of life in the midst of considerations bent upon its destruction.

If, on the other hand, the appropriate changes take place through minute variations, "it follows that during most of the period over which the process is going on there has been *no* advantage derived from the variations, and no reason, therefore, why they should have been preserved by 'natural selection.' "[16] Thus in either case, the argument for prospective contrivance, and hence for intelligent guidance, is not impaired in the slightest degree. Have your evolutionary

I conclude that organic evolution, even if thoroughly valid, does not constitute an explanation which eliminates the necessity of supposing a transcendent intelligence to account for the internal adaptedness of organic beings. The structure of such beings and their action in the environment evince such adaptation to previsioned ends that the whole of these processes is explicable only in terms of just such an intelligent will.

(3) The Intelligibility of the World and Its Instrumentality in the Realization of Humanly Previsioned Ends

The argument stated.—At the summit of the cosmic process, so far as we know it, appears a being that possesses more than a mere adaptation to environment, more than internal adaptedness of its organic constituents: this being is man, and this more that he possesses is intelligence, or mind, or self-conscious personality.

This mind consists, in part, of a rational structure with which the data of experience are approached and made intelligible: and the remarkable thing is that when intelligence approaches experience, it finds a world constituted through the very categories that are basic in the structure of rationality itself. The world is a cosmos, a rational order: and as such it is amenable to interpretation by a rational mind. "There must be one rational order in the universe and in us."[17] The categories of thought and the categories of things are identical in their significance and reciprocal relations.

Thus it appears that the intelligence of man is adapted to understanding the world that envelops him: and just as the former cases

[16]*Ibid.*, pp. 60, 61, and note.
[17]W. N. Clarke, *An Outline of Christian Theology*, p. 107.

of adaptation in the world of nature have shown us, so we may infer that the prospective adaptation of the whole natural world to an intelligence that was last to appear on the cosmic scene, the shaping of nature as if it were meant to be understood and of mind as if it were meant to understand—we may infer, I say, from these facts that the whole integration and adaptation of thought to things bespeaks an intelligent will moving toward the realization of just this end.

But not only does human intelligence understand the world through a categorical structure that characterizes both itself and its world: such intelligence finds that the world is amenable to the realization of humanly previsioned ends. Because the world is a causal order, it is amenable to control by a rational being that seeks to comprehend its causal structure. The whole advance of science proclaims that nature may be bent to subserve human ends: and yet it is conceivable, from a purely naturalistic point of view, that the world might have been so constituted as to elude such an instrumental significance.

We have already attempted to illustrate our point with the analogy of the flute: any other human contrivance might have served as well. Every instance, in which intelligent adaptation uses a means to effect some anticipated end, implies that the environment of man has been constructed *as if* it were intended thus to make subservience to intelligent manipulation by individual minds possible. But again, such anticipatory adaptation to the realization of a future end is itself, as we have often observed, the mark of intelligent will, which must therefore undergird the total cosmic process. The conclusion that James Ward draws therefore seems justified: *"Nature itself* is teleological, and *that* in two respects: (1) it is conformable to human intelligence and (2), in consequence, it is amenable to human ends."[18]

The possibility of chance.—Again the question presses upon us: could all this have occurred by chance? Could the remarkable adaptation of human intelligence to the understanding and manipulating of its environment be merely a special case of natural selection, a mere concretion of the allegedly ateleological evolutionary process?

Our previous analysis already enables us to formulate the answer: if mere natural selection does not explain the complex adaptation of organic beings to their environment, neither will such an explana-

[18]James Ward, *Naturalism and Agnosticism*, pp. 543, 544.

tion serve, in the present context, to explain the adaptation of the environment to subserve rational ends.

But aside from the general insufficiency of the evolutionary hypothesis at this point, two particularly pertinent remarks are in order. In the first place, is the emergence of mind what would naturally be expected as the climax of a naturalistically explicable evolutionary process? Apparently not. As Taylor points out:

> What such a process by itself should logically lead to would be a vast multiplicity of definite adjustments to definite situations, each being in fact conducive to some future result beneficial to the individual, or its species, or both. There is no reason in the nature of the case why these adjustments should be accompanied in man with foresight of the benefit to which they conduce. . . . And there is still less reason why the supposed process should lead to the kindling of an intelligence which is not content to adapt its behavior to the situations furnished by the environment as they arise, but sets itself to transform the environment into conformity to its own demands.[19]

This reasoning seems to me to be unanswerable: mind is simply *not* what would logically be expected to result from the evolutionary process if it operated without initial and subsequent intelligent guidance.

In the second place, is mind explicable as having risen from a series of proximate causes that are themselves devoid of self-conscious nature? Mind, as we shall presently attempt to establish, is so transcendent of the possibilities of matter that its rise from purely material proximate causes is impossible. Further discussion of this point is deferred for consideration of the teleological argument from the microcosmic point of view.

(4) The Temporal Progressiveness of the Cosmic Process

The argument stated.—W. E. Hocking points out that one of the characteristic marks of a process which we denominate consciously purposive is that the process produces results of assignable value:[20] and beyond that these results should appear in a general order that progressively involves increasing assignable value with respect to some telic frame of reference. Thus, for example, I may habitually pass a certain lot near my home in the course of frequent walks. On

[19] Taylor, *op. cit.*, pp. 70, 71.
[20] Hocking, *op. cit.*, p. 111.

a given day I notice that a hole has been dug on the lot, and subsequently I note that concrete floor and walls (as I take them to be) are taking shape in the hole: and so the several steps toward the building of a house ensue. Now I call this process consciously purposive for numerous reasons: but certainly one of these reasons is that I note a certain production of increasingly valuable effects which are oriented to the production of an over-all end or goal. Nor do I need to know the specific character of the end in order to make the inference: what I do need to observe is the increased complexity of mutual interrelation which the parts of the project progressively embody.

Now consider the temporal advance of the whole cosmic process itself: it proceeds through levels of matter, life, and mind in this very order. Each level has an increasing assignable value as over against preceding levels: for each of the later levels not only embodies a more complex adaptiveness to its environment but also itself appears, as we have seen, to be an end toward the production of which the preceding levels are adapted as means. Thus matter is so constituted as to be consonant with the possibility of life, and the stream of life is so directed as to provide in man an organic counterpart for the realization of rational experience.

Matter so exists *as if* it were intended as the environment of organic life. This life in turn is so directed *as if* it were intended to be the scene of intelligent being. As Lecomte du Noüy says: "This amounts to the recognition of the existence of a goal, of an end. . . . Therefore, everything has taken place as if, ever since the birth of the original cell, Man had been *willed*. . . ."[21]

Now this progressive determination of events with respect to a previsioned future is, as always, explicable only in terms of an intelligent will whose purpose is ever rising to realization in the cosmic process. And if the temporal order gives us a hint concerning the specific ultimate purpose of the Divine Will, we may reasonably expect to find the key to teleology in the rational experience of that intelligent being that crowns creation: i.e., in man himself. To this rational expectation we shall presently address our consideration.

Conclusion

Stepping back from the picture that a rational analysis of the macrocosm has thus painted for us, the overwhelming impression of the

[21]P. Lecomte du Noüy, *Human Destiny*, p. 225.

whole and all its parts is that all this bundle of prospective adaptation in the contingencies of nature is borne upon the giant shoulders of Divine Will and Purpose. The summary conclusion of Taylor seems amply justified:

> If intelligence has always been active in the world, then we may assume that it has been active in the way which is characteristic and distinctive of intelligence, as working towards the realization of purpose. Thus the thought which is at the basis of the familiar 'argument from design' will be thoroughly justified.[22]

FORMULATION OF THE ARGUMENT: MICROCOSMIC POINT OF VIEW

Introduction

Not only does the cosmic process move progressively through a series of adaptations to the ultimate appearance of mind at the summit, but this highest realized level of contingent reality itself possesses a nature that utterly transcends the potentialities and possibilities of the lower levels of life and matter: transcends them in such a way that mind is inexplicable as purely a development from such levels.

The transcension of mind, if we may thus speak, comes significantly to the fore in two distinct but closely related aspects of intelligence: (1) the *metaphysical:* the very nature of thought, as the characteristic action of mind, and the very nature of self-consciousness as the mode of mind's existence—these factors show mind to be so disparate from matter that the sufficient cause of the former necessarily transcends the latter; (2) the *moral:* not only is mind metaphysically beyond all the possibilities of a material base, but it also has a further capacity that nowhere else appears in the whole advance of the cosmic process—the capacity, that is, of turning back upon itself and its actions to consider, not merely what it is and does in a descriptive sense, but what it *ought* to be and do in a moral sense. Man as rational faces an imperative which specifies the goal of his rational experience.

The very crowning point of teleological argumentation—indeed, of theistic argumentation—consists in showing that such an imperative for rational life is absolute, and explicable only when thought moves to the assertion that the absolutely necessary being, the intelligence that guides the cosmic process, is a being who supports the absoluteness of the moral imperative and whose nature is therefore that of absolute goodness. When this climax is reached, natural revelation will have run its course in establishing theism as the only sufficient explanation of the total gamut of experience. To the detailed consideration of the metaphysical and moral aspects of mind we now therefore direct our attention.

The Metaphysical Argument: from the Nature of Mind

A. The Naturalistic View of Mind

To account for the presence of mind in the cosmos without appeal to an Ultimate Mind as its sufficient explanation, it is necessary to show how mind might conceivably have arisen from an ultimate material base and be explicable in terms of constituents which are themselves ultimately material in their nature.

In general, the attempt, to meet this need has been executed in two distinct ways: (1) *Materialism* or *Behaviorism* alleges that mind is itself materially constituted, that thought is explicable as itself a series of material elements: perhaps, for example, as a series of motions in the brain. (2) *Functionalism* urges that while the mind is certainly not a series of motions in the crass materialistic sense, it is explicable as a set of functions, which could not exist without the physical organism (especially the brain and the central nervous system) and which are therefore understandable as having originated from an ultimate material base.

One of the principal variants of this last view is epiphenomenalism, or the doctrine that consciousness is an inconsequential by-product of neural states with no reciprocal causal efficacy of its own. What I call functionalism is sometimes criticized as being purely identical with epiphenomenalism: but the relation is rather that the latter is a minor subtype of the former. In our discussion only the general position of functionalism will be considered, it being taken for granted that the refutation of the general theory will also expose the inadequacy of its subtypes.

Materialism or Behaviorism.— (i) The doctrine stated: according to the materialistic or behavioristic theory of mind, thought is explicable in physical terms because it consists purely and simply in a series of physical motions. Classical Watsonian behaviorism in psychology takes the position, originally, that the motions in question are those of the speech organism or of some other physical process that acts as a substitute for speech: thinking is merely talking with concealed musculature.[23] But the more usual view would be that thought is a series of motions in the brain: in any case, the general thesis is that *some physical process* is to be identified with thought and that therefore any explanation of mind by appeal to some supraphysical cause is utterly superfluous.

(ii) Refutation of the doctrine: this view has been so frequently and so thoroughly refuted that scarcely more than a brief catalogue of decisive objections needs to be mentioned.[24] As for the behavioristic suggestion that thinking is talking with concealed musculature, the objections of Blanshard seem decisive. He points out the following crucial facts: first, language may vary while thought is the same, as in the expression of the same thought in three different languages; second, thought may vary while speech remains the same, as in the pronunciation of an expression twice when only the second time its meaning is discerned; third, thought may be present without speech, subvocal or not, as in a simple act of perception, or in cases where an argument is read silently while numbers are being repeated aloud; and finally, language mechanisms may be at work where thought is not present, as in the repetition of nonsense syllables or the talking of a parrot.[25]

As for the general assertion that thought is to be identified with some physical process, such as motion in the brain, this theory is open to at least seven conclusive objections:

(a) The theory cannot account for memory and communication. If thought is identified with motion in the brain (or anywhere else in the organism), how is it ever possible to remember a previous experience? For when a motion has once become past it is never repeated as the same motion. But it may be insisted that while all the given motions are numerically distinct, they may be generically the same: yet how could we know this or be aware of it? To classify two entities as in the same genus, it is necessary to observe a similarity between them. But on a materialistic basis, the thought of similarity would have to be a motion also: and before it occurs, the

[23]Cf. B. Blanshard, *The Nature of Thought*, I, p. 317f.
[24]Cf. G. H. Clark, *A Christian View of Men and Things*, pp. 319-321, for a very brief but cogent refutation; Blanshard, *op. cit.*, I, pp. 317-338, for a more lengthy and completely overwhelming refutation.
[25]Blanshard, *op. cit.*, I, pp. 320-326.

motion of the original experience and the motion of the alleged memory experience would be past. And the question arises: how could any motion connect two motions that no longer exist?[26] Thus the very possibility of thinking generically similar thoughts—a possibility essential to the process we call memory—exists only on the supposition that materialism is false.

But if memory impugns materialism, so also does the communication of thought from one mind to another: for here again there is a generic similarity of thought that is materialistically inexplicable. In communication, when it is effected, the generically same idea exists in two minds at once: and an awareness of this similarity is possible—if not, the long hours I have spent on this book are certainly futile. But if the generically same motion existed in two minds at once, this fact could never be known except by discovering their similarity, a discovery which we have already shown to be impossible on the materialistic hypothesis. And in communication, there is this added difficulty: that if a thought is a motion, then the decision to communicate it is also a motion. And how can I connect *this* motion with the former that no longer exists? Communication therefore seems to be impossible on a materialistic view of mind. And "if, in opposition, anyone wishes to deny that an immaterial idea can exist in two minds at once, his denial must be conceived to exist in his own mind only . . ."[27] and there is no need to refute it.

(b) The theory cannot explain qualities, like color, for example. This point is elaborated by W. E. Hocking.[28] Scientific analysis reduces the external world to quantitative factors. The existence of qualities like color, taste, odor, etc., depends on a relation to the percipient: "The color is merely our personal view of a certain vibration rate, and similarly with sounds and other qualities which appeal to sense."[29]

But on the materialistic view, the quality is merely a vibratory disturbance of the nerves and brain of the percipient: yet these last are also physical objects by hypothesis, so that, for example, "if there is no color in the wave, neither is there any color in the eye or brain."[30] But qualities certainly do exist *as qualities* somewhere, for

[26] So Clark, *op. cit.*, p. 320; although I have altered his argument considerably.
[27] *Idem.*
[28] Hocking, *op. cit.*, p. 95f.
[29] *Ibid.*, p. 95.
[30] *Idem.*

they are integral parts of our experience: and if they do not exist in any physical object as physical, they must exist in a consciousness that transcends the physical. Consequently, materialism is again impugned.

(c) The theory fails to explain either truth or logical sequence. If a thought is a motion, it must be completely determined by antecedently and contemporaneously existing motions to which it is related. But in this case, no thought could be either true or false as compared with any other, since all thoughts would be equally determined effects of other motions and hence on an absolute par with one another. How, indeed, can we speak of a motion as erroneous or correct?[31] In the face of such considerations, Hocking facetiously but justly remarks: "Of what temperamental bias or atmospheric influence is naturalism the effect?"[32]

But of equal importance is the observation that what determines a logical sequence of thought is not the operation of physicochemical elements as such, but the perception of rationally necessary connection. What determines the conclusion of a syllogism? For example: All men are fools; husbands are men; therefore husbands are fools. If we grant these premises—which I hope are false—what determines the conclusion? Is it a series of motions in the brain? Or is it the logical relations that subsist between or among the premises? And surely no one would argue that the physical and the rationally necessary thus happily coincide by accident, especially if one is motivated to deny teleology: for not only would we suspect at once that this situation was no accident but an arrangement; we would also ask how a mistake in argument could then ever be made, since all conclusions would be equally determined by motions. "To suppose that the physical laws are so adjusted as to turn out a product exactly parallel to the steps of a rational demonstration is an assumption of design so stupendous that it would cast all other proof of teleology into the shade."[33]

Thus neither truth nor valid logical sequence can exist in a materialistic universe, not to mention error and invalidity: and if it occurs to anyone to deny that truth exists, he must *ipso facto* admit that even his denial is devoid of truth or significance.

(d) The theory cannot account for the characteristic purposive

---

[31]Cf. Blanshard, *op. cit.*, I, pp. 337, 338.
[32]Hocking, *op. cit.*, p. 102.
[33]James, Orr, *The Christian View of God and the World*, p. 149.

function of mind. The characteristic action of mind, as we have seen, is the adaptation of existing means to the production of previsioned ends: and in this function mind is, by anticipation, extended into the future. Yet the brain is entirely in the present: in what sense can an existing and present physical motion anticipate some future set of motions? As Hocking suggests, nothing can locate an image in the future except a mind which holds an anticipated future before it.[34] Such adaptation of present means to a previsioned end is therefore inexplicable except on the hypothesis that the intelligence which executes this function is qualitatively distinct from the physical or material.

(e) The theory fails to explain the fact that conscious states and bodily movements have mutually exclusive attributes. This is Blanshard's point and he states it well.[35] An idea, for example, is clear or confused, witty or dull, etc.; a motion has velocity, direction, and what have you. Now then, how will the behaviorist or materialist answer such questions as the following: what is the average velocity of the concept *man?* Or do concepts of relativity proceed in a northeasterly or some other direction? How witty is the motion of the planet Mars? Or what is meant by the assertion that the motion of an electric fan is confused? Could existences with such mutually exclusive attributes possibly be identical? Obviously not.

(f) The theory fails to explain the fact that an elaborate knowledge of a given conscious state may be had without any knowledge of the physical correlates, and vice versa: whereas, if the conscious states *are* the physical correlates, the knowledge of what one is would involve the knowledge of the other. Yet obviously I can and do understand complex trains of thought without understanding anything about motions in the brain with which they might be correlated, and vice versa. Materialism, if true, would at least relieve the mind of the student: for he could choose between physiology and psychology, knowing that the knowledge of the one was neither more nor less than that of the other. I suppose that even a casual glance through textbooks in these two fields would rapidly bring such an innocent to a repudiation both of his assumption and of the materialism on which it rests.

(g) Finally, the very process by which the materialistic theory is developed involves its falsity.[36] Beginning with differences of consciousness, say in the perception of red and yellow, the materialist then seeks correlates for these in the nerves and brain of the organism. But this very procedure assumes that the conscious state is distinct from the sought physical correlate, so that the two are not identical.

A final blow may be struck by noting that we do after all experience conscious states as something totally distinct from the motion of material constituents: and how does such an illusory appearance arise in a materialistic universe? Thus Blanshard writes:

> In spite of the fact that nothing exists but matter in motion, we have managed to conjure up a luxuriant jungle of mythology, in the way of sensations, pleasures and displeasures, emotions and ideas, which has not the least foundation in anything that anyone has ever observed. The thing is as inexplicable as it is scandalous.[37]

What may justly be concluded from the foregoing considerations? It is surely not an overstatement to say that no explanation of mind, as derived from an ultimate material base, is possible in terms of the assertion that the mental and the physical subsist in a relation of identity.

Functionalism.— (i) The doctrine stated. In the face of difficulties like the foregoing, functionalism attempts to find a middle road by asserting that, while the mind and its thoughts cannot be equated with physical motion *simpliciter,* nevertheless mind *can* be explained as a function which could not exist without the physical organism and which is therefore explicable as ultimately having arisen from a material base.[38]

How are we to describe mind? Mental images, on the one hand, are clearly not identical with the physical-chemical processes which make their occurrence possible.[39] " 'Mind' . . . signifies a *set of functions* and not a simple entity or thing (whether brain or spiritual substance) ; it comprises a wide range of both capacities and activities on the part of the human organism. Mind is therefore an aspect of the organism's behavior."[40]

---

[36]*Ibid.,* pp. 330, 331.
[37]*Ibid.,* pp. 334, 335.
[38]J. H. Randall, and J. Buchler, *Philosophy: An Introduction,* p. 238.
[39]*Idem.*
[40]*Idem.*

But if mind is clearly not matter in motion, how can we explain its origin from an ultimate material base? In the first place, we should forbear assuming "that no causes can give rise to products of a more precious or elevated kind than themselves. . . . How vastly nobler and more precious, for instance, are the higher vegetables and animals than the soil and manure out of which, and by the properties of which, they are raised up."[41]

But by way of particular explanation: the effect of a cause may involve conditions different, in some respect, from those which give rise to it. Water, for example, is neither hydrogen nor oxygen but a new product different from either of its constituents. Thus new causal factors may continually rise and at the same time influence the circumstances under which the old operate.[42] Further, the laws of nature are illustrated repeatedly, but the specific conditions under which they are illustrated are never exactly the same: the laws are constant, the facts vary.

Now among the new facts a new pattern or repeated relationship may be exhibited, so that a new law is added. Thus physical laws could produce, under differing conditions, that set of functions we call life: and physical and biological laws could produce, by similar interaction, the set of functions we call mind.[43] Thus the functionalist would describe the origin of life, and particularly of mind, from an ultimate material base.

(ii) Refutation of the doctrine. The question whether life is explicable in the manner suggested is not germane to my present purpose and I therefore omit the detailed consideration of it, except as it bears on the proposed explanation for the origin of mind. In either case, it has already been shown that the appearance of life and mind at all, regardless of its proximate mode, is inexplicable apart from the supposition of an ultimate intelligent will.

But to consider the doctrine at hand: in the first place, what is the meaning of the allegation that mind, while it is not to be identified with physicochemical processes, is nevertheless a set of functions executed by the organism and not the activity of an immaterial self? A function must be a function of something or it does not exist: has anyone ever seen a function out by itself for an afternoon walk?

Now either the functions which we call mind are operations of the

[41]J. S. Mill, *Three Essays on Religion*, p. 67.
[42]Randall and Buchler, *op. cit.*, p. 233f.
[43]*Idem.*

physical organism or not. If they are, then they must be completely explicable in physical terms. Digestion, for example, is a function or aspect of the organism's behavior: but every part of the process is physical in its nature. The food, the stomach, the intestinal walls, etc., are all physical entities, as are their motion and action in the digestive process.

And so generally we may say that whatever is a function of the physical organism is completely explicable in physical terms: nor will it help to suggest that physical operations may produce non-physical by-products, for this is either false directly, or else it begs the question for the functionalist theory itself. If mind therefore is a function of the physical organism, it must be completely explicable in physical terms: in terms, i.e., of the motion of physical constituents. But this is simply the materialist view all over again and has already been refuted decisively.

It must therefore be that the set of functions we call mind is not that of the physical organism: but of what then are they the function, since a function must be *of something* and not of nothing, as we mentioned previously? And the only answer is that mental operations are the functions of an immaterial or spiritual substance which we call by the name *soul* or *self*. I know of no *tertium quid*, and I challenge all the naturalists of the ages from Thales to Santayana to suggest one.

But in the second place, is the naturalistic explanation of the origin of mind—however constituted—adequate to show its derivation from a material base? The naturalist urges that mind could nevertheless come from matter since effects are often radically different from the series of their proximate causes. Muscle, for example, does not resemble particularly the food which helps to build it. But in all such cases of transformation, the causes and effects, though different, are nonetheless physical: a traceable continuity of physical constituents characterizes the entire process. Yet there is no such traceable continuity from matter to mind: "if we start with a supposed unconscious matter, we can trace no continuity between it and consciousness; we find no atoms or electrons whatever as constituents of our thoughts or feelings."[44] The appearance of mind is therefore not like the appearance or production of one form of physical existence from another: for mind is not a physical entity.[45]

[44] E. S. Brightman, *The Problem of God*, p. 156.
[45] Cf. Taylor, *op. cit.*, pp. 45, 46, for a good statement of this point.

The laws of nature, it is urged, may concrete in the production of life and ultimately of mind by virtue of the fact that the specific conditions under which these laws operate are always different. But how, without begging the question, can it be shown that a nonphysical entity like mind could be produced in this manner? The effect of a physical cause, in every case except the one in dispute, is itself always physical: water may be neither hydrogen nor oxygen, but it, like them, is for all that still a physical entity, whereas mind is nonphysical by the functionalist hypothesis itself.

If therefore mind appears in a physical universe, it must be because a nonphysical causal factor is operating to produce this effect: and it is this factor that the original physical laws, in any form of expression or operation, cannot explain. Such a nonphysical factor can only be a mind or an intelligent will: both because the mind it produces is, like itself, nonphysical, and because the production of mind, as we have seen, appears to be an end toward which the whole physical realm is oriented as means—such adaptation being explicable only in terms of conscious purpose.

Thus pointedly does mind deny explanation of itself in terms of ultimate material causes. The sum of the matter is that functionalism, like materialism or behaviorism, fails to explain the origin of mind from an ultimate material base. Naturalism therefore fails to explain—indeed, *cannot* explain—the existence of mind in a universe which must be ultimately explicable in purely physical terms, if the naturalistic hypothesis is correct.

B. *The Ultimate Explanation of Mind*

How, then, is the presence of mind at the summit of the cosmic process to be explained? We have already suggested the answer. Mind, as utterly nonphysical, is explicable only in terms of a nonphysical cause, or—what is the same thing—a mind. The same intelligent will that spoke in the whole range of adaptations from the constitution of matter to the appearance of mind speaks in a more special way at this last level of existence. For the appearance of mind, while it occurs in an adapted physical context, so transcends its context as to be explicable only in terms of a transcendent spiritual Cause.

Yet man as a thinking, reasoning being has likewise an end in self-realization of the highest use to which his rationality can be put.

To the consideration of this moral end we now turn for the last step which teleology proffers to establish the existence and character of God.

The Moral Argument: from the Nature of Obligation and Value

A. *Summary of the Argument*

The characteristic action of mind is its adaptation of means to pre-visioned and desired ends: such action, in fact, prescribes the very meaning of intelligence itself from a functional point of view. But such a constitutional behavior of mind, in thus moving toward the realization of purposes, raises the question whether the pursuit of ends is ultimately no more than an interrelated series of specific adaptations, or whether at the summit of rational vision there is a supreme end to which the whole series of our subordinate ends might be related as itself a series of means.

That such an ultimate end of rational life exists would seem ante-cedently probable from a consideration of two facts: (1) First, the cosmic process itself, as we have seen, is directed toward the realiza-tion of a series of ends to which previous ends become subordinated as means, until the climax is reached in the production of mind "after the image" of the Ultimate Intelligence. By analogy it seems reasonable that rational life itself, while existing as the end or pur-pose of the cosmic process, should have a compelling goal of action which would enrich and fulfill its own status as the climax of Divine Purpose.

(2) But in the second place, the very fact that we *do* adapt means to ends is basically insignificant without the recognition of an ulti-mate end which rational life ought to realize. Action toward *any* end implies the existence of a *supreme* end.

An illustration will clarify the point: suppose I work as a ditch digger, and some bystander, seeing me at my customary employment, asks me why I spend my time digging ditches. Of course, he expects a teleological or purposive answer. So I explain that I dig ditches to make money so as to procure for myself and my family the conditions for satisfactory biological adjustment—food, clothing, shelter, etc.

Now suppose he raises the question: why do you want to make this adjustment? Perhaps I might answer that it gives me pleasure, or that it enables me to have opportunity for various casual pursuits, or what have you. But in any case, I will never return to the ditch-digging as an end in my explanation, for then the whole series of ends would collapse and it would result that there *is* no intelligent purpose or reason for my ditch-digging. That which is done for the sake of something else can never become that for the sake of which the something else is ultimately done.

Somewhere, therefore, in the series of such embarrassing questions, I must reach a point where I answer that a certain desired end is supreme and sought for its own sake alone. And thus it is that the pursuit of *any end* at all is either not an intelligent action in the final analysis, or it implies the existence of a *supreme* end that faces me as absolute and unconditional, and toward the realization of which action is being either implicitly or explicitly directed.

Now the moral argument for God is built upon this very assertion that rational life faces a supreme end that ought to be unconditionally sought. *What is the nature of this supreme end or summum bonum?* While specific and detailed answers to this question differ, there is, among ethical theories, a common core of univocity with regard to the nature of this supreme end.

(1) First, it possesses *absolute* or *intrinsic* value. This means, initially, that its status as the supreme end depends upon its own inherent nature and not upon its instrumental significance in any context whatsoever. Thus, for example, if pleasure be defined as the highest good, it is meaningless to ask why pleasure ought to be sought: for the only appropriate answer is that it simply ought to be sought and that that is the end of the matter. And thus with any other proposed specific which might be called this highest good.

Again, that the highest good possesses absolute value means that its status as the supreme end is objective to any particular human self which strives toward its realization. To say that I first impose the supreme end myself and then strive to realize it, seems meaningless: I do not impose this end, I recognize it as inherently valuable irrespective of my subjective impositions. For suppose that I myself do impose the supreme end: it follows that either I imposed it for some reason or for no reason.

Now if I imposed the end for some reason or reasons, these must lie either within the end itself or outside it. But if the reason lies outside the end, then the alleged end is not supreme but has only instrumental value— and so on until I come to an end that is recognized as supreme with no reason but its own nature. But if the reason thus lies within the end itself, this means that the end is not actually imposed but rather *recognized* as thus absolute.

But if on the other hand I impose this supreme end for no reason, the result is the same: for here again, this is just the same as saying that I impose it for its own sake, and hence that I do not *impose* it at all but merely recognize its supremacy. Consequently, the supreme end of rational life is objective to, or independent of, the wish of any particular human self: if *x is* the highest good, it is thus supreme independently of your or my personal imposition.

Finally, the absolute or intrinsic value of the highest good means that its status as the supreme end transcends temporal change: the highest good is not subject to alteration. If it were capable of change or temporal transition, it would not be the *supreme* good at *any* point in the transition: but this would mean that at *no* point is it the supreme good. It follows that the supreme end possesses a certain eternal or timelessly necessary validity as absolute.

(2) Second, the realization of this *summum bonum* imposes an absolute imperative for human activity: if there is an objective and intrinsically valuable end, then the very nature of such an end implies that human selves are rationally and unconditionally obligated to its realization. There is, to use Kant's familiar terminology, a *categorical* imperative for action, an imperative that is unconditional. And all actions become right or wrong in proportion as they embody an advance toward, or a retrogression from, this supreme end itself.

In the light of these considerations, the *moral argument for God* may be briefly formulated as follows:

First Premise.—Rational selves are confronted with a transsubjective and transtemporal supreme end to the realization of which they are unconditionally obligated.

Second Premise.—Such an eternally valid end cannot subsist alone but must be existentially based in an eternal mind whose nature both recognizes and embodies the absolute good.

Conclusion.—There exists, consequently, just such an eternal mind whose nature is absolute goodness.

This whole argument is masterfully summarized by Sorley:

> Persons are conscious of values and of an ideal of goodness, which they recognize as having undoubted authority for the di-

rection of their activity; the validity of these values or laws and of this ideal, however, does not depend upon their recognition: it is objective and eternal; and how could this eternal validity stand alone, not embodied in matter and neither seen nor realized by finite minds, unless there were an eternal mind whose thought and will were therein expressed? God must therefore exist and his nature be goodness.[1]

Perhaps the second premise requires some additional explanation: why must an eternally valid end be thus existentially grounded in an eternal mind? Because value can exist only for a mind or in relation to a mind. A value *is* an end proposed for intelligent action; it is by its very nature a projected goal that intelligence previsions or directly discerns as an end.

But we have already seen that the effecting of ends at all implies the transsubjective and transtemporal reality of a supreme end, the validity of which is therefore not established by *my* discernment of it. Now this can only mean that the supreme end exists independently of particular finite selves *and* that it exists ultimately as embodied or fully realized: for on the opposite supposition, it would not be a supreme end, since it would be in process of transition, there being no other alternative to its full realization except the supposition that there is no such end— and this we have shown to be false.

There may be ever so many intermediate existences or minds that *partially* realize the supreme end: as you and I attempt to do, for example. But unless there is ultimately a being that fully embodies the highest good, such a highest good could not exist at all: but this is contrary to our whole analysis of human purposive activity.

There is, consequently, a being that completely realizes the absolute good. What are the immediately implied further characteristics of this being? It must be a mind, since the realization of good as such is possible only in and for a mind; it must be eternal or timelessly necessary, for the supreme end itself is thus eternal. Hence, the rationale of the second premise, and the consequent assertion that an eternal mind exists whose nature is absolute goodness.

B. *Proposed Alternatives to the Moral Argument*

   (1) Attack on the *first premise:* the denial that value is objectively valid.

[1]W. R. Sorley, *Moral Values and the Idea of God*, p. 349.

(a) *Positivism:* value statements an expression of feeling.

(i) The position stated.—It is meaningless to speak of values as objectively or transsubjectively valid: for all valuational and ethical statements are merely *verbal expressions* of the speaker's *feelings.* As such expressions are not statements of empirical fact, they do not even qualify as meaningful propositions that may be true or false: in fact, they make no assertion at all.

Thus if I say, for example, that you ought not to beat your wife, I am really not making a true or false proposition at all but am merely expressing my own personal feeling of horror at your action. It is just as if I had exclaimed with apparent and obvious horror: "You beat your wife!"

The result is that so-called ethical judgments are no different from other expressions of mere feeling or inclination. "Thou shalt not kill!" has the same status as the expression: "Ahhhh! T-bone steak!" Both express mere feelings and make no actual assertion at all. A feeling is neither true nor false: it just is!

How then can we speak of any such thing as the objective validity of moral (or any other) values? The whole of ethics is but a catalogue of verbal ejaculations which are of no more significance than a shriek of pain.[2]

(ii) The position refuted.—Very thorough and, may I say, completely decisive refutations of this position have already been made. The work of Joad is particularly significant in this respect, although he himself has undergone, if rumor is correct, some transition of thought since his criticisms were formulated.[3]

(a) In the first place, the theory is self-contradictory by virtue of its base in an extreme or radical empiricism. The theory maintains that only statements of empirical fact admit of being true or false. But this proposition itself is certainly not a statement of empirical fact: what relevant data in sense-perception may be cited to substantiate it? I have no idea what the answer might be. And if the proposition is not a statement of empirical fact, it does not admit of being either true or false. The result is that since all noncognitive statements (i.e., statements which are neither true or false and therefore assert nothing) are *emotive,* the proposition must be

---

[2] For a summary of this view, cf., P. E. Wheelwright, *A Critical Introduction to Ethics,* Chapter II; C. E. M. Joad, *A Critique of Logical Positivism,* p. 114f.

[3] Cf. *Philosophical Review* (October, 1952), p. 607. Since the completion of this MS, Joad has died (1953).

just an emotive expression and no more: it is all the same as if I had said: "Ahhhh! Empirical facts!" —and said it with an expression of delight.

Now on this line of analysis I will reach the position that all propositions are emotive or merely expressions of feeling: for any given proposition about facts could be true or false for that reason *only* if the proposition—only statements of empirical fact may be true or false—were true. But it is not true: and this by its own criterion, since it is not a statement of empirical fact. It is a mere verbal ejaculation! Thus I come at last to the assertion that truth does not exist, or—what is the same thing—that knowledge is impossible. But this is self-contradictory skepticism!

Consequently, it is false to say that only statements of empirical fact admit of being true or false: for the statement ultimately involves its own denial. How, then, can it purport to deny that value is objective in its validity? The statement of a self-contradiction, as I have often noted in these pages, is a denial of nothing but itself.

(b) But with specific reference to ethical judgments: how is it possible to classify ethical judgments as mere expressions of feeling, whether this last be understood as emotion or attitude? As for emotion: An emotion is the "effect of some prior psychological and/or physiological event which is [its] completely determining cause."[4] We cannot *will* to feel a certain emotion or not. But an ethical judgment frequently envisages my duty as something I do *not* like: such friction between duty and desire can only mean that the criterion for approval of an ethical judgment is not mere desiring or liking.[5]

As for attitude: no reduction of ethical judgment to feeling is possible on this line either. For an attitude includes an element of rational volition which apprehends an objective situation and then *wills* a particular line of conduct relatively to it.[6]

In fact, it may be said in this context that the reduction of ethical judgments to expressions of feeling overlooks the entire character of intelligent action as directed toward previsioned ends. This characteristic action of intelligence implies that moral judgments embody an attitude toward particular situations in terms of their relation to an end that we consciously espouse as supremely desirable. To say, then, that ethical judgments are mere expressions of feeling is to

[4]Joad, *op. cit.*, p. 125.
[5]*Ibid.*, pp. 125, 126.
[6]*Ibid.*, p. 126.

overlook the nature of intelligence itself as directing its activity toward such an end. And one might facetiously remark that the very considerable number of books that have been propounded by the logical positivists themselves assume just such a conscious orientation of action to ends as the theory propounded in the books implicitly denies.

On either line of analysis an ethical judgment is not a mere expression of feeling or a verbal ejaculation!

(c) The whole position of logical positivism in ethics is unintelligible except on the supposition of its falsity. Ethical judgments are declared to be *mere expressions* of feeling, or of approval and disapproval: and of course, a logical positivist expects that I know what he means by an ethical judgment. Yet if his theory were true, there would be *no way whatever* of distinguishing moral from any other kind of approval or disapproval.[7]

I ask the logical positivist to tell me what it is he is impugning when he impugns an ethical judgment by denying it truth status. And if his answer distinguishes moral approval from other types, then his theory is refuted: for the only mode of distinction would be in terms of an ascription to moral approval of something more than mere expression of feeling. But if he *fails* to tell me what he means by an ethical judgment, his assertions about such judgments will be unintelligible. Consequently, the positivist theory of ethics is unintelligible except on the supposition of its falsehood.

(d) Finally, we may ask with Joad: if ethical judgments are mere expressions of feeling, whence the luxuriant abundance of ethical terms and their distinctive usage?[8] Strange that I should say: a man *ought* to love his neighbor, or he *ought* to act rationally. But it never occurs to me to say: a man ought to like spinach; for at any given point, either he does or does not like it, period! Thus logical positivism is unable to explain the whole range of distinctive ethical terms!

I conclude that since the logical positivist theory of ethics is self-contradictory, since it fails to explain even the empirical data of ethical experience, and since its position is unintelligible apart from the supposition of its falsity; therefore it is invalid and constitutes no denial of the objectivity of value.

[7] Cf. *Ibid.*, pp. 131, 132.
[8] *Ibid.*, p. 127f.

(b) *Relativism or Subjectivism:* value statements an assertion of feeling.

(i) The position stated.—Relativism in ethics is the theory that while ethical assertions are judgments that may be either true or false, their validity or invalidity is determined solely with reference to the individual who makes the assertion: the assertion is true or false, but it is so only for the one who asserts it: "the validity of ethical judgments is determined by the feelings of some person or persons."[9]

This position is therefore at least apparently distinguishable from that of logical positivism: for the latter asserts that ethical judgments have *no* validity and make *no* assertions, while subjectivism asserts that such judgments are valid (or invalid) and do make an assertion, which however possesses truth or falsity only in relation to the feelings of the person who states the assertion. Thus when I say: I ought not to steal; what I state is an assertion which is thoroughly relative to my own personal feelings. It is true-for-me.

Since the validity of values is therefore purely subjective in its determination, no argument which asserts the *trans*subjective character of values can possibly be valid. And just such an assertion is involved in the moral argument for God.

(ii) The position refuted.—This view, like that of logical positivism, has been subjected to constant refutation. As early a writer as Plato himself clearly destroyed the fundamental relativistic basis of the argument.[10] A contemporary refutation may be found in C. H. Patterson's *Moral Standards* and in W. R. Sorley's *Moral Values and the Idea of God.*

(a) First, the position is either self-contradictory or insignificant. Relativism asserts that an ethical judgment is true only for the one who makes it and not objectively true for all minds. Man, as Protagoras said, is the measure of all things. But this statement is itself either objectively true or not. If it is not objectively true, then it is merely an assertion of the subjectivist's feelings and can lay no claim to philosophical acceptance as an ethical theory. If it is objectively true, then the relativists "contradict their own position, which is a denial of any universal truth in moral matters."[11]

Nor is there any escape in terms of the suggestion that the state-

[9]*Ibid.*, p. 115.
[10]Cf. *Theaetetus.*
[11]C. H. Patterson, *Moral Standards*, p. 63.

ment of the theory is not an ethical statement: for every alleged true statement is actually ethical in character. When I say that a proposition is true, I mean that a rational man *ought* to believe it because it is supported by rational evidence. Truth, in other words, is among the values that would be made subjective by a relativist theory. Consequently, it turns out that if relativism is taken as objectively true, it is false by its own assertion—which is self-contradictory.

(b) Second, the same point may be set in a slightly different context. If values are wholly relative to the individual valuer, there is no way of explaining how two persons can differ concerning an ethical question, or any other question, for that matter. The fact is that men do dispute such problems: even the relativist himself is disputing ethical problems in propounding his theory. But that ethical problems may be thus disputed assumes that ethical statements *do* have *objective* reference to an ultimate end which is intrinsically valuable: otherwise, debate would be impossible, just as it is impossible to debate with a man who says: I like carrots.[12]

If the hedonist and the humanist, in ethics, disagree about the nature of the good, it is not that either of them "intends something else in using the term 'good' but that, addressing himself to the intrinsically desirable, he reads the nature of it differently. Otherwise, no debatable issue would lie between these points of view."[13]

(c) Third, the relativist implies that—it being undeniable that men *do* direct their activities toward an espoused intrinsically valuable end—therefore the individual himself imposes this end as thus desirable: but we have already shown, in our analysis of the moral argument itself, that the self-imposition of a truly supreme end is unthinkable.

(d) Finally, it may be questioned whether relativism can maintain a separate identity from logical positivism: if not, then it will have already been shown to be implausible. If ethical judgments are true only with relation to their proponent and each such judgment is only true-for-me, how does such a judgment differ, in the final analysis, from a mere *expression* of feeling? Can a truth-for-me or a good-for-me be anything more than a verbal ejaculation after all? When I say, I ought to tell the truth in a given situation, I either mean that *anyone* ought to do so in a similar situation (but this con-

[12]Cf. D. E. Trueblood, *The Logic of Belief*, pp. 167, 168.
[13]C. I. Lewis, *An Analysis of Knowledge and Valuation*, p. x.

travenes subjectivism), or I mean no more than that I personally prefer the truth in this situation and that I might have said, with equal significance: "Ahhhhh! Truth!" But this would be the pure emotive theory which has already been discarded.

I therefore conclude that relativism, as a theory of value, fails to proscribe the objectivity of the good, since the basic relativist postulate is self-contradictory. And with regard to the attack on the first premise of the moral argument in general, I conclude that neither positivism nor relativism, therefore, succeeds in destroying the objective validity of value; in fact, it is only in terms of such an objective validity that human actions become meaningful at all.

(2) Attack on the *second premise:* the denial that the objectivity of value implies its complete embodiment in an eternal mind.

(a) *Logical Idealism:* the supreme end subsists eternally without embodiment in mind.[14]

(i) The position stated.—Logical idealism holds that, while the objectivity of value is undeniable, the supreme end may yet subsist eternally without being fully embodied in any particular mind: the realm of value is transsubjective and subsists eternally as a universal ideal or group of ideals. Thus the position may be characterized as: *Logical,* since it asserts that value transcends, in its eternal validity, any psychological dependence on particular finite selves which envisage the supreme end; *Idealism,* since it nevertheless denies that the supreme end is fully embodied in an existent being. Since therefore the supreme end is not thus embodied, the inference to God from the objectivity of value is unjustified.

(ii) The position refuted.—It seems to me that this view has already been refuted in my summary statement of the moral argument itself, for we there argued that it is of the very nature of a supreme end that it be thus fully embodied in an existent eternal mind. But to consider the theory on its own merits:

(a) The assertion that the good is transsubjective but not embodied in an existent being is ultimately self-contradictory. For what is meant by saying that the supreme end is objectively valid independently of its recognition by any particular finite mind?

Either this realm of values exists or not. If it does not exist, what is the significance of asserting its objective validity? The attribution of such a predicate *means* that the datum in question possesses an ob-

[14]The phrase *logical idealism* is borrowed from D. C. Macintosh, *The Problem of Religious Knowledge,* p. 147f.

jective reality which is determinative of propositions about it. If it does exist, what is the meaning of abstracting from it the predicate of *being?* I should think anyone would admit that whatever exists has being. Thus in either case, it turns out that objectively valid and eternal value has objective and eternal being: and this means that the proposition—the good is objective and eternal but not existentially embodied—is self-contradictory; for it amounts to stating that an entity which is objective is nevertheless not objective.

But to say that the good has objective and eternal being is precisely the same as saying that the good is a fully embodied existent or reality: and thus logical idealism is transcended.

(b) The same point may be stated in another way: if the supreme end has objective and absolute validity, there must be a metaphysical ground of this absoluteness: for nothing exists which does not possess the determinate conditions of its existence. Now either the supreme end contains its own ground of existence or not. But if it does not, then it is not the supreme end; for the validity of a supreme end, and hence its objectivity and reality, must be self-contained, else the alleged end would not be supreme, since its status even as an end would then depend upon some other reality. Thus the supreme end contains its own ground of existence: i.e., it is the self-existent being, the absolute that thought had originally posited in the cosmological argument. And thus again the conclusion emerges that the supreme end is fully realized in a self-existent being.

It is concluded that logical idealism is self-contradictory in its assertion that absolute value or the supreme end is not objectively embodied in a self-existent being. That such a being is an eternal mind has already been explained above in our summary of the moral argument itself.

(b) *Postulationism:* the objective existence of God as a regulative ideal.

(i) The position stated.—This view, as expounded by Kant for example, holds that the unconditional character of moral obligation involves the existence of God as a regulative ideal or postulate of practical reason: i.e., the existence of God is a hypothesis which renders the concept of the highest good intelligible and reasonable to us, but this condition of intelligibility is not a condition of objective existence.

Thus Kant says:

I find that the moral principle admits this concept [of the highest good] as possible only under the presupposition of an Author of the world having the highest perfection. . . . These postulates are not theoretical dogmas but presuppositions of necessarily practical import; thus, while they *do not extend speculative knowledge,* they give objective reality to the ideas of speculative reason in general . . . and they justify it in holding to concepts the possibility of which it could not otherwise even venture to affirm. . . . We thereby know neither the nature of our soul . . . nor the Supreme Being as they are in themselves. . . . All that is comprehended is that such a causality is postulated through the moral law and for its sake.[15]

Kant's primary argument from the categorical imperative to the theistic postulate is that the highest good must involve happiness proportional to morality and the existence of God is the sole cause adequate to this effect.[16] Since this argument seems to me vague and ambiguous, I have no intention of attempting to justify theism on such a basis.

But Kant has a second argument—similar to that expounded in the preceding pages—that the possibility of a highest *derived* good, say in the world or in our individual moral experience, involves and rests upon "the postulate of the reality of a highest original good, namely, the existence of God."[17] Here, as it seems to me, Kant is on solid ground. Yet as noted above, theism for Kant has only a regulative or postulational or hypothetical character.

Thus Kant's point in response to our argument from the objectivity of value would be that we have illegitimately pushed what is no more than a postulate to that which is objectively existent: the conditions of intelligibility should not be made conditions of objective existence in this manner.[18]

(ii) The position refuted.

(a) The principal thrust of postulationism is thus that while we necessarily posit the existence of God as the only mode of making the highest good intelligible to us, this does not mean that God necessarily exists. The general contention underlying this assertion—that

[15]I. Kant, *Critique of Practical Reason and Other Writings in Moral Philosophy,* pp. 242, 234, 236.
[16]*Ibid.,* p. 227f.
[17]*Ibid.,* p. 228.
[18]For modern exponents of the categorical imperative along Kantian lines, see W. G. de Burgh, in British.Academy (1935), pp. 75-99; W. A. Wick, in *Philosophical Review* (January, 1953), p. 19f.

the categories of thought are not necessarily those of things—has already been refuted in our analysis of Kant in Part I and it is to be subjected to further refutation in Section B of the present part, Chapter III. The reader is therefore referred to these contexts for the detailed refutation.

(b) In general, the assertion that the conditions of intelligibility are not conditions of objective existence reduces to a self-contradictory skepticism which makes knowledge impossible by hypothesis. If what I must conceive, when starting from existential premises—in this case, the objectivity of value and the unconditional character of the moral law—is not *objectively* the case, then knowledge at every level is impossible. For everything that I know is known in terms of what I must rationally conceive, for various existential reasons. And this is as true of the moral law as of anything else. But the position that knowledge is impossible is self-contradictory.

Since the whole position of postulationism rests on such a skeptical theory of knowledge and is thus self-contradictory, I conclude that the position in no way debars the moral argument from concluding the existence of an absolute and eternal being whose nature fully embodies the highest good.

(3) *Conclusion* on the proposed alternatives. Every proposed barrier to the moral argument—from positivism to postulationism—has been shown to be self-contradictory and invalid. And thus the gate of reason opens at last upon the borders of her promised land: the facts of intelligent activity and moral experience bring us face to face with the fullest embodiment of the highest good, or God!

CONCLUSION ON THE TELEOLOGICAL ARGUMENT

The whole gamut of experience, from the constituency of the basal material elements to the highest reaches of moral life that are humanly attainable, thus implies, involves, and necessitates the rational conclusion that beyond and beneath this whole system of expanding cosmic realization there stands an eternal intelligent will whose nature is absolute goodness and whose name is God!

And thus reason stands upon the limit of nature's revelation, confident that her fruits have fully ripened in a theistic world. And when all has been said she dares to stand on the scaffold of the world itself and declare as over against this complex structure of experience that nature cries aloud with her message of hope that God is real!

Part III

NATURAL THEOLOGY AND THE EXISTENCE OF GOD

SECTION B
AN ANSWER TO OBJECTIONS AGAINST THE THEISTIC ARGUMENTS

Chapter I

THE TRANSCENDENTAL ARGUMENT
OF MYSTICISM

INTRODUCTION

C RITICISM OF THE THEISTIC ARGUMENTS has been voluminous, to say
the very least. It would seem to be the case that vast forces of
human genius have conspired together for the express purpose of
destroying the rationality of a theistic philosophy: and thus men have
turned their minds to destroy the very divine purpose for which they
themselves exist. This is not to say that every critic of argumentative
theism is an avowed enemy of theism itself: yet the effect is the same,
for a theism which rests on any but rational and experiential considerations eventually destroys itself in a world where men are basically rational, even if they do volitionally distort the application of
rationality from time to time. Rationality always stands smiling in
the shadows when humanity espouses another lover: for she knows
that men will return to her in the end. The criticism of theistic
argumentation may be classified as emanating from four distinct
sources: first, the transcendental argument of mysticism urges that
all argument for God is invalid because the Divine Reality is not
knowable by rational intellect; such critics are not bent upon the
destruction of theism but on the removal of it to some blissful super-
rational realm. Again, the presuppositionalists urge that such arguments as may be propounded for theism prove no more than the
existence of a finite God, and that if they prove any God at all they
prove a multiplicity of divine beings, there being no reason to suppose that all the arguments converge on the same being; these thinkers too have no appetite for the annihilation of theism but are motivated by a desire to rest the case for theism elsewhere than in the
possibility of a theistic conclusion from argumentative considera-

tions: insofar as this objection, in the mouths of certain Christian thinkers, turns upon the inability of the natural reason to evaluate correctly the natural revelation, we have already offered critical remarks to remove the objection.[1]

Third, the reductive argument offered by Kant himself is a major source of criticism in this context: His is a doubly reductive argument, since he urges that a rational case for God is untenable, both because the rational categories admit of no fruitful application beyond the limits of possible sense-experience—thus reducing the sphere of reason to a specifically restricted area, and because he attempts to show that the whole structure of theistic argumentation reduces to the a priori and invalid form of the ontological argument, so that the entire rational edifice of theism thus vanishes. The principal motivation of Kant is, again, not the elimination of a theistic view, but the shifting of its base from a speculative rational structure to a regulative moral structure: God does indeed exist, even for Kant, but He exists as a regulative ideal for moral life, not as the first cause of either the phenomenal or noumenal worlds.

The three sources of criticism just distinguished are sharply to be differentiated from the destructive argument of critical naturalism. Whereas the former criticisms are designed to reorient the case for theism, the principal motivation of the naturalistic camp in philosophy is the crucifixion of theism on the cross of nature without the hope of subsequent resurrection. The argument proceeds by attacking the theistic evidences in isolation with the express purpose, usually, of destroying theism in favor of a bias which asserts nature itself to be the only reality.

With such prefatory remarks in view, we proceed to address our mind to the task of undercutting this entire structure of objection. While few may have gone our way before, yet it is true that a million philosophers, like Frenchmen, can be wrong.

THE TRANSCENDENTAL ARGUMENT OF MYSTICISM
THE ARGUMENT STATED

The proponent of this first major type of objection urges that God cannot be known by intellectual processes because He is ineffable, indescribable, and intellectually incomprehensible. Consequently, any process of argument that purports to result in meaningful predi-

[1] Cf. Part II, Chapter III.

cation about God is impossible. This does not mean that God is *absolutely* unknowable, but merely that He is unknowable by thought: He can be known in an immediate experience or intuitive consciousness of union with the One through a process of renunciation which is primarily moral rather than intellectual.

Thus the mystics express their objection in words like the following: "The superessential Trinity and Over-God . . . is neither an object of intellectual nor of sensible perception, nor is he absolutely anything of things existing. . . . He can neither be affirmed nor denied. . . . God is far above all predicates."[2] Or again: "To know God is to know Him as unknowable."[3] And again: "All that the understanding may comprehend, all that the will may be satisfied with, all that the imagination may conceive, is most unlike God and most disproportionate to him."[4] The objection is therefore that although God can be known directly and immediately through an inner experience, yet *what* He is cannot be conceptually known, for God, as the absolute Being, is indescribable, since any alleged description could not be true without prescribing limitations to His absoluteness.

THE ARGUMENT CRITICIZED

Difficulties of the Position

There is a sense in which a critical analysis of this transcendental argument of mysticism is love's labor lost: for if the objection is characterized by the denial that rationality may be fruitfully applied in the knowledge of God, then all rational objections will fall on deaf ears so far as the mystic himself is concerned. On the other hand, if we can show that the very contention itself is self-contradictory and unintelligible, the objection will at least be allocated to the region of insignificance. One further introductory remark is appropriate: while it is our intention to destroy the objection itself as an obstacle to the possibility of argumentative theism, it is not our motive to deny the possibility of an intimate personal knowledge of God through spiritual experience.

The objection is either self-contradictory or meaningless.—It must be the case that either the assertion, that God is unknowable, is intended to be rationally apprehensible or not: either it is itself a theory about God or it is meaningless. If it is itself a theory, it so far

[2]Dionysius; quoted in D. C. Macintosh, *The Problem of Religious Knowledge*, p. 18.
[3]Eckhart; *Ibid.* p. 19.
[4]St. John of the Cross; *Ibid.*, p. 20.

renounces its own foundations and turns back upon itself: for it is the theory that no theory about God is possible, which is self-contradictory. Furthermore, as a theory, it purports to be an interpretation of factors in human experience: in this case, of the factors involved in a specialized mystical experience with God. Hence, no argument against the possibility of concluding God from facts of experience can be asserted, for this last theory is generically similar to the mystical assertion itself in that both approaches claim to be an interpretation of factors in experience. To sum up the whole point: because the mystical objection is itself a theory, it cannot impugn argumentative theism on the ground that *it* is an intellectual theory; yet this criticism is precisely the point of the objection.

But suppose that the original assertion is not intended to be rationally apprehensible and is therefore not a theory. In this case, the objection is meaningless: it is merely a jumble of noises or a collection of unintelligible marks on a sheet of paper. And it follows that no objection is possible, for meaningless noises and unintelligible marks hardly constitute an objection. At any rate, it does not occur to us to refute this type of criticism.

The assertion, that God is unknowable by intellect but knowable by experience, embodies a basic confusion.—Even granting the possibility of an intuitive or direct knowledge of God without the mediation of *sensa,* this knowledge must be apprehended by the rational or categorical structure of the intellect, else it cannot appear as experience at all. To recognize an object of experience in particular is the function of the intellect or mind. Now if the experience of God is not the experience of something in particular, then it is the experience of nothing in particular and hence not of God or of anything else.

Does the mystic know experientially that God exists? If not, then the whole position reduces to the baseless assumption that God is unknowable—an assumption yet to be refuted in the sequel. If so, then the mystic must have an awareness of God as an experienced object: now such an awareness would either involve the intellectual functioning of the categorical structure, or it would be a completely indeterminate experience. But a completely indeterminate experience is an experience of nothing and hence not an experience at all. It must be then that the experience of God is either nonexistent or it involves an intellectual awareness of the Object: in either case, there can be no objection on principle to argumentative theism.

The theory involves a double self-contradiction.—In the first place, the objection denies the application of predicates to God and yet predicates of Him that He is indescribable, unlimited, existent, unitary, and so on. Either these terms are themselves predicates or they are meaningless: hence, the criticism asserts that predicates both can and cannot be predicated of God at the same time and in the same manner—which is logically ridiculous. The predication of indescribability itself is grounded in the conviction that God is unlimited and absolute: now either the predicate *absoluteness* is itself meaningful and hence God is not indescribable, or else the predicate is meaningless and then there is no ground for asserting indescribability. In either case, the objection is invalid.

Again, if the criticism is taken as an intellectual theory, it asserts that God both is and is not unknowable in precisely the same way. If God is unknowable, then it cannot be known that He is such. But if He is knowable, then He cannot be described as unknowable. It follows that either God does not exist at all (which is not a question in point here) or He is describable and knowable. Unless definite predicates can be asserted of God He resolves into nothing: and surely an experience of nothing is hardly one of God.

A final remark might be made to the effect that when God is described as incomprehensible out of the motivation to save His absoluteness, such absoluteness is denied in any case, both because an indescribable God is nothing and hence is not absolute, and because such a God would lack the powers of self-limitation and self-revelation, powers which enter into the meaning of absoluteness itself, as our subsequent discussion will abundantly verify.

Conclusion

It is therefore concluded that the objection reduces at every level to self-contradiction and hence forms no valid argument against the attempt to conclude God's existence from the data of objective and subjective experience. The objection is guilty either of meaninglessness or of the very inductive and rational procedures for the use of which it attempts to impugn natural theology. Hence the criticism is unsustained and argumentative theism is so far forth victorious.

Chapter II

THE EXPANSIVE-LIMITING ARGUMENT OF PRESUPPOSITIONALISM

THE SECOND TYPE OF OBJECTION to be considered is that which urges that the only God that can be established on the basis of natural revelation is a finite god and that therefore the arguments may be interpreted to establish, if anything, the existence of a plurality of gods, since no argument leads to an infinite God and since there is no reason why all the arguments conclude the same God.

THE ARGUMENT THAT GOD IS FINITE

Summary of the Argument

The assertion that a consideration of the natural revelation leads, if to any God, to the existence of a God who is but finite, has proceeded upon four similar but distinguishable grounds: the first is that the cause need be no more than finite, since the effect to be accounted for is itself finite—a finite universe does not require explanation by positing the existence of an absolutely infinite being; the second ground is that any argument to a first cause, being based on experience, can do no more than refund or exchange the qualities of experience itself—and if this is the case, we may as well rest content with the self-sufficiency of the world whole; the third ground is that the cause thus found is necessarily related to the world as to an effect and is therefore, by virtue of this relation, not an infinite or necessary being; the final ground for asserting that experience yields only a finite god is that the existence of an infinite and necessary being is incompatible either with the required goodness of such a being or with the presence in the world of ultimate and irreducible evils. This last ground of objection, since it emanates primarily from the naturalistic camp of philosophers, will be considered in connection with the refutation of naturalistic objections in Chapter IV of this present section. We proceed immediately therefore to the consideration of the first three grounds of objection as outlined above.

First Ground of Finitude in God: the Finiteness of the Effect to Be Explained

Statement of the argument.—Even if a causal argument for the existence of God is valid, the god concluded is no more than finite, for the world itself, if the causal argument is applicable, is a finite effect. This point has been urged by numerous classes of thinkers: Carnell,[1] Clark,[2] Henry,[3] Hume,[4] Strong,[5] and a host of others have given it expression. Carnell's statement may be taken as typical: and indeed it is the presuppositionalist school that has championed this criticism in contemporary theological and philosophical circles. Thus Carnell, following Hume, writes: "One may inductively introduce no more to explain an effect than a cause great enough to account for the effect, but no greater. . . . The finite universe does not *require* for its explanation the existence of an infinite cause."[6] It is quite true that the cause of the universe *may* be infinite, but the finite universe affords no ground for asserting this to be the case. After all, a mechanic may have on purple socks when he fixes your car, but the repaired automobile can give no evidence of this unless he leaves the socks in your car. And by common consent, God does not leave His infinity in the finite universe: otherwise no causal argument would be broached at all.

Refutation of the argument.—In point of fact, the objection, that the theistic arguments prove only a finite god, seems to involve a complete misunderstanding of the entire structure of theistic argumentation. It is certainly the case that a cause need be no greater than is sufficient for the explanation of its effect. But when the whole finite, space-time universe is explained in terms of some extraneous cause posited to explain its existence is it a sufficient explanation of such a universe to assert that its cause need be no more than finite? A finite being is one that stands in such relations to some other ex-

---

[1] E. J. Carnell, *An Introduction to Christian Apologetics*, pp. 129, 131.
[2] G. H. Clark, *A Christian Philosophy of Education*, p. 40.
[3] C. F. H. Henry, *Remaking the Modern Mind*, p. 198.
[4] David Hume, *Hume Selections* (Scribner), p. 329.
[5] A. H. Strong, *Systematic Theology*, p. 74.
[6] *Op. cit.*, pp. 129, 131.

istence or existences that its own being is subject to limitations that are not self-involved: or briefly a finite being is one which depends upon some other reality for its existence. But upon what such reality does God Himself depend? Upon the world? But then the world would not have required explanation in terms of God's existence in the first place. Upon what being then does this finite god depend for his existence? Upon some other, as yet unknown finite being? But then the same question remains. And since, as we have tried to show and will yet establish more firmly, an endless series of such finite beings is logically inconceivable, the series must end in the positing of an absolutely infinite being as the only sufficient explanation of any finite reality, be it god or world.

The causal argument, then, does not state merely that a finite world requires a cause, but that the whole series of finite causes must logically mount to the assertion that an absolutely necessary being exists. Now such a being is one which contains the grounds of its existence within itself and which sustains relations only to such other realities as are its own concretions or, if you like, creations. But self-existence is exactly the meaning of infinity as an attribute of God: an infinite being is precisely a being the determinate conditions of whose existence are entirely self-contained. If therefore the causal argument is valid at all, it establishes the existence of an absolutely infinite being. If God were finite, then rationality would conclude from that very finite being the existence of an absolutely infinite being as its ultimate ground of existence, and then such a finite god would not be the conclusion of the argument. Multiply your finite gods as you will: beyond them all stands that one infinite Being that is truly God and that robs all lesser gods of their premature claim to deity. Consequently, we conclude that no ground for asserting the finiteness of God exists by virtue of the finite status of the total space-time universe, but that rather the admission that the universe is finite involves the very truth that the objection purports to deny.

Second Ground of Finitude in God: the Reciprocal Character of Any Argument from Experience

Statement of the argument.—This phase of the objection is most effectively stated by W. E. Hocking:

> If we could prove a first and conscious cause, still we could prove only such cause as is equivalent to his effect. . . . A very

limited Being would this be, a God who is only as great as his
world . . . and finally *only as real*. By such ways we can only
reach a being in whom the qualities of experience are refunded,
without change or heightening. But in such case, we may as well
believe in the world as we find it; and proceed with our work
of mastering it, without reference to God.[7]

The substance of the objection is therefore this: any argument to a
first cause, being based on experience, can do no more than refund
or exchange the qualities of experience itself. And if this is the case
we may as well rest content with the world as we find it and not attempt to argue to a first cause in the first place.

Refutation of the argument.—This argument is basically the Kantian criticism that the rational categories cannot be meaningfully employed to assert, on the basis of experience, existences which transcend the realm of possible experience in sensation. In the degree
to which Hocking's criticism embodies this Kantian point of view,
we have already refuted the contention in our criticism of Kant's
point of view itself by showing that the objection ultimately results
in skepticism.[8]

Yet a brief analysis of the application of this contention in the
present context will serve to establish the invalidity of the objection.
It is true that the arguments for God are formulated to account for
the total data of experience. But the very heart of theistic argumentation, especially in the cosmological argument, is that a mere refund
or exchange does not account for these very data in question. If the
world needs *any* explanation in terms of an adequate cause, such
cause must transcend finitude and contingency in an embodiment of
infinity and necessity. This follows, in the first instance, from a consideration of the fact that if an alleged cause of the world really were
the first cause, its existence would not involve dependence on any
factors except those within its own nature: and such self-existence is
the meaning of necessity and infinity. The same conclusion follows,
in the second instance, from the fact that if the argument did not
lead to such an infinite and necessary being, the *same* logic, that led
from the present world order to a "first" cause, would, in the case of
a mere "refunded" cause, lead beyond the so-called first cause itself
to a necessary and infinite being as *its* only adequate explanation.

[7]W. E. Hocking, *The Meaning of God in Human Experience*, p. 305.
[8]Cf. Part I, Chapters I, II.

Multiply intermediate "first" causes as you like: the last stand of logical analysis concludes an absolutely infinite existence.

A mere refund of experience, then, explains no more than the present world order, since it would be of the same finite and contingent character. Consequently, either *no* causal argument is possible and rationally necessary, or such an argument leads, not to a "refund of experience," but to an absolutely necessary and infinite being. But a causal explanation of the world order is necessary, as we have attempted to show, both in terms of the contingency of that order and in terms of the logical impossibility of an infinite series of actual existents. Consequently, the causal argument does conclude the existence of a being that transcends the contingencies of experience itself, and hence the second ground for asserting finitude in God is likewise invalid.

Third Ground of Finitude in God: the Necessary Relation of the Cause to the World as an Effect

Statement of the argument.—Since the cause posited to explain the world is necessarily related to the world as to an effect, it therefore stands under a limitation and is consequently not an infinite or necessary being. This argument is urged, for example, by Cornelius Van-Til in his critique of the ontological argument and, by implication, of the whole structure of theistic argumentation. VanTil affirms that since the argument depends on the idea of the imperfect or relative in order to get to the idea of a most perfect or absolute, it therefore proves no more than a finite god, if that. "It proves an Absolute Being who is necessarily related to a finite being. Thus non-being is given an original status as over against God."[9] John Caird states the objection in a slightly different, though basically similar, fashion: God is neither infinite nor necessary in terms of the cosmological argument, he urges. He is not infinite, for the world still exists as a limit to such a being and reduces it to a finite; He is not necessary, for, like any cause, the ground of the world is as much conditioned by the effect as the effect is conditioned by it. Hence, the causal argument concludes no more than a finite being.[10]

Refutation of the argument.—Insofar as this argument depends upon the general assertion that the cause of the world is finite, it is open to all the objections mentioned under the preceding headings.

[9]Cornelius VanTil, *Christian Apologetics*, p. 34.
[10]John Caird, *An Introduction to the Philosophy of Religion*, p. 138.

Supposing the objection to be valid and the cause of the world to be finite then the same logic which led to the positing of a cause for the world at all would lead to the positing of a cause for this finite cause and so on until logic rests in an infinite being. Now either logic and intellect cannot conceive or know the outcome of this problem, or the series of causes cannot go on to infinity. Now if the former is the case, then no argument of any kind is possible, there being no reason for restricting the sphere of rational activity without discrediting its validity altogether; moreover, to put it differently, there is reduction to self-contradiction, for the very statement—this problem is logically insoluble—depends upon the assumed validity of logic to understand the problem. It follows that logic and intellect can broach an answer to this problem and that therefore the series of causes cannot go on to infinity, so that at some point an infinite and necessary cause must be posited.

But that aspect of the present objection, which differentiates it from preceding objections, is the assertion that the posited cause, being necessarily related to the effect (whether metaphysically, as suggested by Caird, or epistemologically, as suggested by VanTil), must by that very fact be finite. Now in the first place, the objection is grounded upon false concepts of infinity and necessity: for these concepts do not mean that God stands in *no* necessary relation to any other reality, but rather that He stands only in such necessary relations as are self-involved or posited by His own nature. On any theistic view God sustains necessary relations to the whole realm of contingent being. But the necessity springs, not from any extraneous cause, but from the moral and metaphysical necessity of His own being. After all, everything that God does is a necessary concretion from the interrelation of the divine attributes: otherwise, God's creation of the present universe would either be totally uncaused (which is logically absurd), or it would be conditioned by an extraneous cause (which would mean He was not God at all). But all this merely means that the rationality of God's nature eternally determines His will to action: far from making God finite, it is only such a determination that makes Him infinite; for if God were determined to act by anything except the rational and moral character of His own being, He would then stand under an external limitation and be certainly finite.

To put the answer in slightly different terms, we may pose the question: does not the present objection undermine *any* theistic view of the world whatever? From the standpoint of metaphysics, the objection, as already suggested, moves to the assertion of an infinite series of finite causes for the world, or else to no extraneous cause at all. But if an infinite series of any kind is accepted, there is no reason for transcending the series of finite causes and effects which constitute the present world order: and the idea of such a self-sufficient world is precisely the naturalistic metaphysic. It need hardly be said that if we assert no extraneous cause for the world, a naturalistic view is posited at once.

From the standpoint of epistemology (and here VanTil is especially in view: since his argument seems to assert that God's finitude is involved in the notion that He can be known through a necessary relation to finite being) the result is ultimately the same. VanTil seems to me to be ambiguous here. Does he mean this necessary relation to finite being as a dependence of the idea of the absolute being on the idea of relative being? Or does he mean that the Absolute Being is thus known as necessarily related to a finite knower who uses the argument? In the first case two observations are in order: first, why should the fact that God is concluded from the existence of relative being mean that God is finite? Would it not mean the very opposite? For a relative and contingent being requires the existence of an absolute and necessary being for its adequate explanation, as I have already attempted to show. Again, that God's being known from the existence of finite being would involve God's finitude can be the case only on the assumption that no passage whatever is possible from factors in experience to the existence of an absolutely infinite being: but if this is the case, either God is unknowable or He does not exist. The first alternative is self-contradictory; the second is naturalism.

But suppose VanTil intends the second possible meaning suggested: that the absolute being is finite because He is shown to be necessarily related to a finite knower who argues through to His existence. This objection would then apply against any view that maintains the knowability of God. For suppose God's existence to be revealed in some other way than through facts of experience available to all rational minds—through special revelation, for example, the possibility and actuality of which I do not in the least deny. God's reality will either be known through this revelation or not. If it is known, it is still known relatively to a finite knower: and this is true regardless of the mode of revelation, so that either God's existence as absolute is unknowable or else the fact that He is always known by a finite knower does not deprive Him of infinity and necessity in the least. On the other hand, if God's reality is not known through such a proposed revelation, the argument ceases at once. In any case the objection is either directly invalid and unsustained, or it is indirectly thus by asserting the self-contradictory proposition that God is unknowable.

Therefore, whichever meaning is put on VanTil's words, his objection reduces to the assertion that God is unknowable, which is in turn either self-contradictory or equivalent to the bare assertion that God does not exist. Again we land in the territory of a naturalistic world view. I consequently conclude that the entire objection, both metaphysically and epistemologically, undermines any theistic view of the world whatever.

And thus the third ground for asserting finitude in God is exposed as inadequate through rational analysis. Either no argument to God is possible at all or else the fact that God is necessarily related to finite being does not impose any limit whatever upon His infinite and necessary existence. The first alternative is not here in point, and the second destroys the objection.

Conclusion

Assuming the validity of our subsequent solution to the problem of evil, it appears that no ground actually exists for asserting that the God proved by the arguments for theism is a finite god. It is rather the case that He is either no god at all, or else He is the absolutely infinite God of the highest conceivable theism.

THE ARGUMENT THAT THE THEISTIC EVIDENCES PROVE A PLURALITY OF GODS

Statement of the Argument

The expansive-limiting argument not only attempts to whittle the God of nature down to finite proportions, it attempts to show that He has comrades in the creative enterprise: not only is it asserted that He is a limited being, it is further urged that the argument from nature expands God's being by alleging that the various arguments prove a plurality of gods. Thus Carnell argues: "How can we be assured that the God who is proved in the first argument is the same

Deity who is the Moral Governor of the world? . . . There is room for . . . thousands of gods."[11] How can we show that the arguments all conclude the same being?

Refutation of the Argument

Granting the validity of our refutation of the finitude of God, we must likewise proscribe the present assertion. For if the arguments lead to a God that is absolute and infinite at all, then a plurality of such gods is logically impossible. This will become apparent if we consider in detail the possibility of such a plurality.

Each argument used, it is alleged, leads to a different god. But obviously, if there are a number of gods, they nevertheless collaborated in the production of the present universe. Their effects are so intricately interwoven that they must be conceived as co-operating creators. Influential thinkers have, from this consideration itself, concluded the impossibility of a plurality of gods. Thus no less a philosopher than John Stuart Mill himself urges: "Monotheism . . . is the only Theism which can claim for itself any footing on scientific ground. Every theory of the government of the universe by supernatural beings is inconsistent, either with the carrying on of that government through a continual series of natural antecedents according to fixed laws, or with the interdependence of each of these series upon all the rest, which are the two most general results of science."[12] And G. P. Fisher argues in a similar way when he urges that we do after all have at least three considerations which preclude polytheism: first, while the world contains a plurality of causes, the analogy of our own wills in putting forth a plurality of effects should lead us to posit unity in the Deity; second, all the data can be accounted for by supposing a single self-sufficient being, so that any supposition to the contrary would be inconsistent with the law of parsimony (called Occam's razor, both because it was clearly stated by Occam and because it reduces, or "shaves away," excessive explanatory entities) according to which explanatory hypotheses are not to be multiplied beyond necessity; third, "the fact that nature is one coherent system proves that the operations of nature spring from one and only one Cause."[13]

[11]*Introduction to Christian Apologetics*, pp. 129, 131; cf. also C. F. H. Henry, *Remaking the Modern Mind*, p. 200.
[12]John Stuart Mill, *Three Essays on Religion*, p. 60.
[13]G. P. Fisher, *Manual of Natural Theology*, pp. 17, 18.

It must be conceded, however, that both Mill and Fisher overstate the case: for while the human will does show us that a single cause can produce a plurality of effects, human experience also teaches us that a single, systematically integrated effect can be produced by a number of numerically different agents. As Hume puts the point: "A great number of men join in building a house or ship . . . why may not several deities combine in contriving and framing a world?"[14] The mere analogy of human experience simply teaches us that the creation of the world by a single Deity is logically possible: it does not establish the necessity of the case. As for the law of parsimony, it applies only in purely hypothetical cases: and theism, so far as I embrace it, has no interest in a hypothetical status. It ought rather to assert that a theistic explanation is, not merely *a* possible, but the *only* possible explanation of the gamut of experience.

Fortunately, however, the argument against the objection can be put in logical form to the effect that, whether the creators are infinites or finites, the hypothesis of their plurality is self-contradictory. For consider the possibility of such co-operating creators. Either they are infinites, and thus stand under no limitations that are not self-involved; or they are finites, and thus stand in limiting relations to one another. Now they cannot be absolutes or infinites, for there are two considerations that render such a supposition logically untenable. In the first place, an absolutely necessary or infinite being is, by definition, the ground for the existence of all beings extraneous to itself and related to it. Furthermore, if these creators were absolutes, there would be no mode for their achieving co-operation in the production of a world, for as absolutes they would be totally unrelated. If the proposed absolutes are related at all, then they are finites, for a finite being is just exactly a being that stands in some extraneous relation which is not self-imposed. If it be objected that such absolutes might be aware of each others' existence and hence be able to co-operate in the production of a universe after all, then the answer is that this very awareness destroys their absoluteness, since then they do stand in a relation of awareness that did not proceed from a self-imposed or self-involved condition. And if it be objected that such awareness might be self-imposed, this could only mean that the objects of that awareness have their ground of existence in the particular absolute in question, so that in point of fact these absolutes

[14]*Hume Selections*, pp. 330, 331.

are illusory and only one of them is a true Absolute: namely, the one in whose being the awareness of the rest was self-involved. Consequently, the notion of a plurality of absolute or infinite beings is absurd.

But suppose the co-operating creators were finites in a relation of interdependence. Yet this hypothesis, as we have already indicated, is likewise untenable, for then these interrelated finites need a necessary existence as the explanation of their ground of being and their existence, so that an Absolute God is therefore reached at the last outpost of rationality. If the universe implies the existence of any God at all, that God is an absolutely infinite being, there being no reason, on the opposite supposition, for positing a cause of the world at all. E. A. Burtt, though he hesitates to press reason to our conclusion, finds that if the arguments are sound at all, they do point to a single Being: "The creative ultimate established by these reasonings is therefore one entity, not a plurality of beings. If the arguments are sound, we have proved a single, original, unchangeable, intelligent, supremely perfect being as the necessary ground of everything in the cosmos, and such a being is what we mean by the word God."[15]

Conclusion

The expansive-limiting argument against the theistic evidences attempted to show that the arguments, if valid, prove no more than a finite god and that the effect of the same arguments would be to conclude a plurality of gods, there being no reason for supposing the arguments to converge on the same being. Both of these assertions have been shown to be baseless. If God is knowable on the basis of the revelation in nature at all, the God thus known is a single, absolutely infinite being. Consequently, the original objection is invalid.

---

[15]*Types of Religious Philosophy*, pp. 110, 111.

Chapter III

THE REDUCTIVE ARGUMENT OF IMMANUEL KANT

The Reductive Character of the Kantian Objection

K ANT'S CRITICISM of argumentative theism is properly characterized as reductive on a twofold basis: in the first place, Kant attempts to reduce the application of the rational categories to the limits of possible sense experience, and then he attempts to show that
when these limits are superceded, as in the argument to an absolutely
necessary being distinct from the world, the result is a series of mutually contradictory assertions called antinomies. In the second place,
Kant endeavors to show that the great arguments for God all reduce
ultimately to the invalid a priori ontological argument and therefore share its invalidity. As we have already indicated, Kant's motive
is not the destruction of theism itself, but the shifting of its orientation from the realm of theoretical to that of practical reason: the existence of God is a regulative ideal that gives ultimate significance to
an ultimate moral absolute.

Analysis and Criticism of the First Reduction: The Argument from the Antinomies

The General Thesis

Kant's contention is that when the rational categories are applied
beyond the limits of possible sensation, mutually contradictory assertions inevitably result. Now insofar as this argument thus denies
that the categories can be applied beyond the limits of sense-experience, we have already answered the objection and shown that in
terms of any a priori epistemology this objection is invalid, and, further, that empiricism, the only possible alternative, in the final analy-

sis, reduces to self-contradiction.[1] Consequently our present task is merely the negative one of showing that the application of the categories beyond the limits suggested by Kant, in order to conclude the existence of an absolutely necessary being, need not and does not imply the contradictions alleged. Now in this connection the only relevant antinomies of Kant concern: first, the conception that the world has a beginning in time (although the cosmological argument has been stated in forms that do not raise this problem, yet it must ultimately *be* raised); and second, the conception of the existence of an absolutely necessary being. Consequently, we limit our analysis and critique to these two antinomies.

Kant's argument is that in the case of both the above conceptions, it is possible to argue with equal cogency for either the validity or the invalidity of the concepts in question: to argue, that is, that the world both has and has not a beginning in time; and that an absolutely necessary being both does and does not exist. If this is the case, he urges, then reason must be endeavoring to operate in a sphere where, in its theoretical aspect, it does not legitimately belong.

First Antinomy: the World Both Has and Has Not a Beginning in Time

Statement of Kant's argument.—On the one hand, Kant argues, the world must have had a beginning in time (and this is the alternative espoused by an adequate natural theology). For on the opposite supposition it follows that at any given moment of time an eternity must have elapsed and hence an infinite series of successive conditions or states of things must have taken place. But this is impossible since the very notion of infinity implies that it never can be completed by such a successive synthesis. Therefore, the only alternative to an infinite series being a beginning in time, "a beginning of the world is a necessary condition of its existence."[2]

On the other hand, it is equally necessary to argue that the world has had no beginning in time. For on the opposite supposition there must have been a void time in which the world did not exist, since "a beginning is an existence which is preceded by a time in which the thing did not exist."[3] But in such a void or empty time, no origin of the world is possible, since "no part of such time contains a dis-

[1]Part I, Chapters I, II.
[2]*Critique of Pure Reason*, p. 241.
[3]*Idem.*

tinctive condition of being in preference to that of nonbeing."[4] It follows that the world has had no beginning in time. Therefore, since both of these positions are at the same time logically necessary and logically impossible, it appears that any view which incorporates either of them is an untenable position and that in this sphere theoretical reason has transcended its legitimate field of operation.

Answer to the argument.—It appears to us that Kant has argued validly in the thesis that the world has had a beginning in time. We have ourselves defended such a position in Section A of this part of our entire argument. Nor does the thesis involve the difficulties that Kant attempts to establish in the proposed antithesis that the world has had no beginning in time. Kant himself suggests the way out when he says that an escape is possible in terms of a different view of time itself, viz., that there is no such thing as absolute time, but that time is a form of either external or internal perception and not an object at all.[5] Kant's own view is that time is merely a form of our sensibility which we impose upon the raw material of sensation. If so, then the contention that the beginning of the world in time involves the assumption of void time from which no origin could be made is invalid.

But it is not necessary to assume Kant's purely subjective view of time in order to escape the difficulty. We need only point out that time is merely a relation among objects that are apprehended in an order of succession or that objectively exist in such an order: time is a form of perceptual experience and of objective processes in the external (to the mind) world. Thus the fact that time is a relation among objects or experiences of a successive character *voids* the objection that the beginning of the world implies an antecedent void time: for time, as such a relation of succession among experiences or objective processes, has no existence whatever apart from these experiences or processes themselves. In like manner, for example, the relation of fatherhood has no existence apart from a father and his progeny. Certainly no one would argue that the existence of the relation fatherhood involves a preceding void fatherhood and is therefore impossible. In an analogous sense time itself, though real enough as a relation, does not need for its beginning an antecedently existing void time. Hence I conclude that from the fact that the world began,

[4]*Idem.*
[5]*Ibid.*, pp. 243, 244.

it does not follow that it therefore must have originated out of a void time: for time has no existence apart from the experiences and processes that constitute the world itself.

Furthermore, the assertion that a beginning of the world involves an antecedently existing void time implies the assumption that no existence apart from the succession of time is possible, that temporal existence could spring only from an antecedent temporal framework. But this would involve an infinite series of times. If present temporal existence must have arisen from antecedent temporal existence, then that antecedent time, void or not, must have arisen from a still more antecedent time, and so on. But an infinite series of such successions is inconceivable, as I have indicated in many contexts and as Kant himself argues in the thesis. Hence either an origin from an existence that transcends temporal sequence is possible and actual, or nothing at all can logically exist—which is absurd. This, of course, is just the point to which the cosmological argument has already brought us; for it argued, in one of its forms, from the impossibility of an infinite temporal series to the assertion of the existence of an absolutely infinite being devoid of succession in its essential nature. The problem of how such a being could be related to a world of temporal sequence is considered most fully in several contexts of the following chapter.

It is therefore concluded that the world has had a beginning in time and that Kant's attempt to involve this conception in self-contradiction is unsuccessful. Reason has thus far tried her wings, then, and found them fully able to bear her upward.

Second Antinomy: an Absolutely Necessary Being Both Does and Does Not Exist

Statement of Kant's argument.—On the one hand, "there exists either in, or in connection with the world—either as part of it, or as the cause of it—an absolutely necessary being."[6] For the world of experience contains a series of changes, each of which results from a condition which precedes it in time and renders it necessary. But then there must be a complete series of conditions up to the absolutely unconditioned, which is therefore absolutely necessary: "it follows that something that is absolutely necessary must exist, if change exists as its consequence."[7] Kant then proceeds to argue that this being itself must belong to the temporal series "if it gives the series of

[6] *Ibid.*, p. 257.
[7] *Idem.*

cosmical changes its beginning."[8] "For, as the beginning of a series in time is determined only by that which precedes it in time, the supreme condition of the beginning of a series of changes must exist in the time in which this series itself did not exist."[9] Kant further suggests that this being may be "the whole cosmical series itself, or only a part of it."[10]

On the other hand, it is likewise rationally necessary to assert that no absolutely necessary being exists, either in the world or out of it, as the cause of the world's existence. Such a being could not exist in the world, either as the whole series of changes and events or as a part of it; for of two possible cases, each is self-contradictory. There could not be, in the series of cosmical changes, a beginning that is unconditionally necessary and uncaused; for this would mean that the beginning was not determined in time, and then, by definition, it could not be a member of the series of changes which are in time. But neither could the whole series be such a necessary being, since then we would be asserting, as a necessary being, a whole whose parts were all contingent and conditioned: but this is self-contradictory, "for the existence of an aggregate cannot be necessary, if no single part of it possesses necessary existence."[11]

But neither could such a being exist out of and apart from the world. For such a cause must originate the cosmical series: hence it must begin to act, "and its causality would therefore belong to time, and consequently to the sum-total of phenomena, that is, to the world."[12] Or as Kant puts it elsewhere, it is illegitimate to pass from a series of conditioned things "to something which is not itself a member of the series. The condition must be taken in exactly the same signification as the relation of the conditioned to its condition in the series has been taken."[13]

In a later passage, Kant attempts to show that it is not possible to escape this difficulty by passing from the sphere of empirical contingency to that of intellectual contingency (that is, from the fact that entities change and become different, to the assertion that any given entity might be replaced by its contradictory opposite).[14] In

[8]*Idem.*
[9]*Idem.*
[10]*Ibid.*, p. 258.
[11]*Ibid.*, p. 257.
[12]*Idem.*
[13]*Ibid.*, p. 259.
[14]*Ibid.*, pp. 260, 261.

order thus to move the discussion to the sphere of intellectual contingency—and thus escape the objection that the absolutely necessary being must be a part of the temporal series—it would be necessary to show "that in the same time in which the preceding state existed, its opposite could have existed in its place."[15] But the mere fact that a thing changes does not establish such a contingency.

From these considerations, it follows that an absolutely necessary being cannot exist out of the world either.[16] And thus the result is that no absolutely necessary being exists, since it neither exists in the world nor apart from it. Thus reason seems to be able to establish both the necessity and the impossibility of the existence of an absolutely necessary being: hence the categories of rationality are not fruitfully applicable in this problem, and no theoretical conclusion can be drawn.

Answer to the argument.—In the case of this second antinomy (actually the fourth in Kant's own list), it is impossible to espouse the whole thesis as correct, since Kant not only asserts there the existence of an absolutely necessary being, but attempts to argue that this being must itself be a member of the temporal series. The argument for an absolutely necessary being appears to be valid enough and is in fact merely the formulation of the cosmological argument. But the second part of the thesis—that the absolute being must belong to the temporal series—is a wholly untenable position. Not only has such a view been amply refuted in numerous previous contexts, but Kant himself, in his formulation of the antithesis that there is no absolutely necessary being, clearly and cogently refutes the notion that such a being can be either a part of the temporal series or the whole of it, since either of these positions reduces to self-contradiction.

Hence our only relevant task in this connection is to show that the assertion of an absolutely necessary being existing *apart* from the world is not subject to the self-contradiction that Kant alleges. His relevant argument here is that, since the cause of the world must initiate the temporal series, it must be a member of the series—and this he has already shown to be impossible. Now there are two ways of escaping the charge that is thus leveled against argumentative theism, both of which ways seem to me to be legitimate, though the first admittedly postpones the ultimate problem. The first mode of

[15]*Idem.*
[16]*Ibid.*, pp. 257, 258.

escape consists in the fact that the whole question may be abstracted from the temporal framework by considering the totality of existence at a given isolated moment.

Take, for example, the present moment in which I am writing these words. I am holding the pen which writes the words, but a whole series of conditions is at this very moment sustaining my existence, that of the pen, the paper, the ink, and so on, until I reach an unconditioned existence which is the cause of the totality of present conditions now operating. For the sum total of dependent conditions cannot be infinite in number, since an infinite number of contemporaneously actual existents is logically absurd. Now it can hardly be said that the argument assumes the antecedent existence of this extraneously unconditioned cause in the temporal series, for the whole series of causes up to the unconditioned exists simultaneously. Therefore, the objection that the absolutely necessary being does not exist apart from the world cannot be maintained on the ground that this being itself must have *antecedently* existed in the temporal series, for the being exists now and it is just this present existence that does sustain the whole series of dependent causes.

Kant's answer here would be, I presume, that I have moved the discussion from the sphere of empirical to that of intellectual contingency, and that this is illegitimate, as indicated previously in our discussion of the antinomy itself. But such an answer cannot be sustained. For in the first place, the present moment, which I considered in the argument, is a real moment and hence has empirical existence; so that actually I have not moved the argument as alleged, but have merely focused attention on the totality of conditions at a given moment; and if it is not possible to do this, nothing is possible in argument, for every argument abstracts certain elements from a total context for the purpose of discussion. But in the second place, it is possible anyway to consider whether an entity, say x, as known, is a contingent or a necessary being, even apart from its relation to the temporal sequence. Of any given particular, it is possible to consider the question: can I conceive the nonexistence of this datum without self-contradiction? If Kant urges that there may be something unknown about the object which imposes the impossibility of such conception, I will answer that objects can only be considered insofar as they are known or knowable; that, as I have shown repeatedly in other contexts, there could be only one such object anyway, a plurality of infinite beings involving logical absurdity; that Kant himself has shown that the absolutely necessary being does not exist in the world, either as a whole or as a part of it.

It is granted, however, that this answer to Kant in terms of a consideration of the sum total of existing conditions at a given moment does postpone the final question, since after all the whole temporal series is real, and logical analysis does seek an adequate explanation of it. I pass therefore to the second answer.

Now Kant maintains that any cause of the temporal series must itself be a member of the series. But this assertion can be met in two ways: first, if the allegation is true, then the cause itself, since it exists in the series of temporal events, must likewise have temporal antecedents or it could not exist, and so on to infinity. But an infinite series of such causes is inconceivable; and furthermore, if the cause does have antecedents—which it must have if it belongs to the temporal series—it is not the absolutely necessary being which thought necessarily posits, for its existence depends on previously existing antecedents: which is contrary to the meaning of absolutely necessary existence as completely self-contained. Consequently, either nothing exists, or an absolute being exists which is not a link in an antecedently existing temporal series: and since the former alternative is absurd, the latter must be affirmed.

But in the second place, if it be said that our analysis does not show how a transtemporal cause could bring a temporal series into existence, the answer is that *time exists* only as a relation among successive experiences and processes, so that it comes into being in connection with the positing of the world sequences by the absolutely necessary being. Again we conclude that either nothing exists, or there exists a transtemporal reality whose being is characterized by absolute necessity.

In view of these considerations, we may affirm that while every alternative is self-contradictory, the concept of an absolutely necessary being, existing in transcendence of the temporal series, is not thus contradictory. Consequently, the argument of this second antinomy collapses.

Conclusion Concerning the First Reduction

Since both of Kant's relevant antinomies have been solved, we can only conclude that no objection can be brought against natural theology on the ground that reason encounters insoluble self-contradiction in the realms which transcend the immediate data of possible sensation. On the contrary, reason herself contributes the solution.

ANALYSIS AND CRITICISM OF THE SECOND REDUCTION: THE ARGUMENT FROM DEPENDENCE ON THE ONTOLOGICAL PROOF

Summary of Kant's Argument

In what we have called the second reduction, Kant urges that the teleological argument, since it shows the contingency only of the form of the world and not of its matter, depends upon the cosmological argument as its necessary supplement; but the cosmological argument itself reduces to the purely a priori form of the ontological argument, as that argument was formulated, say, by Anselm or Descartes. Now since the ontological argument itself is thus invalid, this means that the whole structure of theistic argumentation either collapses or results merely in the establishment of an architect of the world's form. Thus the argument involves a double reduction: from the teleological to the cosmological, and from the cosmological to the ontological. Our answer will attempt to show: first, that the former of these reductions, while possibly valid, does not vitally affect the structure of argumentative theism; and second, that the latter reduction is totally invalid.

Reduction of the Teleological Argument to the Cosmological

Statement of the reduction.—Kant thinks very highly of the teleological argument, as the following passage abundantly indicates:

> The world around us opens before our view so magnificent a spectacle of order, variety, beauty, and conformity to ends, that whether we pursue our observations into the infinity of space in the one direction, or into its illimitable divisions on the other, whether we regard the world in its greatest or its least manifestations—even after we have attained to the highest summit of knowledge which our weak minds can reach, we find that language in the presence of wonders so inconceivable has lost its force, and number its power to reckon, nay, even thought fails to conceive adequately, and our conception of the whole

dissolves into an astonishment without the power of expression—
all the more eloquent that it is dumb. .... And thus the universe
must sink into the abyss of nothingness, unless we admit, that
besides this infinite [?] chain of contingencies, there exists something that is primal and self-subsistent—something which, as the
cause of this phenomenal world, secures its continuance and
preservation.[17]

Thus the sage of Koenigsburg paid tribute to the foe he was about
to attack. Kant further admits that the positing of a supreme cause
is a necessity of the human mind in order to account for the existence,
order, and purpose that the world manifests, and that such an implication of God's existence both satisfies the rational requirement for
parsimony in principles and is free from self-contradiction.[18] While
therefore this procedure is admitted to be reasonable, "we cannot
approve of the claims which this argument advances to demonstrative
certainty and to a reception upon its own merits, apart from favor or
support by other arguments."[19]

The chief Kantian objection against the teleological argument is
that it depends upon the cosmological and in turn upon the ontological argument which, though it contains the only possible ground of
proof for the existence of God in the speculative sense, is nevertheless invalid.[20] After all, "the connection and harmony existing in the
world evidence the contingency of the form merely, but not of the
matter, that is, of the substance of the world. . . . This proof can at
most, therefore, demonstrate the existence of an *architect of the
world,* whose efforts are limited by the capabilities of the material
with which he works, but not of a *creator of the world* to whom all
things are subject."[21] Just so, I cannot infer from a watch, for example, that the watchmaker created the materials, but merely that he
oriented them to a previsioned end. Since therefore the argument
does not indicate the existence of an all-sufficient being, it must here
fall back on the cosmological argument and then upon the invalid
ontological argument. Thus, so far as the case for theism is concerned, the entire structure collapses. "Thus the physicotheo-

---

[17] *Critique of Pure Reason,* p. 348.
[18] *Ibid.,* pp. 348, 349.
[19] *Ibid.,* p. 349.
[20] *Ibid.,* p. 350.
[21] *Ibid.,* p. 351.

logical [teleological], failing in its undertaking, recurs in its embarrassment to the cosmological argument; and, as this is merely the ontological argument in disguise, it executes its design solely by the aid of pure reason, although it at first professed to have no connection with this faculty."[22]

In another place, our philosopher levels a further minor objection against the teleological argument. The assumption of a designing intelligence, he says, is a necessary condition for making the world comprehensible to our reason. But this does not mean that the cause of the world actually is or possesses intelligence, for there is no necessary analogy between rational conceivability and objective fact. It is indeed legitimate to render a concept intelligible by the use of an analogy; yet it cannot be inferred that because, in this case, I need the analogy of purposive adaptation to render the cause of the world conceivable, therefore the cause is actually a purposing intelligence. For it is illegitimate to argue from the conditions of conceivability to those of objective existence.[23]

Criticism of the reduction.—Two remarks of considerable detail may be made about Kant's main reduction here. In the first place, all that he actually maintains is that the teleological argument is not adequate when considered independently of the cosmological. Now this can be readily admitted, since, in the final analysis, there are not several arguments for theism, but one integrated structure of argumentation proceeding through various phases. Consequently, we do not ask the teleological argument to evince an all-sufficient being, but merely to show us in detail what kind of cause—namely, personal, intelligent, and voluntary—we have found in the causal argument. That all the arguments, if valid, converge ultimately on the same being has already been established. To demand of one of the argumentative phases that it teach us everything that can be known of God is a demand that would destroy any knowledge of God at all: for no one holds that God has completely exhausted Himself in His revelation, whether special or natural.

On the other hand, certain proponents of the design argument have attempted to invalidate Kant's reduction and to show that the argument does involve creation of the materials of the world. Thus

[22]*Ibid.*, p. 352.
[23]*Religion within the Limits of Reason Alone*, p. 59, footnote.

G. P. Fisher argues that since the properties of matter are inseparable from its existence, and since it is "in these properties that there lies the capacity of being moulded and shaped into the forms that bespeak intelligence,"[24] therefore the realization of purposive ends within the potentialities of matter implies the creation of matter with this structure of potentiality.

More recently, Tennant has propounded the same argument in more convincing form. If the cosmic process involves the existence of purposive intelligence, it must be the case that the general trend of the process was implicit in the primary collocations of matter.[25] If it be objected that such properties may have emerged from the original basal stuff through an evolutionary process without being implicit in the stuff, Tennant's answer is that "the universe has no environment to evoke from it . . . the emergent."[26] And he might have added that such a position merely shifts the problem to another level without solving it at all: for the potentiality of such properties must then have been implicit in the original basal stuff, and so on. In other words, to state the whole point differently, the arrangement of particles so that they build a cosmos involves and implies the initial determination of the nature of the particles themselves: and such a determination is ultimately creation.

Now we ourselves have already granted the substantial validity of the point that these thinkers propound: if it is a thoroughly valid analysis, then Kant's reduction is unsustained. Nor do I think the objection valid that on this line of reasoning every adaptation of means to ends by human intelligence would therefore involve creation by that intelligence: for a human intelligence, as we have shown in Section A, is already in an environment, the adaptability of which itself requires explanation in terms of ultimate purposive intelligence. Matter possessed these properties before human intelligence manipulated it. And it is this very fact, in part, that points to an ultimate purposive intelligence. To say, on the other hand, that God Himself found an environment susceptible of adaptation would merely indicate that He was not God and would require the positing of some still higher purposive intelligence in the metaphysical background.

In fact, however, the teleological argument does reduce to the

[24]*Manual of Natural Theology*, pp. 54, 55.
[25]F. R. Tennant, *Philosophical Theology*, II, p. 123.
[26]*Idem.*

cosmological in at least two further ways. First, the cosmological argument is required to change the *almost* infinite improbability of chance explanation for the order in the universe to an *absolute* improbability and thus raise the argument to the demonstrative level. As we saw in our discussion of the teleological argument itself, the hypothesis of chance explanation in terms of an eternal motion of material elements is almost infinitely improbable. But to assert the absolute improbability, it was necessary to appeal to the reduction of infinite series to self-contradiction. And this last point is an essential element in the cosmological argument itself. Second, the teleological argument is actually a specialized form of the cosmological. For it argues that the properties of matter, even as originally situated, are not self-explanatory or self-sufficient, but are contingent and dependent on some higher cause. But this passage from contingency to an ultimate cause is the very heart of the cosmological argument itself.

Kant's minor objection to the teleological argument was that although I must necessarily conceive the universe in terms of purposive intelligence, in order to make the universe comprehensible, this does not impose any condition on the objective existence of the cause itself. Now while this objection was seriously proposed by Kant, I hardly think that it will appear serious to many minds. For if it be granted that the universe is rationally unintelligible apart from the assumption of a purposive intelligence, such an admission will carry the validity of the inference with every mind except that of the skeptic, whose position reduces to self-contradiction.

The objection, of course, is a special case of Kant's contention that the categories of the understanding cannot be meaningfully applied beyond the realm of possible sense-experience: and we have, in fact, already refuted this position in our discussion of the Kantian epistemology. If, when I start from existential premises (for example, the existence of adaptation in the universe), what I must logically conceive is not existentially necessary, certain tragic results ensue. First of all, there emerges a skeptical theory which reduces to self-contradiction and is therefore invalid. For at every level of knowledge, either what I must rationally conceive is existentially necessary, when I start from existential premises, or knowledge is impossible at every such level: but this last alternative is self-contradictory and therefore the first must be affirmed.

In the next place, how and why should I reach the concept of any cause at all for the universe? For I reach the positing of any cause at all—purposive or not—only in terms of what must rationally be conceived. Hence either no cause of the universe need be sought— which again is inconceivable because it requires the self-contradictory infinite series—or what I must rationally conceive when starting from existential premises, is true and valid for objective existence itself.

But finally, the objection reduces to self-contradiction immediately, and not merely in the indirect ways already suggested. If there is really no analogy between the objectively existent and the rationally conceivable, then this fact itself could not be known, since the knowledge of it would depend upon the existence of the very analogy it denies. For how could I affirm, of a reality that is not related to my rational conceptions, that it is not thus related? I therefore con- clude that this minor objection of Kant is self-contradictory and invalid.

In connection with the general reduction of the teleological argu- ment to the cosmological, we conclude that while the former argu- ment does depend upon the latter for its fullest cogency, this fact does not undermine its positive significance in the structure of theistic argumentation, unless the cosmological argument itself reduces to in- validity—a reduction that we are now to refute.

Reduction of the Cosmological Argument to the Ontological

Statement of the reduction.—The cosmological argument begins with experience and passes to the positing of an absolutely necessary being which is then identified with the *ens realissimum* or most real being.[27] "But it is evident that reason has here presupposed that the conception of an *ens realissimum* is perfectly adequate to the con- ception of a being of absolute necessity, that is, that we may infer the existence of the latter from that of the former—a proposition which formed the base of the ontological argument."[28] That is, what we have done is to assume that we can argue from the mere concep- tion of a most real being to the absolute necessity of its existence: and this is exactly the ontological argument.

[27] *Critique of Pure Reason*, p. 339.
[28] *Ibid.*, pp. 339, 340.

At first sight, Kant's assertion seems arbitrary, but his own explanation clarifies the argument. The proposition—every absolutely necessary being is an *ens realissimum*—converts to: some *entia realissima* are absolutely necessary beings; and then—since no *ens realissimum* is different from any other—to the proposition: Every *ens realissimum* is a necessary being. But since this proposition is determined from the very conception involved, Kant urges, it follows that "the mere conception of an *ens realissimum* must possess the additional attribute of absolute necessity. But this is exactly what was maintained in the ontological argument. . ."[29] Therefore, since the ontological argument is invalid, the cosmological shares its fate.

Several minor objections to the cosmological argument are likewise suggested by Kant. First, the argument involves an application of the causal category beyond the limits of the sensuous world; second, it assumes "the impossibility of an infinite ascending series of causes in the world of sense" and passes to a first cause; third, reason conceives the first cause as the necessary completion of the series and as removed from all conditions, but without conditions no concept of necessity is possible; and finally, the argument involves the conception of a total reality, whereas no empirical experience confirms this conception. This last point calls for a word of explanation. While the conception of such a total reality is admitted by Kant to be logically possible (the criterion of it being the absence of contradiction), yet in order to be empirically legitimate, the argument should proceed from the actuality of such a synthesis of the parts as experience presents: but experience can obviously present no whole of reality. How then can we argue the contingency of such a whole reality?[30]

Answer to the argument.—To prevent needless repetition, the minor objections will be considered first in the order in which they have just been cited. With respect to the first, we answer that the argument has already been refuted. To deny the applicability of the causal category in concluding a nonsensuous reality is to deny the real applicability of the category in the sensuous world. For all we have done in the cosmological argument is not to apply the category to some abstractly conceived ideal, but to apply it to the total world of experience and infer the necessity of that world's base in an

[29]*Ibid.*, pp. 340, 341.
[30]*Ibid.*, p. 341.

Ultimate Necessary Reality. To the second minor objection, we answer that Kant's own analysis in the antinomies has shown the impossibility of an infinite series of contingent realities. To the third objection, we answer, first, that it confuses absolute necessity of existence with necessary contingency, since a datum, the necessity of which is determined by antecedent or extraneous conditions, is not an absolutely necessary being, but a contingent being; second, that the absolute necessity of God's existence means, not the absence of all conditions, but the complete determination of all conditions within God's being: that is, that the absolutely necessary being is completely self-conditioned or self-contained.

To the fourth objection, we answer that the essential structure of the cosmological argument has no such dependence upon the concept of a total reality, since it argues initially from the admission that anything at all exists to the assertion that an absolutely necessary being exists. Furthermore, the conception of a total reality is not actually unjustified. After all, we do experience *something* empirically, as Kant himself would admit. Now, either we experience the total of reality or a part of it: if the former, then an empirically grounded concept of the total reality is admitted at once; if the latter, then this part must be situated in a larger whole with which it is existentially continuous—but then, the conception of a total reality is implied or involved in experience likewise. Thus, in either case, the conception of such a reality is not merely logical, but follows from a rational analysis of any experience at all. Hence the objection is invalid.

But to consider Kant's main objection: Kant maintains that the reduction of the cosmological argument to the ontological follows, as Kemp Smith says, from the fact that "if the concept of a Being of the highest reality is so completely adequate to the concept of necessary existence that they can be regarded as identical, the latter must be capable of being derived from the former."[31] But is this really the case and does this really constitute a reduction of one argument to the other? The ontological argument passes from the mere idea that the concept of a most real being implies necessity of existence, to the assertion of the objective and actual existence of the Being. But the cosmological argument does not do this: it first establishes the existence of an absolutely necessary being on existential premises (for

[31]Norman Kemp Smith, *A Commentary to Kant's Critique of Pure Reason*, p. 532.

example, that I exist). And only then does it explain the conclusion of absolutely necessary existence: this existence is precisely the ultimate reality to which all other reals stand in a relation of contingency; the absolutely necessary being means the basic reality or most real being. If it be objected that the argument assumes that the two concepts are convertible, this is readily admitted, but it is denied that I have concluded the existence of God from either of these concepts or from their conceptual identity: rather, I have established His existence in an empirical fashion by a consistent application of the rational categories to experience. It is to be granted that from either of the two concepts in question, the other may be inferred, but the objective existence of God is inferred, not from such an interchange of concepts, but from the necessity of positing His objective existence in terms of these concepts in order to account for a world that is not self-existent.

If it be objected that "we cannot deny the possibility of any being whatever, however limited, being absolutely necessary. . ."[32] then the answer is: Kant himself has shown that the absolutely necessary being cannot be identified with either the whole or a part of the phenomenal world and that "the condition of absolute necessity can be discovered in but a single being."[33] Hence such a being must exist apart from the world of phenomena.

It is therefore concluded that the cosmological argument does not reduce to the a priori ontological, but is existentially based and therefore valid. Consequently, Kant's attempted reduction is unsustained and fallacious.

Conclusion on the Kantian Criticism of Argumentative Theism

Our conclusion can be both brief and decisive: both general phases of the Kantian reduction are invalid, not only with respect to his attempt to reduce the implications of argumentative theism to self-contradiction, but also with respect to his alleged reduction of all the theistic arguments to the ontological. So far as Kant is concerned, therefore, the arguments stand, and reason has successfully rested her case.

---

[32]A. C. Ewing, *A Short Commentary on Kant's Critique of Pure Reason*, p. 243.
[33]*Critique of Pure Reason*, p. 342.

Chapter IV

THE DESTRUCTIVE ARGUMENT OF CRITICAL NATURALISM

Preliminary Considerations

IN CONTRAST to the motivation that stimulated the three foregoing types of criticism, the express intention of the naturalistic approach to argumentative theism is that of destroying altogether the validity of the idea that any Supreme Being exists precisely in the sense we have suggested. Although many such critics are brilliant exponents of religion *qua* religion, they deny that God has any ontological existence except as an idea in the mind of the religious devotee. The method of the destructive attack consists in considering the argument in piecemeal fashion, picking away one implicate after another until every frame of reference for theism is eliminated, just as an ax eventually fells a tree by cutting out one chip at a time. Carl F. H. Henry, referring particularly to the teleological argument, aptly characterizes this approach when he comments: "Everywhere the edge of the argument was blunted by the naturalists, who overexercised Occam's razor by whittling away every point of reference for design and purpose other than evolutionary process."[1]

Our formulation up to this point has already anticipated and answered the vast bulk of these objections *en masse:* where detailed consideration has already been granted to a particular objection, only a brief summary criticism will appear. In the sequel, an attempt has been made to summarize all the major objections that have been brought against the structure of theistic argumentation: but only such objections as apply to a correctly constructed argument will be considered. I certainly think it no part of my task to defend every formulation of argumentative theism that has ever been propounded

[1] *The Protestant Dilemma*, p. 34.

from a philosopher's desk. Not all the spokesmen cited are philosophical naturalists in the strict sense, but all attempt to undermine the rational case for theism as built upon the foundations of an initial natural theology: hence their lot is implicitly cast with the naturalistic approach even though their own metaphysical positions may, in some cases, be supernaturalistic or even theistic.

The objections will be considered in the order that follows our own positive consideration of the theistic argument itself, attention being first given to the criticism of the cosmological argument and then of the teleological. The ontological argument has already been sufficiently criticized and shown to be, in its a priori form, invalid.

AN ANSWER TO THE OBJECTIONS AGAINST THE COSMOLOGICAL ARGUMENT

A. *Logical Objections:* which attempt to show that the argument is logically deficient.

Because it presupposes that nature must satisfy the intellect.—As stated by C. D. Broad, this objection urges that the cosmological argument is quite correct in its assertion that ordinary causal explanations, e.g., in terms of a possible infinite series, do not prove ultimately satisfying from the intellectual or rational point of view: "It rightly denies that explanations in terms of ordinary causation, however far back they may be carried, have any tendency to produce this kind of intellectual satisfaction."[2] But while an explanation in terms of an absolutely necessary being may be a rational necessity for the satisfaction of the intellect, "it is not in the least evident that nature must be in principle capable of satisfying the intellect in this way."[3] In brief, the basic supposition, "that nature must be, in principle, capable of satisfying the intellect in the way in which it can be satisfied in pure mathematics," is unjustified and unjustifiable.[4] Consequently, the argument is invalid, or at least subject to an arbitrary acceptance of the presupposition.

This objection is generically similar to Kant's minor objection to the teleological argument in that it urges that the conditions of rational intelligibility are not necessarily conditions of objective fact or existence. The answer will therefore be approximately the same with only a difference of application.

[2]C. D. Broad, *Religion, Philosophy, and Psychical Research*, p. 187.
[3]*Ibid.*, p. 188.
[4]*Ibid.*, p. 187.

It is true that the argument assumes the intelligibility of the universe; assumes, in other words, that the rational categories may be fruitfully applied in the understanding of reality at every level. Now Broad admits that the argument is thus needed to make the universe thoroughly intelligible and rational: to say, then, that this is true, will carry the validity of the argument for every mind except that of the skeptic, whose position reduces to self-contradiction. It appears, then, that Broad's argument allows the causal proof to carry off the palm of victory.

Our contention is that the objection reduces to self-contradiction. If what I must logically conceive, when I start from existential premises (in this case, the contingency of the phenomenal world, or the existence of anything at all) is not existentially applicable and necessary, then knowledge at every level of experience is impossible. For at every level, knowledge exists only when it is rationally intelligible, only when it results from a self-consistent application of the mind's categorical structure to the data of experience. Therefore, either what I must rationally conceive, on existential premises, is objectively the case, or no knowledge is possible at all. But the position that knowledge is impossible is self-contradictory, since its truth involves its falsity. Therefore, what I must rationally conceive, on existential premises, is objectively the case.

More immediately, the proposition—the rationally necessary is not necessarily the objectively real—reduces directly to self-contradiction. Either this proposition itself is rationally conceivable or not. If it is not, then it is meaningless and the objection vanishes. If it is rationally conceivable and intelligible, then it must be either a statement about what is objectively and actually the case or not. If it is not objectively and actually the case, it is false and again the objection collapses. But if it is objectively and actually the case, then it is also false, since it itself claims that what is rationally necessary is *not* necessarily actually the case. Thus the objection is self-contradictory.

Now it may be suggested that the word *necessarily* changes the situation and removes the difficulty, since it is maintained that the rationally necessary is not necessarily the objectively real, and not that it simply *is* not the objectively real. But this objection to our answer also melts before analysis as does the objection itself. For that which is not necessarily the case, or not necessarily actual, is either false or without sufficient rational grounds. If false, then the objection cancels out and is invalid, for the word *necessarily* may be dropped. If believed without sufficient rational grounds, then we answer: the definition may be substituted in the original proposition —the rationally necessary is what is believed, without sufficient rational grounds, to be actually the case. But surely the proposition— the rationally necessary is devoid of sufficient rational grounds—is self-contradictory. In either case, then, the original objection to our answer is invalid.

Finally, if it be objected that we have used the rational categories to refute an argument which purports to deny their universal applicability, then the simple answer is that neither an objection nor an answer can be intelligible without the use of these categories. I conclude therefore that Broad's objection is self-contradictory and hence invalid.

Because it transfers, to the sphere of objective existence, the concept of necessity, which belongs only to the sphere of logical validity. —The cosmological argument purports to establish the existence of an absolutely necessary being. But as a matter of fact, the words *necessary existence* have no meaning. For in the first place, necessity is a modal predicate that belongs purely to a relation between the subject and predicate of a proposition which follows logically from given premises, and is not existentially meaningful: "Modal assertions cannot be part of any primary proposition but belong to a group of secondary propositions. That is the group that describes a certain type of relation between the subject and the predicate of a primary proposition."[5]

But in the second place, to state the matter differently, no matter of fact or existence can be demonstrated: "Nothing is demonstrable, unless the contrary implies a contradiction. Nothing that is distinctly conceivable implies a contradiction. Whatever we conceive as existent, we can also conceive as nonexistent. There is no being, therefore, whose nonexistence implies a contradiction. Consequently, there is no being whose existence is demonstrable."[6]

From these two considerations, it follows that the words *necessary existence* have no meaning and that hence the cosmological argument is invalid in its assertion that an absolutely necessary being exists.

As stated by Laird, the objection may be shown to be spurious in

[5]John Laird, *Theism and Cosmology*, p. 99.
[6]*Hume Selections*, p. 355.

the following manner: it is true that necessity is a modal predicate that does belong (I do not say exclusively) to second-order propositions which follow from preceding propositions. But if I begin with existential premises and with the epistemology that has already been defended, why should I bar the conclusion of a syllogism from being existentially meaningful, that is, from applying to objective fact? In other words, if the premises are existentially and epistemologically solid, how can I bar the conclusion from being necessary, not only logically, but objectively and really?

The only means of escaping this application from necessary validity to necessary existence are two: first, to deny the existential or epistemological truth of the premises (for example, to say that the facts may lead to a different conclusion, or that the concept of causality involved is untenable—such objections are answered in the sequel), but the objection of Laird does not make this claim; second, to deny that the logically necessary is existentially actual, but this position is self-contradictory as shown in our consideration of Broad's objection above. In either case, the objection is unsustained.

What we have just said is, by implication, also an answer to Hume's argument, which is essentially similar to Laird's as it assumes that demonstration, or the assertion of necessity, belongs only to the sphere of logical conceptions. But a criticism of Hume's form of the argument may be enlightening. It is true that nothing is demonstrable unless the contrary implies a contradiction. But it is not true that whatever we conceive as existent we can also conceive as nonexistent without self-contradiction: for a series of such contingent entities could not logically be infinite, the idea of an infinite series of actual existents involving, as it does, a direct contradiction. That the nonexistence of which is conceivable, must derive its existence from another and so on, until the mind must ultimately come to rest in the affirmation that there exists a being that is absolutely necessary and cannot be conceived as nonexistent. The idea of such an absolutely necessary being is a distinctly conceivable and coherent concept: it is that self-contained existence to which all other reals are dependently related. Now if it be objected that what the mind must conceive on existential premises is not necessarily actual, even the slowest of my readers knows the answer to that one by now. Consequently, Hume's form of the objection is unsustained. And it follows that the entire objection, being self-contradictory, is invalid.

Because it involves the fallacy of composition.—"The fallacy of composition occurs when one reasons from properties of constituent parts of a whole to the properties of the whole itself."[7] Now it is objected that the cosmological argument commits this fallacy in at least two ways. In the first place, the argument assumes that because particular parts of the world, or even everything in the world, might be contingent or be effects, therefore the world itself is contingent or is an effect. Thus Laird argues that "even if everything in the world were an effect . . . the world itself need not be an effect."[8] Or as Hume puts the point, most ironically: "Can a conclusion, with any propriety, be transferred from parts to the whole? Does not the great disproportion bar all comparison and inference? From observing the growth of a hair, can we learn anything concerning the generation of a man?"[9]

But the same fallacy is allegedly committed in another manner: the cosmological argument assumes that, because parts of the world may be made the subject of empirically justifiable propositions, therefore such propositions may be made about the world-as-a-whole: but "it seems questionable whether the world-as-a-whole can ever be the subject of empirically justifiable propositions."[10]

Since the argument in question commits the proposed fallacy in the manners alleged, it is invalid.

Against the charge that the compositional fallacy is committed by inferring from the contingency of parts of the world that the world-whole is contingent, we answer as follows: first, the argument can be formulated in such a way that no such transfer is involved. The detailed attempt to accomplish this task is found in our previous positive formulation of the cosmological argument, to which reference should here be made.

But even if the argument could not be formulated without such a transfer, it would not, on that account, be invalid, for the fallacy of composition is not actually committed in the transfer. Some illustrations will clarify this point. While it is impossible to argue that because every part of a desk is light, the desk as a whole is light; it is possible to argue that if every part of the desk is light (or of a certain determinate weight), the desk as a whole does not possess infinite

[7] W. H. Werkmeister, *An Introduction to Critical Thinking*, p. 32.
[8] Laird, *op. cit.*, p. 95.
[9] *Op. cit.*, p. 308.
[10] S. P. Lamprecht, "Naturalism and Religion." In Krikorian, Y. H. (ed.) *Naturalism and the Human Spirit*, p. 34.

weight: for it is rationally evident that no summation of actual determinate weights could ever equal infinite weight. And so with every alleged instance of the fallacy: while it is not possible to transfer a conclusion from parts to the whole *simpliciter*, it is always possible to conclude that, if the parts, or any one of them, should be known to possess a certain determinate quality, the summation of the parts cannot possess the opposite quality in absolute degree.

For example,[11] while we cannot conclude that because Joe Smith is an exceptionally good football player, the team on which he plays is an exceptionally good team; we can conclude that the team is not an absolutely poor team. And so with other examples.

Now it is just such a conclusion that is made in the cosmological argument when it is correctly formulated. It argues that every part of the phenomenal world is contingent in its being. But then this must mean that all the parts together in the whole do not possess absolute necessity of existence: for, as no quantity of determinate weights could equal an infinite weight, so no quantity of contingent, finite beings could ever equal necessary and infinite being; hence the whole is contingent. Yet as I have shown repeatedly, a necessary and infinite being must exist if anything at all exists. I therefore conclude that while the argument in this form does involve a transfer of conclusion from parts to whole, it does not involve the fallacy of composition; for it passes, not from the contingency of the parts to the contingency of the whole directly, but from the contingency of the parts to the affirmation that the whole cannot possess absolute necessity of existence; and thence, since the only alternative to absolutely necessary existence is contingent existence, to the affirmation that the world-whole is contingent. Consequently, the accusation of fallacy is unjustified.

As for the accusation that the empirical knowability of a part does not imply the empirical knowability of the whole, this is actually Kant's fourth minor objection to the cosmological argument and has already been refuted in the preceding chapter.

It is therefore concluded that the cosmological argument, when correctly formulated, does not involve the fallacy of composition and is consequently free from the objection.

Because it concludes a cause whose relation to the temporal series is unintelligible.—The cosmological argument concludes that the

[11] I use Werkmeister's examples here.

ground of the temporal series is an eternal and infinite Being which transcends the series itself. But this hypothesis either involves the same difficulties as would the eternal existence of the temporal series itself, or it involves an unintelligible and self-contradictory concept of the relation between the eternal ground and the series. If God's eternity is defined as an infinite extension of time, then we are confronted with a *higher* infinite series of successive moments in the divine experience, in which case we may as well rest content with the naturalistic view of the world as itself constituting an infinitely extended series: "the idea of God as a first cause presents exactly the same difficulties and contradictions and offers no solution of them. For the existence of God . . . runs back into an infinite past in exactly the same way as the suggested chain of causes."[12]

If, in the face of such a difficulty, God's eternity is defined as timeless necessity of existence, or as involving transcension of the temporal series entirely, then we are faced with a twofold problem: first, there is the inconceivability of time having a beginning; "the conception of time beginning *at* a time, which was not itself in time, i.e., had no time before it, is self-contradictory."[13] Second, we are confronted with the impossibility of explaining how a transtemporal cause can effect the temporal series at all. So Whitehead remarks: "The vicious separation of the flux from the permanence leads to the concept of an entirely static God, with eminent reality, in relation to an entirely fluent world, with deficient reality."[14] In view of this allegedly irrational abyss, the naturalistic thinker declares that "a pragmatic analysis raises the question whether, in asserting that 'God is eternal and infinite' we are asserting any more than we would if we said that '*x* is *y* and *z*.' "[15] Not only is there the problem of the relation between time and eternity at the conceived beginning of time, then, there is the problem of God's present awareness of, and efficiency in, the temporal series: how are either of these last possible without assuming succession in God? But then we are right back to the impossible infinite series.

Consequently, whether God's eternity is conceived as endless duration or as timeless necessity of existence, the relation between God

---

[12]W. T. Stace, *Religion and the Modern Mind*, p. 219.
[13]*Idem.*
[14]*Process and Reality*, p. 526.
[15]J. H. Randall, and J. Buchler, *Philosophy: An Introduction*, p. 177.

and the temporal series is ultimately either superfluous or unintelligible.

In answer to this objection: we grant that God's existence and eternity are not to be defined in terms of an infinite extension of time, and that if it were, the objection of a still higher infinite series would be valid meat for naturalistic mouths. But we deny that the concept of a supratemporal cause is unintelligible. The objection that time could not conceivably have had a beginning has already been analyzed in our discussion of the Kantian antinomies: and it seems to me that a valid and satisfactory refutation of the objection has there been given. Yet we did not there explain with sufficient detail how a transtemporal cause could effect, and sustain meaningful relations to, the temporal series.

In answer to this last-mentioned requirement: such a cause could effect time just for the reason that it is changeless and does transcend the temporal series itself. For as Wild remarks: "How can that which is itself still in flux have a determinate influence on anything else? Secondary instrumental causes may involve change. But they must be determined by a first cause that remains fixed throughout the process."[16]

Time is a name for the relation of succession that holds among changing experiences and processes. But any such succession must originally be grounded in a changeless first cause, or no determinate changes would occur at all in the process of succession. For example, my purpose in expressing the meaning of the above sentence must be fixed or the progressive expression would not be effected: and so with the whole series of successive changes.

To put the matter bluntly, then: either change is itself an illusion or the process of change has a changeless first cause. If change is an illusion, then we concede a changeless being immediately; but we have merely shifted the problem, since now we have the difficulty of explaining the origin of the illusion. There must therefore be a changeless first cause.

But how could this rationally necessitated changeless being or eternal ground sustain meaningful relations to the temporal series: relations of awareness, for example? The answer is that such a being could sustain relations of awareness to the temporal series because, being transtemporal, it apprehends the whole content of the temporal

[16]John Wild, *Introduction to Realistic Philosophy*, p. 359.

series in a single eternal intuition. That is, it is impossible and illegitimate to argue that if God is aware of the succession of events in time, he must have succession in His own experience: for all the parts of time, as it were, are immediately present to His Mind as properly related in the whole. Thus when I apprehend a single object in sensation—say a circle. Now there are indeed parts in the circle and I comprehend the circle as thus composed. But it is not possible to argue that a succession of parts in the circle implies necessarily and of itself a succession of parts or of successive experiences in the percipient: for all the parts are apprehended as properly related in a single sensory intuition. Just so, God apprehends the whole content of the temporal series in a single intuition: and as my analogous apprehension of the parts of the circle does not negate the reality of the circle or its parts, neither does God's apprehension negate the reality of succession in the temporal series.

But how can such a changeless ground sustain the progress of effects in the temporal series? Again, the answer is that he can—or it can—do so because, being the changeless ground of the series, it sustains, in the timeless necessity of its existence, the whole ultimate basis of the temporal series itself. Thus every possibility of the temporal series is eternally grounded in God: or, to put it differently, is an integral part of His eternal plan or purpose. Hence, it cannot be said that the progressive realization of the temporal process implies a progressive development, and hence temporality, in God: for it is contained in the very meaning of an eternal ground that it imposes *all* the conditions within which the possibilities of the temporal series are concreted. Such a ground must be changeless because if it were not, it would necessarily be subject to extraneous conditions and hence not be the eternal ground at all but merely a link in the temporal series.

We conclude therefore that the relation of an eternal ground to the temporal series is not unintelligible and that the objection is therefore invalid.

B. *Metaphysical Objections:* which attempt to show that the cosmological argument rests on erroneous concepts about the nature of reality and the relations within it.

> *Objections which attempt to show that the argument rests on a fallacious concept of causality:*

Because it assumes the universality of the causal law.—The argument under fire assumes that the causal category is universally applicable, whereas the assertion that an event occurs by chance, while it may be false, is not self-contradictory; and to prove the universality of the causal law, it would be necessary to show that the hypothesis of chance *is* self-contradictory.[17]

But in answer: even if the causal law were an empirical generalization, it is supported by every case in which it has been tested; so that it rests upon strong empirical evidence that the naturalist himself accepts in every sphere of investigation except the present one: his rejection of the axiom in this case is therefore extremely arbitrary.

Yet the causal axiom is not a mere empirical generalization from experience. We have already defended a rational empiricism which attempted to show that the causal category, far from being derived from experience as such, is a condition for the existence of any intelligible experience at all. Without the categorical structure of rationality—which includes the category of causality—there is no such thing as experience. Hence the assumption of the causal axiom can only be denied by the skeptic whose position is self-contradictory, as I have already suggested repeatedly.

But finally, the objection rests on the ambiguity of the word *chance*. When we speak of a chance event, we do not mean an event for which there are no operating causes, for an event occurs only when all antecedent conditions suited to its actuality are present. For anything that occurs is a determinate event: and it is surely self-contradictory to say that a determinate event might occur without being determinate, that is, without possessing the conditions of its specific actuality. What we do mean by a chance event is an event whose occurrence is determined by causal factors of which the percipient is ignorant: or, more simply, that we do not know the factors which unite one causal nexus with another, as, for example, when two friends chance to meet on the street. Thus the occurrence of a so-called chance event is not an opposite alternative to the assertion that the causal axiom is universally applicable. Yet the objection turns upon just the idea that a chance event occurs without a cause. I therefore conclude the universal applicability of the causal axiom and the invalidity of the objection.

Because it involves a nonscientific concept of causation.—The cos-

[17]Randall and Buchler, *op. cit.*, p. 160.

mological argument assumes that the cause of a given event is the sum total of conditions necessary to the production of the effect and every relation exhibited in it, whereas modern science holds a cause to be an antecedent occurrence to which the effect merely stands in a relation of dependable sequence.[18] Now this scientific concept of causality has certain important implications. First, it means that only what is a later term in some sequence can be appropriately called an effect. Again, the concept implies that "a single experience of an event affords no basis for the use of this concept. . . . We must have two temporally contiguous events whose conjunction has been repeated in various experiences."[19]

What do these implications involve when they are applied to the cosmological argument? Since the world is not a later term in a sequence—the very point of the argument being that an infinite series of sequences is unthinkable and that the temporal sequence must depend on a nontemporal cause, the world cannot be said to be an effect. Laird argues similarly but fails, in his formulation of the objection, to push his point to the final form, since he mentions only that "we have no experience of anything that came before the world."[20] But in the next place, since the world—in the largest sense of the term—is unique, there is likewise no basis in an experience of repeated events for affirming that it is an effect. If we infer causal connection only from experience of repeatable sequences, how can we infer anything about the unique world-whole as an effect?[21] The outcome of our analysis is that the cosmological argument is invalid, since, when the scientific concept of causality is applied, no inference can be drawn that the world is an effect: yet the argument depends on this very inference.

In answer to the objection: does the scientific concept of causality purport, at the outset, to be a complete explanation of the causal origin of a given event or entity? It is true that science is interested in that aspect of the causal nexus, underlying a given event, which is the antecedent whose presence always involves the presence of the effect and whose absence always involves the absence of the effect. But this interest springs from the practical motive for scientific pursuits, the scientist being interested primarily in *controlling* natural

---

[18]E. A. Burtt, *Types of Religious Philosophy*, pp. 104-105.
[19]*Ibid.*, p. 218.
[20]Laird, *op. cit.*, p. 96.
[21]Burtt, *op. cit.*, p. 219 (commenting on Hume).

sequences to bring about some events and prevent others. This certainly does not mean, however, that there are no other causal factors operating: while it may be true, for example, that heat is always present subsequent upon the presence of motion and absent when motion is thus absent, this does not mean that the presence of motion is the whole explanation of any particular instance of heat; it merely means that it is the factor of interest to the person who wishes, in any given case, to produce or prevent heat. But does anyone imagine that heat or anything else of similar nature could be present without the sum total of conditions that determine the existence and structure of the whole material universe itself? It appears therefore that the scientific concept of causality is a function of practical interest in the control of sequences and does not purport to offer a complete causal explanation of any given event: the scientific concept, briefly, is merely a part of the meaning of causality. A complete causal explanation would involve the sum total of antecedent and contemporaneous factors necessary to the production of a given event. Consequently, the rest of the present objection, being based on the assumption that the scientific concept of causality embraces the full meaning of causality, is invalid.

The same conclusion may be effected by analyzing the implications of the scientific concept itself. First, is it true that only what is a later term in some sequence can be called an effect and only for that reason? Obviously not, unless nothing that now exists may be called an effect. For example, I am now writing this sentence: and I fancy that it is an effect, in part, of my writing and that I call it an effect for that reason among others; but the sentence is *contemporaneous* with my writing of it, so that either it is not an effect by virtue of its being written thus (in which case I hope no one reads it) or it is false to say that nothing is an effect which is not a later term in some sequence. A given event or entity is rather an effect because it sustains a present dependence on extraneous conditions. To state the point in general terms: all the conditions that determine any event are contemporaneous with it, for otherwise, the conditions for its particular existence being partly absent, the event would not occur, even though the present conditions may be and are temporally continuous with the past. It follows that either there are no effects at all now existing, or it is false to say that only a later term in some sequence can be an effect and only for that reason. I hardly think that much choice is involved.

It must be then that the scientific concept of causality is grossly incomplete, although it may be a valuable guide to the control of sequences. With special reference to the cosmological argument, it would seem to follow that no objection can be brought against the argument on the ground that the world is not a later term in some sequence.

But again, is it true that we infer causal connection only from the experience of repeatable sequences? And again, obviously not, unless there are no events at all and the world is nothing but a geometrical figure. For whatever happens either has some unique feature which differentiates it from what went before, or it has no such unique feature. If it has no such feature, then why is it a different entity? It must be the same thing; or at least if it were not the same thing, we would not know it. On the other hand, if the event has such a unique feature, then it is indeed a different entity: but this feature itself, even though it is *not* a mere repetition, is nevertheless an effect. Otherwise, we would be denying the universal applicability of the law of causality: and this denial has already been refuted. Our predicament is this, then: either there are no unique features which distinguish similar events, or it is false to say that we can infer causal connection only from experience of repeatable sequence. In the first case, we would be denying the existence of distinct events—which is absurd. In the second case, we have again shown the insufficiency of the scientific concept of causality.

An illustration may help. I am a distinct being: and it seems to me obvious that I am, in my constituent nature, an effect of operating causes. But my being an effect extends, not merely to the general similarities between myself and other men, but also to the positively unique features which distinguish me from them. Now on the basis of the scientific concept of causality, I could infer as effects only such aspects of my being as had been repeated in previous instances. But while this would enable me to say that the possession of hands, for example, is an effect, it would not enable me to say that the possession of these particular unique hands is an effect, for no repeatable sequence is involved. Hence either I have no particular and unique hands at all as effects, or the idea is false that causal connection is only inferable from repeated sequence. Nor is the case essentially different when more closely similar objects are considered: say, for example, pennies struck from the same mold. For they too are either distinct or not, and so the argument presses ruthlessly forward to its irresistible conclusion.

It would appear then that this second implication of the causal axiom is likewise an insufficient account of causality: for, if taken as a sufficient explanation, it leads us to the curious position that no particular and determinate events exist at all as effects, but only events in general—which in fact have no ontological reality. As applied to the cosmological argument, the analysis would seem to imply that no objection can be brought against the argument on the ground that the world cannot be an effect because it is a unique existent.

It is therefore concluded that the entire objection—which charges the cosmological argument with employing a nonscientific concept of causality—is invalid since it leads to experiential and logical contradiction.

Because it fails to explain why God Himself does not need an extraneous cause.—As usually stated, the cosmological argument assumes that God is exempted from the principle of causation, but the argument fails to explain this exception which is so rigidly insisted upon in every other context.[22] Perhaps Burtt puts the objection most cogently: "If it is legitimate and necessary to ask for the cause of other things and to find it in God, is it not just as legitimate and necessary to ask for the cause of God's existence?"[23] But if this is true and if we are thus left with the same predicament as exists in the case of the world itself, why not stop with the world and decline to push through to the conclusion of an extramundane cause? The cosmological argument would therefore appear to be invalid.

In answer: the argument, if properly formulated, does not at all exempt God's being from the causal axiom; it certainly is legitimate and necessary to ask for the cause of God's existence. But the argument does explain why God does not need an extraneous cause. For when we ask for the cause of God's existence, there are two possible answers: either he contains the ground of His existence within Himself, i.e., He is self-existent or self-conditioned; or He depends for existence upon some extraneous cause. But this last is impossible, for the same problem would arise about the extraneous cause and so on to supposed infinity. Now it is just the point of the cosmological argument that an infinite series of causes and effects is impossible, as we have shown already in our consideration of the argument and will present again in the sequel. At some point, it is rationally necessary to posit a self-existent cause or reality.

If it be objected that the rationally necessary may not be the existentially real, we have already shown that this objection is self-contradictory. If it be said that since we must posit a self-existent cause, why not grant this status to the world itself, this objection has also been answered and will likewise be met in greater detail below.

It therefore becomes evident that while the cosmological argument does not exempt God from the causal axiom, it does show why it is that His existence requires no extraneous cause: namely, because His self-existence is the only alternative to a self-contradictory infinite series. I therefore conclude the invalidity of the objection.

Objections which grant that the universe requires explanation but which attempt to show that it can be explained in terms which do not involve the concept of absolute necessity, whether of existence or not

Because an infinite series of causes and effects is possible.—The status of the cosmological argument depends upon the assumption that an infinite series of causes and effects is impossible. But such a series may actually be conceivable after all.[24] We are, in fact, familiar with the infinite series in mathematics: for example . . . −3, −2,−1,0,1,2,3 . . . ; and we do not say that such a series involves self-contradiction. Why, then, should we say that such a series does involve self-contradiction in the realm of being?[25]

Furthermore, the argument that such a series is inconceivable "may be represented as merely expressing the inability of the human mind to go on thinking backwards indefinitely. But the point at which it stops is purely arbitrary. No positive argument can fairly be based on this incapacity."[26]

I conceive that it will be a sufficient answer to this objection if I show that the hypothesis of an infinite series of actual existents in-

[24]So Burtt, *op. cit.*, pp. 102, 103, 218; W. H. Moberly, "God and the Absolute," p. 432; Randall and Buchler, *op. cit.*, p. 160; W. T. Stace, *op. cit.*, p. 219; A. H. Strong, *Systematic Theology*, p. 74.
[25]Randall and Buchler, *op cit.*, p. 160.
[26]Moberly, *op. cit.*, p. 432.

volves self-contradiction. And this is precisely the case, for either such a series consists of determinate parts, or it does not. If it does not, the series would have no applicability to the present universe, since, both spatially and temporally, the total manifest universe consists of determinate parts. But if the proposed series is thus constituted of such parts, self-contradiction is manifestly involved: for no series of determinate parts could add up to an actually infinite series. Yet such an actually infinite series must exist unless the series culminates in the absolutely self-conditioned being or God, which is contrary to the hypothesis that the series is actually infinite.

Furthermore, suppose that there does exist such an infinite series of causes and effects. At any given point in time, the series would be infinite, yet greater than at any previous time: but this is self-contradictory since an actually infinite series does not admit of increase or decrease. Therefore, either the series is not infinite, or the progression of temporal events is an illusion; but then there is no way to account for the illusion.

I therefore conclude that an infinite series of actual existents is inconceivable because self-contradictory and that therefore the objection is invalid. And if someone should deny that the law of contradiction applies here, I answer that this type of objection is self-annihilating and has been refuted previously at length.

As for the appeal to the mathematical infinite: the so-called infinite series in mathematics is not a series that is *actually* infinite in the sense of existence; it merely approaches infinity by reason of the fact that no definite limits are assigned to the series. Should I write ever so many numbers in either direction in such a series, I would never arrive at an infinite number; for betwixt the highest possible number that I might write and an infinite number, the distance always remains infinite. Were I therefore an eternal spirit and should I continue to write through all eternity, I would not even have begun the task. It follows that there is no such thing as an infinite number, no such thing as an *actual* infinite.

The fact that there is no such thing as an actual infinite was pointed out by Aristotle himself more than two thousand years ago; yet history has failed to assimilate his point, if we may judge from the popularity of the objection now under consideration. Whether we consider an infinite by addition or by reduction, as in the division of a determinate magnitude into progressively smaller parts, "it will always be possible to take something *ab extra*. Yet the sum of the parts taken will not exceed every determinate magnitude, just as in the direction of division every determinate magnitude is surpassed in smallness and there will be a smaller part. . . . The infinite [so far as it is meaningful] turns out to be the contrary of what it is said to be. It is not what has nothing outside it that is infinite, but what always has something outside it."[27]

The conclusion that there is no actual infinite is further confirmed by the contradictions that arise if we *do* conceive the mathematical infinite as actual: for example, that the series of whole numbers is equal to the series of odd numbers—which is logically ridiculous.

Thus no appeal can be made against the cosmological argument on the basis of an analogy to the mathematical infinite, since this last is merely a series with no assigned limit and not an infinite number of actual existents. But the concept of just such an infinite number of actuals *is* involved in the concept that the series of causes and effects might be infinite.

As for the assertion that the impossibility of the infinite series rests on an incapacity of the human mind to think backwards indefinitely: if this means that the rationally necessary is not the existentially actual, all readers know the answer by now. If it means I posit an absolutely necessary being merely because I am tired of enumerating proximate causes, then the assertion is false. For I do not posit the being on such a ground but on the ground that it is rationally evident that no such enumeration could conceivably add up to infinity; it is not that I tire of counting, but that I see at once the futility of it.

In the light of these criticisms, I therefore conclude that this objection, like its predecessors, has gone the way of all flesh to self-contradiction and invalidity.

Because the concept of a dynamic universe in process may be taken as given.—The cosmological argument assumes that the occurrence of processes must be accounted for by reference to a changeless ground. But "modern science is built on a dynamic rather than a static foundation. It assumes that the things which make up the world are by their very nature in process rather than at rest. . . . Motion needs no explanation."[28] The proposed argument for a first cause is thus in-

[27]*Physics*, 206b, 207a.
[28]Burtt, *op. cit.*, p. 102.

valid since it seeks an explanation of that which should be taken as given.

This alleged difficulty merely restates the basic assumption of the naturalist; viz., that the ingredients of the world, their quantity, proportion, arrangement, and activity in the causal nexus are all given. But this is exactly what the objector should establish: the mere statement of a contrary hypothesis is no refutation of its opposite. Furthermore, scientific concepts themselves, as we saw in the positive formulation of the cosmological argument, seem to indicate a point in the past when all energy was equally distributed: so that it would then be false to say that motion, or the action of energy, requires no explanation.

In point of fact, the concept of a universe in eternal process is actually a restatement of the preceding objection that an infinite series of causes and effects is possible. For it is the nature of a process that it embodies a series of successive states (from the temporal standpoint) and a series of interrelated, dependent causal factors (from the standpoint of the existence of the process at any given moment). In either case, the series of such states and factors is either infinite or finite: but it cannot be infinite, since an infinite series is rationally inconceivable. And it cannot be finite unless it depends for its existence on an absolutely necessary and self-conditioned being which transcends the process itself. Therefore, the assertion that nature is ultimately explicable as a dynamic process is false; for the conception of such a nature leads either to self-contradiction or to the assertion that an absolutely necessary being exists as the ground of the process itself, which consequently is not an ultimate explanation of the world-whole.

Because the existence of the universe may be explained in terms of aboriginal becoming or creativity.—Instead of choosing between the absolutely necessary being and the infinite regress, it is possible to hold that the universe emerged out of an aboriginal becoming, or creativity, or mere possibility.[29] As a matter of fact, "many philosophers have maintained that it is not true that everything that exists, or even everything that has a beginning, is an effect. The world . . . contains 'spontaneous,' free, or uncaused and unoriginated events. In any case . . . there is no way of proving that such uncaused events do not occur. . . . If, then, it cannot be (or has not been) shown

[29] D. C. Macintosh, *The Problem of Religious Knowledge*, pp. 219, 220.

that every event must have a cause, how can it be shown that the world must have a cause?"[30] It appears therefore that the proposed argument for a first cause is invalid and that an explanation of the universe is possible in terms of creativity without the infinite regress.

But this objection too melts before rational analysis. Insofar as the objection rests on the denial that the causal axiom is universally applicable, it has already been refuted above: and this consideration actually vitiates the entire objection by implication.

The hypothesis of aboriginal becoming, or creativity, or possibility, either requires an absolutely necessary being as its explanation or reduces to the self-contradictory infinite regress. Becoming and creativity, for example, must be functions of an existing entity or entities, else they are inconceivable. If they are functions of an existent being or beings, then they are functions either of the succession and contemporaneous series of causes and effects, or of the absolutely necessary being in originating and sustaining the causal series. In the first case, we again reach either the self-contradictory infinite regress or the absolute being which the cosmological argument itself maintains. In the second case, we reach such an absolute being immediately. Hence, in either case, the hypothesis of explanation in terms of creativity or becoming is either not ultimate directly or else it is the old infinite series again and is therefore likewise an inadequate explanation.

As for the emergence of being out of nonbeing in terms of mere possibility: either this possibility has an extraneous ground of being or not. If it has such a ground, it is either an infinite series of dependent grounds (which is untenable) or ultimately the absolutely necessary being. On the other hand, if the proposed possibility has no extraneous ground of existence, it is either self-existent or it is nothing; for that only can be something whose determinate conditions are present. In the first case, possibility is another name for the absolute being itself; in the second case, it does not exist and therefore cannot explain the existing universe. In any case, therefore, the hypothesis of an absolutely necessary being is rationally inescapable.

I therefore conclude that aboriginal becoming, creativity, and mere possibility are not ultimate explanations of reality and that thus the objection is invalid. Again the argument has emerged triumphant.

[30]Laird, *op. cit.*, pp. 95, 96.

*Objections which hypothetically grant the validity of the
argument but which attempt to show that its conclusion
may be something less than an absolutely necessary
and transcendent being.*

*Because the argument proves only necessity of causation and not
necessity of existence.*—This objection, so far as I know, is the peculiar possession of John Caird: "Even if this argument proved
necessity, it would not be a necessity of existence but merely a
necessity of causation. You may form a conception of two beings of
which, if they existed, one would be the necessary cause of the other;
but this does not prove that the former, though it has a necessity
relatively to the latter, possesses any absolute necessity of existence."[31]

But what is a necessity of causation that does not involve a necessity of existence? Take any two events in the series of dependent
effects and assume that the first is the proximate cause of the second.
Now the first must exist if it is the cause of the second: otherwise,
what is the meaning of naming it the cause? For a cause is a series
of conditions that determine the presence of a given effect: no existing conditions, no existing effect.

The objection must therefore mean either that the alleged second
event has no extraneous cause but is its own ground of existence, or
that the alleged second event does not exist other than as a figment
in some mind or other. In the first case, the cosmological argument
is valid; in the second case, the point is irrelevant, since the universe
obviously does exist as more than a figment of mind except for the
solipsist, whose position has already been discredited.

But perhaps Caird means to assert that no event in the temporal
series is absolutely existent or self-existent, since it can always be
traced to other proximate causes: this I grant, but then the series
must either culminate in the self-conditioned or take refuge in the
self-contradictory infinite regress again. On any line of analysis, the
absolutely necessary being is ultimately posited from the presence of
necessary causation. Hence, the objection collapses.

*Because the material (phenomenal) universe or some part of it may
be the absolutely necessary being.*—The cosmological argument alleges that the cause of the universe must be a being that transcends
the material universe. But is this allegation justified? Even if there
is an absolutely necessary being, it might be the material universe

[31]*An Introduction to the Philosophy of Religion*, p. 138.

or some part of it.[32] After all, while we legitimately seek the cause of changes, yet "there is in every object another and a permanent element—viz., the specific elementary substance or substances of which it consists and their inherent properties. These are not known to us as beginning to exist: within the range of human knowledge, they had no beginning, consequently no cause. . . . As a fact of experience, then, causation cannot legitimately be extended to the material universe itself, but only to its changeable phenomena."[33] The first cause which we seek would therefore seem to be the basic quantity of force in the universe.

Again, the only reason for asserting that this first cause is a mind is "that the hypothesis of a mind is the only one which will explain the evidence of purpose. . . ."[34] Yet the hypothesis of a mind to explain apparent purpose in the universe is itself extremely questionable.

It would therefore seem that there is no reason why the absolutely necessary being may not be the material universe itself or some entity within it. If this is the case, then the argument falls grossly short of its alleged goal.

This objection has already received substantial treatment in the positive formulation of the cosmological argument, in the consideration of the Kantian antinomies, and in the refutation of the objection that the argument involves the fallacy of composition. Hence only a brief summary of the refutation has an appropriate position in the present context.

First, every composite being is a contingent being, since it does not contain within itself the ground of the togetherness of its constituent parts. Yet every reasonable view of the world regards it as a composite existence. It follows that the material universe as a whole cannot be the absolutely necessary being, since it is thus contingent; and it follows by implication that no part of it, being a dependent factor in the whole, can be the absolute being either.

Second, the present existence and status of the material world is an effect of antecedent conditions in the temporal series and of the given conditions existing at any particular moment of time. This is also true of any particular part of the material world. But it belongs to the existence of anything in the temporal causal series that its be-

[32]*Hume Selections*, p. 355.
[33]J. S. Mill, *Three Essays on Religion*, p. 63.
[34]Stace, *op. cit.*, pp. 219, 220.

ing what it is does not arise from itself but from extraneous conditions which determine its particular character. It therefore follows either that the material world (or any part of it) has no particular character, or that it is not the result of temporal antecedents and causal interrelations, or that it is not the absolutely necessary and self-conditioned being. But the first two alternatives contradict the conditions for the existence of a material universe at all. Hence neither the material universe nor any part of it is the absolutely necessary being.

Third, if the material universe is the absolutely necessary being, then it must be that an infinite series of causes and effects is conceivable. For the material universe embodies a series of successive and contemporaneous actualities. This series, viewed from either standpoint, is either infinite or finite in extent: that is, it either consists of a determinate number of parts or not. If it were finite, then it would depend on some extraneous cause, which is contrary to the hypothesis. It must therefore be infinite. But it has already been shown that an infinite series of actual existents is impossible: so that the absolutely necessary being must transcend the space-time universe.

Fourth, if some part of the material universe were the absolutely necessary being, then it would not be a part of the material universe: which is absurd. For any part of the material universe is such by being a member of the causal series, both in the temporal and in the contemporaneous sense. But every member of the causal series is dependent upon the other members of the series for its particular status. Hence such part is either not the absolutely necessary being —which is contrary to the hypothesis, or it is not a part of the material universe—which is self-contradictory.

As for the suggestion that the being we seek is the basic quantity of force in the universe, this could be true only if this quantity were absolutely simple and indeterminate. For suppose it to be composed of parts which are determinate—and this, I take it, is the status of the existing universe. These determinate parts would then either derive their determinate nature from extraneous conditions or they would be self-determinate. But in the first case, the series would either be infinite or finite and so on to the irresistible conclusion. In the second case, as shown above, they could not be parts of the basic quantity of force—which contradicts the nature of this quantity and is contrary to our experience of the real world, however defined. Therefore the basic quantity of force is either not composed of determinate parts or it is not the absolutely necessary being: the former being absurd, the latter must be affirmed.

As for the point that the only reason for calling the absolutely necessary being a mind is that this would explain the allegedly questionable presence of purpose, the assertion is false. For it has been shown that no material being can occupy the status of absolute necessity of existence by reason of its composite character. If it is reasonable to suppose that mind is the only alternative to matter, then it is also reasonable to suppose that the absolutely necessary being is a mind. And it may be added that the traditional design argument, even if it were the basis for calling the absolute being a mind, may not be as worthless as the critics imagine.

From such considerations, it may be legitimately concluded that neither the material universe nor any part of it is the absolute being which reason necessitates in its interpretation of experience, and that therefore this present objection is unsustained.

Because the ground of the universe might be epistemological rather than metaphysical.—Why should the ground of the universe be an existent being at all? It might be merely a totality of truth, or set of first principles, or system of universals instead. So suggests Professor Lamprecht.[35]

Although I hardly think that Lamprecht, as a philosophical naturalist, proposes this as a serious hypothesis, it will bear some analysis. What is the nature of this supposed totality of truth, or set of first principles, or series of universals? It would seem to be of the nature of truth that it bears an essential relation to existence. If truth is predicable only of judgments or propositions, then a totality of truth could exist only in a mind; for judgments exist only in minds or for minds. In this case the totality of truth would be dependent upon a knowing mind for its reality, so that if the first cause is of this character, it *is* an existing being.

If truth, on the other hand, is independent of mind, it must be objectively real else it could not be said to explain the present existing world. If truth is thus objectively real, it is by that very fact existent. And it exists either as self-conditioned or as conditioned by extraneous factors. It cannot exist as extraneously conditioned, for

[35]Lamprecht, *op. cit.*, p. 35.

then it would not be the absolutely necessary ground. It must there-fore be a self-conditioned existent: which is contrary to the original hypothesis.

It therefore seems that either truth is not an ultimate expla-nation or else it is another name for the absolutely necessary being. I therefore conclude that the objection is invalid.

C. *Conclusion:* on the objections against the cosmological argument

All the proposed objections against the argument have been shown to melt away before analysis as wax before the fire's warmth: each has been shown to be invalid and either experientially or logically contradictory, or both. It is therefore concluded that the cosmologi-cal argument establishes the existence of an absolutely necessary be-ing, which is the ground of existence for the total space-time uni-verse, and which transcends the causal nexus that such universe em-bodies. With this conclusion firmly in hand, reason proceeds silently but inexorably to her final task: the similar destruction of the criti-cism against teleology.

*An Answer to the Objections against the Teleological
Argument*

A. *Mode of Approach*

While the universe itself may have resulted from a churning of the elements with mindless and accidental motion, our order of con-sideration in dealing with such criticisms is nevertheless deliberate and designed: for we now take it for granted that the existence of an absolutely necessary being, as the ground of the space-time universe, has been established and defended against all major objections. It is therefore with this conclusion that we approach the destructive criti-cism of the teleological argument. If it be objected that we ought to consider the teleological argument on its own merits, without refer-ence to the cosmological argument, then we answer: first, that there are not so many separate arguments for theism, but one progressive argument, the parts of which must be considered together if their full significance is to be apprehended; second, that we have already admitted the insufficiency of the teleological argument when it is considered as an independent structure. Nor does the fact that numerous exponents of the Argument have considered it to possess complete self-sufficiency debar us here, any more than the fact that there are persons who have added two and two incorrectly should preclude our uniting them without such error.

The objections will be considered in the following order:

1. Logical objections which charge the argument with some logical *non sequitur* or invalidity.
2. Epistemological objections which charge that the argument has no sufficient experiential basis.
3. Metaphysical objections which charge either that all the data can be otherwise explained than in the manner which the argument alleges or that the argument does not conclude a full theism.
4. The ethical objection which charges that the existence of an omnipotent and benevolent being as the world's ground is incompatible with the existence of evil in the universe.

B. *Logical Objections:* which attempt to show that any inference to the existence of ends in the universe, other than such ends as are espoused by human selves, is logically fallacious

Because any arrangement of existing elements is almost infinitely improbable: so that no argument can be based on the complexity of conspiring causes.—No one can observe an end or the realization of purpose as such, "for we can observe only successions of events and things."[36] It is evident, then, that the assertion of existing ends in the universe is an inference from some facts which are observable. The question then becomes: from what facts is it inferred that various effects were aimed at by a mind? Two answers are common: the complexity of conspiring causes, and the production of valuable entities in a significant order. These two processes of inference form the basis of this and the following objection.

The inference that certain effects are ends is therefore based, in the first instance, on "the extreme complexity of the causes, the fact that a vast variety of causes have had to work together to produce the effect. . . ."[37] If, it is argued, there had been only the operation of chance, any arrangement of existing elements might have occurred, so that the chances of this particular arrangement (say, of the solar

[36]Stace, *op. cit.*, p. 77.
[37]*Idem.*

system, or of the parts of the eye, or of the passage from matter to life to mind) are practically infinite.[38] Since this particular arrangement has appeared, we suppose that it is the concretion of the purpose or end of an intelligent mind.

But consider the argument: suppose that the solar system were differently arranged, or the eye differently constructed. This altered arrangement would be equally improbable, so that the fact that these entities exist as they do is no argument in favor of their having been planned.[39] Or to put the matter generally: *"Whatever happens in the world is almost infinitely improbable,* for there are always an infinite number of other things which could have happened instead."[40] Consequently, the argument from the extreme complexity of causes is "wholly fallacious."[41]

As Randall and Buchler put the point: since any arrangement of the world would be an order, how is it possible to argue the existence of an intelligent being to account for the present order?[42] It follows that the argument on this basis is invalid.

By way of answer: we grant at once that an end *qua* end is not observed but inferred, that one reason for the inference is the necessary complexity of conspiring causes, and that whatever happens in the universe is almost infinitely improbable from the standpoint of chance. But does it follow that the teleological argument is therefore invalid? We think not.

In the first place, the existence of an absolutely necessary and transcendent being has already been established and rationally defended against objections. It therefore follows that the existence of the basal elements of the world, the laws of their interaction, and their intrinsic possibilities, are dependent for their being upon a nonmaterial and supratemporal reality. If this is the case, then the general results of the interaction of the basal elements are also attributable to the Ultimate Cause, so that if adaptation does arise in the complex of determinate conditions, it cannot be attributed purely to the elements themselves but must be referred to the Cause of these elements. Hence before we even approach the objection, there is a rational presupposition in favor of the inference to intelligent will: a presupposition which depends upon the obvious fact that the

[38]*Ibid.,* p. 78.
[39]*Ibid.,* p. 79.
[40]*Idem.*
[41]*Ibid.,* p. 80.
[42]*Op. cit.,* pp. 163, 164.

possibilities of any given universe depend, in part, upon the original structure of its elements. If the concretions of the elements produced any effects *not* made possible by the absolutely necessary being, then another cause would be operating, and the former would not be the absolutely necessary basis of reality after all.

But with particular reference to the objection itself: note that it makes two definite admissions. First, it admits the presence of adaptation in the very fabric of the universe. Thus Stace, commenting on the solar system, says: "It has to be admitted as a fact that the various masses, velocities, and distances of the planets, being what they are, have produced the effect that the planets move as they do around the sun."[43] Second, the objection admits the practically infinite improbability, on the hypothesis of chance concatenation, that any arrangement exists as it does.

Now these admissions—which form the basis of the objection— would seem to vitiate the contention of the objection entirely. If any arrangement of the elements is almost infinitely improbable on the basis of chance, then are we to affirm that therefore chance explains the present universe or any other? Would you write a check on your bank if I could show you that it was almost infinitely improbable that the bank had any funds? The opposite conclusion is the rational one: namely, that chance does not explain any arrangement whatever, but that recourse must be had to mind to explain the existence of a universe, whatever its order. It scarcely seems reasonable that I should accept an explanation which by hypothesis is almost infinitely improbable—and accept it for the very reason that it is thus improbable. Certainly, this is not the ordinary mode of procedure in any other investigation. Of course, the word *almost* makes the hypothesis of chance still barely possible: but the cosmological argument, as we have seen, plus the impossibility of explaining the origin of mind from a material base, destroys even that bare possibility.

Now add in the other admission of the objection: namely, that the universe is replete with instances where the complex of causes conspires to produce effects which *are* suited to ends that could not have been previsioned by the elements themselves (except on the hypothesis of an untenable panpsychism). Not only is this a universe which, in terms of chance, is almost infinitely improbable: it is

[43]*Op. cit.*, p. 76.

one in which the complex of causes does result in the adaptation of means to what turn out to be ends; the structure of the eye, for example, conspiring to make vision possible. The hypothesis of chance now appears to be reducing to the vanishing point: the whole structure of the universe is *as if* it had been produced by an intelligent will; chance, the only alternative, is almost infinitely improbable and is made completely so by the cosmological argument.[44] Are we therefore foolish to believe that the universe is the product of intelligent will?

If it be objected that I have assumed the identity of the intelligent will and the absolutely necessary being, I answer that I have already demonstrated the absurdity of a plurality of ultimate beings. The only rational conclusion seems to be that the complexity of conspiring causes *does* serve to indicate that the universe is the product of intelligent will, and that therefore the objection to the contrary is invalid.

Because it commits the fallacy of consequent.—The teleological argument is guilty of this fallacy because it reasons from the fact that virtuous minds tend to produce valuable things to the conclusion that valuable things must have been produced by a virtuous mind. It will be recalled that the second ground of the inference to effects as ends, according to the teleological argument, is the progressive production of increasingly valuable things in the cosmic process. Now "valuable things are the kind of things which we, assuming that we are virtuous persons, would aim at producing if we were creating a world. We therefore think that, if there are valuable things in the world, they have probably been produced by a mind with purposes similar to our own."[45]

But this argument commits a common logical error called the fallacy of consequent. Such fallacy consists in supposing that a condition and its consequent are convertible, so that it is possible to argue from the presence of the consequent to the existence of the condition. Thus, for example, the fallacy is committed if I assume a theory proved when facts are present which *should* be present *if* the theory were true: this, however, is only verification, not proof, which would require that I show all logically possible alternatives to be untenable.

---

[44] The possibility of a third alternative—that of unconscious purpose—is considered in the sequel.

[45] Stace, *op. cit.*, p. 81.

From the mere fact that x causes y, I cannot conclude that y exists if, and only if, x exists.

Now this confusion of verification with proof is exactly what the teleological argument commits:[46] virtuous minds tend to produce valuable things; the cosmic process has resulted in the production of valuable things; therefore it must be the effect and end of a virtuous mind. Clearly, such argument is fallacious.

Suppose, in the face of this difficulty, that refuge is taken in mere verification, so that the existence of God becomes no more than an hypothesis in the strict scientific sense. This is certainly a possible position, but it is open to the charge that it fails to explain the existence of bad things in the universe:

> Although this may be a good hypothesis insofar as it explains some of the facts, it is not so good as the hypothesis, that 'chance,' i.e., the laws of nature operating without design, produces all the events and things in the world. . . . If the world is *not* ruled by a designing mind, but only by the blind laws of nature, then that the world would be an indiscriminate mixture of good and bad things—as it is—is precisely what we should expect.[47]

The conclusion to be drawn is that "the argument from design turns out to be worthless."[48]

In answer to this objection: we readily grant that the argument from the progressive realization of valuable entities in an order of increasing significance is a basic aspect of teleology; and that if the argument rested *merely* on the analogy from experience (i.e., that virtuous minds tend to produce valuable things), it would either involve the fallacy of consequent or be no more than a hypothesis. But we deny that these considerations establish the invalidity of the argument.

In the first place, let us suppose that the theistic postulate *is* only hypothetical and admits of no more than verification. Stace's point is that it is not as simple an hypothesis as chance, nor as adequate, since it fails to explain the existence of bad things, while chance explains both good and bad. Now the following remarks become appropriate: Stace assumes that theism cannot explain the presence of evil; if it is possible to show that evil *is* explicable in a theistic

[46] *Idem.*
[47] *Ibid.*, p. 82.
[48] *Idem.*

universe, then the two hypotheses will stand so far on equal footing. In the sequel just such a theistic explanation of evil is proffered for consideration.

Assume then for the present that the problem of evil is soluble in theistic terms: this means that the theistic and chance hypotheses are equally plausible in this respect. But actually the theistic hypothesis is *far more* plausible, for every case or instance of valuable things, except the one in dispute, does involve conscious purpose. If appeal is made to any of the whole range of adaptations in nature, the appeal is unjustified, for these are the very cases in dispute. The objector to teleology can point to no instance of valuable things which does not involve conscious purpose, unless he does so in the area of dispute, which would beg the question. Now, of two otherwise equally plausible hypotheses is it not rationally admissible to accept the alternative which every analogy of human experience supports in other spheres than the one in question? True, there is no compulsion, but the rational case is for the theistic hypothesis: to say that the case in question *may* be the result of blind elements churning the universe with motion is begging the question for the naturalist or at most stating a bare possibility.

As a matter of fact, however, the theistic postulate is not a mere hypothesis: for it can be shown that the hypothesis of chance is rationally inadmissible; hence that theism admits of proof, since its alternative is impossible. We have already shown, in our answer to the preceding objection, that the chance motion of material elements is thus inadmissible as an hypothesis: first, because the cosmological argument has already established the existence of an absolutely necessary being which transcends the space-time universe and is its ground of existence; second, because it is impossible to explain the origin of mind from a material base, as would be necessary on the chance hypothesis. But a proposition is considered proved when (1) those facts follow which ought to follow if it were true, and (2) all logically possible alternatives are eliminated. Therefore the case for theism admits, not merely of hypothetical verification, but of demonstrative proof.

I therefore conclude that the theistic postulate does not involve the fallacy of consequent when properly formulated, and that *consequently* the objection is invalid and unsustained.

C. *Epistemological Objections:* which attempt to show that the argument to design or purpose is without a sufficient experiential foundation

Because the design argument does no more than make explanation in terms of intelligence a possibility (converse of the preceding objection).—The teleological argument rests on the assumption that where there is order there is mind, whereas this conclusion is extremely doubtful. So Lamprecht (who by some accident poses this as an objection to the cosmological argument): the argument "rests on the supposition that where there is order there is manifestation of mind; but for that supposition there is no empirical evidence, and indeed the supposition, being highly general, is more doubtful than the conclusion it is designed to support."[49]

Of course, the analogy of human experience makes the supposition of an intelligent will possible, perhaps even probable. Thus Mill (who sharply distinguishes design and purpose aspects of teleology): "The resemblances between some of the arrangements in nature and some of those made by men are considerable, and even as mere resemblances afford a certain presumption of similarity of cause; but how great that presumption is it is hard to say. All that can be said with certainty is that these likenesses make creation by intelligence considerably more probable than if the likenesses had been less, or than if there had been no likenesses at all."[50] It therefore seems that explanation in terms of intelligent will is at best possible or probable.

By way of answer: we need only observe that this objection is merely the preceding objection in converse form. Whereas the former argued that the inference to ends involved the fallacy of consequent, this present statement asserts that the argument is *no more* than hypothetical or possible. Therefore, the argument has already been refuted; and I state it in this form merely for the convenience of those persons who might encounter the objection thus and fail to recognize it as a restatement of the preceding allegation. I pass therefore to a consideration of the next objection.

Because the inference to design is justifiable only on the basis of a past experience of association: and we have no such experience, either of the world as a whole, or of the particular instances of design in it.—The teleological argument assumes that, in arguing to a

---

[49]Lamprecht, *op. cit.,* p. 32.
[50]Mill, *op. cit.,* p. 72.

designer, we know "what sort of a thing a universe due to intelligent design would be, and what sort of thing one due to no design would be. But in fact we have not any such antecedent knowledge."[51] In fact, we are justified in the inference to design merely on the basis of a past experience of association: thus, to use Mill's example, when I find a watch, the reason I infer a watchmaker is not that the watch has designed structure, but that I already know by direct experience that watches are made by men.[52]

Thus if we had seen worlds made by an intelligent will, or particular natural instances of adaptation thus brought about, we might infer from the present world, or from the experienced instances of adaptation, that the cause involved was an intelligent will. But we have had no such experience. Hence the inference to an intelligent will is unjustified, if it is to be regarded as a true induction. In fairness to Mill, it ought to be said that he does not push the objection this far, but it seems to me that he was inconsistent in not doing so.

By way of answer: this objection (and every other which admits the presence of adaptation at all) has already been refuted by implication in the preceding sections. Of course, if I try to show that the universe contains evidence of design or purpose, I do assume that I know what sort of thing a universe due to intelligent design and purpose would be. That I have no such antecedent knowledge would appear to me to be a strange objection, to say the very least. For if I did not know what purpose and design were, if I were not familiar with my own experience of adapting means to ends, I would *never attempt* an explanation of the universe in terms of design or purpose: certainly I should not be so absurd as to explain *anything* by something that I do not know. But this is no objection to the teleological argument, or to any other, so far as I can see.

But more importantly: even if it were true that we infer design from an experience of past association, the assertion that we are justified in asserting design *only* on the basis of such past association, involves that very fallacy of consequent which previously had been directed against the teleological argument itself. Just because I *do* infer design on the basis of past experience, this does not mean that I can infer design only on this basis. It may be that a bolt of lightning will effect the burning down of a house, but it may also be

[51]A. E. Taylor, *Does God Exist?*, p. 101; cited for purpose of refutation.
[52]Mill, *op. cit.*, p. 72.

the case that this effect is accomplished by the lighting of a match, or even atomic disintegration. And so the teleologist can also charge the fallacy of consequent, and that with justice.

The objection that we thus infer design only from experience of past association is, in fact, either nonexistent or self-contradictory. I infer a watchmaker from a watch, it is alleged, because of my past direct experience that watches are made by men. But when I find a *particular* watch on a sandy beach, I have had no experience of its origin: although I may have seen many similar articles made by men, I have not seen *this* one thus made, for it is a distinct, unique, particular, determinate watch. Now either I am justified in the induction that this watch was made by an intelligent will or not. If not, then it is false that I may infer design from a past experience that similar objects were produced by intelligent will—but this contradicts the original hypothesis. Yet if I *am* justified in the induction, then the original hypothesis is no longer an objection, for it involves the same passage of thought as is involved in the teleological argument itself. In the one case, I pass from an entity, of whose origin I have had no experience, to the inference of an intelligent will, for the reason that in the past similar objects were experienced by me to have been effects of intelligent will: thus, according to the objection, I reason from this particular watch to a watchmaker. In the other case, I do exactly the same thing: I pass from an instance of adaptation, for example, to an intelligent will as its cause, because every one of my own past experiences of adaptation is thus explicable. Consequently, the original hypothesis is not an objection but a support for the teleological argument.

It may be objected that in the case of the watch, I can corroborate my induction by other considerations; but this is not an objection. It still is true that I can never see any particular watch made, once it is given in experience as completed. The teleological argument also has numerous other corroborations, e.g., the reduction of the alternatives to self-contradiction. It must therefore be that the original objection either disappears or is self-contradictory.

As a matter of fact, however, it is not true that I infer design only on the basis of an experience of past association, unless it is true in such a way as would involve the validity of the teleological argument itself. As A. E. Taylor points out: if an explorer finds certain objects which, because of the coadaptation of the various parts, appear to be artifacts, he concludes the existence of intelligent beings as their author, even though no other evidence of the existence of such a race or tribe or individual might be available.[53] Similarly, if we found a watch in the sand, even though we had never seen one before, the coadaptation of the various parts to produce a unitary result would argue purposive contrivance: and it is just such contrivance that nature everywhere discloses.

Thus it appears that either the objection is false that I may infer intelligent will only on the basis of past experience of association, or that the objection is true in such a way that it admits the validity of the teleological argument itself and therefore is not an objection at all.

Because the argument from the progressive realization of ends is purely anthropomorphic and anthropocentric.—The teleological argument, in its emphasis upon the progressive realization of ends in the universe in an order of increasingly significant value from matter to life to mind, assumes that man, as the embodiment of the stage of mind, is the goal of the creative process. But this self-glorification is pure anthropocentrism, or to let Bertrand Russell speak for himself:

> Is there not something a trifle absurd in the spectacle of human beings holding a mirror before themselves, and thinking what they behold so excellent as to prove that a Cosmic Purpose must have been aiming at it all along? . . . Only abysmal self-complacency can see in Man a reason which Omniscience could consider adequate as a motive for the Creator.[54]

Surely the teleological argument rests on the most extreme and unbridled self-centeredness and self-preoccupation.

By way of answer: even if this objection were valid, it would not destroy the teleological argument, for *that* argument rests, not merely on the culmination of the cosmic process in man, but on the whole structure of the adaptation of means to ends in the general order of nature. Even if it were false that man is the "highest product in respect of value, and in the light of whose emergence all Nature, to which he is akin, seems to have its *raison d'etre*,"[55] still the teleologi-

[53]*Op. cit.*, pp. 103-105.
[54]*Religion and Science*, pp. 221, 222.
[55]F. R. Tennant, *Philosophical Theology*, II, p. 114.

cal argument would stand. For, as Tennant also observes, "the forcibleness of Nature's suggestion that she is the outcome of intelligent design lies not in particular cases of adaptedness in the world, nor even in the multiplicity of them . . . [but] consists rather in the conspiration of innumerable causes to produce, by their united and reciprocal action, and to maintain, a general order of Nature."[56]

Furthermore, the objection as usually put is somewhat overstated: for the argument does not, or should not, assert that man is the highest being under God; for the most ardent teleologist ought to admit that there may be in the universe other orders of rational beings beside man; what the argument does imply is that man affords some hint regarding the designed end of the world process and that "whereas in the realm of nature beneath man no final purpose can be discerned, such purpose may be discerned in beings possessed of rationality, appreciation, self-determination, and morality."[57]

But, in fact, the objection is unsustained in any case. From a purely evolutionary point of view—which we here assume for the sake of argument—is it not the case that man is the highest product of the process? He is such in at least two distinct ways: first, he embodies, both by virtue of his physical structure and primarily by his possession of rational nature, the greatest capacity for complex adjustment to environment—and evolution is just the passage from a simpler to a more complex adjustment; second, man is the last principal species to appear in the evolutionary process—about this point there is little dispute.

It seems therefore reasonable to argue that what, as a matter of empirical fact, is the (so far) final achievement of the evolutionary process, is also the end of the intelligent will that underlies the process, if there be any such end or will at all: and this last point is not here in dispute. Where *else* in the process should the end be located? If the end exists somewhere in "nature beneath man," why has the process of evolution gone on to achieve man? Man could only exist as means to subserve the assumed ultimate end. Now the concept of means admits of at least two meanings: (1) conditions for the existence of a presumed end, as hydrogen and oxygen are means to the existence of water; (2) conditions employed by a presumed end for the realization of its own ends, as sticks are among the means whereby a man builds a fire for some reason. Now the first of these two mean-

---

[56]*Ibid.*, p. 79.
[57]*Ibid.*, pp. 113, 114.

ings is inapplicable, because one thing cannot be the condition of the existence of another unless it possesses prior or at least contemporaneous existence: and man was the last principal species to appear. The second meaning is applicable only to the activity of rational nature and therefore must either assert panpsychism or admit that rational nature (as in man) is the end of the process after all.

But again: either rational and self-conscious existence *has* an assignable value as over against brute matter and mere life, or it has no such assignable value. If it has such an assignable value in this context, then Russell's objection is invalid at once, for that which has greater assignable value is by that very fact more appropriate as an end.

Suppose, however, I assert that self-conscious and rational existence has no assignable value as over against matter and life. This assertion is a judgment and therefore possesses two sets of characteristics: first, it is possible only on the condition that rational nature exists, since judgment is a capacity of mind alone; second, it is either true or false. If it is false, then the objection against the teleological argument is at once removed. Suppose therefore that the assertion **is** true: it would then be self-contradictory. For truth itself has no existence apart from the judgments which rational minds construct on the basis of experience: and the statement asserts that rational nature has no assignable value as over against matter and life. It therefore follows that truth has no such assignable value and hence, for that reason, must be either false or meaningless; since if it is really true that it has no such value, the statement itself, if considered true, has no such value. It results, consequently, that the truth of the proposition—rational existence has no assignable value as over against matter and life—involves its own falsity and is therefore self-contradictory.

It may be objected that the analysis is faulty, since the objector asserts, not that truth has no value, but that, as possible only for rational nature, it has no value greater than that of matter or life. But this objection is also to no avail. For the assertion that anything at all has value—whether matter, life, or mind—is possible only for a mind, both because it is a judgment and because value is predicated only with respect to the experienced or anticipated utility of a given entity—and only mind has a capacity thus to judge with respect to given entities. It therefore is the case that matter and life have no assignable value apart from mind, since only minds can assign values.

Now then: if truth and, more basically, mind have the same value as matter and life considered independently, they therefore have no value. But we have already shown that the assertion—truth has no assignable value—is self-contradictory. It is concluded that the whole objection—that mind has no assignable value as over against matter and life—is self-contradictory and hence invalid.

While I think the objection already stands refuted, one final set of remarks might be made from a more positive point of view. The implication of the preceding analysis is that rational, moral nature is the only conceivable end of the cosmic process, since any other assumption about such end involves either material or logical contradiction. After all, if God is Himself rational and moral, it is *prima facie* reasonable that He would create a universe in which rational and therefore moral being was the chief end.

I therefore conclude that the whole objection is invalid and that the teleological argument is anthropocentric only in being rational and for the very reason that the chief end of the universe is rational.

Because any given entity has no single function and hence not a single purpose.—The teleological argument assumes that "everything has its 'purpose' in the total scheme of nature, whether animate or inanimate."[58] But as a matter of fact, many, if not all, entities have no single purpose or function. "No object has an *absolute* or *single* 'purpose' under all circumstances. If a random stone is to be spoken of as having a purpose or function, this is not something with which the stone is intrinsically endowed or antecedently equipped; it is determined only *after* the stone is found to function within its environment in a definite way."[59] It follows that "the assumption of a single purpose on which this teleological argument rests is far from being the only interpretation of the facts."[60]

In answer: we readily grant that a given object in the environment of man may be put to a multiplicity of purposes; although the higher we go in the cosmic process, the more definitely assignable are the functions of various entities: for example, in the structure of organic beings, definite and particular functions are to a large extent precisely definable.

But how are we to explain the fact that intelligence *has* appeared

[58]Randall and Buchler, *op. cit.*, p. 162.
[59]*Ibid.*, p. 163.
[60]*Idem.*

and *can* adapt its environment to a multiplicity of purposes? If the objection means anything, it means that nature is so constructed that it can be instrumental in the realization of ends which intelligence may envisage. And if this be granted, the case for a teleological principle in the structure of reality is but strengthened: it is the very fitness of the inorganic to be instrumental in the development of life and mind that needs to be explained by reference to intelligent will.

Now the objector may insist that we have merely skirted the objection: he may say that after all, if the universe admits of teleological explanation, then every part of it must be thus explicable ultimately and have an assignable purpose, whereas experience does show that given entities may execute numerous functions. In reply: we grant at once that if the universe is teleologically explicable, it must be thoroughly so from an ultimate point of view, so that all things and events must be traceable to the total set of conditions necessary for the realization of the Divine Purpose. Now we have already indicated the desired purpose by implication. Man is the chief end of the cosmic process, so far as that process is known: and therefore other aspects of the process are significant primarily as means for the development of rational and moral existence.

What then is the purpose of a stone, or a planet, or a universe—excluding the specified chief end? The purpose of all these is the instrumental one of constituting an environment for rational and moral being. I have therefore given a teleological explanation, in general terms, of every given entity in the environment of rational and moral being. And if it be asked how any given entity contributes specifically to this end, the answer is twofold: first, that, while I am not omniscient, experience—both on scientific and popular levels—is progressively unfolding the answer; second, that the reply to this question need not be exhaustive, if I have already shown that rational and moral being is the chief end of the cosmic process. It is therefore concluded that the original objection is invalid and that its basic assertion of the adaptiveness of environment to intelligent ends is actually a consideration in support of teleology.

Because the teleological principle is practically barren.—We regard an hypothesis as fruitful if it can be used to predict future events; and the aim of such prediction is one of the basic motives of scientific investigation. But how does the teleological and theistic explanation enable us to predict future events? That a given entity has a purpose does not enable me to say anything about its future action or significance. Randall and Buchler state essentially this objection: "The supernaturalistic hypothesis is regarded as unsatisfactory because . . . it explains nothing in a scientific sense but rather limits inquiry and the search for objective evidence."[61] It therefore follows that the theistic hypothesis is pragmatically useless.

In answer: we have already shown that the theistic explanation does not occupy the status of an hypothesis but rather that of objective validity; the objection is therefore invalid because it erroneously assumes that theism is purely hypothetical. If the evidence establishes the existence of x beyond question, its existence cannot be impaled on the cross of pragmatic barrenness.

But with regard to the objection itself: how are we to explain the possibility of successful prediction at all? Such prediction is possible only on the condition that a general order of nature is continuously maintained in accordance with generally fixed laws. The force which maintains this uniformity must be either the material world, or some part of it, or an extraneous cause: and the untenable character of the first two alternatives has already been shown in the discussion of the cosmological argument. It follows that such a cause or force must be an extraneous reality that thus transcends the space-time universe, or what is the same thing, the absolutely necessary being. Consequently, God, or the absolute being, is the unexpressed premise of every predictive hypothesis: and far from being unfruitful, the existence of God is the only ultimate principle that does enable us to predict the future; for it makes it possible for us to predict what is the *sine qua non* for prediction itself: namely, the continued maintenance of the system of nature and therefore of predictability itself.

The present objection is thus doubly invalid, both by making God's existence hypothetical, and by denying that theism explains anything about the future.

D. *Metaphysical Objections:* which attempt to show that the argument from teleology does not give a valid explanation of ultimate reality

Because the apparent presence of design and purpose may conceivably have resulted from the chance interaction of elements in a material base.—On the *cosmic* level: life and mind might have arisen

[61] *Ibid.,* p. 227.

by accident from the chance concatenation of material constituents. Thus Russell, after suggesting this possibility, singles out the existence of life and remarks: "It may seem odd that life should occur by accident, but in such a large universe accidents will happen."[62] And so Tennant represents an opponent as suggesting: "Rich suggestions of design in the known world yield no proof of design in the universe, since our ordered fragment may be but a temporary and casual episode in the history of the universe . . . a chance product of mindless agency in a universe which has had opportunity to produce all sorts of local and ephemeral worlds within a World."[63]

On the *biological* level: the fitness of the inorganic to minister to life and the internal adaptedness of organic beings may have resulted from natural interaction with the environment. So Mill, although he thinks that "the adaptations in nature afford a large balance of probability in favor of creation by intelligence."[64] On the evolutionary hypothesis, it is no marvel that the parts of an organism should be adapted to perform particular functions or that the inorganic serves to minister to life, for these functions of the organism were developed through natural selection of those particular forms of life which, being accidentally produced, were most fit to survive in a given environment. If it be objected that just those conditions which are present had to be present for the development of life and its forms, the answer is that if conditions had been different, other forms of life, consonant with them, might have emerged.

On the *psychic* level: the intelligibility of the world may be a special case of adaptation which, as at lower levels, results from environmental interaction. Mind itself being a construct on a material base, it is no object of astonishment that it should be adapted to the understanding of a nature from which it sprang by natural selection. So G. P. Conger writes: "Arguments based on the wonders of epistemology lose their point when one regards the world of nature as capable of moulding mind in its own matrix and keeping in contact with it during the process."[65]

Thus the evolutionary hypothesis cuts away every implicate for design and purpose by enumerating a series of proximate causes which render an adequate explanation of the whole range of adapta-

[62]*Religion and Science*, p. 216.
[63]*Op. cit.*, II, p. 80.
[64]*Op. cit.*, pp. 74, 75.
[65]G. P. Conger, *The Ideologies of Religion*, p. 119.

tion and the progressive realization of ends: consequently, the teleological argument is invalid and the assertion of an ultimate intelligent will therefore is superfluous.

In answer: The basic assumption and *sine qua non* of the entire objection is that the whole space-time universe is explicable in terms of chance interaction of material elements: but we have already refuted this basic assumption *ad nauseam* in our consideration of the preceding objections. And with the general discrediting of the chance hypothesis goes the refutation of the specific applications involved in the present objection. To summarize, we have shown that the basic assumption of chance is untenable for three main reasons. First, because, even if we were to grant the existence of a self-subsistent material base (which we do not grant), any explanation of the structure or action of these elements in terms of chance is almost infinitely improbable and therefore untenable as an ultimate theory: consult our answer to the first logical objection above. Second, because the cosmological argument has already shown that a material universe in interaction, when offered as an ultimate explanation, involves the rationally impossible infinite series and therefore must be grounded in an absolutely necessary being that transcends the space-time universe. Third, because mind could not have arisen from a material base, since there is no continuity of essential structure that is common to both matter and mind, in terms of the naturalistic hypothesis. In point of fact, therefore, the entire objection stands guilty at reason's bar before it even faces the jury.

But to consider the objection on its own merits: the suggestion that order (in the sense of apparent design and purpose) in our fragment of the world, whether from a temporal or spatial point of view, may be a merely casual episode in a vast space-time universe is actually untenable in any case. Not only is it the case that any chance universe is absolutely improbable, it is also true that order in the fragment implies order in the assumed whole. Either our isolable (?) fragment is causally related to the assumed whole of the space-time universe, or not. If not, then there is no basis for speaking of the fragment as part of the whole and no reason for even affirming that this extraneous whole exists. It must therefore be that our ordered fragment is an integral part of the whole and is causally related to it. But this must mean that the two are interdependent, that order in our fragment springs from order in the whole and reciprocally conditions the whole: "The ordered oasis is not an isolable fragment. It and the supposed desert or 'chaos' are interdependent. It is because the desert is what it is that the oasis is what it is; and the one has orderedness only by permission, so to say, of the other."[66] Hence the order of our fragment springs from a nexus of conditions in the assumed chaos, which is therefore not a chaos at all, since that which contains the conditions of order is by that very fact itself an order. And if it occurs to someone to suggest that the present "fragmentary" order did not spring from conditions in the assumed "chaos," then either he will have to repudiate the causal axiom—which we have already shown to be an impossible procedure—or he will himself give explicit support to the teleological argument.

Again, even if the whole effect of the cosmic process were explicable in terms of successive proximate causes, this fact would not be incompatible with teleological explanation—although, as the cosmological argument has already shown, the series of proximate causes itself must rest in the existence of an absolutely ultimate cause. The teleological argument does not need to resort to a *deus ex machina:* it need not assert that God supervenes on the evolutionary process at every point and produces adaptations thus by direct intervention— any more than when I set a series of causes in motion to attain a certain effect, it must be held that I directly perform the operation of each intermediary factor, if I am to be the ultimate explanation of the particular orientation of the series. Similarly with God, although it is true that God sustains the operation of second causes in a manner that transcends my sustaining of the operation of intermediary factors by my intent, purpose, and initial action in a given situation. So Tennant, commenting on the organic realm: "The fact of organic evolution, even when the maximum of instrumentality is accredited to what is figuratively called natural selection, is not incompatible with teleology on a grander scale. . . . This kind of teleology does not set out from the particular adaptations in individual organisms or species so much as from considerations as to the progressiveness of the evolutionary process and as to the organic realm as a whole."[67] Explanation in terms of proximate causes, even if it were possible on a completely exhaustive scale, does not therefore eliminate appeal to intelligent will as the ultimate explanation of the whole progress of successive adaptations in nature.

[66]F. R. Tennant, *op. cit.*, II, p. 80.
[67]*Ibid.*, p. 84.

But as a matter of fact, even if the evolutionary explanation of the organic realm were granted, it appears that the process is not explicable merely in terms of proximate causes, but that it requires a progressive and continuing intelligent guidance for its sufficient explanation. Of course, this does not mean that proximate causes are not operative at every point in the process; what it does mean is that the particular mode of their operation is explicable only in teleological terms.

The "survival of the fittest" presupposes the arrival of the fit, and, as Tennant remarks, "throws no light thereupon."[68] This is not to say that there are no proximate causes from which the "fittest" arrives: but rather that, merely because a *chance* arrival of anything at all is, as we have already explained at length, absolutely improbable, the fittest could not conceivably appear without the guidance of intelligent will in setting up the whole series of proximate causes and maintaining its operation. The suggestion that, had there been different conditions, other forms of life consonant with them might have appeared is actually pointless: for "the existence of any forms of life that we may conceive, the necessary environment, whatever its nature, must be complex and dependent upon a multiplicity of conditions, such as are not reasonably attributable to blind forces or to pure mechanism."[69] In other words, any environment of life would depend on a complex of conditions that is absolutely improbable from the standpoint of chance alone. It follows therefore that any complex of conditions from which any form of life arises, requires explanation in terms of guidance by intelligent will.

The same point can be cast in a different light with a similar result, if we ask whether natural selection does explain specific adaptations at all, and particularly the progress of the cosmic process as a whole in the biological realm. In the first place, in the case of any given adaptation, the mutations required to achieve the complex structure are, in almost innumerable instances, a burden and a handicap, rather than a means to more adequate adjustment to environment. If pure natural selection were operative, mutations of this type would die out because not so fit to survive as their hardier, but less complex, relatives: and yet on the theory of natural selection, it is just such mutations which account for the progressive realization of more

[68]*Ibid.*, p. 85.
[69]*Ibid.*, p. 87.

complex forms. But according to the theory itself, these variants ought to die out as not fit to survive.

Burtt, though noncommittal on the point, gives this illustration: he speaks of the complex of conditions involved in the development of a bird's wings, through which it is fitted to fly, and then remarks:

> Can this remarkably complex adaptation be accounted for mechanically, by the principle of gradual natural selection . . . ? No . . . because the first rudiments of a wing could hardly enable their possessor to fly; they would not only bring no positive advantage in the struggle for existence, but would be a useless burden and therefore a handicap. Their possessors would be less adapted to the needs of life rather than more. Yet, according to the Darwinian theory of natural selection, such adaptations are acquired through the accumulation of specific variations of structure, each of which when it occurs is preserved because it provides its possessor with a distinct advantage over others who compete with it for the privileges of existence. There is no such advantage in a quarter or half of a wing; to explain the gradual growth of a complete wing enabling its possessor actually to fly, we must leave natural selection and suppose an intelligent cause directing the entire process toward the attainment of its appropriate end.[70]

Again, chance adaptation and natural selection, even if operative, would not explain the radical steps in the evolutionary process. If a given form is well adapted to its environment, a stabilization results and the process becomes fixed at that point. On the other hand, if it is not well adapted it dies out in favor of forms which are and which therefore become fixed. This point is developed at considerable length by Prof. Wild, who points out that forms especially well adapted to a given environment are by that very fact ruled out of the main progress of evolutionary advance. Adaptation to environment "has been on the whole a conservative factor which has produced, not advance, but flexible stability like that of certain forms which became so well adapted in the Cambrian period that they have suffered no major change down to the present day."[71] Yet as a matter of fact, the higher forms of life *have* arrived; and this fact therefore seems explicable only in terms of the activity of directive intelligence.

[70]E. A. Burtt, *Types of Religious Philosophy*, p. 109.
[71]John Wild, *Introduction to Realistic Philosophy*, p. 367.

In the light of the above considerations, I therefore conclude that the apparent presence of design and purpose in the universe is inexplicable in terms of the chance interaction of elements in a material base, and that hence the entire objection is invalid.

Because the argument, if valid, does not involve theism in the fullest sense.—

> *Because all the phenomena, while they require explanation teleologically, may be accounted for in terms of unconscious purpose, or impersonal intelligence and will.*

An objector might try to escape the dilemma posed by a necessary choice between chance and theism, by the accusation that, while we have all along assumed that self-conscious intelligence and chance are the only alternatives of explanation, this basic assumption is false. For we have overlooked the possibility of unconscious purpose or impersonal intelligence.[72] Might there not be an *élan vital* which strives blindly toward what happen to become significant and progressively realized ends, when viewed from the standpoint of intelligence? After all, if our own actions may often concrete in ends which, though not previsioned, are nevertheless significant, could not this be true of nature itself?[73] It appears therefore that the teleological argument need conclude no more than such an unconscious purposive factor, and not the personal God of theism.

In answer: aside from the cases here in question—which therefore cannot be the basis of argument without begging the question—every analogy of human experience supports the contention that no purpose exists except a conscious one and no intelligence except a personal one. In other words, the hypothesis of unconscious purpose is of such a character that it admits of absolutely no experiential support without appeal to the very cases that are in dispute. If it be said that our actions sometimes result in effects which we do not anticipate, this is true: but it cannot be said that these effects are ends or are purposed in any intelligible sense of those terms. They are rather the concomitants of purposive activity which, due to our ignorance, were not previsioned. Such effects may *become* ends, or means to further ends, but they do so only on the basis of conscious espousal. Hence experiential analogy is entirely on the side of the position that teleology is personal or self-conscious in character.

[72] A. H. Strong, *Systematic Theology*, p. 78.
[73] Cf. Tennant, *op. cit.*, II, pp. 107-108.

The same point may be sharpened in effectiveness by the assertion that the expressions, "unconscious purpose" and "impersonal intelligence," are self-contradictory. For when do we call a process purposive or intelligent? Only when it is the result of an action consciously calculated to produce a previsioned end: and it is only with respect to such an end that predicates of purposiveness and intelligence are appropriate.

It may be, for example, that Benjamin Franklin discovered electricity while flying a kite in a storm: but we do not say that this effect was Franklin's purpose in flying a kite. His action was an intelligent action, I presume: but it was so only with reference to some previsioned end—for example, that Franklin took pleasure in kite flying, or perhaps even that he flew the kite to escape boredom. The concomitant, but unforeseen, effect of an action is not its purpose.

If I should, while driving in my car, strike down and kill a small child without any prevision of this effect, would it be said that I killed the child purposely or that the killing *qua* killing was an intelligent action? The answer is no: in fact, the degree of my responsibility is determined precisely by the extent to which I did or could foresee the effect. It follows from such considerations as these that an unforeseen effect is not *as such* either purposive or intelligent.

What then is an unconscious purpose? It is an unpurposed purpose—which is nonsense. Or what is an impersonal intelligence? Since self-consciousness is involved in the direction of action toward a previsioned end, an impersonal intelligence is an unintelligent intelligence—which, again, is nonsense. Therefore the expressions, "unconscious purpose" and "impersonal intelligence," are self-contradictory and meaningless.

The preceding considerations have already shown that the production of unforeseen effects in human experience is no support for the hypothesis of unconscious purpose. But the same point can be reached in another manner.[74] The unforeseen effects of human action are sometimes advantageous and sometimes not: hence they require redirection through intelligent action which does prevision its end. But, by hypothesis, nature has no such previsioning intelligence: consequently, she must inevitably go straight to her mark or end without intelligent manipulation, if there is to be progressive realiza-

[74]*Ibid.*, p. 108 f.

tion of ends at all. But this would imply, not that the teleological principle was *un*conscious, but if anything *super*conscious.

For "nature's 'unconscious wisdom,' in other words, must vastly exceed the sapience and foresight of humanity, liable as that is to errors which, save for reasoned amendment, might prove fatal."[75] That nature does go straight to her mark would imply, in other words, not the absence of previsioning intelligence, but the complete and exhaustive presence of it, unless we beg the question by referring to instances of the case in dispute—such as animal instinct, etc. It turns out therefore that the assertion—nature is not the result of previsioning intelligence—is self-contradictory.

Finally, it may be asserted that either *no* teleological explanation is necessary at all, or else it is necessary by reference to intelligent will. If unconscious purpose may be all that is required as a teleological explanation, then such purposes can be attributed separately to all the individual instances of adaptation that present themselves in nature. The eye, for example, may be said to have in itself the unconscious purpose of seeing, etc. There seems to be no reason why all the adaptations should be attributed to a single vital force: if we may make the purposive aspects of nature unconscious, contrary to the analogy of human experience, we may also impugn their unity. But it was to explain just such individual instances of adaptation that the teleological principle was suggested in the first place. Consequently, the hypothesis of unconscious purpose really means no more than that although the cosmic process proceeds *as if* it were purposive, as a matter of fact, it is not purposive but merely happens to act as though it were. But this explanation is thus shown to be nothing but the old appeal to chance appearing in a new guise. Since the chance hypothesis has already been shown to be absolutely improbable, it follows that either no teleological explanation is required at all or such an explanation involves personal intelligence and conscious purpose.

It is therefore concluded that conscious purpose and chance are the only alternatives and that the suggested middle alternative of unconscious purpose is either self-contradictory or a mere repetition of the chance hypothesis. And since chance is likewise not a rationally admissible alternative, the ultimate result of our investigation must be the affirmation that intelligent and conscious purpose is the

[75] *Idem.*

only explanation of the gamut of experience that will finally suffice from a rational point of view.

Because the progressive and gradual realization of purpose, through the use of means, is inconsistent with omnipotence as an attribute of God.

Theism involves the assertion of God's omnipotence: but the use of means to gain an end—which is the very meaning of purpose and the characteristic action of intelligence—is inconsistent with this attribute, since the use of means implies limitaton of power. Thus Mill points out:

> Every indication of Design in the Kosmos is so much evidence against the omnipotence of the designer. For what is meant by design? Contrivance: the adaptation of means to an end. But the necessity for contrivance—the need of employing means—is a consequence of the limitation of power. . . . Who would have recourse to means if to attain his end his mere word was sufficient? . . . The evidences, therefore, of Natural Theology distinctly imply that the Author of the Kosmos worked under limitations; that he was obliged to adapt himself to conditions independent of his will. . . .[76]

And Russell bitingly remarks: "The conception of purpose is a natural one to apply to a human artificer. . . . But Omnipotence is subject to no such limitations [as a human artificer]. If God really thinks well of the human race . . . why not proceed, as in Genesis, to create man at once?"[77] The use of means to attain an end would thus seem to outlaw omnipotence: and thus theism, in the fullest sense, is unjustified by the very design argument which purports to support it.

In answer: this objection has already been refuted by implication in our answer to objections against the cosmological argument and in our answer to the expansive—limiting argument of presuppositionalism. In the latter context, we attempted to show that the hypothesis of a finite ultimate, or of a plurality of infinite ultimates, is logically self-contradictory and therefore rationally untenable. Yet it is the very conception of a plurality of ultimates that the present objection embodies, since it implies that God works under conditions which are extraneously applied and imposed. In the former

[76]Mill, *op. cit.*, pp. 75, 76.
[77]*Religion and Science*, pp. 193, 194.

context, it was established that the only rational explanation of existence must be cast in terms of the reality of an absolutely necessary being: that is, a being that contains all the ultimate conditions of existence and therefore faces no extraneous limitations whatsoever in the final analysis.

At the very outset, therefore, the objection is faced with the insuperable difficulty that its basic assumption—namely, that of a finite ultimate—is rationally impossible. But in this case, the real alternatives are not a finite God or an infinite God, but an infinite God or no God at all! And this conclusion is reached without reference to teleology at all. Now we have already shown that no explanation of the universe is possible on the assumption that there *is* no absolutely necessary being or God. Again the alternatives shift: for the choice now is confined to explanation in terms of an infinite God or no explanation at all; since the latter position reduces to a self-contradictory skepticism—asserting, as it does, that no explanation of reality is possible—the former position must be accepted.

Since therefore the refutation of the objection already confronts us, our sole task in the present context is to show that the progressive realization of ends through the use of means is not inconsistent with the existence of an omnipotent and infinite God. That such a God exists has already been established.

Now the objection insists that the use of means to gain an end is inconsistent with the divine omnipotence. But such an objection, pressed to its ultimate implications, would be, not that an omnipotent God cannot use means, but that either He can do nothing, or else all that He can do has been done from eternity. For consider: the objector urges that the use of means to an end is inconsistent with God's omnipotence, since omnipotence ought to achieve its end at once, without means. But the objection applies just as much against the attainment of the end as it does against the use of the means: for how could an omnipotent and all-sufficient God have any end to realize at all?

Such an end would either exist within God, in which case there would be no need of its realization. Or it would exist outside God as a possibility yet to be realized; but then God would not be an omnipotent and absolutely necessary being, for He would be limited by the existence of an end not yet realized. It therefore follows that either an omnipotent God can do nothing or else every possibility of His being has been realized from eternity. If omnipotence cannot employ means and achieve ends, then these two alternatives are the only logical possibilities.

But suppose that an omnipotent God can do nothing: this position is liable to a double objection. First, it contradicts the whole structure of argumentation which asserts that an absolutely necessary being is the only rational explanation of the existing universe: it is just the fact that God *has* done something that led us to conclude *His* existence as an absolute being. Second, the assertion is directly self-contradictory: for a God that can do nothing is utterly devoid of omnipotence, so that the assertion says that an omnipotent God is absolutely impotent—which is absurd.

Now consider the other alternative involved in the ultimate form of the present objection: suppose that all that an omnipotent God can do must have been done from eternity. This position is also objectionable. It contradicts the empirical fact that successive processes *are* going on in the experienced universe: if this is false, at least the illusion of these changes is in process, and the problem is the same. Again, the position would mean that the material universe is eternal: but then there must have been an infinite series of successive changes in the universe, and we have already demonstrated *ad nauseam* the impossibility of an infinite series of actual existents. Thus the supposition that all God's acts must have been executed from eternity is either experientially or logically self-contradictory, or both.

It follows that neither an omnipotent God who can do nothing, nor an omnipotent God who has done all things from eternity, is rationally conceivable. The outcome of the whole argument is that either an omnipotent God can use means in some explicable sense, or no explanation of reality is possible: since this last alternative is self-contradictory, the former must be affirmed.

From a more positive point of view, what is really implied in the divine omnipotence, and how can it be shown that such an omnipotent God may be conceived, without self-contradiction, as using means?

The meaning of divine omnipotence is not the ridiculous doctrine that there are *no* conditions that limit the expression of divine power, but rather it is the doctrine that all such conditions are self-involved and constitute the very structure of God's own being. And since every limit is thus imposed by God's own nature and is therefore timelessly necessary, it follows that every expression of God's power is completely determined by His nature and also timelessly necessary. Consequently, God is called omnipotent for the very reason that the sum total of His actions is completely determined by His nature without the action of any ultimately extraneous conditions. God is not the whole of reality: but every aspect of subordinate reality springs from conditions that were ultimately imposed by the self-determination of the divine Being. Omnipotence therefore may be defined as that attribute of God by virtue of which the total expression of His power is timelessly necessary and completely determined by His nature, independently of extraneous conditions.

Now this very conception of omnipotence involves the concept of means: for the limiting conditions of the divine nature are themselves, from one point of view, so many means to the achievement of the expression of God's power, since a means is by definition a limiting condition necessary to the achievement of a given end. Thus omnipotence is not inconsistent with the use of means, but rather it cannot exist without them, since its very meaning is the complete determination of action by self-involved limiting conditions.

Yet all the ends must therefore coexist with the means in God, and hence it might be insisted that we have actually returned to the already-refuted position that all God's actions have been executed from eternity. Such an objection is, however, invalid; for the absolutely necessary being or God, as we have shown elsewhere, transcends the space-time universe without negating its character as spatial and temporal. This means that the whole content of the temporal series, for example, is directly perceived by God in a single intuition; so that the series is apprehended as a nexus of related parts, the reality of which is not destroyed by their being thus perceived. Thus all God's ends *do* coexist with timeless necessity in what may be called the divine plan: but they so coexist, not because they are not progressively realized in the space-time universe, but because God, as transcending that universe, both imposes all the conditions for its existence and intuits directly the total space-time expression of these conditions in our developing world.

Should I be asked to put this whole point in simple language, I would say: omnipotence is not inconsistent with the use of means because all the means, as well as the end, are an unfolding expression of God's timelessly necessary plan. Since therefore the objection has been shown to be self-contradictory when traced to its ultimate implications, and since omnipotence has been shown necessarily to involve the use of means, I conclude that this objection, like all others before it, has melted before rational analysis.

Because, if the end of the cosmic process is the production of mind, the puny extent of its realization is unsuited to the nature of a Supreme Existence.

Thus Bertrand Russell writes: "if it is the purpose of the Cosmos to evolve mind, we must regard it as rather incompetent in having produced so little in such a long time."[78] In point of fact, such an objection is largely evasive. It implies that the Divine Purposer was faced with conditions not originally imposed by His will: but this has already been shown to be rationally untenable, since the absolutely necessary being ultimately imposes *all* the conditions for the existence of the entire space-time universe.

Does the appearance of mind require explanation in terms of intelligent will, or not? If it does require such explanation at all, the question of whether the number of minds is ten or ten billion, is irrelevant to the validity of the teleological conclusion. After all, suppose God had created ten times—or a million times, if you like— the number of minds that have appeared. Russell could always say that God was incompetent since He could have created a still larger number, an infinite number of actually existing minds being inconceivable. It would seem, then, that either no explanation of a teleological nature is required, or else the question of the number of minds thus to be explained is irrelevant: and since the former position is already discredited, the latter must be allowed to stand.

Again, how, in any case, does Russell know how many minds the universe has produced? There may be uncounted orders of rational beings beside those which have appeared on our terrestrial ball. If the naturalist can speak of the experienced world as but a tiny fragment of the whole, the teleologist can do the same and suggest the possibility that the minds present in this fragment are likewise dwarfed in number by the total production of self-conscious beings

[78] *Ibid.*, p. 216.

in the whole universe. At least, there seems to be no way of denying such a possibility.

Finally, it may be pointed out that intrinsic value is not a function of quantity at all. Is a musician, for example, more competent because he composes ten symphonies instead of one? The point is not decided in this way at all, but rather by a consideration of whether, in such symphonies as he *has* written, something of great aesthetic worth has been achieved. Shall I impugn a Beethoven or a Brahms on the ground that each might have written more musical classics? If it be said that a musician who composes ten symphonies of aesthetic worth is more competent than one who composes two, this may be true: but it is true, not because of the greater number of the products as such, but because they all evince the single, sustained capacity to produce objects of aesthetic worth. The production of a greater number of symphonies simply convinces us that the ability therein expressed is a continuous capacity of the composer. In a similar way, it should hardly be said that God is incompetent be-cause He did not produce a greater number of minds: both because God is the *only* composer of minds so that no comparison with the ability of a rival is possible; and because if rational and moral being *is* the true end of His purpose, then it is of intrinsic worth in an ultimate sense and cannot be judged by quantitative criteria.

Such considerations suffice, I think, to justify the consignment of the entire objection to the abyss of unreason.

> *Because every purpose of God is doomed to defeat in*
> *the future equal distribution of energy in*
> *the space-time universe.*

Life and mind, the teleological argument asserts, are explicable only in terms of an ultimate intelligent will. But in fact, these levels of reality will eventually suffer dissolution in the death of the space-time universe through the eventual equal distribution of energy in the universe. "The second law of thermodynamics tells us that, on the whole, energy is always passing from more concentrated to less concentrated forms, and that, in the end, it will have all passed into a form in which further change is impossible. When that has happened, if not before, life must cease."[79] When therefore life, and presumably finite minds as well, passes into dissolution, the cosmic

[79]*Ibid.*, p. 218.

purpose will be defeated. But surely, it might be urged, a purpose doomed to defeat is not the purpose of an infinite God, and hence not that of the God of the highest theism.

In answer: the objection implies a naturalistic, if not materialistic, view of mind, since it assumes that the dissolution of the series of material or physical changes will involve also the dissolution of mind. But mind has already been shown to be qualitatively distinct from matter, since it is inexplicable either as a series of material constituents in motion or as a mere function of such constituents. Now the production of mind (that is, of rational and moral being) has been shown to be the chief end of the cosmic process: and since mind transcends material constituents, the death of the solar system need not involve the dissolution of mind at all and thus not the defeat of the divine purpose either. The contemplated equality of energy distribution will therefore be, not the extinction of God's purpose, but the transcension of its instrumental and temporary environment. It is not our purpose here to argue for the survival of the self-conscious mind after physical death: but the established nature of mind makes such survival at least possible—and this is all that is required to vitiate the objection that the "death" of the physical universe will dissolve the cosmic purpose in a mist of utter stability.

And this consideration suggests a further point. The dependence of the universe on God has already been established: the conditions for its existence rest in the absolute necessity of God's existence. Now if, as seems to be the case, God conditioned the existence of the present space-time universe as an environment for His purpose, no objection can be brought, in principle, against the assertion that such a God might also condition the existence of a new environment for the further development of rational and moral being.

I therefore conclude that God's purpose is not necessarily doomed to defeat and that hence the objection is unsustained.

Because intelligence in God must differ so radically
from human intelligence as to make any
analogy meaningless.

If God is described as a personal intelligence, His intelligence must be so different from ours that the analogy between the two is meaningless: a mind without progressive, successive apprehension is not a mind at all.[80] Theism grants that intelligence in God is devoid

[80] Cf. Burtt, *op. cit.*, p. 222, in a comment on Hume's position.

of temporal succession and discursive process. Otherwise, time would be a form of His experience and He would be neither omnipotent nor omniscient. God, that is, does not think a succession of ideas, but rather He thinks the totality of ideas in an eternal or timelessly necessary intuition. But are not discursive reasoning and successive apprehension essential to the very existence of an intelligent mind? If God therefore lacks these characteristics, can He be described as a personal intelligence at all?

In answer: actually, the appropriate reply to this objection has already been given in numerous other contexts. For it has already been established that the existence of an absolutely necessary being possessed of intelligent will is the only ultimately possible explanation of the existence of the space-time universe; and, further, that the essential characteristic of intelligence—namely, the adaptation of means to ends—is not inconsistent with God's transcendence of the temporal series, but is, on the contrary, actually involved in that transcension.

It therefore appears that intelligence in God and intelligence in man are not *essentially* different but only—if we may say so in the language of technical logic—*accidentally* different. It certainly is essential to intelligence that it have a structure in which limiting conditions prescribe the existence of ends that are willed. In God, the totality of this structure, as previously explained, is necessarily co-existent, while in man it is necessarily successive. But in each case, the necessity is imposed, not by the essential nature of intelligence as such, but by transcension of the temporal series and inclusion within that series in the two cases respectively. Hence intelligence in God and man are essentially the same, and the original objection is unsustained.

But suppose, for the sake of argument, that we grant the validity of the objection; what alternatives are left? Either intelligence in God is progressive and successive in a temporal sense, or no explanation in terms of an intelligent and absolutely necessary being is required. But both of these alternatives are rationally untenable.

If intelligence in God is progressive and successive in a temporal sense, then either the series of such successions is infinite, or its ground lies in the existence of a being that does transcend the temporal series as its ultimate cause. The first case is rationally self-contradictory and would prompt the objection that if God can be an infinite series, so can the space-time universe, and thus God vanishes in thin air. The second case would imply that we had not properly located God, for the ultimate transtemporal being would in reality be the absolutely necessary being that thought posits—and this would contradict the hypothesis that God's intelligence is progressive.

On the other hand, if *no* explanation in terms of an absolutely necessary and intelligent being is required, then the whole structure of our argument so far would be thus arbitrarily set aside.

It must therefore be that the universe is explicable only in terms of an ultimate being that is both intelligent personality and transtemporal existence, the only alternative being a self-contradictory skepticism. I therefore conclude that intelligence in God and man are essentially similar, that the objection to the contrary reduces, on any line of argument, to self-contradiction, and that consequently the allegation of the original difficulty is unsustained and the objection baseless.

E. *The Ethical Objection:* that the presence of evil in the universe is incompatible with the thesitic explanation as formulated on a teleological basis.

FORMULATION OF THE OBJECTION

The teleological argument professes to explain the apparent purpose and design in the experienced universe by reference to an ultimate intelligence that is both omnipotent and benevolent. But such an hypothesis completely bypasses the existence of evil in the world. As Randall and Buchler put the matter:

> If God is omnipotent, it was within his power to create a universe without evil. Since he did not do so, he is [as] responsible for the existence of evil as of everything else, and is therefore not benevolent. . . . If, however, we start by assuming that he is benevolent, and that it was not within his power to prevent the existence of evil in creation, he cannot be regarded as omnipotent. . . . But the denial of either attribute is a denial of the perfection . . . of a supernatural being.[81]

Or, to put the point briefly, how can a being that is both omnipotent and benevolent create a universe that includes evil, if evil is that which, in itself, absolutely ought not to be?

[81]*Op. cit.,* p. 173.

Much aesthetic ardor and intellectual labor has been put forth to state the objection in its most serious and perplexing form. Perhaps Mill has succeeded in stating the point in the most devastating fashion:

> In sober truth, nearly all the things which men are hanged or imprisoned for doing to one another are nature's every-day performances. . . . Not even on the most distorted and contrasted theory of good which ever was framed by religious or philosophical fanaticism can the government of Nature be made to resemble the work of a being at once good and omnipotent. . . . If a tenth part of the pains which have been expended in finding benevolent adaptations in all nature had been employed in collecting evidence to blacken the character of the Creator, what scope for comment would not have been found . . . [!] [82]

Hume writes in a similar spirit when he urges that there is so much pain and suffering in the world that "the whole presents nothing but the idea of a blind Nature, impregnated by a great vivifying principle, and pouring forth from her lap, without discernment or parental care, her maimed and abortive children."[83] On the other hand, Hume admits that "if the goodness of the Deity (I mean a goodness like the human) could be established on any tolerable reasons a priori, these phenomena [the evils of existence], however untoward, would not be sufficient to subvert that principle. . . ."[84] But Hume denies that any such evidence is forthcoming and therefore asserts that there is no ground for asserting God's goodness, "while there are so many ills in the universe, and while these ills might so easily have been remedied, as far as human understanding can be allowed to judge on such a subject."[85]

More specifically, the evils of existence may be classified as: first, moral evil, which springs from the abuse of freedom by rational, moral agents; second, so-called natural evil, which springs from the structure of the natural world and is called evil because it affects the organic realm—especially at the human level—with pain, suffering, disease, and ultimately physical death. Of course, natural evil ultimately reduces to moral evil, since it is called evil significantly only in a moral context. Only that is denominated evil of which it

[82]*Op. cit.*, pp. 17, 21, 30.
[83]*Dialogues*, XI; quoted in Burtt, *op. cit.*, p. 224.
[84]*Hume Selections*, p. 380.
[85]*Idem.*

could be said that it *ought* to be otherwise than it is. And the underlying motive for describing natural events as evil is that they are regarded as originating in God, so that if any of these events are really evil, God is morally at fault, in the final analysis.

It is therefore the task of any explanation of the problem of evil to suggest how it is that the presence of such evils as do exist *may* exist consistently with any proposed metaphysical interpretation of reality. And in particular, the theist must explain how a good God could create a universe which contains evils that appear to spring ultimately from the divine causation.

Since moral evils admit of fairly ready explanation in terms of the necessary freedom of finite moral agents, it is natural evil that receives the greatest emphasis in any objection, against theistic philosophy. How, for example, can the theist explain the birth of an idiot, if he assumes the goodness and supreme power of God? Or what kind of theology can be built on the adaptiveness of the tiny organisms that cause disease and physical death? Or what does a destructive earthquake teach us about the goodness of God? Again, a hunter entangled in the coils of a crushing python might wish that God had not so well adapted its organic structure to its environment.

IMMEDIATE LOGICAL POSSIBILITIES FOR A SOLUTION

It will contribute greatly to a clarification of this problem if we note the various solutions that are logically possible in terms of the concepts involved in the statement of evil's dilemma. Thoughtful consideration will reveal that there are three concepts or terms of explanation which constitute the motif of the problem: (1) an omniscient, omnipotent and benevolent God, as the posited ultimate of explanation; (2) evil, as the datum of experience to be explained; (3) rational capacity or analysis, as the method of solution. As a matter of historical fact, attempts have been made to solve the problem of evil by almost every conceivable alteration or transposition of these three terms. No attempt will be made here to present a detailed analysis of these formulations from the historical standpoint. Instead, the possibilities themselves will be expounded and criticized from a purely theoretical point of view, although, of course, some historical reference will be unavoidable.

First Set of Solutions: by Alteration of the Concept of God

Naturalism: the denial of God's existence.—The most radical solution is to eliminate the problem by denying that there is any God at all. If there is no God, as an ultimate of power and goodness, the problem vanishes. First, there is no moral evil: for there is no ultimate or absolute standard—namely, the character of God—over against which a given action by some individual may be classified as morally reprehensible. The most that could be said would be that a certain action is socially undesirable, or what have you, but not that it is morally evil in any ultimate sense.

On the other hand, there is no natural evil either, ultimately for the same reason that eliminated moral evil; but more immediately because the so-called evils of existence are merely the unavoidable effects of the accidental churning of the universe with mindless motion. These effects may be obstacles for organic life, but they are not evils in any ultimately significant sense. Thus the problem is solved by the simple expedient of abandoning the theistic explanation altogether.

By way of objection to this solution: after so much energy has been expended to establish the existence of God, it will scarcely be necessary to do anything more than point out that naturalism is totally inadequate as a solution to this or any other ultimate problem. We have already attempted to show that the existence of an absolutely necessary being of intelligent nature is the only rational explanation of the space-time universe, since every supposition to the contrary leads to the self-contradiction of skepticism. Hence it may be put down as established that the naturalistic solution is eliminated at once: the solution to the problem of evil must be sought in terms of a viewpoint that transcends any posited self-sufficiency of nature.

But the proposed solution of naturalism is also ethically, as well as metaphysically, self-contradictory. Naturalism, in this context, discards the existence of God on the ground that theistic explanation is incompatible with the presence of evil in the world. But in a naturalistic universe, there *is* no evil in any ultimately significant sense, as we have indicated above; for evil exists only as over against an ultimate standard of goodness which has no validity for the naturalist. It follows that the naturalist has denied God's existence on grounds which are valid only in terms of the position he is trying to subvert. If evils *are* real, then they cannot be used as a basis for denying the existence of an ultimate standard of good, or what is ultimately the same thing, God: for evils exist only on the supposition that such an absolute good exists. On the other hand, if evils do not exist, they certainly cannot form the basis for a denial of God's existence. If, to avoid this predicament, the naturalist *begins* by denying that there are any evils, then he must take one of two grounds: he must hold either that statements about good and evil are cognitively meaningless (logical positivism), or that such statements are true or false only for their proponents (relativism). But both of these positions have already been refuted in Section A, Chapter IV, of the present part. Thus the naturalistic solution to the problem of evil is self-contradictory, because it necessarily assumes as a premise what it denies in its conclusion.

Pessimism: the denial of God's benevolence.—An explanation of the universe is necessary in terms of some Ultimate World Will; but this will is utterly devoid of purpose, intelligence, or goodness: all is merely blind striving and progressively frustrated desire. This, then, is the worst of all possible worlds and would not have been created by an ultimate being whose nature is goodness. Such, approximately, is the position of Schopenhauer.[86] The problem of evil is therefore solved by denying the goodness of the Ultimate Being.

By way of objection to this solution: Pessimism, as a solution to the problem of evil, faces a difficulty similar to that of naturalism. For on what basis is it asserted that this world is the worst possible one? If there is really no ultimate *good*, then there would appear to be no significant basis for declaring that this world is evil; and just for the reason that unless there is an absolute good, all attempts to call an entity, an experience, or a world evil, are baseless. In other words, the assertion that this is the worst of all possible worlds is self-contradictory in an ultimate context, because it can be significant only by assuming the existence of the very good it denies: or in brief it can be true only by being false.

Supposing that the ultimate self-contradiction of Pessimism might be soluble, the concept, that the World Will is devoid of conscious intelligence, is also open to serious objection. Such a World Will would be an unconscious will: and we have already refuted the idea that there could be any such thing as an unconscious ultimate.

[86]Cf. W. K. Wright, *A History of Modern Philosophy*, p. 363f.

A proposed alternative of this type would reduce to naturalism and would therefore fail to explain the whole range of telic aspects in nature, such as we have outlined with some fullness in previous contexts: only on the basis of conscious, intelligent will is the range of adaptations in nature explicable.

Again, if the World Will is actually devoid of intelligence and rationality, why should any rational explanation at all be attempted? Even Schopenhauer explained the world by the fourfold root of sufficient reason: but if rationality is not basic in the structure of ultimate reality, why assert that a rational explanation in terms of an ultimate World Will is necessary at all? Either no explanation is necessary, or rationality is a basic feature of ultimate reality. The former alternative contradicts the already established fact that the universe does not contain its own ground of explanation: therefore, the latter must be affirmed, but it is contrary to the original hypothesis of a World Will devoid of conscious intelligence. Consequently, the original hypothesis is self-contradictory.

I therefore conclude that Pessimism is untenable as a solution to the problem of evil which therefore is inexplicable on the assumption that God's benevolence is denied.

Finitism: the denial of God's omnipotence.—Since it is not tenable to deny God's benevolence, the problem of evil may appear to be soluble in terms of a denial of His omnipotence: if God Himself faces conditions that have not originated ultimately from situations established by His own will, then it is no marvel that the world contains even so-called surd evils—evils which, because they contain or involve no principle of improvement, are inherently and irreducibly evil.

Contemporary proponents of this viewpoint usually point out that much so-called evil may spring from conditions whose original imposition may be perfectly consonant with the existence and action of a benevolent God in establishing them.[87] But there are at least some inexplicable evils *if* we regard God as absolute in power. Such evils can be accounted for only on the supposition that God Himself faces problems that do not arise from His active and creative will.

Brightman attempts to locate this original problem datum as a passive element within God's very nature:

[87]E. S. Brightman, *The Problem of God*, p. 160.

There is within him, in addition to his reason and his active creative will, a passive element which enters into every one of his conscious states . . . and constitutes a problem for him. This element we call the Given. The evils of life and the delays in the attainment of value, insofar as they come from God and not from human freedom, are thus due to his nature, yet not wholly to his deliberate choice. His will and reason acting on the Given produce the world and achieve value in it.[88]

Insofar therefore as God is active and creative, His nature is goodness. But He also includes within His nature a Given that conditions and limits His every action. Thus the problem of evil is soluble by positing limits to the divine power: God Himself is finite.

By way of objection to this solution: at the outset, it may be observed that we have already shown that a finite God is an impossibility of rational thought: consider our discussion of the expansive-limiting argument of presuppositionalism. If God and evil ultimately limit each other, if evil springs from conditions not originally imposed by the divine will; then both God and evil are finites, and it is exactly the existence of a plurality of finites that leads us to posit beyond them a deeper ultimate that is their explanation and ground of existence.

Nor do I think that the situation is relieved by Brightman's assumption that evil springs from a Given or passive element within the very nature of God—as if I could transform a pair of finites into an infinite by drawing a circle around them. For if the existence of evil is actually a self-involvement in God's being, what is the real meaning, in the final analysis, of saying that God is good in any absolute sense? If evil *qua* evil necessarily springs from God, then God's nature can scarcely be said to consist essentially in goodness.

Or to put the matter in another way, either the Given is a necessary aspect of God's nature or not. If not, then it is no aspect of His nature at all, since every such aspect must be necessary in an absolutely necessary being. If, on the other hand, the Given is a necessary aspect of God's nature, then God is necessarily evil. It therefore results either that the original source of this element is an extraneous factor—in which case we must posit a deeper ultimate to explain both God and evil; or that God is necessarily evil as such, in which case His benevolence has not been saved by positing an internal limit to His power. In any case, no real solution to the problem of evil is proffered.

Nor can finitism solve the problem of evil from a purely practical point of view. If God and evil limit each other, then the following alternatives are possible: (1) God and evil have been struggling from all eternity, conceived as endless duration; (2) God and evil both transcend the temporal series and are in a relation of timelessly necessary opposition; (3) Evil transcends the series, but God does not; (4) God transcends the series, but evil does not.

But none of these alternatives is actually valid. If God and evil have been struggling through infinite time, two problems appear: first, the rationally impossible infinite series results; second, since evil is a present reality, no real prospect exists for conquering it, for, in infinite time, God must either have already conquered evil or He never will. Again, if God and evil are timelessly necessary, two problems appear here also: first, this amounts to the contention that two infinite beings exist—a position that has already been refuted; second, an absolute stalemate follows as in the case of the first alternative: no conquest of evil is possible if it is timelessly necessary.

If, to consider the third alternative, evil is timelessly necessary and God is not, again two problems confront us: first, evil is then the absolutely necessary being and is therefore God—but this is Pessimism and has already been refuted; second, the so-called God must therefore have sprung from that which is absolutely evil—but if God's nature is goodness, this is absurd. Finally, if God is timelessly necessary and evil is not, then evil must have sprung from conditions which, though originally posited by God, are not in themselves evil. But this is contrary to the hypothesis that evil is to be explained by supposing God not to be omnipotent.

Thus the hypothesis of a finite God makes the conquest of evil impossible so that instead of solving the problem, it makes it eternal. I therefore conclude that no solution of the problem of evil is possible, either theoretically or practically, in terms of a denial that God is omnipotent.

Nescientism: the denial of God's omniscience. A possible mode of approach to the problem of evil may also be cast in terms of a denial that God is omniscient: but while the divine omniscience has frequently been denied to explain the "true" freedom of moral agents, I know of no serious attempt to solve the problem of evil itself along this line of argument. But a proponent of this hypothesis might state his case as follows:

If God is both omniscient and omnipotent, He cannot be conceived as benevolent. For if He foresaw the existence of irreducible evils, His omnipotence could presumably have avoided them. Now, since the denial of neither omnipotence nor benevolence offers any solution to the problem, it must be the case that God is not omniscient and that evil springs from concomitants which even His great wisdom could not and did not foresee or anticipate. Just as we do not blame one another for unforeseeable effects of our actions, so we ought not to blame God for surd evil, if, in fact, it resulted from a similar situation. God therefore is benevolent: and the ultimate or irreducible evils are unforeseen effects of His benevolent activity.

By way of objection to this solution: at the outset, it should be observed that the denial of the divine omniscience is in reality a denial of omnipotence, and is therefore open to the whole range of objections that are above cited against finitism. For if God is not omniscient, then He is subject to a limit not imposed by His active will: namely, the potential existence of a future that is unforeseen and unforeseeable. But the presence of such a limit is precisely what is meant by a denial of omnipotence.

Nor can the divine omnipotence be saved by suggesting that, in spite of the divine nescience, still all the conditions of existence spring from God's will, and He is therefore omnipotent nonetheless. For God still lacks the power to control the operation of the conditions He imposes. And if He does lack this power, then such lack must either spring necessarily from His nature or not. If not, then an extraneous condition exists as a limit of His power and He is finite, hence not omnipotent. If, on the other hand, these conditions spring necessarily from His nature, then either they must result in evil, or they are conditions which need not result in evil.

In the first case, God is necessarily evil and hence not benevolent. Nor will it help to say that God's lack of benevolence is no fault of His own, just as ours is not in a similar situation: for our ignorance in such a situation is precisely the effect of our finitude, whereas if God is finite in this way, then omnipotence is denied at once and our point is established. In the second case, no reason exists for the denial of the divine omniscience, since the denial was posited in the first place to explain why irreducible evils exist: and on the supposition that the conditions imposed by God are not necessarily productive of evil, there *are* no such irreducible evils.

It seems, then, that the denial of omniscience either vanishes or reduces to a denial of omnipotence and therefore stands refuted with finitism.

A serious logical objection likewise confronts nescientism. For if God is conditioned by a future that is not known by Him, then God must be conceived as subject to temporal limitations: that is, He must be conceived as passing through a succession of moments, since He is limited by a future that does not yet exist even for Him. But we have already shown that the absolutely necessary being must be transtemporal, both because on any other supposition He would not be the absolutely necessary being, and because a time composed of an infinite succession of moments is logically absurd. Consequently, the denial of the divine omniscience is untenable because it implies that time is a form of God's experience.

I therefore conclude that the denial of God's omniscience does not yield a solution to the problem of evil. And not only so: but I further assert that no solution is possible through any alteration of the concept of God in the various ways suggested.

Second Set of Solutions: by Alteration of the Concept of Evil

Illusionism: the denial of evil's existence.—As naturalism attempted to solve the problem of evil by denying the reality of God, illusionism makes its solution by denying the reality of evil. If evil is merely an illusion or an appearance, then again there is no problem of evil at all. That which does not exist can scarcely constitute a problem: and thus the whole situation vanishes in thin air, just as a mirage on the road vanishes when it is is approached.

This solution is very ancient. It is imbedded in the Vedanta philosophy of Hinduism,[89] and is popular in the Western world through the doctrines of Christian science. The Augustinian solution that evil is a privation of essence or being[90] is likewise basically an illusionist theory of evil. For to say that everything that is, insofar as it is, is good, is to say no evil actually exists, which is precisely the allegation that evil has only an illusory existence.

---

[89] Cf. Sri Aurobindo Ghose, *The Life Divine*, Book II, Chapter XIV, for a modern exposition in this context.
[90] Augustine, *The Confessions of Saint Augustine*, pp. 153, 154, *et passim*.

By way of objection to this solution: the solution is self-contradictory. First, because it is an indisputable fact that some evil exists; at least the evil of our thinking evil to exist when it does not—so that the proposition that all evil is illusory is thus false for the very reason that it is true, which is self-contradictory. Second, to put the same point differently: if all evil is really illusory, then why is this offered as an explanation at all? If no evil exists, then it does not require explanation. If it does exist, then it is not illusory, in which case the original hypothesis is contravened.

We may state our criticism more positively by saying that illusionism merely moves the problem of evil to another context: for the explanation of the origin and power of the illusion of evil is exactly as problematical as the explanation of evil itself. Evil then possesses at least an illusory reality, just as the mirage on the road is real as a mirage. And just as the mirage is not explained by calling it a mirage, neither is evil explained by calling it an illusion.

Since illusionism thus reduces to self-contradiction, no solution to our problem is possible in terms of a denial that evil exists.

Instrumentalism: the denial of evil's ultimate character as evil, and the assertion that it is an instrument for good.—According to this particular approach to the problem, evil is declared to be emphatically genuine: the evils of life are not illusory.

Yet on the other hand, it is only from a relative and limited point of view that evil appears to be ultimately real: to the mind of God the passing evils of experience, though genuinely evil from our limited point of view, are necessary parts of the eternal good. If only we could see things through the eyes of God, we would apprehend that ultimately evil enhances the good.

Since this solution is difficult to conceive, an illustration may be of some help. Take the infinite series of whole numbers: 1, 2, 3, 4 . . . to infinity. Now every part of this series is finite and limited: and as long as we view its parts, there is no transcension of this limitation. But if we view the series as a whole it is infinite: now this does not mean that the parts are not really finite—it merely means that their reality as finite is apparent only from a limited point of view. From the over-all vantage point, the series is infinite. Now just as the mathematical series can be both infinite and finite, depending on the point of view from which it is considered, so evil can possess independent reality and yet be transcended in the eternal good.

This solution is common in idealistic circles, being propounded, for example, by Leibniz and Royce.[91] And it is essentially the solution, or a part of the solution, offered by Prof. Edward John Carnell. Thus he writes:

> If one loved God, he would be willing to believe God when he says that the creation of evil is but an expedient; and that through such means a perfect plan conceived in the counsels of eternity, is being fulfilled. . . . This solution does not reduce evil to an illusion. Both God and man agree that idiocy [for example] is an evil. The issue is whether or not God has the right to use evil to accomplish good ends. The Christian answers yes, for he trusts the person of God.[92]

Every attempt to solve the problem of evil by saying that what God does is good because He wills it[93] is also essentially of this type: for if God does the evil deliberately and remains good, then this evil too is a part of the eternal good.

The instrumental theory of evil is perhaps set in its best terms in the late G. F. Stout's *God and Nature:*

> The complete good, though its goodness can never be evil, must in some way include the evil which we actually find in the universe. The good must be essentially incomplete without the evil. . . . The absolute good essentially involves struggle against evil, evil corresponding to the incomprehensible immensity of the complete good. . . . God must will a good which includes evil as something not to be tolerated, but hated, opposed, and destroyed.[94]

By way of objection to this solution: the insuperable objection to the instrumentalist theory is that, as a proffered explanation of evil, it reduces logically to illusionism, and is therefore subject to the whole range of objections against that theory which have already been indicated. This reduction to illusionism may be shown in two essentially similar ways.

The simplest way is to point out that if what we call evil is actually an instrument for the realization of good, then by no stretch of the imagination can it be significantly called evil. For evil is, presumably,

[91]Wright, *op. cit.*, pp. 131, 132; 500, 501.
[92]E. J. Carnell, *A Philosophy of the Christian Religion*, p. 314 and note.
[93]So also Carnell, *Ibid.*, pp. 313, 315.
[94]*Ibid.*, pp. 313, 319.

that which ought not to be: but it surely cannot be said that the instruments for the achieving of the absolute good ought not to be. This would be the same as saying that the good ought not to be, whereas, if the good is anything in an ultimate sense, it is precisely that which ought to be. And unless we deny the reality of the good itself, then evil, as its instrument, must be good. If we take the alternative and maintain that the evil ought to be, then it is indistinguishable from the good at once. In either case the evil is shown to be actually the good: but this is the same as saying that evil as evil does not exist, or in other words, that its reality is basically an illusion.

If an attempt is made to escape this reduction by saying that God takes what is *really* evil, even in an ultimate sense, and uses it to accomplish His ends in spite of its evil character, this may be true: but then no solution of the evil *qua* evil is involved and the justification of the existence of the evil itself must be sought along other lines. To say that God accomplishes His purposes in spite of evil, while it may be correct, does not explain the *presence* of evil in the universe of an omnipotent and benevolent God.

The alternate method of reducing instrumentalism to illusionism is to show that an evil, whose reality is relative to the viewpoint of only a finite knower, is not evil at all, in the last analysis. Even if it were possible to make this distinction between a relative and an absolute vantage point, the question would be, in case of a conflict between the two points of view, which is to be taken as final and decisive? The only reasonable answer is that since our viewpoint is subject to limitations of finitude, it is the viewpoint of God which ultimately reads the nature of evil correctly. But in God's eyes, evil is not basically opposed to good: it is rather among the means to the realization of the eternal good itself. Evil therefore is ultimately unreal: and this is the position of illusionism.

The mathematical analogy that I outlined will likewise illustrate the refutation. For if we say that an infinite series is actually made up of finite entities (in this case, numbers) then the only alternatives available are to deny that the series is infinite and thus cling to the reality of the parts, or to deny the reality of the parts (i.e., the composite character of the series) in the infinite whole. Similarly, if we say that the ultimate good is actually made up of parts, some of which are evil, then the only alternatives available are either to deny that the whole is good, or to deny that the good actually has evil parts. In the first case, either evil is not explained by the theory or the benevolence of God is denied. In the second case, the theory is pure illusionism.

Thus the instrumentalist theory of evil is untenable because it either is no explanation of evil at all, or it reduces to illusionism and thus is self-contradictory.

Third Type of Solution: Irrationalism: the Denial of Rational Capacity as a Mode for Solving the Problem.

Throughout our discussion of this problem, it has been assumed that a rational solution to the problem of evil is possible. But this is the whole source of our difficulty: in point of fact, the solution of the problem transcends the ability of reason. Are not God's ways incomprehensible? Who are we to pretend to solve the problem of evil in a universe that is the product of such a God? Here then is the answer: the problem of evil is rationally insoluble. After all, we would never attempt to dissect an atom bomb with no tool but a toothpick; we should not, similarly, attempt to explain evil with no tool but reason.

As a parenthetical remark, I might suggest that this seems to me to be the solution most common in Calvinist theology, at least in its less guarded moments: although I readily concede that in careful exposition Calvinists commonly take instrumentalist ground.

By way of objection to this solution: irrationalism has already been criticized in so many other contexts that no detailed attempt at refutation will be made here: we have shown repeatedly that every attempt to limit the applicability of the rational categories, or to define a sphere into which reason cannot enter, is self-contradictory and therefore untenable. About the only appropriate thing to say to an irrationalist is that well-worn remark of J. M. E. McTaggart to the effect that no one ever tried to break logic but that logic finally broke him. A few remarks in the context of the problem of evil may nevertheless be appropriate as a supplement to such comment.

In the first place, is a problem solved by denying the possibility of its solution? It would seem to be no explanation of evil at all that its presence in the universe is inexplicable. If someone objects that while finite intelligence may not be able to solve the problem, the infinite intelligence of God has the answer, then we counter that intelligence in God is not essentially different from intelligence in man and that therefore reason ought to be able to evolve at least the principles of the solution, even though the reason employed be finite and human. Further, we answer that the theory would then reduce to instrumentalism by suggesting that evil is a problem only from our limited point of view: but instrumentalism has already been defeated.

To state the matter in more complete fashion: if we say that the problem of evil is rationally insoluble, then we must select one of the following alternatives: first, that the problem is rationally insoluble only to us, but admits of solution rationally from God's point of view—but this is instrumentalism. Or we may allege that the problem is absolutely without rational solution. And this in turn involves two further alternatives: that God Himself, since His reason is essentially analogous to ours, does not have the solution to the problem—but this is either finitism, or nescientism, or both; that the problem is soluble to God, but not through the instrumentality of reason.

But consider this last possibility: what is meant by a nonrational solution to any given problem? Such a solution would either be intelligible or not. And so the argument goes its inevitable way to the conclusion that either the solution is a rational one or it is no solution at all. But to shift the context slightly: is this assertion itself—that the problem is soluble to God but not through reason—intended to be rationally intelligible as a solution to the problem of evil? If so, then it is a rational solution and the original hypothesis is contradicted. If not, then, since the assertion is unintelligible, it hardly occurs to me to refute it. Thus the position is either meaningless or self-contradictory.

On any line of argument, therefore, the hypothesis that the problem of evil is insoluble is rationally untenable, so that irrationalism, like its predecessors, has brought us no relief.

Conclusion on the Immediate Logical Possibilities of Solution

The primary result of our investigation is that no solution to the problem of evil is possible in terms of a denial or essential alteration of any of the basic concepts involved in the problem.

It might appear that we have ourselves slipped into the abyss of irrationalism by discrediting all the apparent logical possibilities for a solution to the problem of evil. But there is yet a different alternative. Since irrationalism is not a solution, there necessarily exists a rational explanation of evil. Such an explanation must embrace the following facts: (1) the existence of an omnipotent, omniscient, and benevolent God as the ultimate ground of reality: all suppositions to the contrary having been rationally discredited; (2) the reality of evil *qua* evil; (3) the capacity of rationality to solve the problem.

The explanation, furthermore, must be cast in terms of principles which reason may regard as sufficient for the solution of the problem: but it is impossible to ask that the principles be applied to every specific instance of evil that might be cited. For in any particular case we may be ignorant of data which would enable us to apply the sufficient principles to a given situation. Of course, increased knowledge of the total background of the specific case would render the determination of the exact explanation of the given evil more possible.

An illustration will serve to clarify this situation. Suppose that I have a house that is so constructed that access to it can be had only through unlocking the front door with a given key type. Suppose, further, that my wife and I are the only ones who possess keys and that our two keys are not identical but are basic variants of the given key type. Suppose, finally, that I come home one afternoon and find the door ajar. Now as I stand at the door, a problem confronts me; I know that there are only two keys in existence that will unlock this door, but the question is: *which* key unlocked the door and *who* used it to do so? Can I decide at once?

The answer may be yes and it may be no, depending on the further simplicity or complexity of the actual situation. If I enter the house and make certain that my wife and I both have our keys, and if my wife assures me that her key has not been thus used, it must be that I left the door ajar when I departed originally—assuming, that is, that someone has not taken my key on the particular day, unlocked the door, and then replaced the key without my knowledge. But perhaps my wife did go out that morning and has forgotten her escapade. Or it may be that when I enter the house, my wife is not there, and so the possibilities begin to mount. Perhaps she has gone to the store and left the door open; or perhaps she locked the door, but a thief stole her key. And so the plot thickens.

In all of my perplexity, I know that the two keys are the sufficient explanation for opening the door; but as to who opened the door with which key, a satisfactory explanation is possible only after a careful scrutiny of the entire situation. In fact, if my wife never returns and I never see again either her or the key she had, I may never be able to answer the question as to which key was used by what person to open that door! But I will still be satisfied that someone or something opened that door with one of the keys.

Just so with any given evil of specific character: while I may be in possession or cognizance of certain principles (keys) that separately or together are a sufficient explanation of the particular evil, only a careful scrutiny of all the details will enable me to apply the principles in the proper degree and extent to the particular case. And as with the keys, so here: the data for determining the specific application may be entirely out of reach—imbedded in an unknown history or in unascertained present facts. But this will hardly discredit the principles themselves, since the inability to apply them is a function, not of the principles themselves, but of the absence of determining data.

The Proposed Solution of the Problem of Evil[95]

Preliminary Considerations

Because no solution to the problem of evil has been found possible in terms of the previously considered alternatives, we are now in a position to assert that Hume's demands have, in any case, been satisfied. For, it will be recalled, he admitted that if the goodness of the Deity could be established in some way on a priori grounds—not, I take it, absolutely a priori, but a priori so far as the particulars of evil are concerned, the difficulties of the problem of evil would not be insuperable. This demand has been satisfied in two ways:

First, by showing, positively, that the existence of an absolutely necessary being characterized by personal intelligence and absolute

---

[95] May I say that a hint toward this type of solution is expressed, in general terms, in an article by B. Bosanquet, "The Meaning of Teleology." Proceedings of the British Academy, 1905-1906, pp. 235-245.

goodness is required by the whole cumulative argument for theism. The cosmological argument established the existence of an absolutely necessary being that transcends the space-time universe and is the ground of its existence. The teleological argument established the nature of this ultimate being as personal intelligence, and, through a consideration of the nature of values, as absolute goodness.

Second, Hume's demand has also been met, negatively, by showing that no solution of the problem of evil is actually possible through the denial of God's existence, omnipotence, or benevolence; through the denial of the reality of evil; or through the denial of reason's capacity to solve the problem. These considerations forced us to the conclusion that some solution of the problem of evil is rationally possible and necessary in terms which admit the existence of a God who is both omnipotent and benevolent, the reality of evil, and the ability of reason. Thus we approach the solution to the problem of evil with the confidence that though the solution may be difficult, it is both possible and necessary: we are like the scientist who approaches a causal problem in the laboratory with the confidence that although the location of the cause may be difficult, it will eventually bare itself to rational scrutiny, and that for the very reason that the causal axiom is antecedently taken as universally valid.

One word of caution before we proffer our solution: it is unfair and arbitrary to approach the problem with any preconceived notion of what the good must be. In particular the problem should not be approached, for example, in terms of an assumed hedonistic ethical theory. Such an approach, as Taylor says, "rests throughout on the assumption that if there were a God directing the course of events, His purpose *could* only be to make the 'good' happy and the 'bad' unhappy in respect of their earthly fortunes. But this assumption is wholly arbitrary. . . . All that is proved by the calamities of the 'good' and the undeserved worldly success of the 'bad' is that, if there is a divine purpose, it is nothing so crude as remunerating righteousness with worldly felicity."[96]

[96]*Does God Exist?*, pp. 9-10.

Brief Statement of the Solution

The existence of irreducible or real evil results in every case from a contingency that is necessarily involved in those determinate conditions which are themselves essential to the creation of a universe whose ultimate end is the production and progressive development of rational, moral selves.

Expansion of the Solution

General implications of the proposed solution.—Scrutiny of the above summary statement will reveal that the existence of evil in the universe of an omnipotent, benevolent God is held to be explicable in terms of two basic and equally ultimate principles: the principle of law or causality, and the principle of purpose or teleology.

According to the principle of law, the totality of real entities exists only in and with the presence of determinate conditions, and the ultimate purpose of the universe is given in the determinate conditions of God's being. In the case of the absolutely necessary being, these determinate conditions are completely self-involved: and in our previous discussion, we have already indicated that omnipotence in God, rather than consisting in the absence of all determining conditions, is constituted instead by the complete self-conditioned and timeless necessity of God's being. In the case of realities dependent on the absolutely necessary being—and that includes all other realities, their determinate conditions of existence are ultimately derived from the self-conditioned necessity of divine existence. Thus every aspect of reality admits of causal explanation, or explanation in terms of the presence of determinate conditions of existence: if any of these conditions were wanting, in the case of a given entity, the entity would not exist.

According to the principle of purpose, the ultimate end of the universe both prescribes the proximate determinate conditions essential to its realization and itself imposes the determinate conditions of God's Being. Thus the divine purpose is an eternally necessary aspect of His being and imposes upon that being its determinate character. In the case of all dependent realities, their teleological or purposive significance is ultimately dependent upon the eternal purpose of God. The total environment of rational, moral being is *instrumentally* significant in the achievement and development of that being. The existence of moral beings themselves is *ultimately* significant as God's end in creation. Thus every aspect of reality admits of teleological explanation, or explanation in terms of the progressive realization of the ultimate Divine Purpose; if some aspect of that purpose had been different, the ultimate and instrumental results of it would exist otherwise than as they do.

These two principles of law and purpose are completely coextensive: each offers a complete explanation of reality from a different point of view. Neither is ultimate and basic as over against the other. On the one hand, law is the necessary instrument for the existence of a determinate Divine Purpose and for the creation of a moral universe to embody that purpose. On the other hand, the ultimate moral purpose of God is itself grounded in the absolute necessity or self-conditioned character of God's being. Thus each principle is instrumental and basic to the other.

Lest there should be any misunderstanding of what is meant here, some illustrative explanation may be helpful. As I write with my pen on this paper, all the determinate conditions for writing are present: paper, ink, a pen with a point through which the ink is dispensed, the grasping and moving of the pen with my hand, and so forth: the process is completely explicable in causal terms. Yet the process also admits of complete purposive explanation: my intent in writing, the adapted structure of the paper and pen, the selected consistency of the ink, and so on—all these are what they are in terms of an adaptation to the fulfillment of some purpose. And thus with all the actions of a rational being: the purposive and causal sequences are both complete, yet both basic to the existence and functioning of the other. Now a theistic interpretation of the universe—as I profess it—asserts exactly such a correlation to be significant for the sum total of real entities. And it is in terms of such a relationship that the problem of evil is soluble.

For more advanced students of philosophy, an illustration from Spinoza will clarify the point: just as Spinoza held that substance was completely comprehended by a multiplicity of attributes, each of which was a complete embodiment from its own point of view of substance itself, so we maintain that all reality is completely explicable in terms of two principles—law and purpose—each of which is a complete account, from its own point of view, of reality itself.

In the following section, the implications of this viewpoint are traced in detail, so far as the principles of law and purpose render evil explicable. The account appears in parallel columns so that the correlation of the principles may be more readily discerned, and so that the whole of the problem may be considered separately from either point of view.

Detailed application of the principles to the problem of evil.—

LAW	PURPOSE

LAW

1. *Ultimate Law:* the absolute necessity of God's being; but the law necessarily embodies God's eternal purpose.

2. *Proximate Principles* for the explanation of evil.

a. The Law-abidingness of the universe.

(1) A law-abiding universe is the necessary rational environment for moral experience and organic life, which is, now at least, the sphere of moral realization. Organic life could not be maintained either in its own structure or in relation to the physical world, if there were not determinate and regular conditions of its existence which were sustained in continuous operation: and the very meaning of law is the existence and functioning of a system according to such determinate and regular conditions.

Moral experience depends, as we have shown previously, upon rationality, since morality is, in the final analysis, the rational conduct of life: but the rational conduct of life would be impossible in a world not sustained by regular laws and explicable in causal terms. So Tennant writes: "A world which is to be a moral order must be a physi-

PURPOSE

1. *Ultimate Purpose:* the production and development of rational, moral beings; but this purpose is determined by the law of God's being.

2. *Proximate Principles* for the explanation of evil.

a. The Freedom of moral agents.

(1) Moral freedom is the necessary condition for the existence of rational and moral beings: for a moral being is precisely one that engages in the self-determination of actions in relation to some proposed standard. Now freedom is precisely such self-determination in view of motives that operate in our experience. Consequently, if the ultimate Divine Purpose is the production and development of rational, moral selves, such an end must prescribe the reality of ethical freedom in such beings.

Nor is the freedom of finite selves inconsistent with the divine omnipotence, since the conditional existence of these selves and their freedom rests, causally and teleologically, in the absolute necessity of God's being.

cal order characterized by law or regularity. . . . [Otherwise] no man could employ his reason in the conduct of life. And without rationality, morality is impossible."[97]

(2) Yet a law-abiding universe would not exist except as the environment of moral life: every causal nexus has therefore a complete teleological explanation, for its determinate conditions would not exist apart from the ultimate divine purpose.

(2) Yet ethical freedom would not exist apart from its determination from the law of God's being and the existence of a law-abiding universe which makes free acts possible: every free act has therefore, a complete causal explanation for, as a real entity, it could only exist if all the determinate conditions of its being were present. The reason that an act is free lies, not in its status as indeterminate, but in the fact that the decisive causal factor is the self-determination of the agent.

(3) *But* a law-abiding universe involves the possibility of *natural evil:* just because nature operates through determinate conditions, these very conditions may issue in adverse results through misappropriate adjustment to the order of natural law.

(3) *But* moral freedom involves the possibility of *moral evil:* just because a rational being possesses the power of self-determination, this very power may issue in acts which contravene the moral law of God. The possibility of evil is a necessary condition for the existence of an ethical being, except in the case of that Ultimate Being (namely, God) whose nature itself determines the standard of absolute goodness.

(4) *Range of Coverage.*
(a) In general: the law-abidingness of the universe explains the existence of every evil, both natural and moral.

(4) *Range of Coverage.*
(a) In general: moral freedom explains the existence of every evil, both natural and moral.

[97]Tennant, *op. cit.,* II, pp. 199, 200.

(i) A universe of law means that all effects follow from the complete presence of necessary and determining factors; and a free act is no exception.

(ii) Now every evil is an effect of this kind: it could not exist unless all its determining conditions were present.

(iii) Since a universe of law is the necessary instrument of God's ultimate moral purpose, such a universe is justified in its existence.

(iv) Yet this does *not* mean that every evil is a *necessary* result of the existence of a law-abiding universe: it is merely a contingency that is contained in such a universe.

(b) More specifically, the functioning of law accounts for:

(i) *Specific instances* of natural evil: for example, the occurrence of accidents which involve pain and suffering. Were it not for the laws which operate in such cases, the accident might not happen; but then, apart from these same laws, no adaptation of means to ends by rational selves would be possible.

(a) The occurrence of such pain and suffering is made possible through the constitution of sentient beings as suited to organic life: if pain and suffering were not possible, it is questionable whether organic life could exist in a universe which is necessarily law-abiding: for pain has a protective and prophylactic character, and is

(i) A universe of law, which contains the possibility of natural evil, is essential to the functioning of moral freedom.

(ii) The possibility of moral evil is essential to the existence of freedom itself.

(iii) Since a moral universe is the purpose of God's determinate being, such a universe is justified in its existence.

(iv) Yet this does *not* mean that every evil is a *necessary* result of the existence of a moral universe: it is merely a contingency that is contained in such a universe.

(b) More specifically, the functioning of moral freedom accounts for:

(i) *Specific instances* of moral evil: for example, the breaking of a promise, the misrepresentation of facts, etc. Were it not for the reality of freedom, such breaches of obligation might not occur; but then, apart from this same freedom, moral obligation and moral experience generally would be impossible.

(a) The occurrence of such evils is made possible through the constitution of rational beings for ethical life: if moral evil were not possible, it is questionable whether moral experience could exist in a universe which is teleologically explicable: for the existence of freedom is also the *sine qua non* for the realization of moral good. Mor-

merely the intensification of experiences which make interaction with an environment possible. Light, for example, is essential to vision, though a very bright light causes pain in the visual mechanism.

al evil is merely the abuse of conditions which make interaction with an ethical environment possible.

(b) The specific occurrence of such accidents is made possible through the complex interaction of various causal nexi: and the multiplicity of such factors in any given case is uncalculated. For example, as in the factors which result in the head-on crash of two automobiles. The extremely complex results of such accidents are likewise uncalculated and may be the cause of further pain and suffering: for example, as a severe fall in childhood may concur with other factors to cause paralysis at a later period in life.

(b) The specific occurrence of evil acts is made possible through the complex interaction of various purposive nexi: and the multiplicity of such factors in any given case is uncalculated. For example, factors which result in the stealing of a loaf of bread to feed a starving family. The extremely complex results of such acts are likewise uncalculated and may be the occasion of further acts of moral evil: for example, as the stealing of a diamond may occasion the telling of lies to cover up the theft.

(ii) *Alteration of the whole series of natural causes* through the conditioning of specific instances:

(ii) *Alteration of the orientation of moral character* through the conditioning of specific instances:

(a) Particular cases of natural evil tend to produce an uncalculated number of further adverse effects, as the above example indicates, though in numerous cases the results are likewise beneficial. This last fact does not make the antecedent evil good, but it does indicate that natural evils do not necessarily defeat the good.

(a) Particular acts of moral evil tend to produce an uncalculated degree of influence upon the orientation of personal character, as the above example indicates: a proclivity toward evil follows on the committing of an ethical breach;[98] though in numerous cases, such acts may be the occasion of morally good acts. This last fact does not make the antecedent evil good, but

[98]A poem from Tennyson comes to mind:
Vice is a monster of such dreadful mien,
That to be hated is but to be seen.
But seen too oft, too familiar with her face,
We first endure, then pity, then embrace.

it does indicate that moral evils do not necessarily defeat the good.

(b) The accumulation of cases thus produces an alteration of the whole succeeding series of instances and determines, along with the general operation of law, the occurrence of future effects.

(b) The accumulation of cases thus produces an alteration in the orientation of moral character and occasions, along with the general operation of freedom itself, the occurrence of future acts.

(iii) *Resultant infliction of pain and suffering* at numerous other points in the causal series, as already suggested, on:

(iii) *Resultant infliction*, through acts of moral evil, *of pain and suffering* on:

(a) Orders of sentient being below the human: as when a newborn fawn starves to death because its mother has been accidentally killed from running in the path of a moving auto.

(a) Orders of sentient being below the human: as when I beat my horse in a fit of temper, the latter being itself an expression of misoriented character.

(b) Moral beings: as when a wife suffers economic poverty because her husband has been accidentally killed at his work.

(b) Other Moral Beings: as when a victim of assault suffers physical pain and other inconveniences from the experience: nor is this factor necessarily confined to the action of human agents, for there may be, so far as we know, other spiritual and moral beings in the universe whose morally evil acts issue in human suffering, as when Job was inflicted with boils through the evil act of Satan, according to the Biblical tradition.

(iv) *Distortion in the operation of telic or purposive factors* through the conditioning of the causal series:

(iv) *Distortion in the operation of the causal series* through the conditioning of purposive acts:

(a) In numerous ways, the causal series may result in the prevention of the fulfillment of purpose or moral obligation.

(a) In numerous ways, the causal series may be turned to the production of evil effects through the purposive acts of human selves.

(b) For example: while the purpose of human life is rational and moral development, the conspiration of a multiplicity of causal factors may eventuate in the birth of an idiot who cannot fulfill this purpose.

Again, the fulfillment of a moral obligation may be prevented through the coincidence of accidental causes: as when a man cannot pay a debt because his money unforeseeably drops from his pocket at an unknown place.

Again, a wrong ethical decision may be occasioned by the influence of environmental factors, as when a man commits suicide to escape some experience of pain.

(c) *The status of the order of law,* as essential to the existence of moral and rational being in the process of development, implies the *secondary* significance of all incidental concretions of pain and suffering which result from the general maintenance of uniform law: natural evil is possible and has become actual; but if it were not possible the supreme divine end could not be realized.

(b) For example: the danger of specific natural evils may be ignorantly increased by the purposive alteration of the causal series: as when the danger of a flood is increased through the removal of large forest areas.

Or the production of specific natural evils may be augmented through consciously inappropriate actions: as when the birth of a deformed child results, in part, from acts of carelessness in the parental line.

(c) *The status of rational, moral being* as the ultimate end of the divine purpose, implies the *instrumental* significance of all lower levels of reality—even including the higher orders of sentient being and the sentient nature of man himself.

(i) Thus the maintenance of the general balance of the entire organic realm, through the reciprocal instrumentality of the various forms of organic life in sustaining one another, is not an insoluble problem at all, since the whole organic realm has a predominantly (and I think exclusively) instrumental significance.

(a) Various forms of life do prey upon one another: cats do eat mice; micro-organisms do cause decay and disease in sentient beings.

(b) But all this would be inexplicable only on the supposition that mere organic life as such had intrinsic and ultimate significance as an end: that this is the case has been disproved in a previous context.

(ii) Furthermore, the reciprocation among various forms of organic life does maintain the general balance of the whole organic realm as a proximate environment for moral realization: this plan provides for the removal of organisms "in the way which least pollutes nature with corruption."[99]

(iii) Finally, we shall presently see that human disease and suffering have a still deeper purposive significance in the development of moral character.

b. *Reaction of divine purpose to the evil effects of the law-abiding-ness of the universe: Restitution*

b. *Reaction of divine law to the evil effects of freedom: Retribution*

(1) On the *personal* level,

(1) On the *personal* level,

(a) The various specific effects of natural evil may, though genuinely evil, serve as a discipline for the development, toward righteousness, of a character already distorted by evil at the moral level: pain and suffering may thus be turned to a disciplinary purpose, so that they become the occasion of reascent to the divine ideal.

(a) The various specific effects of moral evil—for example, the misorientation of moral character—may constitute in part a just retribution for the evil itself: an aspect of the reaction of divine law against the misuse of the contingency essential to the existence of moral freedom itself. Moral freedom thus results in an evil which becomes its own punishment by effecting moral depravity.

[99]James Orr, *The Christian View of God and the World*, p. 189.

(b) Yet the restitution is not complete at this present level of experience:

(i) Pain and suffering are often conspicuously maladjusted to the ends of discipline and education: but this merely means that only a part of pain and suffering are of disciplinary significance; much of such suffering springs from the complexity of contingencies that we have already elaborated above.

(ii) If, moreover, human selves, as we have shown to be possible, transcend their present environment at death and occupy another, even the excessive sufferings of the present, which arise from the complex causal nexus, may be adjusted to the divine purpose of moral realization. But even this ultimate adjustment is not required to solve the problem, if suffering springs causally from a contingency that is involved in the conditions necessary to rational and moral life.

(b) Yet the retribution is not complete at this present level of experience:

(i) The distortion of moral character is not always proportionate to the evil acts of the individual: but this merely means that only a part of the explanation for the status of moral character, is to be found in the conditioning of specific morally evil acts; much of the explanation lies in the complexity of contingencies that we have already elaborated above.

(ii) If, moreover, human selves, as we have shown to be possible, transcend their present environment at death and occupy another, the disproportion of moral character and evil acts, which arises from the complex causal nexus, may be adjusted to the divine law of reaction against evil: for in such a survival of the self, there would be an essential continuity of moral character from the present environment to the next; as Socrates long since observed, what a man receives into his soul cannot be idly stored in another vessel, but rather becomes a determination of harm or benefit to the soul itself.[100] But even this ultimate adjustment is not required to solve the problem, if the disproportion springs causally from a contingency that is involved in the maintenance of a determinate world order.

[100]Plato, *Protagoras*, 314.

(2) On the *cosmic* level,

(a) Much natural evil can be eliminated by the expansion of our knowledge of the proximate causal factors operating in given cases.

(i) Just for the reason that pain and suffering are explicable in causal terms, the possibility of control exists, so that the very conditions from which the evils resulted become the means for the conquest of these evils, at least to a large extent.

(ii) The rational structure, of minds and their environment, may thus progressively transcend the accidental evils of existence.

(b) Yet the expansion of knowledge cannot effect the progressive conquest of pain and suffering in the cosmos apart from the ethical transformation of human, moral selves: for an uncalculated quantity of such pain and suffering is the effect of morally evil acts as they are related to the whole moral community of selves.

(It is not my purpose to consider here the means for such a transformation: suffice it to say that it is effected, in my opinion, by an experience of spiritual conversion and regeneration. All that the present context requires is the recognition that such a transformation seems necessary.)

(2) On the *cosmic* level,

(a) The existence of natural evil may likewise constitute a part of the just retribution for moral evil as committed by human selves, so that such natural evil embodies, to some extent, the reaction of divine law against the abuse of freedom.

(i) This by no means implies that every instance of suffering in human life is a retribution for specific moral evil: nothing could be further from the truth.

(ii) Pain and suffering are often conspicuously maladjusted with relation to retribution for moral evil.

(b) What our assertion does mean is that nature is itself in a state of arrested development because of the complex influence of moral evil on the natural order, and that a part of the result of this arrested development is of judicial and punitive significance, as related to a race of men who, being all tinged with moral evil, stand in a certain solidarity of revolt against God.

(3) *Summary:* Thus the divine purpose reacts against the evil effects of the law-abidingness of the universe, both by making these effects a part of the context for moral development, and by rendering a vast number of such effects eliminable through an expanding knowledge of their causal origins and through an ethical transformation of moral selves.

(3) *Summary:* Thus the divine law reacts against the evil effects of freedom by resulting in a retribution which consists partly in the alteration of moral character itself, partly in that experience of pain and suffering which results from natural causes in their complex interaction with the moral.

c. *Application of the Principles*

(1) The proportionate application of these principles to specific instances of evil would appear to be an exceedingly complex affair: why is *this* man blind? Why did *this* flood take place? Why was *this* child stricken with infantile paralysis? Why should *this* man have been slain by a wild beast?

(2) The answer to such questions involves the knowledge of an intricate causal and purposive nexus in every case; and, due to the limitation of our knowledge of specific cases, may not be precisely formulable: the more we expand our knowledge, however, the less will be our percentage of error in applying the correct proximate principles.

(3) But the difficulty of application does not undermine the principles themselves, any more than the difficulty of solving a particularly intricate mathematical problem undermines the validity of the system of mathematical principles which the problem presupposes.

d. *The contingency of natural evil:*
(1) While natural evils spring from the determinate conditions essential to the environment of moral realization, such evils are a contingent, and not an ultimately necessary result of these conditions.

d. *The contingency of moral evil:*
(1) While moral evil springs from the determinate conditions essential to the existence of moral beings, such evils are a contingent, and not an ultimately necessary result of these conditions.

(2) Since natural laws operate with a general fixity, failure to adjust to them may be disastrous; but just because the laws do thus op-

(2) Since moral freedom operates as it does, failure to choose the good may be disastrous; but just because moral freedom is a reality,

erate, they may become the means for an elimination of disastrous consequences through an expansion of our knowledge of these very laws.

it may become the means for an elimination of moral evil through progressive orientation of character toward the good.

(3) And who can say, but that if the sources of maladjustment, whether moral or natural, are progressively eliminated, natural evils may yet bow to decisive defeat in a universe of divine purpose?

(3) And who can say, but that if human selves thus respond to the possibilities of freedom, moral evil may yet bow to decisive defeat in a universe of divine law!

e. Conclusion on the Ethical Objection

What then is the issue of our consideration of evil? Since the totality of natural and moral evil springs from conditions essential to the existence of a moral universe, and since every specific evil is merely a possibility and not a necessity of these conditions, and since evil is definable only as over against the existence of an absolute good, therefore, the presence of evil in the universe is not inconsistent with the existence of an omnipotent, benevolent God as the ultimate explanation of the total space-time universe. Consequently, the ethical objection against the teleological argument is invalid.

F. Conclusion on the Objections to the Teleological Argument

Since the whole range of objections against the teleological argument as correctly formulated has been found to be invalid and freighted with both logical and experiential contradiction, I therefore conclude that the teleological argument is valid and that the absolutely necessary being is a personal intelligence whose nature is absolute goodness.

CONCLUSION ON THE WHOLE DESTRUCTIVE ARGUMENT OF CRITICAL NATURALISM

The rational case for theism has at last emerged triumphant over its foes at every point of debate: the clouds of objection fade into mist and the mist vanishes into oblivion until now we stand unquestionably confronted with the divine Being Himself. Since both the cosmological and the teleological arguments have been defended against the objections of a destructive naturalism, I therefore conclude that these arguments are valid, that God exists as the ultimate explanation and ground of the whole complex of reality: God, that is, as the absolutely necessary being of intelligent nature which embodies absolute goodness.

CONCLUSION

Our path has been long, but it has brought us at last to the general answer for the questions with which our investigation began: the broad outlines of a philosophy may now be asserted.

The problem of epistemology has been solved in terms of a rational empiricism which teaches that all knowledge is a union of categorical and experiential elements: the mind comes to experience with certain forms of thought, or synthetic a priori categories, in terms of which it understands the data upon which it is dependent for valid content knowledge. This rational empiricism involved, in turn, both epistemological dualism and the coherence theory of truth. Such a comprehensive epistemology was seen thus to be basic to the ultimate justification of beliefs, so that metaphysics was necessarily the second, and not the first, object of pursuit. The knowledge of knowledge is basic, finally, to the knowledge of being.

With such a view clearly established, we turned, in the next place, to a consideration of proposed alternate approaches to the understanding of Being, so far as those approaches were proposed as possible bases for Christian Apology. Empirical, pragmatic, and voluntaristic approaches were all subjected to rational criticism with the result that our original rational empiricism emerged as the only ultimate and satisfactory epistemological approach to a theistic apologetic.

Finally, natural revelation itself became the basis for a demonstrative theistic world view. The traditional arguments for God led us at last to the firm conclusion that theism alone actually poses a solution to the metaphysical problem. The whole range of critical objections against such a view was found to vanish in the mist before the searching eyes of rational analysis until at the end of the way we found at last that man is not alone, but finds his highest destiny in the knowledge of God.

Now at last the tables may be turned and theism may call its opponents before the bar of reason, as those opponents had thought thus to summon her. And with apologies to Bertrand Russell, we might assert a new creed for the Free Man's Worship:

> That man is the product of a Cause which had an eternal pre-vision of the end it was achieving; that his origin, his growth, his hopes and fears, his loves and his beliefs, transcend the colloca-tions of atoms in his material environment and achieve sig-nificance in the light of a spiritual destiny; that no argument, no distorted cunning, no intensity of thought and feeling, can pro-tect an individual life from supreme moral responsibility to the Divine; that all the labors of the ages, all the devotion, all the in-spiration, all the noonday brightness of human genius, insofar as these express the realization of man's true spiritual purpose, are destined for an eternal fulfillment as over against the vast death of the solar system, and that the whole temple of God's achievement must rise inevitably from its eternal source, despite its sinful consignment to burial beneath the débris of a universe in ethical ruins—all these things are so far beyond dispute and so certain, that no philosophy which rejects them can hope to stand. Only within the scaffolding of these truths, only on the firm foundation of unyielding Divine purpose, can the soul's habitation, now as always, be built.[101]

God is not dead, nor is theistic philosophy hopelessly impaled on any cross of destructive criticism. On the contrary, this cross of criti-cism is succeeded by a theism vibrant with resurrection life—a life all the more triumphant because it has victoriously borne its at-tempted crucifixion.

---

[101]*Selected Papers of Bertrand Russell*, p. 3: transformed from its original natu-ralistic orientation.

BIBLIOGRAPHY

ANSELM, ST. *Proslogium; Monologium, An Appendix in Behalf of the Fool by Gaunilon;* and *Cur Deus Homo*. Trans. from Latin by SIDNEY NORTON DEANE. LaSalle, Illinois: The Open Court Publishing Co., 1948.

AQUINAS, ST. THOMAS. *Basic Writings of Saint Thomas Aquinas*. Vol. I, ed. A. C. PEGIS. New York: Random House, c. 1945.

ARISTOTLE. *The Basic Works of Aristotle,* ed. RICHARD MCKEON. Random House: New York, c. 1941.

AUGUSTINE. *The Confessions of St. Augustine*. Trans. by J. G. PILKINGTON. Liveright Publishing Corp., 1943.

BAILLIE, JOHN. *Our Knowledge of God*. New York: Charles Scribner's Sons, 1939.

BALFOUR, A. J. *The Foundations of Belief*. New York: Longmans, Green, and Co., 1895.

———. *Theism and Humanism*. New York: George H. Doran Company, c. 1915.

———. *Theism and Thought*. London: Hodder and Stoughton, 1923.

BARTH, KARL. *The Doctrine of the Word of God*. Trans. by G. T. THOMSON. Edinburgh: T. & T. Clark, 1936.

———. *Dogmatics in Outline*. Trans. by G. T. THOMSON. New York: Philosophical Library, 1947 (original German ed.).

———. *The Knowledge of God and the Service of God According to the Teaching of the Reformation*. Trans. by J. L. M. HAIRE and I. HENDERSON. New York: Charles Scribner's Sons, 1939.

BERGSON, HENRI. *Creative Evolution*. Trans. by A. MITCHELL. New York: Henry Holt and Co.

———. *The Two Sources of Morality and Religion*. Trans. by ANDRA, BRERETON, and CARTER. New York: Henry Holt and Co., c. 1935.

BERKELEY, GEORGE. *A New Theory of Vision and Other Writings*. Everyman's Library. New York: E. P. Dutton and Co., Inc., 1910.

BERTOCCI, PETER A. *Introduction to the Philosophy of Religion*. New York: Prentice-Hall, Inc., 1951.

BLANSHARD, BRAND. *The Nature of Thought*, 2 vols. London: George Allen and Unwin, 1939.

BOSANQUET, B. "The Meaning of Teleology." Proceedings of the British Academy, 1905-1906. London: Henry Frowde, Oxford University Press, pp. 235-245.

BRIGHTMAN, E. S. *A Philosophy of Religion*. New York: Prentice-Hall, Inc., 1940.

————. *The Problem of God.* New York: The Abingdon Press, c. 1930.

BROAD, C. D. *Religion, Philosophy, and Psychical Research.* New York: Harcourt, Brace and Co., Inc., 1953.

BRUNNER, EMIL. *Revelation and Reason: The Christian Doctrine of Faith and Knowledge.* Trans. by OLIVE WYON. Philadelphia: The Westminster Press, c. 1946.

BURTT, EDWIN A. *Types of Religious Philosophy.* Rev. ed. New York: Harper and Bros., c. 1939, 1951.

CAIRD, JOHN. *An Introduction to the Philosophy of Religion.* Glasgow: James Maclehose, 1880.

CALVIN, JOHN. *Institutes of the Christian Religion.* Trans. by JOHN ALLEN. 6th Am. ed. rev. and corrected. Vol. I. Philadelphia: Presbyterian Board of Publication, n. d.

CARNELL, EDWARD J. *An Introduction to Christian Apologetics.* 2nd ed. Grand Rapids: Eerdmans Publishing Co., 1948.

————. *A Philosophy of the Christian Religion.* Grand Rapids: Eerdmans Publishing Co., 1952.

CHADBOURNE, P. A. *Lectures on Natural Theology:* 7th ed. New York: G. P. Putnam's Sons, 1874.

CHRISTLIEB, THEODORE. *Modern Doubt and Christian Belief.* Trans. by H. U. WEITBRECHT. Edinburgh: T. & T. Clark, 1874.

CLARK, GORDON H. *A Christian Philosophy of Education.* Grand Rapids: Eerdmans Publishing Co., c. 1946.

————. *A Christian View of Men and Things.* Grand Rapids: Eerdmans Publishing Co., 1952.

————. *Studies of the Doctrines of "The Complaint."* Unpublished material in my possession: circulated in mimeographed form.

CLARKE, WILLIAM N. *An Outline of Christian Theology.* 5th ed. New York: Charles Scribner's Sons, 1899.

CONGER, GEORGE P. *The Ideologies of Religion.* New York: Round Table Press, Inc., 1940.

DE BURGH, W. G. "The Relations of Morality to Religion." Proceedings of the British Academy, 1935, pp. 75-99. London: Humphrey Milford, Oxford University Press.

DESCARTES, RENE. *Descartes Selections.* Ed. by RALPH M. EATON. New York: Charles Scribner's Sons, c. 1927.

DEWEY, JOHN. *A Common Faith.* New Haven: Yale University Press, c. 1934.

————. *Logic: The Theory of Inquiry.* New York: Henry Holt and Co., c. 1938.

————. *Reconstruction in Philosophy.* New York: Henry Holt and Co., 1920.

EMMET, DOROTHY M. *The Nature of Metaphysical Thinking.* London: Macmillan and Co., 1946.

EWING, A. C. *A Short Commentary on Kant's Critique of Pure Reason.* Chicago: University of Chicago Press, 1938.

FICHTE, JOHANN GOTTLIEB. *The Vocation of Man.* Trans. by WM. SMITH. La Salle, Illinois: Open Court Publishing Co., 1940.

FISHER, G. P. *Manual of Natural Theology.* New York: Charles Scribner's Sons, 1893.

GALLOWAY, GEORGE. *The Philosophy of Religion.* New York: Charles Scribner's Sons, 1927.

GHOSE, SRI AUROBINDO. *The Life Divine.* New York: The Greystone Press, c. 1949.

GILSON, ETIENNE. *God and Philosophy.* New Haven: Yale University Press, 1941.

———. *The Philosophy of St. Thomas Aquinas.* Trans. by E. BULLOUGH. Cambridge: W. Heffer and Sons, Ltd., 1929.

HENRY, CARL F. H. *The Drift of Western Thought.* Grand Rapids: Eerdmans Publishing Co., 1951.

———. *Giving a Reason for Our Hope.* Boston: W. A. Wilde Company, c. 1949.

———. *Notes on the Doctrine of God.* Boston: W. A. Wilde Company, c. 1948.

———. *The Protestant Dilemma.* Grand Rapids: Eerdmans Publishing Co., 1949.

———. *Remaking the Modern Mind.* Grand Rapids: Eerdmans Publishing Company, c. 1946.

———. *Remaking the Modern Mind.* 2nd ed. Grand Rapids: Eerdmans Publishing Co., 1948.

HOCKING, W. E. *The Meaning of God in Human Experience.* New Haven: Yale University Press, 1924.

———. *Types of Philosophy.* Rev. ed. New York: Charles Scribner's Sons, c. 1939.

HODGE, CHARLES. *Systematic Theology,* vol. I. Grand Rapids: Eerdmans Publishing Co., 1946. (First published, 1871.)

HUME, DAVID. *An Enquiry Concerning Human Understanding and Selections from a Treatise of Human Nature.* La Salle, Illinois: Open Court Publishing Co., 1949.

———. HUME SELECTIONS. Ed. CHARLES W. HENDEL, JR. New York: Charles Scribner's Sons, c. 1927.

———. *A Treatise of Human Nature.* Ed. L. A. SELBY-BIGGE. Oxford: The Clarendon Press, 1st ed., 1888, reprinted 1949.

JAMES, WILLIAM. *The Meaning of Truth.* New York: Longmans, Green, and Co., 1910.

———. *Pragmatism.* New York: Longmans, Green, and Co., 1909. New impression (1st ed. 1907).

JOAD, C. E. M. *A Critique of Logical Positivism.* Chicago: University of Chicago Press, 1950.

JOSEPH, H. W. B. *An Introduction to Logic.* 2nd ed., rev. Oxford: Clarendon Press, 1916.

KANT, IMMANUEL. *Critique of Practical Reason and Other Writings in Moral Philosophy.* Trans. and ed. by L. W. BECK. Chicago: University of Chicago Press, c. 1949.

———. *Critique of Pure Reason.* Revised Edition. Trans. by J. M. D. MEIKLEJOHN. New York: Willey Book Co., 1943.

———. *Prolegomena to Any Future Metaphysics.* Chicago: Open Court Publishing Co., 1949.

———. *Religion within the Limits of Reason Alone.* Trans. by GREENE and HUDSON. Chicago: Open Court Publishing Co., c. 1934.

KAUFMAN, ARNOLD S. "The Analytic and the Synthetic: A Tenable 'Dualism.'" *Phil. Review*, Vol. LXII, No. 3, July, 1953.

KRIKORIAN, Y. H. (ed.) *Naturalism and the Human Spirit*. New York: Columbia University Press, 1944.

LAIRD, JOHN. *Knowledge, Belief and Opinion*. New York and London: Century Co., c. 1930.

———. *Theism and Cosmology*. London: George Allen and Unwin Ltd., 1940.

LARRABEE, HAROLD A. *Reliable Knowledge*. Boston: Houghton Mifflin Co., c. 1945.

LECOMTE DU NOUY, P. *Human Destiny*. New York: Longmans, Green, and Co., 1947.

LEWIS, CLARENCE IRVING. *An Analysis of Knowledge and Valuation*. La Salle, Illinois: The Open Court Publishing Co., c. 1946.

MACINTOSH, D. C. *The Problem of Religious Knowledge*. New York: Harper and Bros., c. 1940.

MAHAFFY, J. P. and BERNARD, J. H. *Kant's Critical Philosophy for English Readers*. Rev. ed. London: Macmillan and Co., 1889.

MARITAIN, JACQUES. *The Degrees of Knowledge*. New York: Charles Scribner's Sons, 1938.

———. *An Introduction to Philosophy*. Trans. by E. I. Watkin. New York: Sheed and Ward, n. d.

MCKEON, RICHARD. *Selections from Medieval Philosophers*. Vol. II. New York: Charles Scribner's Sons, c. 1930.

MILL, JOHN STUART. *Nature, The Utility of Religion, and Theism*. (Three Essays on Religion). London: Watts and Co., 1925.

MOBERLY, W. H. "God and the Absolute." In *Foundations: A Statement of Christian Belief in Terms of Modern Thought*. London: Macmillan and Co., 1912.

MONTAGUE, W. P. *The Ways of Knowing*. London: George Allen and Unwin, Ltd., New York: Macmillan Co., 1925.

MORRISON, A. CRESSY. *Man Does Not Stand Alone*. New York: Fleming H. Revell Co., c. 1944; rev., 1946.

ORR, JAMES. *The Christian View of God and the World*. 3rd ed. Edinburgh: Andrew Elliot, 1897.

PALEY, WILLIAM. *Natural Theology*. Boston: Gould and Lincoln, 1858.

PATON, H. J. *Kant's Metaphysic of Experience*, vol. I. London: George Allen and Unwin, 1936.

PATTERSON, C. H. *Moral Standards*. New York: Ronald Press Co., c. 1949.

PHILLIPS, R. P. *Modern Thomistic Philosophy*, vol. II. London: Burns Oates and Washbourne, Ltd., 1935.

PLATO. *The Dialogues of Plato*. Ed. by B. JOWETT. 3rd ed., 5 vols. London: Oxford University Press, 1892 (impression of 1931).

———. *The Republic*. Ed. C. M. BAKWELL. New York: Charles Scribner's Sons, c. 1928.

PRATT, JAMES BISSETT. *Naturalism*. New Haven: Yale University Press, 1939.

QUINE, W. V. "Two Dogmas of Empiricism." *The Philosophical Review*, Vol. LX, No. 1, pp. 20-43.

RAMM, BERNARD. *Problems in Christian Apologetics.* Portland: Western Baptist Theological Seminary, 1949.

——. *Types of Apologetic Systems.* Wheaton, Illinois: Van Kampen Press, c. 1953.

RANDALL, J. H. and BUCHLER, J. *Philosophy: An Introduction.* New York: Barnes and Noble, Inc., c. 1942.

RASHDALL, HASTINGS. *Philosophy and Religion.* New York: Charles Scribner's Sons, 1910.

RECEJAC, E. *Essay on the Bases of the Mystic Knowledge.* Trans. by S. C. Upton. London: Kegan Paul, Trench, Trübner, and Co., Ltd., 1899.

REICHENBACH, HANS. "Are Phenomenal Reports Absolutely Certain?" *The Philosophical Review,* April, 1952, pp. 147-159.

RILEY, WOODBRIDGE. *The Meaning of Mysticism.* New York: Richard R. Smith, Inc., 1930.

RUSSELL, BERTRAND. *Dictionary of Mind, Matter and Morals.* New York: Philosophical Library. c. 1952.

——. *Human Knowledge: Its Scope and Limits.* New York: Simon and Schuster, 1948.

——. *The Problems of Philosophy.* New York: Henry Holt and Co., n. d.

——. *Religion and Science.* London: Oxford University Press, 1935.

——. *Selected Papers of Bertrand Russell.* New York: Random House— The Modern Library, 1927.

SCHILLER, F. C. S. *Formal Logic: A Scientific and Social Problem.* London: Macmillan and Co., 1912.

SHEDD, W. G. T. *Dogmatic Theology,* Vol. I. Grand Rapids: Zondervan Publishing House, n. d. (published first, 1888).

SMITH, NORMAN KEMP. *A Commentary to Kant's Critique of Pure Reason.* 2nd ed. London: Macmillan and Co., 1923.

SORLEY, W. R. *Moral Values and the Idea of God.* 2nd ed. Cambridge: University Press, 1921.

SPINOZA, B. *Ethics.* New York: E. P. Dutton & Co. Inc., 1910.

STACE, W. T. *Religion and the Modern Mind.* Philadelphia: J. B. Lippincott Co., c. 1952.

STOUT, G. F. *God and Nature.* Cambridge: University Press, 1952.

STRONG, A. H. *Systematic Theology.* Philadelphia: The Judson Press, c. 1907.

TAYLOR, A. E. *Does God Exist?* New York: The Macmillan Company, 1947.

TENNANT, F. R. *Philosophical Theology,* 2 vols. Cambridge: University Press, 1935.

THILLY, FRANK. *A History of Philosophy.* New York: Henry Holt and Co., c. 1914.

TRUEBLOOD, DAVID ELTON. *The Logic of Belief.* New York: Harper and Bros., c. 1942.

VANTIL, CORNELIUS. *Christian Apologetics.* Philadelphia: Printed by The Theological Seminary of the Reformed Episcopal Church, 25 S. 43rd Street; rev. and printed, January, 1939.

———. *Common Grace.* Philadelphia: Presbyterian and Reformed Publishing Co., 1947.

———. *Junior Systematics.* Philadelphia: The Theological Seminary of the Reformed Episcopal Church, 25 S. 43rd Street, 1940.

———. "Nature and Scripture," chap. in *The Infallible Word: A Symposium by the members of the Faculty of Westminster Theological Seminary.* Philadelphia: The Presbyterian Guardian Publishing Corp., 1946.

WARD, JAMES. *Naturalism and Agnosticism.* 4th ed. London: A. and C. Black, 1915.

WARFIELD, B. B. *The Inspiration and Authority of the Bible.* Introduction by CORNELIUS VANTIL. Philadelphia: The Presbyterian and Reformed Publishing Co., 1948.

WATSON, JOHN. *Kant and His English Critics.* Glasgow: James Maclehose, publisher to the university, 1881.

WELDON, T. D. *Introduction to Kant's Critique of Pure Reason.* Oxford: Clarendon Press, 1945.

WERKMEISTER, W. H. *An Introduction to Critical Thinking.* Lincoln, Nebraska: Johnsen Publishing Co., c. 1948.

WHEELWRIGHT, PHILIP ELLIS. *A Critical Introduction to Ethics.* Rev. ed. New York: The Odyssey Press, c. 1949.

WHITE, MORTON G. "The Analytic and the Synthetic: an Untenable Dualism," in *John Dewey: Philosopher of Science and Freedom,* ed. by SIDNEY HOOK. New York: The Dial Press, 1950, pp. 316-330.

WHITEHEAD, ALFRED NORTH. *Process and Reality.* New York: The Macmillan Company, 1929.

WICK, WARNER. "Moral Problems, Moral Philosophy, and Meta-ethics: Some Further Dogmas of Empiricism." *The Philosophical Review,* Vol. XLII, No. 1, January, 1953.

WILD, JOHN. *Introduction to Realistic Philosophy.* New York: Harper and Bros., c. 1948.

WRIGHT, WILLIAM KELLEY. *A History of Modern Philosophy.* New York: The Macmillan Company, c. 1941.

INDEX

Twin Brooks Series

Hort, Fenton John Anthony
Judaistic Christianity

Jerome
Commentary on Daniel

Kevan, Ernest F.
The Grace of Law

Klotsche, E. H.
The History of Christian Doctrine

Kuiper, R. B.
God-Centered Evangelism

Kurtz, J. H.
Sacrificial Worship of the Old
Testament

Kuyper, Abraham
Principles of Sacred Theology

Law, Robert
The Tests of Life

Lecerf, Auguste
An Introduction to Reformed
Dogmatics

Lightfoot, J. B.
The Apostolic Fathers

Longenecker, Richard N.
The Christology of Early Jewish
Christianity
Paul, Apostle of Liberty

Machen, J. Gresham
The Virgin Birth of Christ

Manson, T. W.
The Servant-Messiah

Mayor, Joseph B.
The Epistle of James
The Epistles of Jude and II Peter

McDonald, H. D.
Theories of Revelation

Meeter, H. Henry
The Basic Ideas of Calvinism

Niesel, Wilhelm
The Theology of Calvin

Orr, James
Revelation and Inspiration

Rackham, Richard Belward
The Acts of the Apostles

Ramm, Bernard
The Evangelical Heritage
Varieties of Christian Apologetics

Raven, John Howard
The History of the Religion of Israel

Sandeen, Ernest R.
The Roots of Fundamentalism

Seeberg, Reinhold
Textbook of the History of
Doctrines

Sherwin-White, A. N.
Roman Society and Roman Law in
the New Testament

Smith, David
The Days of His Flesh

Smith, James
The Voyage and Shipwreck of St.
Paul

Steinmetz, David C.
Reformers in the Wings

Stonehouse, Ned B.
Origins of the Synoptic Gospels
The Witness of the Synoptic Gospels
to Christ

Sweet, William Warren
The Story of Religion in America

Theron, Daniel J.
Evidence of Tradition

Trench, Richard Chenevix
Notes on the Miracles of Our Lord
Notes on the Parables of Our
Lord
Studies in the Gospels

Trueblood, David Elton
General Philosophy
Philosophy of Religion

Turretin, Francis
The Atonement of Christ

Van Til, Henry
The Calvinistic Concept of Culture

Vos, Geerhardus
The Pauline Eschatology

Westcott, B. F.
A General Survey of the History of
the Canon of the New Testament

Wilson, Robert Dick
Studies in the Book of Daniel

Young, Warren C.
A Christian Approach to Philosophy

BAKER BOOK HOUSE   BOX 6287   GRAND RAPIDS, MI 49506